Natopolitanism

Natopolitanism

The Atlantic Alliance
since the Cold War

Edited by Grey Anderson

VERSO

London • New York

First published by Verso 2023
Chapters 6, 7, 12, 13, 15, and 16 © *New Left Review* 2023
All other chapters © The contributors 2023
The Collection © Verso 2023
The publisher would like to express its gratitude to the publications in
which these essays originally appeared

1 3 5 7 9 10 8 6 4 2

Verso
UK: 6 Meard Street, London W1F 0EG
US: 388 Atlantic Avenue, Brooklyn, NY 11217
versobooks.com

Verso is the imprint of New Left Books

ISBN-13: 978-1-80429-237-2
ISBN-13: 978-1-80429-239-6 (US EBK)
ISBN-13: 978-1-80429-238-9 (UK EBK)

British Library Cataloguing in Publication Data
A catalogue record for this book is available from the British Library

Library of Congress Cataloging-in-Publication Data
A catalog record for this book is available from the Library of Congress
LCCN: 2023019313

Typeset in Minion Pro by MJ&N Gavan, Truro, Cornwall
Printed and bound by CPI Group (UK) Ltd, Croydon CR0 4YY

Contents

Part Two
OUT OF AREA

Part Three
DRANG NACH KIEV

Part Four
BATTLEFIELD UKRAINE

Part Five
ATLANTICOLOGY

Conclusion

List of Acronyms and Abbreviations

CEPA	Center for European Policy Analysis
CIS	Commonwealth of Independent States
CSCE	Conference on Security and Co-operation in Europe
CSDP	EU Common Security and Defense Policy
CSTO	Collective Security Treaty Organization
EC	European Community, now called the European Union (EU)
FRG	Federal Republic of Germany
GATT	General Agreement on Trade and Tariffs
GDP	Gross Domestic Product
GDR	German Democratic Republic
IMF	International Monetary Fund
ISAF	International Security and Assistance Force in Afghanistan
MAP	Membership Action Plan
NAC	North Atlantic Council
NED	National Endowment for Democracy
NPT	Non-Proliferation Treaty
NSC	American National Security Council
OECD	Organization for Economic Co-operation and Development
OSCE	Organization for Security and Co-operation in Europe
PfP	Partnership for Peace
SACEUR	Supreme Allied Commander Europe
SHAPE	Supreme Headquarters Allied Powers Europe
START	Strategic Arms Reduction Treaty
USIA	United States Information Agency
WEU	Western European Union

Introduction

Pactum de contrahendo

Grey Anderson

Military alliances, by definition, are an agreement on the use of force against a rival. But this is not their only, or even primary, role. Ensuring internal order, encouraging commerce, and disseminating ideology are additional alliance activities, far from exhaustive. They may also serve as *pacta de contrahendo*, through which a strong power controls weaker allies, potential adversaries seek conciliation, or contracting parties pledge mutual restraint.[1] Since its inception in 1949, NATO has assumed all of these functions; each, however, has not been equal in significance, and their relative weight has shifted with time.

From the beginning, the architects of the North Atlantic Treaty were under few illusions as to the military utility of their compact. In the unlikely event of a Soviet offensive on Western Europe, a handful of under-armed American divisions could not be counted on to turn the tide. With the militarization of the alliance at the turn of the 1950s (acquiring its "organization" and integrated command as Chinese troops crossed the Yalu), the forces at the disposal of the Supreme Allied Commander Europe (SACEUR) grew more formidable—by the middle of the decade, equipped

---

1   Paul W. Schroeder, "Alliances, 1815–1945: Weapons of Power and Tools of Management," in *Historical Dimensions of National Security Problems*, ed. Klaus Knorr (Lawrence: University Press of Kansas, 1976), pp. 227–62.

with 280mm M65 atomic cannon—but schemes to mount a defense at the Fulda Gap or on the North German Plains were always far fetched and recognized as such. Of greater concern, in the immediate postwar years, was the enemy at home. European leaders looked to NATO as a bulwark against internal subversion as much as against the Red Army. Such considerations illuminate a further dimension of the alliance. For propagandists then as now, its mandate extended to "values" as well as security: did the 1949 treaty not engage signatories "to safeguard the freedom, common heritage and civilization of their peoples, founded on the principles of democracy, individual liberty and the rule of law"?

At first blush, a congeries that counted the Estado Novo and French colonial Algeria in the ranks of its founding members might not be thought an advertisement for democratic virtue. Nor was its warranty of civilian control impeccable. Within a decade of joining the alliance, both Turkey (admitted in 1952 alongside Greece, the first case of expansion) and France would see elected governments toppled in coups d'état; in 1967, Greek putschists took the outline for their plot from a NATO contingency plan for domestic counter-insurgency operations. Insofar as NATO has claim to be an "alliance of democracies," this is best understood in restrictive terms. By design, not flaw, it has effectively limited the exercise of sovereignty on the part of its constituent publics, insulating existential decisions over war and peace from the hurly-burly of electoral politics.[2] Here, the alliance bears comparison with the institutions of the European Union, which originated in the same conjuncture and matured within the nuclear protectorate directed from Washington.

Untroubled by any immediate prospect of havoc on the Central Front, content to oversee conservative restoration west of the Elbe, US authorities showed no sign of excessive concern for the preamble of the Washington Treaty. Discontent in Canada, Norway, and the Netherlands over the inclusion of Salazar's Portugal subsided in the face of geostrategic imperatives to reinforce a southern flank. Bilateral arrangements between Washington and Madrid sufficed to preempt the uproar augured by possible accession of Francoist Spain. Germany inevitably posed a more intractable conundrum. France, in particular, was loath to agree to the rearmament of its historic rival. The failure of ensuing tractations, which

---

2   This is the main thesis of the most recent archival history of the alliance, a work of impeccably orthodox credentials: Timothy Andrew Sayle, *Enduring Alliance: A History of NATO and the Postwar Global Order* (Ithaca: Cornell University Press, 2019).

hinged on an alternative scheme for a European Defense Community, resulted in a straightforward quid pro quo, US subvention of French colonial counter-insurgency buying acquiescence to a resurrected Wehrmacht in the NATO fold.

With the entry of the Bundesrepublik, formalized in 1955, NATO settled the question, in the words of a Central Intelligence Agency analysis, "of who is going to control German potential and thus hold the balance of power in Europe."[3] Not for the last time, the alliance effectively resolved a problem of its own making. Having opted for remilitarization, the Americans found themselves obliged to garrison hundreds of thousands of troops in Germany, as much to reassure its neighbors as deter the Soviets. For an outspoken minority in the US foreign policy establishment, this represented a fateful error, binding the country to a neo-imperial policy of dominion, as opposed to leadership in a more pluralistic postwar system.[4] By the late 1940s, however, such views were out of season. They ignored both the scale of US superiority and the breadth of its interests: the incorporation of the Pacific Rim, Mediterranean basin, and Europe into a global capitalist order.[5] NATO, in this vast scheme, acted first and foremost to prevent any rival bloc from emerging in the Eurasian heartland, at its geopolitical center the confluence of the Rhine and the Ruhr. Even critics of the treaty typically accepted the underlying logic. In the Senate debate over ratification, its most trenchant opponent, Senator Robert Taft of Ohio, proposed instead that the Monroe Doctrine simply be extended to Europe.[6]

---

3   Central Intelligence Agency, "Review of the World Situation," CIA No. 5-59, May 17, 1949, p. 8; cited in Melvyn Leffler, *A Preponderance of Power: National Security, the Truman Administration, and the Cold War* (Stanford: Stanford University Press, 1992), p. 284.

4   Two senior diplomats at the State Department, Charles Bohlen and George Kennan, shared this opinion. For an overview, see David P. Calleo, "Early American Views of NATO: Then and Now," in *The Troubled Alliance: Atlantic Relations in the 1980s*, ed. Lawrence Freedman (London: Heinemann, 1983), pp. 7–27; and David Calleo, *Beyond American Hegemony: The Future of the Western Alliance* (New York: Basic Books, 1987), pp. 27–43.

5   On the wartime evolution of US strategic planning, see Thomas J. McCormick, *America's Half-Century: United States Foreign Policy in the Cold War and After* (Baltimore: Johns Hopkins University Press, 1995), p. 33; and Gabriel Kolko, *The Politics of War: The World and United States Foreign Policy, 1943–1945* (New York: Random House, 1968), pp. 15–29.

6   "Last Thoughts," *Time*, July 25, 1949. Kennan and others supported a similar alternative, seen to stop short of a guarantee of military intervention in the event of an attack

Other institutions developed in turn to steward postwar reconstruction on the continent, prodromes of the European Community. By relieving constituent states of the responsibility to assure their own defense, NATO encouraged this process while at the same time furnishing a check against unwanted bids for autonomy. It was both a means toward European integration and a hedge against it. A distinctive feature of the Pax Atlantica, by contrast with British imperial precedent, was the close interweaving of economic, military, and ideological spheres, packaged as "security" and retailed as a public good. NATO exemplified this development, by linking defense expenditure to member states' respective national incomes, invigilated in alliance conclaves.[7] From dollar hegemony to international trade, Washington did not hesitate to exploit its military presence for leverage. Threats to withdraw forward-deployed troops secured German cooperation on monetary policy, while periodic escalation against the USSR helped thwart bilateral arrangements with the Soviets in defiance of American diktat. Sanctions and embargoes on the Eastern bloc, first mooted as a component of NATO strategy during the "Second Berlin Crisis" of 1961—to howls of protest from the allies—proved a trickier issue with Europeans, aware of who stood to suffer the brunt of their impact.

Political scientists have puzzled over the persistence of NATO after the dissolution of its putative adversary. But in the councils of power, plans not only to preserve but to expand the alliance in the event of a Soviet collapse dated back decades.[8] The fall of the Berlin Wall, two advisers to George H. W. Bush recalled, had no effect on the rationale for keeping US forces in Europe, as these "had become vital to projections of American power elsewhere in other areas such as the Middle East," not to forget "serv[ing] as the ante to ensure a central place for the United States as a player in

---

on an allied state. In essence this is the compromise solution embodied in Article 5 of the 1949 treaty.

7   Charles S. Maier, "The Making of 'Pax Americana': Formative Moments of United States Ascendancy," in *The Quest for Stability: Problems of West European Security, 1918–1957*, ed. R. Ahmann, Adolf M. Birke, and Michael Howard (Oxford: Oxford University Press, 1993), pp. 389–434.

8   Zbigniew Brzezinski, then attached to the State Department's Policy Planning Council, drafted a memorandum in 1966 that called for a cautious approach to détente and ruled out any mutual agreement to disband the two military blocs. Even US victory in the Cold War would not spell an end to NATO's raison d'être; the US presence in Europe was to remain a vital prerequisite "for building world order on the basis of closer collaboration among the more developed nations, perhaps including eventually some of the Communist states." Cited in Sayle, *Enduring Alliance*, p. 153.

European politics."[9] That settled, Washington's chief interest in the change sweeping the continent was to ensure that Germans not be permitted to accept neutrality or forfeiture of American nuclear weapons on their territory in exchange for reunification.[10] The success of this undertaking, accomplished via a combination of bribery and deception, thrilled US negotiators.[11] A satisfied Bush did not bother to attend the ceremonial recoupling of the two Germanies. From the outset, it was clear that the German Democratic Republic would not be the last Warsaw Pact state to accede to NATO, even if the scope and timing of further expansion remained uncertain. Set into motion by the Bush administration, this was guided by the desire to take advantage of Russian weakness and ensure that no independent European security arrangement emerge to jeopardize US hegemony.[12] Loftier considerations would be adduced in time, as leaders found it convenient to invoke common "values," the entreaties of Central and East European countries, democracy, and so forth. None figured in the cardinal choice.

As a January 1992 report by the CIA concluded, the US held "strong cards to play" on the "military front." NATO guaranteed against resurgent Russian bellicosity and an overweening Germany alike, a priceless resource in obtaining "corresponding European agreement" on "economic security decisions of vital interest to Washington."[13] Berlin, confronted with disquiet over its post-unification heft, did not tarry in expressing gratitude; that June, Foreign Minister Klaus Kinkel promised to support the US over French objections in the finale of the Uruguay Round GATT negotiations. Flush with the glow of victory, American leaders indulged in

9   Philip Zelikow and Condoleezza Rice, *Germany Unified and Europe Transformed: A Study in Statecraft* (Cambridge, MA: Harvard University Press, 1995), p. 169.

10   Mary E. Sarotte, *Not One Inch: America, Russia, and the Making of Post-Cold War Stalemate* (New Haven, CT: Yale University Press, 2021), p. 36.

11   Ibid., 66; Joshua R. Itzkowitz Shifrinson, "Deal or No Deal? The End of the Cold War and the US Offer to Limit NATO Expansion," *International Security* 40:4 (Spring 2016), pp. 7–44. Shifrinson is more categorical than Sarotte that American officials reneged on a formal promise to their Soviet counterparts that NATO, having brought in East Germany, would not expand eastward, but both agree on the basic facts.

12   This argument, substantiated by American archives, is presented in Joshua R. Itzkowitz Shifrinson, "Eastbound and Down: The United States, NATO Enlargement, and Suppressing the Soviet and Western European Alternatives, 1990–1992," *Journal of Strategic Studies* 43:6–7 (2020), pp. 816–46.

13   Liviu Horovitz and Elias Götz, "The Overlooked Importance of Economics: Why the Bush Administration Wanted NATO Enlargement," *Journal of Strategic Studies* 43:6–7 (December 2020), p. 856.

franc-parler unthinkable in Atlanticist circles on the old continent. "Full participation in the international marketplace," Senator Richard Lugar affirmed in August 1993, "requires a degree of stability and security in the international environment that only American power and leadership can provide."[14] Months later, on February 28, 1994, American-piloted F-16s dispatched to enforce a no-fly zone over Bosnia-Herzegovina shot down four Bosnian Serb fighter-bombers, the first combat mission in NATO's forty-five years of existence. Operation Deny Flight, debuted the previous April, marked the inaugural deployment of NATO forces "out of area," opening the way to exploits farther afield. Unpopular at home and in defiance of Franco-British efforts to broker a negotiated settlement, the US air campaign over Bosnia gratified interventionists who stressed the need to take the initiative precisely so as to preempt a solution.

Fissures in the alliance, brought to light in the Balkans and farther afield by the American monopoly over targeting selection and the manifest operational incapacities of European allies, reliant on the US for in-flight refueling, signals intelligence, and command-and-control, were patched over soon enough. The US has always capitalized on material and technological superiority, embodied in its nuclear arsenal, to exact a military division of labor within the alliance. Allies, in this conception, are expected to maintain "interoperability" with the American arsenal while furnishing sepoys on request. At the turn of the millennium, US pressure to embrace the tech-enthralled Revolution in Military Affairs combined with new counter-terrorism and counter-insurgency missions to calamitous result, visible in Afghanistan and Libya. American commanders lament Europeans' shortcomings on the battlefield, yet they have simultaneously worked to exacerbate them, pressuring allied armies either to perform light-infantry expeditionary missions or mop up as "peacekeepers."[15] Hectoring Europe to contribute more to its own defense ("burden sharing") is accompanied by strict limits on the scope of action of any EU force, forbidden from duplicating existing NATO capabilities or discriminating against non-EU alliance members, as well as US right

---

14   Richard Lugar, "NATO: Out of Area or Out of Business. A Call for US Leadership to Revise and Redefine the Alliance," Remarks Delivered to the Open Forum of the US State Department, August 2, 1993, cited in Benjamin C. Schwarz, "'Cold War' Continuities: US Economic and Security Strategy toward Europe," in Part I.

15   Paul van Hooft, "Land Rush: American Grand Strategy, NATO Enlargement, and European Fragmentation," *International Politics* 57:3 (June 2020), pp. 539–41.

of refusal over any operation involving manpower or materiel billeted to NATO—what amounts to blanket veto power.[16] Washington prefers a multilateral fig leaf for American adventures to a hard-power asset free from oversight. Integrated command structures provide an additional advantage from the US perspective, as the officers assigned to them— desirous of preferment, admiring of cutting-edge *quincaillerie*, on the lookout for budgetary windfalls at home—can be counted on as a bastion of Atlanticist fealty.[17]

Containment, it could be admitted at the end of the Cold War, never really fired the imagination. At best, it was the counsel of prudence, a purely negative message. Democratic norms, economic *aggiornamento*, and global governance furnished more energizing material. This was the idiom that animated propagandists for NATO expansion from the 1990s. But the Natopolitan galaxy of think tanks, cenacles, and advisory boards dates back earlier. Its proximate origins are in the revivified Atlanticist offensive of the 1970s, when the alarming progress of West German Ostpolitik prompted a coalition of neoconservative and neoliberal hawks to launch a crusade against "neutralism," harbinger of continental "Finlandization." Led by the US Information Agency, later joined by the National Endowment for Democracy, American psychological warfare—euphemistically described as public diplomacy—obtained relays in institutions like the Atlantic Council and the Ford Foundation, which cultivated biddable European elites.[18]

---

16   Secretary of State Madeleine K. Albright spelled out the "three 'Ds'" ("decoupling," "duplication," and "discrimination") in a 1998 address at NATO headquarters in Brussels, where she described fledgling EU military coordination as "a very useful way to think about burden sharing." Christopher Layne, "Death Knell for NATO?: The Bush Administration Confronts the European Security and Defense Policy," *Policy Analysis* 394 (April 2001), p. 5.

17   Charles de Gaulle, himself returned to power by pronunciamento, privately blamed the praetorian ructions that marred the French retreat from Algeria on officers' participation in NATO integrated command. Generals assigned to Supreme Headquarters Allied Powers Europe, he complained, "de-nationalize themselves, unwittingly." "They [lose] any sense of the state, the nation, of respect for the national hierarchy. ..." Alain Peyrefitte, *C'était de Gaulle* (Paris: Gallimard, 2002), pp. 333–4. On the part played by philo-American French military leaders in thwarting plans for a distinct European "pillar" in NATO (headed by France), see Kori Schake, "NATO after the Cold War, 1991–1995: Institutional Competition and the Collapse of the French Alternative," *Contemporary European History* 7:3 (November 1998), pp. 379–407.

18   Melvin Small, "The Atlantic Council: The Early Years," NATO Report, June 1, 1998; available on the NATO website.

In the twenty-first century, the importance of these bodies has grown in tandem with NATO's ever more capacious concept of "security," now encompassing everything from fossil fuel consumption and pandemic preparedness to digital media. Since the turn of the 2010s, at least, attention has trained on the arena of so-called hybrid threats, where "disinformation" occupies pride of place.[19] This watchword, meant to describe Russian and Chinese meddling in the domestic arrangements of Western states, is better understood as a mechanism to sidestep traditional diplomacy and inflate threats, justifying increased defense spending and "public-private partnerships" across sectors like surveillance, artificial intelligence, and cyberwarfare. Viewed accordingly, the US, partly via organisms like the German Marshall Fund and the Atlantik-Brücke in Berlin, the International Institute for Security Studies (IISS) and Royal United Services Institute (RUSI) in London, and the Center for European Policy Analysis (CEPA) in DC, exercises by some measure the most powerful external influence in European politics. These are complemented by some two dozen NATO "Centers of Excellence," alliance-accredited think tanks that operate in tune with US strategic objectives. As Washington has effected a "pivot" to Asia without letting Russia out of the crosshairs, its ideological apparatuses combat allied complacency amid talk of a new Cold War.

Historical analogies, for what they are worth, may be looked for less in the midcentury freeze of diplomatic relations between the two blocs than in the crisis of détente in the 1970s, catalyzed in the Second Cold War. The reignition of superpower tensions in the Carter and Reagan years took place in a context of relatively diminished American economic and military supremacy, deepening contradictions in the Western camp, and a shift in gravity away from the European theater.[20] After a flurry of protest at the turn of the eighties, these years also witnessed a remarkable reversal of much of the European left, with anti-Soviet feeling trumping antipathy to American imperialism. In the wake of the Russian invasion of Ukraine in February 2022, German leaders instinctively grasped for references to SPD Chancellor Helmut Schmidt's initiative in the *NATO-Doppelbeschluss*, the 1979 resolution to deploy US cruise and Pershing II

---

19   This paragraph is based on the edifying report by Joshua Rahtz and Anne Zetsche, "Rhetoric and Reality of Disinformation in the European Union," Study for the Left in the European Parliament (July 2021).

20   Fred Halliday, *The Making of the Second Cold War* (London: Verso, 1986).

nuclear-armed ballistic missiles to Western Europe if the USSR refused to remove its equivalent theater forces, the SS-20s. The parallels are curious, if unintended, after two decades in which the US unilaterally unwound Cold War–era arms-control agreements, from the scuppering of the Anti-Ballistic Missile Treaty in 2002 to the 2019 abrogation of the ban on intermediate-range nuclear forces, the 1987 accord that brought the so-called Euromissile Crisis to a close.

NATO's formal abandonment of any pretense to comity with Russia, announced at the 2014 alliance summit in Wales, marked the twentieth anniversary of the Partnership for Peace (PfP), sop to Russian angst over expansion and antechamber to membership for other Central and Eastern European states. The Wales summit also coincided with a series of meetings between Russian, Ukrainian, French, and German representatives in Belarus, to negotiate an end to ongoing fighting in southeast Ukraine. Yet well prior to the signature of the Minsk accords, supplemented the following spring by an additional protocol, a powerful coterie of American hawks moved to sabotage any compromise with Moscow. From the outbreak of hostilities in the Donbas following the February 2014 overthrow of Ukrainian president Viktor Yanukovych, Allied Supreme Commander Philip Breedlove took point position in sounding the alert of an imminent, full-fledged Russian offensive. Advised by Wesley Clark, another former NATO supremo, and a network of neoconservative operatives in the orbit of Victoria Nuland, former US ambassador to the alliance and assistant secretary of state for European affairs, Breedlove conspired to undermine German diplomacy and sway the White House into equipping the Ukrainian armed forces for a protracted struggle. Harlan Ullman, senior adviser at the Atlantic Council, and Phillip Karber, veteran Cold War threat-inflater and lobbyist for NATO aspirants, served as go-betweens. In leaked emails, Ullman relayed to Breedlove a request from Secretary General Jens Stoltenberg that they "fashion a NATO strategy to leverage, cajole, convince, or coerce the US to react." "We need to do a [Robert] Komer in reverse," Ullman wrote, in reference to "Blowtorch Bob," architect of the Phoenix assassination program in Indochina.[21] As an adviser to Secretary of Defense Harold Brown, Komer had engineered the "3 Percent Agreement," pledging European allies to scale up their

---

21   Ullman to Breedlove, March 27, 2015; archived at dcleaks.com.

continental commitment, adopted at the NATO Washington summit in
1978. This time alliance command, not the White House, sought to turn
the screws.

For the war party, escalation was self-evident. Decisive action would
not only cow Russia and check German ambitions in the region, but signal
resolve to Beijing. "China is watching closely," Clark wrote to Breedlove
in April 2014,

> China will have four aircraft carriers and airspace dominance in the
> Western Pacific within 5 years, if current trends continue. And if we
> let Ukraine slide away, it definitely raises the risks of conflict in the
> Pacific. For, China will ask, would the US then assert itself for Japan,
> Korea, Taiwan, the Philippines, the South China Sea? ... If Russia takes
> Ukraine, Belarus will join the Eurasian Union, and, presto, the Soviet
> Union (in another name) will be back ... Neither the Baltics nor the
> Balkans will easily resist the political disruptions empowered by a resur-
> gent Russia. And what good is a NATO "security guarantee" against
> internal subversion? ... And then the US will face a much stronger
> Russia, a crumbling NATO, and [a] major challenge in the Western
> Pacific. Far easier to [hold] the line now, in Ukraine than elsewhere,
> later.[22]

Breedlove and his associates stewed over Obama's apparent reluctance
to supply more advanced materiel to Ukraine.[23] In the new year, as a
tenuous ceasefire took hold, the general repeatedly warned of a forthcoming Russian conquest of Donbas, to the astonishment of European
intelligence services. Berlin was sufficiently irked to lodge a complaint
with the North Atlantic Council; German diplomats reported that every
visit to Kiev by senior US commanders and politicians left their Ukrainian
counterparts more gung-ho to retake the separatist oblasts by force.[24]

---

22 Clark to Breedlove, April 13, 2014; cited in Kees van der Pijl, *Flight MH17,
Ukraine, and the New Cold War: Prism of Disaster* (Manchester: Manchester University
Press, 2018), p. 102.

23 "I think POTUS sees us as a threat that must be minimized," Breedlove wrote to
Ullman in September, "ie do not get me into a war????" [*sic*]. Breedlove to Ullman, Sep-
tember 30, 2014; cited in Lee Fang and Zaid Jilani, "Hacked Emails Reveal NATO General
Plotting against Obama on Russia Policy," *Intercept*, July 1, 2016.

24 "Breedlove's Bellicosity: Berlin Alarmed by Aggressive NATO Stance on Ukraine,"
Spiegel, March 6, 2015.

Obama declined to dispatch antitank weapons to Ukraine, despite bipartisan clamor in Congress and prevailing consensus in his own administration, reportedly for fear of compromising German and French support for renewed sanctions against Russia.[25] He acceded, however, to hardliners' demands to boost American presence at the Yavoriv training facility on the Ukrainian border with Poland, site of joint NATO exercises since the mid-1990s. His successor in the White House, withal heretical claims on the stump that the alliance was "obsolete" and Ukraine might not be a foremost national priority, deferred to the same coalition of interests; undermined even before he took office by Democratic connivance with Ukrainian nationalists, Trump's agreement to supply FGM-148 Javelins did not prevent impeachment for insufficient promptness in shipping them out. Outrage greeted his disobliging comments about allied tithes and trade policies on the eve of a 2018 NATO summit in Brussels, complaints voiced by American leaders for generations. Rhetoric, more than substance, grated in the president's cavalier treatment of America's foreign entanglements. "Demeaning those commitments as if they were transactional protection rackets," bemoaned the *New Yorker*, "is corrosive and self-defeating."[26]

In Komer's day, the rationale for pushing Europeans to increase their NATO outlays was to free the US to expand operations farther afield, along what his White House ally Zbigniew Brzezinski called the "arc of crisis," stretching from the Indian Ocean to the Horn of Africa. Proxy wars in Central America, Asia, and Africa—Komer had once managed the struggle against Nasserism in Yemen, before shipping off to Saigon—formed part of a wider, multi-front offensive aimed at weakening and eventually subduing the USSR. Half a century later, US strategy toward Russia self-consciously evoked this legacy. An omnibus digest published by RAND in 2019 cited Andrew Marshall's 1972 report for the think tank, *Long-Term Competition with the Soviets*, as inspiration for "cost imposing" strategies vis-à-vis Moscow. "One historical reference point for such measures," the report noted,

---

25   "I have never seen a more aggressive and emotional debate than I have on this question," commented Matthew Rojansky, director of the Kennan Institute, who added that it was "reminiscent of that when the Soviet Union invaded Afghanistan." Jennifer Steinhauer and David M. Herszenhorn, "Defying Obama, Many in Congress Press to Arm Ukraine," *New York Times*, June 11, 2015.

26   Steve Coll, "Global Trump," *New Yorker*, April 11, 2016.

can be found in the policies of the Jimmy Carter and Ronald Reagan administrations through the 1980s. These included a massive US defense buildup, the launch of the Strategic Defense Initiative (SDI, also known as Star Wars), the deployment of intermediate-range nuclear-armed missiles to Europe, assistance to the anti-Soviet resistance in Afghanistan, the intensification of anti-Soviet rhetoric (the so-called evil empire), and support to dissidents in the Soviet Union and its satellite states.[27]

Beyond deployment of advanced cruise and antiradiation missiles, as well as drones, to compel expenditure on costly electronic warfare and air-defense systems, and increased economic sanctions, stepped-up support for the Ukrainian military—"already bleeding Russia in the Donbas region"—was another means of "extending Russia," raising the likelihood that the Kremlin might counter-escalate, committing more troops and pushing them deeper into Ukraine. Russia might even preempt US action, escalating before any additional US aid arrived. Such escalation might extend Russia; eastern Ukraine was already a drain. Taking more of Ukraine might only increase the burden, albeit at the expense of the Ukrainian people.[28]

Such an approach was not without risk. Were Ukraine overwhelmed, or forced to accept a Carthaginian peace, "US prestige and credibility" could suffer. Flooding the theater with weaponry likewise called to mind undeniable hazards. "On the other hand," the authors observed, "Ukraine is certainly a more capable and reliable partner than others to whom the United States has provided lethal equipment—for instance, the anti-Russian Afghan mujahidin in the 1980s." Updated in a militant synthesis by the Atlantic Council, similar reflections guided the agenda of the Biden administration from January 2021.[29]

Brzezinski, writing as Obama relaunched the war in Afghanistan, cautioned that a NATO defeat would inevitably draw comparisons with the Soviet debacle, entraining catastrophic consequences for American credibility and transatlantic harmony.[30] Around the same time, a

---

27   James Dobbins et al., *Extending Russia: Competing from Advantageous Ground* (Santa Monica: RAND Corporation, 2019), p. 1.

28   Ibid., p. 100.

29   David C. Hendrickson, "Why Washington Has Lost Its Mind over Ukraine," *National Interest*, February 11, 2022.

30   Zbigniew Brzezinski, "An Agenda for NATO: Toward a Global Security Web,"

German Marshall Fund report diagnosed congenital symptoms of "re-nationalization," evident not only within the International Security Assistance Force (ISAF) mission—where the Bundeswehr's legalistic rules of engagement (relaxed not long thereafter) invited mockery—but in debates over NATO's continuing push into the former USSR, revealing the persistence of "national, rather than collective, defense goals" in Western capitals.[31] When Kabul fell to the Taliban on August 15, 2021, the US withdrawing without so much as consultation with its allies, voices resounded to declare the end of Pax Americana. At a cost of $2.3 trillion, the twenty-year war had claimed more than seven thousand lives on the invaders' side and an untold number of Afghans. In December 2021, NATO foreign ministers convened in camera at the ATTA Centre in Riga, Latvia, to discuss the conclusions of an "Afghanistan Lessons Learned Process," disseminated to the public in a page-long fact sheet. This document struck a basically upbeat note, although it regretted the failure of the (non-NATO) "international community" to rebuild a functioning state.[32] In the meantime, the Biden regime retargeted sanctions on Kabul and seized $9 billion in central bank reserves, leaving the country ruined and millions prey to starvation and death.[33]

Months later, as Russian troops and armor poured across the Ukrainian border, all could be forgotten. "NATO has been revitalized, and the United States has reclaimed a mantle of leadership that some feared had vanished in Iraq and Afghanistan," the *New York Times* announced two weeks after the offensive began.[34] With its leading role in arming an embattled Ukraine and orchestrating economic sanctions against the aggressor, the US had reunified an ailing alliance. On the battlefield, Hillary Clinton confirmed in February, precedent lay in "the very motivated, and then funded and armed insurgency [that] drove the Russians out of Afghanistan."[35] Oliver North, onetime Contra bagman, reassured US television viewers at the

---

Foreign Affairs 88:5 (September–October 2009), pp. 2–20.

31   Joseph Wood, "[Re] Nationalization in Europe," Policy Brief, German Marshall Fund of the United States, August 20, 2009; on German RoE, see the pungent digest by Max Boot, "German Rules of Engagement?," *Commentary*, July 29, 2009.

32   "Factsheet: Afghanistan Lessons Learned Process," NATO, November 2021; available on the NATO website.

33   Ezra Klein, "If Joe Biden Doesn't Change Course, This Will Be His Worst Failure," *New York Times*, February 20, 2022.

34   Mark Landler, Katrin Bennhold, and Matina Stevis-Gridneff, "How the West Marshaled a Stunning Show of Unity against Russia," *New York Times*, March 5, 2022.

35   "Transcript: The Rachel Maddow Show," MSNBC, February 28, 2022.

end of the year that the more than $100 billion funneled to Kiev to date under Biden was "money well spent."[36] "In my humble opinion, this is very much like what Ronald Reagan did back in the eighties," North added, hearkening back to US assistance for "freedom fighters" in Afghanistan, Central America, Angola, Guinea-Bissau, and Mozambique. "These people were willing, as the Ukrainian people are, to use their blood and our bullets." Americans concerned about the scale of the largesse could rest easy knowing that much of it was spent back home, "provided to the contractors, defense logisticians, and the kinds of people who build the kind of systems we're getting." "The idea of it," North explained, was to send a signal to the Chinese leadership,

> to make sure that *they* get the right message, and to make sure that Putin gets the right message: no more invasions. And that means that the people of Taiwan are going to need the same kinds of weapons systems we're giving to the Ukrainians. And we'd better get hot at it. Because the Communist Chinese aren't backing down. But they're watching closely what we're doing.

Within the synods of American foreign policy, contrary noises can be heard. For some China hawks, overcommitment to Ukraine is a distraction, not a boon, in light of the imminent showdown over Taiwan.[37] But the quarrel concerns emphasis as much as upshot, permitting Republican legislators to amplify perennial griping over Europeans' insufficient investment in their own defense. And counterarguments are ready to hand. "Why have we achieved the level of success we've achieved in Ukraine?" mused the commander of US Marine Forces Japan, Lieutenant General James Bierman, at the start of the new year.

> [A] big part of that has been because after Russian aggression in 2014 and 2015, we earnestly got after preparing for future conflict: training for the Ukrainians, pre-positioning of supplies, identification of sites from which we could operate support, sustain operations.

---

36   Fox News, December 21, 2022.

37   Elbridge A. Colby, deputy assistance secretary of defense in the Trump administration (and grandson of the former CIA director), is one of the most energetic exponents of this opinion at the commanding heights of the US establishment. See Elbridge Colby and Oriana Skylar Mastro, "Ukraine Is a Distraction from Taiwan," *Wall Street Journal*, February 14, 2022.

We call that setting the theater. And we are setting the theater in Japan, in the Philippines, in other locations.[38]

As hostilities raged along a thousand-kilometer front in eastern Ukraine, observers in Washington found other reasons to rejoice. The expansion of NATO to Finland and Sweden would be a further windfall for American weapons manufacturers, whose share prices soared in 2022 as arms sales to other states in the alliance almost doubled from the previous year, the market largely innocent of competition and buyers bound by treaty covenant. Europe, Biden trumpeted in May, was at last en route to being fully "NATO-ized." Tangible evidence lay in the "F-35-ification of European armies," *Forbes* reported, a bonanza thanks not only to the cost of the combat aircraft themselves, malfunction-plagued fruit of an endless procurement boondoggle, but the "lock-in factor" guaranteed by "corresponding ground support, spare parts, and maintenance." "Europe," in short, "is now committed to American-made gear for decades to come."[39] This was not to mention the underlying cost-benefit calculus of the conflict. An analyst at CEPA, the Atlanticist think tank funded by Lockheed, United States European Command, and Ukrainian billionaire Victor Pinchuk, inter alia, concluded in late 2022 that "continued US support for Ukraine is a no-brainer from a bang for a buck perspective" [*sic*]. At only a fraction of the American defense budget (north of $715 billion for the fiscal year), this assistance underwrote a spectacularly disproportionate degradation of Russia's capability. "The US military might reasonably wish Russia to continue deploying military forces for Ukraine to destroy," given such an impressive return on investment.[40]

"The central importance of America to European security has been reasserted," a German parliamentarian affirmed in April 2022.[41] Finance Minister Robert Habeck, summoned to Washington to discuss promises to allocate 2 percent of GDP to military spending, per a totemic, long-flouted NATO benchmark, neatly summarized Berlin's position: "The

---

38   Kathrin Hille, "US Military Deepens Ties with Japan and Philippines to Prepare for China Threat," *Financial Times*, January 8, 2023.

39   Jon Markman, "Expanded NATO Will Shoot Billions to US Defense Contractors," *Forbes*, May 23, 2022.

40   Timothy Ash, "It's Costing Peanuts for the US to Defeat Russia," CEPA, November 18, 2022; available on the CEPA website.

41   Gideon Rachman, "Putin, Ukraine, and the Revival of the West," *Financial Times*, April 15, 2022.

more Germany serves, the greater its role."[42] Proof, if needed, appeared in the stoicism that greeted the bombing of the Nord Stream pipelines in September. Was this act of sabotage, the most serious attack on the civilian infrastructure of a NATO member state since the Second World War, not perhaps a blessing in disguise? Chancellor Olaf Scholz, in an English-language conspectus of Germany's "Zeitenwende"—a new era of militarism, conjured by the Russo-Chinese hydra—for the house journal of the Council on Foreign Relations, devoted only a sentence to the episode, under the subheading "Good for the Climate, Bad for Russia."[43] Radosław Sikorski, the European MP and former Polish minister of foreign affairs, delivered his own pithy appraisal on the morrow of the detonations: "Thank you, USA."[44] The culprits have yet to be apprehended; an initial wave of accusation against Moscow ebbed for want of a remotely plausible rationale, and the German and Swedish governments have withheld investigative findings on grounds of national security.[45] Whatever the case, American LNG now traversed the Atlantic in record quantities at what Habeck described as "astronomical prices," a "tremendous opportunity," according to Secretary of State Antony Blinken, to end Germany's shameful dependence on Russian fossil fuels.[46]

NATO is not, as such, responsible for sanctions against Russia or arms shipments to Ukraine. Rather it administers US power in Eurasia, as regional satrapy and launchpad for excursions elsewhere. In this respect, the brigading of allied nations into the Sino-American face-off bespeaks broader strategic intentions. In 2019, White House pressure on NATO allies to adopt a more aggressive posture toward Beijing provoked an indignant response from French president Emmanuel Macron. "Is our enemy today Russia? Or China?" he asked rhetorically, at a press conference alongside Stoltenberg. "Is it the goal of NATO to designate them as

---

42   "Habeck sieht 'dienende Führungsrolle,'" *Neue Zürcher Zeitung*, March 2, 2022.

43   Olaf Scholz, "The Global Zeitenwende: How to Avoid a New Cold War in a Multipolar Era," *Foreign Affairs* 102:1 (January–February 2023), pp. 22–38.

44   "Former Polish Foreign Minister Sikorski Thanks US for Damaging Nord Stream," TASS, September 28, 2022.

45   Wolfgang Streeck, "Getting Closer," *Sidecar*, November 8, 2022. According to reporting by Seymour Hersh, the attentats were carried out by US Navy divers on order from the White House. Seymour Hersh, "How America Took Out the Nord Stream Pipeline," *Substack*, February 8, 2023.

46   Thomas Fazi, "Did America Cause Europe's Energy War?," *UnHerd*, October 11, 2022.

enemies? I don't think so."[47] Macron reiterated the question two years later, after Anglo-Saxon treachery euchred France out of a lucrative submarine contract. But subsequent events returned a different verdict. At a June 2022 alliance summit in Madrid, NATO for the first time officially fixed China (labeled a "systemic challenge") in its gunsights, amid US efforts, in the words of allied diplomats, to "leverage the action it had been taking on Ukraine … into more concrete support for its policies in the Indo-Pacific region."[48] How far such leverage will extend cannot be foretold. Beneath avowals of unity, dissensus inevitably lurks, from an increasingly independent Turkey, with the second largest army in the alliance, to Chinese economic diplomacy and fickle opinion in Budapest or Rome.

This reader surveys the balance sheet of NATO-ization from the end of the Cold War to the Russian invasion of Ukraine. Varying in judgment and historical vantage, the contributions all share a critical perspective at odds with prevailing orthodoxy. The volume is divided into five sections. In Part I, Mary Elise Sarotte, Benjamin C. Schwarz, John Lewis Gaddis, and Peter Gowan revisit the initial option to preserve and expand the alliance in the 1990s. In Part II, Gowan, Tariq Ali, Alan J. Kuperman, and Régis Debray assay different episodes in NATO's transformation from a "defensive" alliance into a roving, interventionist cartel, its operations stretching from the Maghreb to the Khyber Pass. Part III turns to the 2014 crisis in Ukraine and its aftermath in the context of deteriorating relations between NATO and Russia, with essays by John J. Mearsheimer, Susan Watkins, and Michael T. Klare. Against that backdrop, Watkins, Tony Wood, and Volodymyr Ishchenko explore the origins of the 2022 conflagration in Part IV.

Part V zooms out to capture the wider landscape of Atlanticist ideology and its possible futures, canvassed from various angles by Richard Seymour, Alexander Zevin, Lily Lynch, Cihan Tuğal, and Wolfgang Streeck, followed—in conclusion—by Thomas Meaney. Written during the war itself, these texts stand in contrast to the pieties and propaganda that saturate the Natopolitan scene.

---

47   Helene Fouquet, "Macron Says NATO Should Shift Its Focus away from Russia," *Bloomberg*, November 28, 2019.

48   Henry Foy and Demetri Sevastopulo, "US Steps Up Pressure on European Allies to Harden China Stance," *Financial Times*, November 29, 2022.

PART ONE
Vae Victis

1

A Broken Promise? What the West Really Told Moscow about NATO Expansion

Mary Elise Sarotte

Twenty-five years ago, in November 1989, an East German Politburo member bungled the announcement of what were meant to be limited changes to travel regulations, thereby inspiring crowds to storm the border dividing East and West Berlin.[1] The result was the iconic moment marking the point of no return in the end of the Cold War: the fall of the Berlin Wall. In the months that followed, the United States, the Soviet Union, and West Germany engaged in fateful negotiations over the withdrawal of Soviet troops and the reunification of Germany. Although these talks eventually resulted in German reunification on October 3, 1990, they also gave rise to a later, bitter dispute between Russia and the West. What, exactly, had been agreed about the future of NATO? Had the United States formally promised the Soviet Union that the alliance would not expand eastward as part of the deal?

---

1 [For complete references for this chapter, see Mary E. Sarotte, *Not One Inch: America, Russia, and the Making of Post–Cold War Stalemate* (New Haven, CT: Yale University Press, 2021).]

Even more than two decades later, the dispute refuses to go away. Russian diplomats regularly assert that Washington made just such a promise in exchange for the Soviet troop withdrawal from East Germany— and then betrayed that promise as NATO added twelve Eastern European countries in three subsequent rounds of enlargement. Writing in *Foreign Policy* in June 2014, the Russian foreign policy thinker Alexander Lukin accused successive US presidents of "forgetting the promises made by Western leaders to Mikhail Gorbachev after the unification of Germany— most notably that they would not expand NATO eastward."[2] Indeed, Russian president Vladimir Putin's aggressive actions in Georgia in 2008 and Ukraine in 2014 were fueled in part by his ongoing resentment about what he sees as the West's broken pact over NATO expansion. But US policymakers and analysts insist that such a promise never existed. In a 2009 *Washington Quarterly* article, for example, the scholar Mark Kramer assured readers not only that Russian claims were a complete "myth" but also that "the issue never came up during the negotiations on German reunification."[3]

Now that increasing numbers of formerly secret documents from 1989 and 1990 have made their way into the public domain, historians can shed new light on this controversy. The evidence demonstrates that contrary to the conventional wisdom in Washington, the issue of NATO's future in not only East Germany but also Eastern Europe arose soon after the Berlin Wall opened, as early as February 1990. US officials, working closely with West German leaders, hinted to Moscow during negotiations that month that the alliance might not expand, not even to the eastern half of a soon-to-be-reunited Germany.

Documents also show that the United States, with the help of West Germany, soon pressured Gorbachev into allowing Germany to reunify, without making any kind of written promise about the alliance's future plans. Put simply, there was never a formal deal, as Russia alleges—but US and West German officials briefly implied that such a deal might be on the table, and in return they received a "green light" to commence the process of German reunification. The dispute over this sequence of events has distorted relations between Washington and Moscow ever since.

---

2   Alexander Lukin, "What the Kremlin Is Thinking," *Foreign Affairs* 93:4 (July– August 2014), pp. 85–93.

3   Mark Kramer, "The Myth of a No-NATO-Enlargement Pledge to Russia," *Washington Quarterly* 32:2 (April 2009), pp. 39–61.

Getting the Green Light

Western leaders quickly realized that the fall of the Berlin Wall had brought seemingly long-settled issues of European security once again into play. By the beginning of 1990, the topic of NATO's future role was coming up frequently during confidential conversations among US president George H. W. Bush; James Baker, the US secretary of state; Helmut Kohl, the West German chancellor; Hans-Dietrich Genscher, the West German foreign minister; and Douglas Hurd, the British foreign minister.

According to documents from the West German Foreign Ministry, for example, Genscher told Hurd on February 6 that Gorbachev would want to rule out the prospect of NATO's future expansion not only to East Germany but also to Eastern Europe. Genscher suggested that the alliance should issue a public statement saying that "NATO does not intend to expand its territory to the East." "Such a statement must refer not just to [East Germany], but rather be of a general nature," he added. "For example, the Soviet Union needs the security of knowing that Hungary, if it has a change of government, will not become part of the Western Alliance." Genscher urged that NATO discuss the matter immediately, and Hurd agreed.

Three days later, in Moscow, Baker talked NATO with Gorbachev directly. During their meeting, Baker took handwritten notes of his own remarks, adding stars next to the key words: "End result: Unified Ger. Anchored in a ★ changed (polit.) NATO — ★ whose juris. Would not move ★ eastward!"[4] Baker's notes appear to be the only place such an assurance was written down on February 9, and they raise an interesting question. If Baker's "end result" was that the jurisdiction of NATO's collective-defense provision would not move eastward, did that mean it would not move into the territory of former East Germany after reunification?

In answering that question, it is fortunate for posterity's sake that Genscher and Kohl were just about to visit Moscow themselves. Baker left behind with the West German ambassador in Moscow a secret letter for Kohl that has been preserved in the German archives. In it, Baker explained that he had put the crucial statement to Gorbachev in the form of a question: "Would you prefer to see a unified Germany outside of NATO, independent and with no US forces," he asked, presumably

---

4   Sarotte, *Not One Inch*, p. 55.

framing the option of an untethered Germany in a way that Gorbachev would find unattractive, "or would you prefer a unified Germany to be tied to NATO, with assurances that NATO's jurisdiction would not shift one inch eastward from its present position?"

Baker's phrasing of the second, more attractive option meant that NATO's jurisdiction would not even extend to East Germany, since NATO's "present position" in February 1990 remained exactly where it had been throughout the Cold War: with its eastern edge on the line still dividing the two Germanies. In other words, a united Germany would be, de facto, half in and half out of the alliance. According to Baker, Gorbachev responded, "Certainly any extension of the zone of NATO would be unacceptable." In Baker's view, Gorbachev's reaction indicated that "NATO in its current zone might be acceptable."

After receiving their own report on what had happened in Moscow, however, staff members on the National Security Council back in Washington felt that such a solution would be unworkable as a practical matter. How could NATO's jurisdiction apply to only half of a country? Such an outcome was neither desirable nor, they suspected, necessary. As a result, the National Security Council put together a letter to Kohl under Bush's name. It arrived just before Kohl departed for his own trip to Moscow.

Instead of implying that NATO would not move eastward, as Baker had done, this letter proposed a "special military status for what is now the territory of [East Germany]." Although the letter did not define exactly what the special status would entail, the implication was clear: all of Germany would be in the alliance, but to make it easier for Moscow to accept this development, some kind of face-saving regulations would apply to its eastern region (restrictions on the activities of certain kinds of NATO troops, as it turned out).

Kohl thus found himself in a complicated position as he prepared to meet with Gorbachev on February 10, 1990. He had received two letters, one on either end of his flight from West Germany to the Soviet Union, the first from Bush and the second from Baker, and the two contained different wording on the same issue. Bush's letter suggested that NATO's border would begin moving eastward; Baker's suggested that it would not.

According to records from Kohl's office, the chancellor chose to echo Baker, not Bush, since Baker's softer line was more likely to produce the results that Kohl wanted: permission from Moscow to start reunifying Germany. Kohl thus assured Gorbachev that "naturally NATO could not expand its territory to the current territory of [East Germany]." In parallel talks, Genscher delivered the same message to his Soviet counterpart, Eduard Shevardnadze, saying, "For us, it stands firm: NATO will not expand itself to the East."

As with Baker's meeting with Gorbachev, no written agreement emerged. After hearing these repeated assurances, Gorbachev gave West Germany what Kohl later called "the green light" to begin creating an economic and monetary union between East and West Germany—the first step of reunification. Kohl held a press conference immediately to lock in this gain. As he recalled in his memoirs, he was so overjoyed that he couldn't sleep that night, and so instead went for a long cold walk through Red Square.

Bribing the Soviets Out

But Kohl's phrasing would quickly become heresy among the key Western decision-makers. Once Baker got back to Washington, in mid-February 1990, he fell in line with the National Security Council's view and adopted its position. From then on, members of Bush's foreign policy team exercised strict message discipline, making no further remarks about NATO holding at the 1989 line.

Kohl, too, brought his rhetoric in line with Bush's, as both US and West German transcripts from the two leaders' February 24–25 summit at Camp David show. Bush made his feelings about compromising with Moscow clear to Kohl: "To hell with that!" he said. "We prevailed, they didn't. We can't let the Soviets clutch victory from the jaws of defeat."[5] Kohl argued that he and Bush would have to find a way to placate Gorbachev, predicting, "It will come down in the end to a question of cash." Bush pointedly noted that West Germany had "deep pockets." A straightforward strategy thus arose: as Robert Gates, then US deputy national security adviser, later explained it, the goal was to "bribe the Soviets out." And West Germany would pay the bribe.[6]

---

5   George H. W. Bush and Brent Scowcroft, *A World Transformed* (New York: Alfred A. Knopf, 1998), p. 253.

6   Robert M. Gates, *From the Shadows: The Ultimate Insider's Story of Five Presidents and How They Won the Cold War* (New York: Touchstone, 1996), pp. 492–3.

In April, Bush spelled out this thinking in a confidential telegram to French president François Mitterrand. US officials worried that the Kremlin might try to outmaneuver them by allying with the United Kingdom or France, both of which were also still occupying Berlin and, given their past encounters with a hostile Germany, potentially had reason to share the Soviets' unease about reunification. So Bush emphasized his top priorities to Mitterrand: that a united Germany enjoy full membership in NATO, that allied forces remain in a united Germany even after Soviet troops withdraw, and that NATO continue to deploy both nuclear and conventional weapons in the region. He warned Mitterrand that no other organization could "replace NATO as the guarantor of Western security and stability." He continued: "Indeed, it is difficult to visualize how a European collective security arrangement including Eastern Europe, and perhaps even the Soviet Union, would have the capability to deter threats to Western Europe."[7]

Bush was making it clear to Mitterrand that the dominant security organization in a post–Cold War Europe had to remain NATO—and not any kind of pan-European alliance. As it happened, the next month, Gorbachev proposed just such a pan-European arrangement, one in which a united Germany would join both NATO and the Warsaw Pact, thus creating one massive security institution. Gorbachev even raised the idea of having the Soviet Union join NATO. "You say that NATO is not directed against us, that it is simply a security structure that is adapting to new realities," Gorbachev told Baker in May, according to Soviet records. "Therefore, we propose to join NATO." Baker refused to consider such a notion, replying dismissively, "Pan-European security is a dream."

Throughout 1990, US and West German diplomats successfully countered such proposals, partly by citing Germany's right to determine its alliance partners itself. As they did so, it became clear that Bush and Kohl had guessed correctly: Gorbachev would, in fact, eventually bow to Western preferences, as long as he was compensated. Put bluntly, he needed the cash. In May 1990, Jack Matlock, the US ambassador to Moscow, reported that Gorbachev was starting to look "less like a man in control and more [like] an embattled leader." The "signs of crisis," Matlock wrote in a cable from Moscow, "are legion: Sharply rising crime

---

7   Mitterrand's top adviser on foreign policy, Hubert Védrine, wrote of Bush after the fall of the Berlin Wall that "the *only* issue that concerned him [was] the survival of NATO." *Les mondes de François Mitterrand: À l'Élysée, 1981–1995* (Paris: Fayard, 1996), p. 443.

rates, proliferating antiregime demonstrations, burgeoning separatist movements, deteriorating economic performance ... and a slow, uncertain transfer of power from party to state and from the center to the periphery."[8]

Moscow would have a hard time addressing these domestic problems without the help of foreign aid and credit, which meant that it might be willing to compromise. The question was whether West Germany could provide such assistance in a manner that would allow Gorbachev to avoid looking as though he was being bribed into accepting a reunified Germany in NATO with no meaningful restrictions on the alliance's movement eastward.

Kohl accomplished this difficult task in two bursts: first, in a bilateral meeting with Gorbachev in July 1990, and then, in a set of emotional follow-up phone calls in September 1990. Gorbachev ultimately gave his assent to a united Germany in NATO in exchange for face-saving measures, such as a four-year grace period for removing Soviet troops and some restrictions on both NATO troops and nuclear weapons on former East German territory. He also received 12 billion Deutsche Marks to construct housing for the withdrawing Soviet troops and another 3 billion in interest-free credit. What he did not receive were any formal guarantees against NATO expansion.

In August 1990, Saddam Hussein's invasion of Kuwait immediately pushed Europe down the White House's list of foreign policy priorities. Then, after Bush lost the 1992 presidential election to Bill Clinton, Bush's staff members had to vacate their offices earlier than they had expected. They appear to have communicated little with the incoming Clinton team. As a result, Clinton's staffers began their tenure with limited or no knowledge of what Washington and Moscow had discussed regarding NATO.

The Seeds of a Future Problem

Contrary to the view of many on the US side, then, the question of NATO expansion arose early and entailed discussions of expansion not only to East Germany but also to Eastern Europe. But contrary to Russian

---

8 "Moscow Embassy Cable," May 11, 1990, released by the State Department via FOIA and reproduced in *Gorbachev and Bush: The Last Superpower Summits*, ed. Svetlana Savranskaya and Thomas S. Blanton (Budapest: Central European University Press, 2020), pp. 141–7.

allegations, Gorbachev never got the West to promise that it would freeze NATO's borders. Rather, Bush's senior advisers had a spell of internal disagreement in early February 1990, which they displayed to Gorbachev. By the time of the Camp David summit, however, all members of Bush's team, along with Kohl, had united behind an offer in which Gorbachev would receive financial assistance from West Germany—and little else— in exchange for allowing Germany to reunify and for allowing a united Germany to be part of NATO.

In the short run, the result was a win for the United States. US officials and their West German counterparts had expertly outmaneuvered Gorbachev, extending NATO to East Germany and avoiding promises about the future of the alliance. One White House staffer under Bush, Robert Hutchings, ranked a dozen possible outcomes, from the "most congenial" (no restrictions at all on NATO as it moved into former East Germany) to the "most inimical" (a united Germany completely outside of NATO). In the end, the United States achieved an outcome somewhere between the best and the second best on the list. Rarely does one country win so much in an international negotiation.

But as Baker presciently wrote in his memoirs of his tenure as secretary of state, "almost every achievement contains within its success the seeds of a future problem."[9] By design, Russia was left on the periphery of a post–Cold War Europe. A young KGB officer serving in East Germany in 1989 offered his own recollection of the era in an interview a decade later, in which he remembered returning to Moscow full of bitterness at how "the Soviet Union had lost its position in Europe."[10] His name was Vladimir Putin, and he would one day have the power to act on that bitterness.

---

9   James Baker with Thomas M. DeFrank, *The Politics of Diplomacy* (New York: G. P. Putnam's Sons, 1995), p. 84.

10   Vladimir Putin, with Nataliya Gevorkyan, Natalya Timakova, and Andrei Kolesnikov, *First Person: An Astonishingly Frank Self-Portrait by Russia's President Putin*, trans. Catherine A. Fitzpatrick (New York: PublicAffairs, 2000), pp. 69–76.

2

"Cold War" Continuities: US Economic and Security Strategy toward Europe

Benjamin C. Schwarz

With the end of the Cold War, the American foreign policy community has been avid to try something new. Having spent decades evaluating the drab minutiae of arms control and in other ways attempting to manage the seemingly eternal US–Soviet rivalry, members of that community have eagerly answered the call to refashion America's national security strategy. The flood of recent reports, articles and books, however, is disappointing. After promising bold new thinking on America's grand strategy, these writings boldly call for the status quo. Some take a nip here: the United States can reduce its troop strength in Europe to a hundred thousand ("although not below that"). Others take a tuck there: "Not all Third World states are equally important to the United States" (although it would be "a mistake to ignore the spillover effects" of Third World instability "on international order and on American interests"). In short, when these alterations are finished, the essentials of America's "Cold War" strategy remain inviolate.

The Clinton administration's "Bottom-Up Review" of US defense policy, released in September 1993, illustrates this stasis. Having promised a fundamental reassessment of America's national security requirements, Pentagon planners concluded after six months of analysis that US security demands military spending of more than \$1.3 trillion over the next five years and the permanent commitment of two hundred thousand US troops in Europe and East Asia—in other words, a strategy remarkably similar to that of the Cold War. Moreover, rather than relinquish America's costly and risky responsibilities by dissolving Cold War alliances, the administration now plans to expand NATO's responsibilities eastward. Those who call for a more modest US defense policy argue that American defense plans are extravagances born of paranoia or of a defense establishment's anxiety to protect its budget. In fact, however, given the way the United States has defined its interests since World War II, the plans are quite prudent. And that is the problem.

The demand for new strategies for a new world springs from the assumption that the Soviet "threat" fundamentally determined US diplomacy from 1945 until the end of the Cold War. Now that the USSR has disappeared, it would seem reasonable that American security policy would change profoundly. But this view presupposes that Washington's Cold War grand strategy was—and that foreign policy in general is—a response to the pressures of other states. If, however, US security policy has been primarily determined not by external threats but by the apparent demands of America's economy, it would follow that, despite the collapse of the Berlin Wall, Washington's global strategy must remain largely unaltered. Persuasively, albeit unwittingly, this is the argument that the foreign policy community advances today in its post–Cold War strategic reassessments. To appreciate the dilemma that arises when the United States seeks its domestic well-being in sources beyond its borders, we must examine those internal imperatives that dictate foreign policy. In other words, we must explore that policy from the inside out.

The US Role in Cold War Europe

Diplomatic historians fall into two general categories. The tradition of *Innenpolitik* argues that internal pressures mainly determine foreign policy. In contrast, the scholarship of *Außenpolitik* views relations among states as a realm apart from domestic politics and holds that a state's foreign policy is determined mostly by the pressures of the international system. In assessing the forces that shape a country's foreign policy, therefore, the *Außenpolitik* approach stresses strategic considerations and perceptions of external threats. This approach dominates the interpretation of American strategy since World War II. The history of US national security policy after 1945 is thus understood as the story of America's response—sometimes paranoid, sometimes clumsy, occasionally prudent—to the threat of a superpower rival.

That such a view is misleading becomes apparent through the critique of US Cold War strategy produced by the school of foreign policy known as "political realism." Realism, which holds that gaining power and security is the primary foreign policy objective of states (in contrast, say, to furthering an ideology or pursuing profits) is, of course, an expression of *Außenpolitik*. Believing that external pressures determined strategy, many realists—including such penetrating American foreign policy thinkers as George Kennan and Walter Lippmann—were convinced that much of America's Cold War security policy was irrational. Neither Kennan nor Lippmann, for example, could understand the US commitment in Vietnam, an area of no intrinsic strategic value. Nor, more important, could they understand why America's foreign policy elite met their suggestions for a mutual superpower disengagement from Europe with such hostility.

Kennan and Lippmann's goals in Europe were limited and specific. Defining America's interest there as preventing the continent's military domination by a single power, they perceived American policy in strategic, rather than ideological or "world order," terms. "It is to the Red Army in Europe and not to ideologies, elections, forms of government, to socialism, to communism, to free enterprise, that a correctly conceived and soundly planned policy should be directed," Lippmann argued in 1947.[1] Similarly, Kennan saw America's European interests in narrow, geopolitical terms.[2]

---

1 Walter Lippmann, *The Cold War: A Study in US Foreign Policy* (New York: Harper, 1947), p. 19.

2 In what he admitted was an oversimplification, Kennan argued in 1948 that there were "only five centers of industrial and military power in the world which are important to us from the standpoint of national security." These were the US, Britain, Germany and Central Europe, the Soviet Union, and Japan. Quoted in John Lewis Gaddis, *Strategies of Containment: A Critical Appraisal of Postwar American National Security Policy* (Oxford: Oxford University Press, 1982), p. 30. See also George Kennan, *Memoirs, 1925–1950* (Boston: Little, Brown, 1967), p. 359. Only one of these power centers was, · at the time, in the hands of the Soviet Union; to Kennan, the primary security interest of the US, therefore, was to see to it that no other area fell under Soviet sway. Kennan did not believe, however, that containing the Soviet Union required America's security leadership in Europe. Memorandum from Kennan to the undersecretary of state, "Policy with Respect to American Aid to Western Europe," in US Department of State, *Foreign*

While most of his government colleagues were inspired by the idea of a
Pax Americana, Kennan had a far more modest view of America's future
European—and global—role. He looked to the restoration of a plural world
in which other powers—the major European states in particular—would
dilute the nascent US–Soviet confrontation.[3]

Disengaging the United States and the Soviet Union from Europe (a
proposal that most historians now believe would have stood a good chance
of success)[4] and thereby restoring a multipolar balance of power would
be, Kennan and Lippmann reasoned, in America's long-term interest,
for it would free the United States from its crushing responsibilities for
others' security and would reduce tensions between the superpowers.
As it happens, the foreign policy community had very clear reasons for
wishing to maintain those responsibilities, but Kennan, Lippmann, and
other realists blamed America's seeming refusal to act realistically on what
they saw as its penchant for viewing foreign policy as a moral crusade.

That realist assumption was wrong. Throughout the post–World War
II era, American interests and security commitments (at least the major
ones) have been pursued deliberately and for consistent—if recondite—
reasons, reasons not obvious to the public nor fully appreciated by the
realist viewpoint. If well-informed Americans had been asked in the mid-
eighties why US troops were deployed in Europe (and East Asia), they
would have answered: to keep the Soviets out. They may have wondered,
however, why the United States persisted in its strategy even after Western
Europe (and Japan and South Korea) had become capable of defending
themselves. Today, they are thoroughly bewildered. Now that the USSR

Relations of the United States 1947, vol. 3 (Washington, DC: US Government Publishing
Office, 1974), pp. 224–5; memo, from Kennan, "North Atlantic Security Pact," ibid., p. 285;
memo, from Kennan to the secretary of state, "Policy Questions Concerning a Possible
German Settlement," US Department of State, *Foreign Relations of the United States 1948*,
vol. 2 (Washington, DC: US Government Publishing Office, 1974), pp. 1287–97. See also
Kennan, *Memoirs*, pp. 406–7. Kennan strongly believed that NATO would, in fact, be
inimical to American interests. A formal military alliance, he argued, would militarize
Europe around a superpower confrontation, thus preventing the political and diplomatic
flexibility needed for later European settlement. Once European territory came to be seen
in a confrontational military perspective, Kennan reasoned, the Soviets could never withdraw from positions they might otherwise view as undesirably overextended. Kennan,
"Policy Questions Concerning a Possible German Settlement" and "North Atlantic Security Pact."

   3   Kennan, "North Atlantic Security Pact." See also Anders Stephanson, *Kennan and
the Art of Foreign Policy* (Cambridge, MA: Harvard University Press, 1989), pp. 145–7.

   4   Ibid., p. 155.

itself has disappeared, why does Washington continue to insist that an American-led NATO and the US defense commitments to East Asia are still indispensable to America's security?

If, on the other hand, National Security Council staffers, think tank analysts, or State Department policy planners were asked about America's globe-girdling security commitments, forty years ago, ten years ago, or now, their answers would be consistent—and noticeably different from those of educated laymen. They would justify American deployments overseas by invoking such terms as "shaping a favorable international environment," "reassurance of allies," and the ongoing need for "leadership," "stability," and "continuing engagement." Even during the Cold War, the "Soviet threat" might not have been mentioned. The question this begs, however, is why has the awesome task of building a stable world been deemed so crucial to America? Why have "stability" and "reassurance" been for nearly fifty years the mantra of the foreign policy cognoscenti?

America's Economically Driven Cold War Policy

To understand the forces that have motivated US foreign policy since 1945, we must look not to the Soviet Union, but to ourselves; not primarily to the superpower's geopolitical rivalry, but to the ascendancy of a vision that saw new requirements for America's prosperity. From the end of World War I through the 1930s, the American political economy was changing dramatically. The most rapidly growing and profitable sector comprised large, capital-intensive, advanced-technology corporations, investment banks, and internationally oriented commercial banks, all of which took the world market for their target. The international economy was America's future—or so it seemed to the architects of America's post–World War II foreign policy elite, who were themselves drawn almost exclusively from the world of East Coast international business and finance.[5]

---

5   On this transformation of the American political economy and its influence on US foreign policy, see Thomas Ferguson, "From Normalcy to New Deal: Industrial Structure, Party Competition, and American Public Policy in the Great Depression," *International Organization* 38:1 (Winter 1984), pp. 41–94; Lynn Rachele Eden, "The Diplomacy of Force: Interests, the State, and the Making of American Military Policy in 1948," PhD diss., University of Michigan, 1985; James R. Kurth, "Travels between Europe and America: The Rise and Decline of the New York Foreign Policy Elite," in *The Capital of*

These men had great hope for the future, for they believed that the United States could, using such implements as the General Agreement on Tariffs and Trade (GATT) and the international monetary arrangements negotiated at Bretton Woods, build and manage a new, liberal, global political economy in which trade and capital flowed across national boundaries in response to the laws of supply and demand. Of course, in such a world, the United States, which dominated the international economy, would benefit enormously, but the rest of the world would benefit as well. America's power at the close of World War II made US policymakers believe that they could translate their vision into a reality.

Such hopes were coupled with an uncomfortable recollection of the Great Depression. Fear of return to depression fueled the drive toward a postwar international order that might guarantee America's economic health. To Secretary of State Dean Acheson and the other designers of America's Cold War foreign policy, there was only one solution. Summarily dismissing schemes to achieve national self-sufficiency through state planning, Acheson declared: "We cannot have full employment and prosperity in the United States without foreign markets."[6] American foreign policy generally, and America's interests in Europe specifically, since World War II cannot be understood except within the context of the project to maintain an open global economy. National policymakers knew that such a goal dictated that the United States fundamentally alter international politics.

The greatest danger to American democracy and prosperity, as US policymakers saw it, came not primarily from the Soviet Union but from Germany and Japan, since their strength was both necessary and potentially disastrous for the multinational capitalist community the United States was intent on constructing. An industrialized Germany, for instance, would be Europe's most cost-competitive producer and its most effective consumer. Without full German participation in the European economy, there could be no revitalization of an international economy, and that, as under secretary of state for economic affairs Will Clayton warned in 1949,

the American Century, ed. Martin Shefter (New York: Russell Sage Foundation, 1993); Franz Schurmann, The Logic of World Power: An Inquiry into the Origins, Currents, and Contradictions of World Politics (New York: Pantheon Books, 1974); and Bruce Cumings, The Origins of the Korean War, vol. 2, The Roaring of the Cataract, 1947–1950 (Princeton: Princeton University, 1990), chaps. 1–5, 22.

6   Quoted in Fred Block, "Economic Instability and Military Strength: Paradoxes of the 1950 Rearmament Decision," Politics and Society 10:1 (January 1980), pp. 35–58.

would spell the beginning of the end for "our democratic free enterprise system."[7] But, as future secretary of state John Foster Dulles explained in a closed Senate hearing in 1949, while Germany's integration with Western Europe was imperative, Western Europeans were "afraid to bring that strong, powerful, highly concentrated group of people into unity with them."[8] Similarly, a strong Japan was at once essential to Asia's economy and intolerable to its neighbors.[9] The problem lay in the inherent contradiction between capitalist economies and international politics.

Capitalist economies prosper most when labor, technology and capital are fluid, so they are driven toward international integration and interdependence. But while all states benefit absolutely in an open international economy, some states benefit more than others. In the normal course of world politics, in which states are driven to compete for their security, this relative distribution of power is a country's principal concern, and it discourages interdependence. In efforts to ensure that power is distributed in its favor at the expense of its actual or potential rivals, a state will "nationalize," that is, pursue autarkic policies—practicing capitalism only within its borders or among countries in a trading bloc. That action restricts both production factors and markets, thereby fragmenting an international economy.

In the normal course of world politics, therefore, international economic interdependence is impossible to achieve. As political economist Robert Gilpin remarks, "what today we call international economic interdependence runs so counter to the great bulk of human experience that only extraordinary changes and novel circumstances could have led to

---

7   Quoted in Thomas McCormick, *America's Half-Century* (Baltimore: Johns Hopkins University Press, 1986), p. 81. See the similar comments by Secretary of State George Marshall in November 1947 in Lloyd C. Gardner, *Architects of Illusion: Men and Ideas in American Foreign Policy, 1941–1949* (Chicago: Quadrangle Books, 1971), p. 231.

8   US Congress, *North Atlantic Treaty: Hearings Before the Senate Foreign Relations Committee on Executive L*, 81st Cong., 1st sess., April–May 1949, pp. 355–6.

9   On the central importance of Japan in the US vision of a postwar international capitalist order, see William S. Borden, *The Pacific Alliance: United States Foreign Economic Policy and Japanese Trade Recovery, 1947–1955* (Madison: University of Wisconsin Press, 1984); Ronald L. McGlothlen, *Controlling the Waves: Dean Acheson and US Foreign Policy in Asia* (NY: Norton, 1993); Bruce Cumings, "The Origins and Development of the Northeast Asian Political Economy: Industrial Sectors, Product Cycles, and Political Consequences," *International Organization* 38:1 (Winter 1984), pp. 1–40; Bruce Cumings, "Power and Plenty in Northeast Asia: The Evolution of US Policy," *World Policy Journal* 5:1 (Winter 1987–88), pp. 79–106; and Cumings, *Origins of the Korean War*, vol. 2.

its innovation and triumph over other means of economic exchange."[10] In fact, as Immanuel Wallerstein and Thomas McCormick point out, international capitalism has enjoyed only two golden ages: the periods following the Napoleonic Wars and the two World Wars.[11] The key to both of these episodes of peace and prosperity has been the same: the ability and will of a single state to play the role of hegemonic power. The only way to overcome the dangers inherent to international capitalism is for a preponderant power to take care of other states' security problems for them, so that they need not pursue autarkic policies or form trading blocs in attempts to improve their relative positions. This suspension of international politics through hegemony has been the fundamental aim of US foreign policy since 1945; the real story of that policy is not the thwarting of the Soviet "threat," but rather the effort to impose a specific economic vision on a recalcitrant world.

After World War II, Washington policymakers recognized that only the United States could achieve the prerequisite for an open world economy—ensuring that Germany and Japan were revitalized as engines of world economic growth, while simultaneously assuaging Western Europe's and Asia's fears about German and Japanese economic, military and political dominance. Thus, Washington committed itself to building and maintaining an international political order based upon an American "preponderance of power." By providing for Germany's and Japan's security and by enmeshing their military and foreign policies into alliances that it dominated, the United States contained its erstwhile enemies, preventing its "partners" from embarking upon independent policies. This stabilized relations among the states of Western Europe and East Asia, for by controlling Germany and Japan, the United States "reassured" their neighbors that these most powerful allies would remain pacific. NATO and the US–Japan Alliance, by banishing power politics and nationalist rivalries, protected the states of Western Europe and East Asia from themselves.[12]

---

10   Robert Gilpin, *War and Change in World Politics* (Cambridge: Cambridge University Press, 1981), p. 130.

11   Immanuel Wallerstein, *The Modern World System: Capitalist Agriculture and the Origins of the European World Economy in the Sixteenth Century* (New York: Academic Press, 1974); Immanuel Wallerstein, *Historical Capitalism* (London: Verso, 1983); and McCormick, *America's Half-Century.*

12   On America's role as Western Europe's and East Asia's "adult supervisor," see the comments of current and former officials cited below and Lawrence Kaplan, *The United States and NATO: The Formative Years* (Lexington, KY: University of Kentucky Press,

Freed from the fears and competitions that had for centuries kept them nervously looking over their shoulders, the West Europeans (and East Asians) were able to cooperate politically and economically. As Secretary of State Dean Rusk argued in 1967: "The presence of our forces in Europe under NATO has also contributed to the development of intra-European cooperation ... But without the visible assurance of a sizeable American contingent, old frictions may revive, and Europe could become unstable once more."[13] From that perspective, restoring Europe to its prewar status risked destroying America's grand design. What Kennan saw as the return to the normal power balance on the continent seemed to most other American statesmen to be a return to the international political and economic fragmentation of the 1930s. It was, after all, an independent Western Europe that had toppled the Pax Britannica and its beneficent global economic order. Recognizing that Europe and East Asia could not be left to their own devices in the post–Cold War world, Washington pursued not Kennan's vision of balance and diversity, but hegemony. This preponderance ensured the tranquil world environment in which an open economic system could operate.

Thus, America's foreign policy has been "imperialist" in the non-pejorative sense of the extension of great-power influence for economic purposes. In this sense, Lenin was right. Imperialism is (or allows for) "the highest stage of capitalism"—an open economy among the industrialized nations.

The fundamental purpose behind America's "Cold War" policy had little to do with containing the Soviet Union, even though the Soviet threat was used to justify that policy to a nationalist public and Congress (a strategy described by Senator Arthur Vandenberg as "scaring hell out of the American people" to secure an internationalist agenda).[14] The

1984); Josef Joffe, "Europe's American Pacifier," *Foreign Policy* 14 (Spring 1984), pp. 64–82; John Mearsheimer, "Back to the Future: Instability in Europe after the Cold War," *International Security* 15:1 (Summer 1990), pp. 5–56; and Bruce Cumings, "Trilateralism and the New World Order," *World Policy Journal* 8:2 (Spring 1991), pp. 195–222.

13   Memorandum from Dean Rusk to Sen. Mike Mansfield, April 17, 1967, Lyndon B. Johnson Library, National Security File, Box 51, "The Trilateral Negotiations and NATO 1966–1967," Tabs 43–63, Memo 153b.

14   That same year, Vandenberg's colleague, the fervently anticommunist Robert Taft, strongly suspected that the supposed dangers to the nation from the USSR failed to explain America's new foreign policy when he complained that he was "more than a bit tired of having the Soviet menace invoked as a reason for doing any- and everything that might or might not be desirable or necessary on its own merits." Quoted in William

Kremlin's irrelevance to America's postwar planning was acknowledged in NSC-68, the National Security Council's 1950 blueprint for America's Cold War strategy, which defined the security policy it advocated "as one designed to foster a world environment in which the American system can survive and flourish." This "policy of attempting to develop a healthy international community," NSC-68's authors went on to assert, was "a policy which we would probably pursue even if there was no Soviet threat."[15] In fact, America's "Cold War" alliances, organized ostensibly to contain the USSR, were formed at a time when US statesmen "did not expect and were not worried about Soviet aggression," as historian Melvyn Leffler, author of the most comprehensive study of the origins of the Cold War, concludes.[16]

Moreover, US officials recognized that their Cold War strategy actually exacerbated Washington–Moscow tensions. Arguing against Kennan's proposal for the neutralization of Germany and the consequent disengagement of the superpowers from the continent, the Central Intelligence Agency insisted, "The real issue is not the settlement of Germany [i.e., relaxing tensions with the Soviets] but the long-term control of German power."[17] By 1957 Kennan, grappling with why his ideas for withdrawing US and Soviet troops from Europe "appear[ed] so dangerous and heretical" to official Washington, was forced to conclude that American statesmen "would not have considered the withdrawal of a single American battalion from Western Germany even if the Russians had been willing to evacuate all of Eastern Germany and Poland by way of compensation."[18] While

---

Appleman Williams, *The Tragedy of American Diplomacy* (New York: Dell Publishing Company, 1972), p. 240. For the argument that the Soviet Union served as a "convenient adversary"—as an instrument to justify at home and abroad America's world order strategy—see Christopher Layne and Benjamin C. Schwarz, "American Hegemony— Without an Enemy," *Foreign Policy* 92 (Fall 1993), pp. 20–1.

15   See Layne and Schwarz, "American Hegemony"; and Block, "Economic Instability and Military Strength."

16   Melvyn P. Leffler, *A Preponderance of Power: National Security, the Truman Administration, and the Cold War* (Stanford: Stanford University Press, 1992). Although Leffler's book has emerged as the central work of Cold War "post-revisionists," the preponderance of his evidence and conclusions reinforces the "revisionist" critique of US Cold War policy. On this point, see the review article by Bruce Cumings, "'Revising Post-revisionism,' or the Poverty of Theory in Diplomatic History," *Diplomatic History* 17:4 (Fall 1993), pp. 539–69.

17   Quoted in Leffler, *A Preponderance of Power*, p. 284.

18   Kennan, *Memoirs, 1925–1950*, p. 260.

Kennan had long believed that America's European policy was motivated by an ill-considered ideological reaction to the Soviets, he now came to realize that US preponderance in Europe served aspirations that were unrelated to the Soviet Union.

American Hegemony and the World Economy

The conviction that America's prosperity depends upon international economic interdependence and that the precondition for economic interdependence is the geopolitical stability and reassurance that flow from America's security commitments continues to animate America's national security strategy. Secretary of State James Byrnes's 1945 explanation of the motive behind American foreign policy—"Our international policies and our domestic policies are inseparable; our foreign relations inevitably affect employment in the United States"[19]—remains the formula Washington follows today.[20] In fact, according to this reasoning, the weaker the US economy grows, the more energetically America must pursue world stability.

As Senator Richard Lugar (Republican from Indiana), explained in August 1993 when he called for American leadership to revive NATO:

> Trading within our own borders is insufficient to lead us out of economic difficulty; sustained economic growth requires an ability to export vigorously abroad. Full participation in the international market place requires a degree of stability and security in the international environment that only American power and leadership can provide.[21]

---

19 Quoted in Walter LaFeber, *America, Russia, and the Cold War, 1945–1966* (New York: Wiley, 1967), p. 6.

20 For examples of such reasoning, see the comments of former secretary of defense Dick Cheney and former national security adviser Brent Scowcroft. Dick Cheney, "The Military We Need in the Future: American Leadership and Security Requirements," September 4, 1992, in *Vital Speeches of the Day*, September–October 1992, pp. 13–14; and Brent Scowcroft, "Who Can Harness History? Only the US," *New York Times*, July 2, 1993.

21 Richard Lugar, "NATO: Out of Area or Out of Business. A Call for US Leadership to Revise and Redefine the Alliance," Remarks Delivered to the Open Forum of the US State Department, August 2, 1993. Lugar's foreign policy philosophy is nicely encapsulated in his assertion that America's "domestic well-being" is "heavily dependent on stability, economic reform and the growth of market economic and democratic institutions abroad."

The apparent connections among the requirements of an international capitalist economy, America's economic well-being, and its defense commitments have been repeated so often that Anthony Lake, President Clinton's national security advisor, conflated the supposed dictates of prosperity with those of national security in announcing the administration's new foreign policy doctrine in September 1993. Explaining that "the expansion of market-based economies abroad helps expand our exports and create American jobs," Lake declared that America's new "security mission" is the "enlargement of the world's community of market democracies."[22]

The now infamous draft of the Pentagon's classified "post–Cold War" Defense Planning Guidance (DPG), which gave the public an unprecedented glimpse into the thinking that informs America's defense strategy when it was leaked in March 1992, merely restates in somewhat undiplomatic language the logic behind America's "Cold War" reassurance strategy. Arguing that American preponderance as a security blanket is essential for stability in Europe and East Asia, the DPG stated that the United States must therefore "discourage the advanced industrialized nations from challenging our leadership or even aspiring to a larger global or regional role." To accomplish this, America must do nothing less than "retain the pre-eminent responsibility for addressing … those wrongs which threaten not only our interests, but those of our allies or friends, or which could seriously unsettle international relations."[23] The United States, in other words, must provide what one of the DPG's authors termed "adult supervision."[24] It must protect the interests of virtually all potential great powers for them so that they need not acquire the capabilities to protect themselves, that is, so that they need not act like great powers. The very existence of truly independent actors would be intolerable to the United States, for it would disrupt American hegemony, the key to a stable world.

The draft DPG's "post–Cold War" strategy of preponderance, then, reflects what Leffler defines as an imperative of America's Cold War national security policy: that "neither an integrated Europe, nor a united Germany nor an independent Japan must be permitted to emerge as a

---

22   Anthony Lake, "From Containment to Enlargement," Speech to the Johns Hopkins University School of Advanced International Studies, September 21, 1993.

23   See the excerpts of the FY 1994–1999 Defense Planning Guidance in Chapter 3 of this volume.

24   Interview, former Defense Department official, September 1993.

third force."[25] America's "allies" were understandably troubled by the impolitic language of the draft DPG, so the Pentagon issued a sanitized, unclassified version in January 1993. While the revised DPG may give less offense, its underlying message is the same and its economically based arguments are even stronger. America's Cold War alliances, it asserts, ensure "a prosperous, largely democratic, market-oriented zone of peace and prosperity that encompasses more than two-thirds of the world's economy." This makes maintaining these alliances America's "most vital" foreign policy priority.[26]

In 1993 President Clinton stated (echoing Byrnes's argument forty-eight years earlier) that "a global economy has changed the linkages between our domestic and foreign policies and, I would argue, has made them indivisible."[27] If this reasoning is accepted, America's security strategy seems to inexorably follow. Economic interdependence, apparently, dictates security commitments.[28] As long as world politics remain what they have always

25 Leffler, *A Preponderance of Power*, p. 17

26 In a similar vein, see the comments in 1990 by Deputy Assistant Secretary of State for European Affairs James Dobbins, who applied the DPG's reasoning to America's post–Cold War role in Europe specifically. US Congress, CSCE, *Implementation of the Helsinki Accords: Hearings*, 101st Cong., 2d sess., April 3, 1990, pp. 8, 18; and US Congress, *The Future of NATO: Hearings before the Senate Foreign Relations Committee*, 101st Cong. 2d sess., February 9, 1990, p. 19. Deputy Assistant Secretary of Defense Alberto Coll's elaboration of that argument in terms of US policy toward East Asia revealed the degree to which Washington sees its national security strategy as serving domestic economic imperatives. See Alberto Coll, "Power, Principles and a Cooperative World Order," *Washington Quarterly* 16:1 (Winter 1993), p. 8. Even America's nuclear preponderance serves this country's economic needs, according to a classified Pentagon report on the strategic importance of America's nuclear superiority in the post–Cold War era, leaked in 1991. Rejecting the notion that the only purpose of nuclear arms is to deter nuclear attack, the report explained that America's nuclear preponderance helps "sustain the nation's prestige and deter Germany and Japan from developing nuclear arsenals of their own." If Washington's former enemies were to acquire nuclear weapons, the report argued, the concomitant political and military "re-nationalization" in Europe and East Asia would close the world economy upon which America's prosperity depends. Thus, the report concluded with the seemingly bizarre assertion that America "must keep nuclear weapons to protect … a healthy and growing US economy." Quoted in R. Jeffrey Smith, "US Urged to Cut 50 Percent of A-Arms," *Washington Post*, January 6, 1992.

27 White House, Office of the Press Secretary, Prepared Remarks of President Clinton to the American Society of Newspaper Editors, "A Strategic Alliance with Russian Reform," April 1, 1993.

28 Since American prosperity presumably hinges "on achieving and maintaining open markets for international trade and investment," as C. Fred Bergsten, former assistant secretary of the treasury and senior adviser to the NSC, argues, then "the containment

been, Europe—and East Asia—will be potentially unstable. And as long as US prosperity is understood to depend upon the stability of those regions, the United States must pacify them, employing the most prominent—and costly—feature of its present security strategy: the military power that ensures America's preeminent place in its Cold War alliances. This leads to a dismal conclusion. America's worldwide security commitments are a truly permanent burden. They amount to taking the wolf by the ears: how could America ever let go? Arguing in 1992 for the maintenance of the US reassurance strategy in Asia and Europe, a high-ranking Pentagon official asked, "If we pull out, who knows what nervousness will result?"[29] The problem, of course, is that the United States can never know and, therefore, according to the assumptions underpinning its security policy, it must always stay.

Post–Cold War NATO and US Economic Renewal

Today's realists, who assume that others view national security policy through a narrow strategic lens rather than through a wider economic and political one, and who therefore argue that conflict in the former Yugoslavia is no danger to the United States, must look again to understand why foreign policy establishment figures as different as Jeane Kirkpatrick and Cyrus Vance agree that vital American interests are ultimately imperiled by Balkan turmoil. Ludicrous as it may seem at first glance, the fighting in the former Yugoslavia worries policymakers not so much for the humanitarian reasons that have received so much attention, but largely because they fear that instability in the Balkans will ultimately damage the global economy.

The interventionists' argument that America must lead efforts to pacify the former Yugoslavia merely extends the argument that America must lead in European security affairs, generally. In a memorandum written before his appointment, Deputy Assistant Secretary of Defense David

---

of the risk of conflict among the economic superpowers" must be "a primary purpose of US foreign policy." C. Fred Bergsten, "The Primacy of Economics," *Foreign Policy* 87 (Summer 1992), pp. 8–11.

29   Quoted in Morton Kondracke, "The Aspin Papers," *New Republic*, April 27, 1992, p. 12. The "wolf by the ears," of course, was Thomas Jefferson's apt phrase describing the dilemma of slavery in America. See Benjamin Schwarz, "From a Founding Father, an Imperfect Vision of America," *Los Angeles Times*, July 4, 1994.

Ochmanek urged US military action in Bosnia, explaining that since American "prosperity is intimately tied to that of the Europeans," the United States must "maintain its capacity to influence decision-making in Europe." Because NATO is "an essential source of US influence," Washington must continue to lead European security efforts—including undertakings to stanch instability in the Balkans. "If we want a seat at the table when the Europeans make decisions about trade and financial policy," Ochmanek reasoned, "we can't pretend that messy security problems in Europe are not our concern as well." If the US-dominated NATO demonstrates that it cannot or will not address Europe's post–Cold War security problems, then the alliance will be impotent. Atlanticists maintain that without an effective NATO—that is, without the Americans providing "adult supervision"—post–Cold War Europe will lapse into those same old bad habits that the alliance was supposed to suppress—power politics.[30]

What would be the result of this scenario? The United States will be greatly harmed *economically*. As General William Odom, former director of the National Security Agency, argues:

> Only a strong NATO with the US centrally involved can prevent Western Europe from drifting into national parochialism and eventual regression from its present level of economic and political cooperation. Failure to act effectively in Yugoslavia will accelerate this drift. That trend toward disorder will not only affect US security interests but also US economic interests. Our economic interdependency with Western Europe creates large numbers of American jobs.[31]

This appreciation of the disastrous consequences regional instability might have for America's hegemonic position and consequently for

30   "Yugoslavia and the Need to Live Up to Our Responsibilities," memorandum by David Ochmanek, RAND Corporation, June 9, 1992. Copy in author's files.

31   William E. Odom, "Yugoslavia: Quagmire or Strategic Challenge?," Hudson Institute Briefing Paper, November 1992. In the same vein, Lugar explains that fundamental American interests are greatly endangered in Bosnia because the "devastating" economic effects in Europe of the spread of Balkan instability would mean a "loss of jobs and loss of income in this country as we try to base a recovery upon our export potential." *MacNeil/ Lehrer NewsHour*, May 6, 1993. Sen. Dennis DeConcini (D-AZ) also argues that "crucial American interests are on the line in Bosnia." The US through NATO, he asserted, must bomb Serbian targets to pacify the former Yugoslavia because "Europe represents America's largest trading partner. An unstable Europe would damage our own economy." Dennis DeConcini, "Bomb the Serbs Now," *New York Times*, May 18, 1993.

international political cooperation and, ultimately, for international economic integration is the missing link that connects instability in the Balkans to American national interests. Unfortunately, there are many other situations in which the same connections can very plausibly be made.

According to the logic of Washington's global strategy, while the end of the superpower rivalry has reduced US security risks and commitments in some respects, it has in other ways expanded the frontiers of America's insecurity. During the Cold War, stability in Europe could be assured by Washington and Moscow smothering their respective clients. In fact, this superpower condominium, while crushing to the Europeans, was probably the best means of insuring America's overriding economic and political interest in the stability of the continent, as American statesmen have often privately acknowledged.[32] With the Soviet Union gone, however, its former charges have become free to make trouble for each other and for Western Europe. As former deputy assistant secretary of defense Zalmay Khalilzad, one of the main architects of the Bush administration's "new world order" policy, asserts, "Western and East Central European stability are becoming increasingly intertwined," and thus Western Europe's prosperity, upon which America's own economic health depends, is increasingly tied to economic relations with Eastern Europe. Moreover, Khalilzad argues, direct US economic interests in the region have also grown considerably, since "East Central Europe offers new and potentially expansive markets for US goods, investments and services."[33]

Even more important, American strategists fear that if the newly independent states of Eastern and Central Europe are not enmeshed in multilateral security arrangements under US "leadership," the region could once again become a political-military tinderbox as it was in the 1920s and 1930s, with the Baltic countries, Russia, Ukraine, Poland, the Czech and Slovak republics, Hungary and Romania worrying about each

32 The American public, for instance, was puzzled by State Department Counselor Helmut Sonnenfeldt's assertion that a Soviet–US condominium in Europe was actually in America's interest. Sonnenfeldt's thinking reflected that of the US foreign policy community, although it was clearly at variance with America's official position. See US Congress, *United States National Security Policy vis-à-vis Eastern Europe (The "Sonnenfeldt Doctrine"): Hearings before the Subcommittee on International Security and Scientific Affairs of the House Committee on International Relations*, 94th Cong., 2d sess., April 12, 1976.

33 See Zalmay Khalilzad, "Extending the Western Alliance to East Central Europe: A New Strategy for NATO," RAND Issue Paper, May 1993.

other and with all of them worrying about Germany. And, the argument goes, as in the past, Germany's involvement in Eastern Europe's rivalries could alarm its Western neighbors as well, threatening the stability of the entire continent.[34]

So America's responsibilities multiply. The Clinton administration and a growing number of the foreign policy elite have joined Khalil-zad in asserting that these conditions dictate that the US-led NATO must be "transformed."[35] As Lugar argues, since European stability "is a *precondition* for American domestic renewal" and since that stability is now threatened by "those areas in the east and south where the seeds of future conflict in Europe lie," the US-led NATO must now stabilize both halves of the continent by extending security guarantees to all of Europe, including, possibly, to Ukraine.[36] In other words, the United States must be prepared to go to war to defend the territorial integrity of states in regions riven by ethnic, religious, and nationalist animosities, regions in which nearly all borders are in dispute. Khalilzad and other proponents of this policy acknowledge that spreading America's security blanket over so inhospitable an area demands that the United States retain a substantial number of troops in Europe.[37] Indeed, this view of threats to America leads inevitably to Cold War–era military budgets. Therefore, it is not surprising that NATO's defense ministers declared in May 1993 that despite the dissolution of the very enemy that NATO was ostensibly formed to contain, cuts in military spending had to be immediately halted, for otherwise the alliance would be unable to fulfill what NATO's secretary general termed its "expanded range of missions."[38]

Since the late 1940s, the United States has, in essence, defined its vital interests in Europe as forestalling normal patterns of economic and security competition among the states of the region. This has required

---

34   Ibid.

35   The Clinton administration's Partnership for Peace (PfP) initiative, designed to increase significantly the military ties between NATO and the states of Eastern Europe, stopped short of providing those states with ironclad security guarantees. Its purpose, however, is to "reassure" those countries by enmeshing them in the NATO military system to such a degree that they become Alliance members in fact, if not in word. Moreover, formal NATO membership for Poland, Hungary, the Czech Republic, and Slovakia, President Clinton declared in July 1994, "is not a question of if, but of when and how." White House, Office of the Press Secretary, Remarks of the President to the Sejm, July 7, 1994.

36   Lugar, "NATO: Out of Area or Out of Business," p. 6. Emphasis in original.

37   Khalilzad, "Extending the Western Alliance," p. 6.

38   "Arms Cuts Worry NATO," *New York Times*, May 27, 1993.

an unprecedented extension of America's overseas responsibilities and commitments. So, while current proposals to extend NATO eastward are characterized by their proponents and detractors alike as radical and bold initiatives, those initiatives are in fact merely an additional payment, made necessary by changing geopolitical circumstances, on what is called America's original "transatlantic bargain."[39]

Realists, the foreign policy community maintains, can argue all they want that the plethora of potential hot spots in Eastern Europe and the former Soviet Union have no immediate strategic importance to the United States, but instability in these regions is intrinsically insidious to America's interests. So America must take the lead in attempts to impose stability. The liberal foreign policy commentator Walter Russell Mead, who in the past has favored reducing America's commitments abroad, says that he favors the United States having a cooperative, rather than a dominant, relationship with its allies. But Mead, reflecting the dilemma of American security policy, is unable to reconcile America's need to lighten its international burdens with his recognition of the dangerous economic consequences of America abdicating its leadership role. The United States, Mead asserts, cannot even allow its "partners" to assume primary responsibility for quelling the instability that, after all, most affects them. Maintaining that an "[economically] closed Europe is a gun pointed at America's head," Mead argues:

> In a well-intentioned effort to stabilize Eastern Europe, Western Europe, led by Germany, could establish something like Napoleon's projected Continental System. Eastern Europe and North Africa would supply the raw materials, certain agricultural products, and low-wage industrial labor. Western Europe would provide capital and host the high-value-added and high-tech industries ... A Europe of this kind would inevitably put most of its capital into its own backyard, and it would close its markets to competitors from the rest of the world. It would produce its VCRs in Poland, not China; it would buy its wheat from Ukraine, rather than the Dakotas.[40]

---

39   See Benjamin C. Schwarz, "NATO at the Crossroads: Reexamining America's Role in Europe," RAND Issue Paper, January 1994.

40   Walter Russell Mead, "An American Grand Strategy: The Quest for Order in a Disordered World," *World Policy Journal* 10:1 (Spring 1993), p. 21. Mead's argument echoes Assistant Secretary of State Breckinridge Long's May 1940 picture of the economic

Given that the actions Washington's allies would take to forestall instability without American leadership would apparently lead to US economic
disaster, it seems that the United States must forever remain—in former
president Bush's words—the world's "sole superpower."[41]

That line of reasoning—that if a hegemon must ensure the stability of a
region on which it apparently depends, it must also secure those areas on
which that region depends—nicely illustrates what historian Paul Kennedy
calls "imperial overstretch." If America must guarantee the stability of a
potentially unstable Europe, then logic seemingly dictates that it must
guard against instability that could infect Europe.[42]

This thinking, so reminiscent of the Cold War domino theory, suggests that the logic of economic interdependence leads to a proliferation
of American "security" commitments in an unstable new world order.
An imperial strategy is necessarily expansive. With awkward syntax, the

---

implications to the US of the subordination of Europe to German control. See *The War
Diary of Breckinridge Long*, ed. Fred L. Israel (Lincoln: University of Nebraska Press,
1966), p. 98.

41   The foreign policy establishment's anxiety concerning the effects of regional
instability on the European political situation and ultimately on international economic
interdependence extends to unstable regions far from Europe. Concern about the potential psychological and political effects of turmoil in the Persian Gulf on Western Europe
and Japan was a major factor underlying James Baker's assertion that the US had to
counter Iraq's invasion of Kuwait to save American jobs. His comment reflects, if over-
simplifies, official opinion on the importance of Persian Gulf security to the United States.
Believing that tranquility and democracy in Germany and Japan are fragile, US officials
fear that a sudden economic downturn in these states could cause a repeat of the 1930s:
recession and unemployment would bring extreme nationalist forces to the fore, which
in turn would intensify regional political tensions and lead to the "re-nationalization" of
foreign and economic policies. According to that reasoning, the open economic system
would slam shut and the world crash into depression. Consequently, Germany and Japan
must have unhampered access to Persian Gulf oil—and not be tempted to develop forces
capable of power projection to secure those supplies. Author's conversations and inter-
views with current and former State and Defense Department and NSC officials, 1991–93.

42   Hence, the foreign policy establishment's recent spate of reports on what is
termed America's "post–Cold War security agenda" argues that NATO must not only
extend security guarantees to Central and Eastern Europe and the European states of the
former Soviet Union, but that it also must ensure stability in the Central Asian states of the
former Soviet Union (since instability there could spread to Turkey, which could, in turn,
spur massive immigration to Western Europe, destabilizing that region) and in North
Africa (again because of the supposed harm to US interests that would result from the
potential political effects of a wave of immigration in Western Europe). See, e.g., Graham
Allison and Gregory F. Treverton, eds., *Rethinking American Security: Beyond Cold War
to the New World Order* (New York: Norton, 1992); and *Changing Our Ways: America and
the New World* (Washington, DC: Carnegie Endowment for International Peace, 1992).

authors of NSC-68 asserted in 1950 that America's freedom and welfare can
only be secured through "the virtual abandonment by the United States of
trying to distinguish national from global security" and that, therefore, "it
is not an adequate objective merely to seek to check the Kremlin design,
for the absence of order among nations is becoming less and less tolerable.
This fact imposes on us, in our own interests, the responsibility of world
leadership."[43] In 1993 the same logic compelled Lugar to argue that the
United States must make itself responsible for the stability of all of Eurasia,
since "there can be no lasting security at the center without security at the
periphery." While such assessments sound excessive, they in fact reflect
the imperial thinking upon which America's security strategy—during
and after the Cold War—rests.[44]

Sustaining the Unsustainable?
The High Cost of Pax Americana

While this strategy fulfills one set of America's perceived economic needs,
it is not viable. For one thing, the United States is in a deep fiscal crisis
that has been gathering for a long time and will damage the country
profoundly if not resolved. Nearly fifty years of world leadership have
taken their toll. The links among heavy military spending, the weakening
of the economy, and fiscal imbalance are too clear to ignore. America
is overconsuming and underinvesting. Too much consumption is still

---

43   Quoted in William Appleman Williams, *Empire as a Way of Life* (Oxford: Oxford
University Press, 1980), p. 186; and Lloyd Gardner, "Response to John Lewis Gaddis,"
Diplomatic History 7:3 (Summer 1983), p. 192.

44   Anyone familiar with the historiography of American foreign relations will find
it difficult to read the arguments used by members of the foreign policy establishment
to define America's post–Cold War security strategy without being struck by their ironic
consonance with the views of the "open-door school"—a quasi-Marxist interpretation of
American diplomacy. Led by the late socialist historian William Appleman Williams in
the 1950s and early 1960s, the open-door school was the most important attempt to apply
the *Innenpolitik* approach to the study of American foreign policy. The open-door school
characterized the imperatives dictating America's global strategy in terms remarkably
similar to those used by the statesmen who currently implement that strategy. To both,
America's global pacification policy is pursued not simply because it "pays," but because
US policymakers believe that the economy demands it. Most important, both the leftist
scholars and current officials believe that America's worldwide defense commitments
are not the product of an indiscriminate and ideologically motivated globalism, but of
careful thought.

devoted to defense, depriving the productive sectors of the economy of urgently needed resources. To be sure, the military budget is now a smaller portion of federal spending than in the 1950s and 1960s. But in constant dollars defense spending is still at Cold War levels: 18 percent of the federal budget—$263.8 billion in fiscal year 1995—is a substantial share to spend on defense, and America continues to spend a far higher portion of its GDP on national security needs than do other major industrial countries. Compounding this fiscal crisis, America faces social and structural economic problems (high rates of infant mortality, illiteracy, malnutrition, and poverty) of a magnitude unknown to other economically advanced states.[45]

To maintain that America can continue at anything like its current level of defense spending without damaging its economy is incorrect and irresponsible. Yet to suggest that the United States can afford to reduce that spending significantly is, given the assumptions underlying the past half century of US strategy, simply wrong. Most foreign policy reformers assert that America's enormous defense costs are the product of globalist overextension. America's strategic dilemma, they argue, can be resolved by simply balancing its commitments and resources. But criticizing US policy for overextension fails to take America's security considerations seriously. To argue that America's defense spending is the result of its being overcommitted begs the question: What commitments involving significant amounts of military spending can be jettisoned?

The driving force behind the US defense posture is the perceived need to ensure order by, in effect, exercising hegemony in regions composed of wealthy and technologically sophisticated states and to take care of such nuisances as Saddam Hussein, Slobodan Milošević, and Kim Jong Il so that potential great powers need not acquire the means to take care of those problems themselves. While retrenchment from these positions may seem economically attractive, it would, following the logic of US security strategy, carry enormous risks. "The United States, as a great power, has essentially taken on the task of sustaining the world order," former secretary of defense James Schlesinger concisely explained. "And any abandonment of major commitments is difficult to reconcile with that task."[46]

---

45 Jonathan Peterson, "Life in US Graded on the Curve," *Los Angeles Times*, April 11, 1993.

46 Cited in Layne and Schwarz, "American Hegemony," p. 19.

"Shaping the strategic environment," to use post–Cold War Pentagon jargon, requires today, as it has for the past forty-five years, the maintenance and deployment of large and technologically advanced armed forces. American defense planners appreciate that to guard against the apparent disaster of political and economic "re-nationalization," US defense commitments must be operationally meaningful. America must convince others not only that it is committed to the security of their regions, but that it is capable of *acting* on that commitment. Imposing a protectorate over the world economy means that the United States must spend more on national security than the rest of the world's countries combined. Reassuring Western Europe, even without a military threat to the continent, is costing the United States $100 billion this year. Stabilizing East Asia is taking another $47 billion. In defense you get what you pay for, and America's "adult supervision" strategy means that the United States—if it is lucky and nothing disastrous happens—must pay forever.

The United States is caught in a dilemma that eventually ensnares all hegemons. Stabilizing the international system is a wasting proposition. While other states benefit from the stability the predominant power provides, they have little incentive to pay their "fair share" of the costs of protection since the hegemon will defend the status quo in its own interests, regardless of what these lesser states contribute. Just as Britain, as the guarantor of world stability in the nineteenth century, spent more than twice as much on defense as France or Germany, even though the latter countries' neighborhood was more perilous, so the United States today spends vastly more on defense than either Japan or Germany, though both countries are less secure than America.

Forced to place such importance on "security," the hegemon directs capital, creativity and attention from the civilian sector, even as its economic rivals, freed from onerous spending for security, add resources to economically productive investments. This leads over time to the erosion of the preponderant power's relative economic strength.[47] As economic, and hence military, capabilities deteriorate, so does the very comparative advantage over other powers upon which hegemony is founded. And as its relative power declines, the international stability that the hegemon assured is, perforce, unsettled.

---

47 These arguments are made in Paul Kennedy, *The Rise and Fall of the Great Powers: Economic Change and Military Conflict from 1500 to 2000* (New York: Random House, 1987); David P. Calleo, *The Imperious Economy* (Cambridge, MA: Harvard University Press, 1982); and Gilpin, *War and Change.*

Thus, even without the burden of high defense spending the United States is simply less and less able to order and pacify the world. The Pax Americana depended upon America's preponderant strength in the decades following World War II; probably never in history did one state so dominate the international system. Yet history affords no more remarkable reversal of fortune in a relatively short time than the erosion of US hegemony in the late twentieth century. The worldwide economic system that America has fostered has, itself, largely determined the country's relative decline, even as it has contributed to America's prosperity. For those concerned with maintaining American predominance, the problem with economic interdependence is that it has worked all too well. Through trade, foreign investment and the spread of technology and managerial expertise, economic power has diffused from the United States to new centers of economic growth, thus rapidly closing the industrial and technological gap between the United States and its global partners.

These developments are not "bad" for America economically. Almost everyone—including US consumers—benefits absolutely from the most efficient production of industrial goods in an open world economy. But with a shift in the international distribution of economic strength, American hegemony, of necessity, has been undermined. Thus, a global economy bites the hegemon that feeds it. America, then, is in a bind. The international open economic system that it believes is necessary for its prosperity weakens the very condition—American preeminence—that makes that system viable. And attempts to maintain its hegemony through security leadership only further weaken its position in the long run.

The United States has defined a very difficult role for itself. Its foreign policy, in fact, is dedicated to sustaining the unsustainable. To be sure, some optimists hold that America can escape this quandary by reaping the reward of hegemony—a global economy—without paying for it. According to that argument, America can "lead" but in "partnership" with other like-minded states.[48] That is an illusion. Multilateral enterprises, from juries to UN police actions, require a leader. The indispensable foundation of cooperation and integration in the Western security and economic systems was—and remains—American hegemony. The rather strident assertions of every American president since Truman of the need for

48   Richard Gardner, "The Return of Internationalism," *Washington Quarterly* 13 (Summer 1990), pp. 23–39; Allison and Treverton, eds., *Rethinking American Security*; and Robert Art, "A US Military Strategy for the 1990s: Reassurance without Dominance," *Survival* 34 (Winter 1992–93), pp. 3–23.

American preeminence in European security affairs stems less from an overbearing chauvinism than from a realization that, as Acheson wrote in 1952, arguing for the necessity of the NATO alliance, "unity in Europe requires the continuing association and support of the United States; without it, [Western] Europe would split apart."[49] To hold that America can safely relinquish its hegemony because the political, economic and military cooperation among the great powers now ensures stability and peace is to put the cart before the horse. Stability in Western Europe and East Asia, guaranteed by American preponderance, was the precondition for cooperation, not vice versa. There is no reason to believe that, without this guarantor, stability will take on a life of its own.

The nature of international politics will not change to solve America's security quandary. In fact, given the inevitable rise of other great powers and trends toward greater regional instability, the wolf the United States is now holding by the ears is likely to grow increasingly feisty, making America's strategy of preponderance more problematic and expensive.[50]

Superpower Hegemony and the Capitalist System

Discussion of US "post–Cold War" foreign policy has revolved around stale generalizations about morality and foreign policy, self-satisfied assertions of the need for America to "remain engaged abroad" and the familiar tactical arguments about when, where, and how to intervene militarily in foreign quarrels. Such a dialogue fails to illuminate the important questions. It is time for Americans to stop debating what is and is not America's "mission" in the world and instead to assess the viability, costs, and benefits of attempting to maintain the international requirements of the US economy. Americans must acknowledge, as did Kennan forty years ago, the dilemma inherent in defining their prosperity in terms of economic security abroad. Despairing over the implications of the new doctrine of "national security," Kennan noted: "To what end—security? For the continuation of our economic expansion? But our economic expansion cannot proceed much further without ... creating

---

49   Quoted in Gardner, *Architects of Illusion*, p. 227.

50   For the argument that the ascendancy of new great powers is inevitable, see Christopher Layne's seminal article, "The Unipolar Illusion: Why New Great Powers Will Arise," *International Security* 17:4 (Spring 1993), pp. 5–51.

new problems of national security much more rapidly than we can ever hope to solve them."[51]

But while America's national security policy may be dangerous and damaging, any significant change in that policy necessarily demands radical change in the US economy, since that strategy, as its makers acknowledge, grows out of the structural requirements of American capitalism. Such changes may—and in anything but the long run will—present as many difficulties as they eliminate.

The late historian Christopher Lasch made what is at first glance the astonishing assertion that any fundamental critique of American foreign policy must "simultaneously take the form of an indictment of capitalism itself."[52] Surely a basic change in security policy can be effected without jettisoning the basis of the US economy.

In fact, economist John Maynard Keynes and historian Charles Beard proposed programs in the 1930s that tried to reconcile capitalism with noninterventionist foreign policies by proposing autarkic capitalism—what Keynes called "national self-sufficiency." They embraced that "solution" even more for what they believed would be the welcome changes it would permit in foreign policy than for what they saw as its enormous domestic social benefits. As Keynes stated, "the progress of economic imperialism" —that is, "a great concentration of national effort on the capture of foreign trade and the ... protection of foreign [economic] interests"—was "a scarcely avoidable part" of economic internationalism. Both Keynes and Beard hoped, therefore, that the domestic economic restructuring each proposed would allow for a more circumscribed and less expensive national security policy.[53]

But plans to alter fundamentally the domestic political economy in the name of national self-sufficiency are even more unthinkable now than they were fifty years ago, when Acheson dismissed them out of hand. Moreover, Keynes's and Beard's schemes originated when the advanced economies were far less interdependent than they are now. National self-sufficiency

---

51   Quoted in Anders Stephanson, "Ideology and Neorealist Mirrors," *Diplomatic History* 17:2 (Spring 1993), p. 289, note 10.

52   Christopher Lasch, "William Appleman Williams on American History," *Marxist Perspectives* 7 (Fall 1978), p. 126.

53   See John Maynard Keynes, "National Self-Sufficiency," *Yale Review* 22:4 (June 1933), pp. 755–69; Charles Beard, *The Open Door at Home: A Trial Philosophy of the National Interest* (New York: MacMillan, 1935); and Beard, *America in Midpassage* (New York: Macmillan, 1939), p. 453.

is not an option at this late date—at least not one that would be freely chosen. America cast its economic lot with liberal internationalism long ago, and it has succeeded in making the internationalists' dream—a world economy—a reality. A global economy is addictive: in embracing a system permeated by international market pressures, a state's economy is perforce restructured profoundly and it becomes bound to the world market by complicated patterns of trade, production, and capital flows. Having lost its economic autonomy, the United States would find a break from the global economy extraordinarily disruptive, requiring years of economic readjustment and, given the strength of international market forces, severe political measures to sustain.

Still, while the price of reversing course, of forsaking economic internationalism, is prohibitively high, the social costs of continuing to depend on the international economy may well be enormous. As Keynes and Beard understood, the more open a state is to the world market, the more vulnerable its population is to international market forces. And, in an increasingly open global economy, a state will be less and less able to modulate, let alone manage or control, the domestic effects of those forces. A state committed to economic internationalism will grow economically, but significant sectors of its population will suffer labor dislocation and a decline in income and will be plagued by economic insecurity, as the domestic economy constantly responds to the global economy's changing demands and accelerating shifts in comparative advantage.

Adhering to America's present political economy and its concomitant national security policy may nevertheless seem the best of bad alternatives. But not only is America's current policy risky and expensive, it is also unsustainable. Therefore, while it may be inconceivable that the United States would choose a non-capitalist "solution" to its foreign policy conundrum, such a "solution" may nevertheless be imposed upon it, as the demands of international capitalism collide with the realities of international politics. As capitalism becomes more complex and "advanced," it becomes more fragile. For instance, today the emergent high-technology industries are the most powerful engines of world economic growth, but they require a level of specialization and a breadth of markets that is possible only in an integrated world economy.

Such a global economy is easily threatened in that disruptions—wars, for example, or reversion to competitive mercantilist policies—within or among any significant national participants send damaging shock waves throughout the entire system. As American hegemony—the political condition that holds such disruptions in check—weakens, "re-nationalized" foreign and economic policies among, say, the states of Northeast Asia or Western Europe would destroy the global economy. Capitalism, certainly as it has developed over the last fifty years, cannot survive without an open world economy. It is difficult to see, therefore, how it can survive the decline of Pax Americana, as the fragmented and discordant nature of international politics reasserts itself over an illusory unity forged by an ephemeral preponderance.

In 1917, Lenin argued that international capitalism would be economically successful but, by growing in a world of competitive states, it would plant the seeds of its own destruction.[54] Although the empire he built is in ruins and his revolution discredited, Lenin may have the last laugh.

The US foreign policy community's definition of America's legitimate interests in Europe cannot be adequately understood if seen through the narrow prism of threats to America's physical security. America's thinking about its interests in Europe rests on a set of interrelated assumptions concerning international politics, international capitalism, and national prosperity and democracy that have driven Washington policymakers since at least the turn of the twentieth century. These assumptions dictate that America pursue an imperial policy, albeit perhaps a benign one. The same assumptions have also informed every grand strategic assessment the United States government has undertaken since the end of World War II. It is no accident, then, that these assessments have concluded that, in essence, American national security policy is what it should be. To arrive at a fundamentally different conception of American interests in Europe—and hence a meaningful change in US security policy toward the continent—either America's assumptions concerning the requirements of international stability in Europe, or the assumptions concerning the requirements of American prosperity, must change radically.

54　V. I. Lenin, *Imperialism: The Highest Stage of Capitalism* (New York: International Publishers, 1939 [1917]).

3

Excerpts from US Department of Defense, FY 1994–1999 Defense Planning Guidance

Early in 1992, a classified, biannual report on US strategic objectives, the Defense Planning Guidance (DPG), provoked furor when extracts of a draft appeared in the press.[1] The document, a sweeping overview of the geopolitical scene after the dissolution of the USSR and victory over Ba'athist Iraq, was attacked from all sides. Patrick Buchanan saw in it "a formula for endless American intervention in quarrels and war when no vital interest of the United States is remotely engaged," while Senator Joseph Biden denounced a charter for "literally a Pax Americana."[2] Written under the direction of Paul Wolfowitz's deputy at the Pentagon (and future Afghan viceroy) Zalmay Khalilzad, together with a coterie of defense intellectuals in the orbit of Secretary of Defense Richard Cheney, the result would long be associated with militant neoconservatism. Yet its content, notwithstanding an indiscreet unilateralist bent and rhetorical flourishes characteristic of the period (from the "full spectrum dominance" concocted by the Joint Chiefs of Staff to the "democratic zone of peace" theorized by Francis Fukuyama,

---

1   Copies of the draft were sent to the *New York Times* and the *Washington Post*. The portions reproduced here are taken from "Excerpts from Pentagon's Plan: 'Prevent the Re-Emergence of a New Rival,'" *New York Times*, March 8, 1992. On the genesis of the document, see James Mann, *Rise of the Vulcans: The History of Bush's War Cabinet* (London: Penguin, 2004), pp. 198–215.

2   Cited in Hal Brands, "Choosing Primacy: US Strategy and Global Order at the Dawn of the Post–Cold War Era," *Texas National Security Review* 1:2 (March 2018), p. 9.

a Wolfowitz protégé who was consulting for the Pentagon at the time the DPG was prepared), reflected time-honored traditions of American thinking about foreign policy. After eight years of Democratic rule in the White House, Wolfowitz could express justified contentment that at the end of the day, critics of the DPG had reconciled themselves easily enough to its overweening vision of American power.[3] The text, still not fully declassified, remains among the pithiest statements of post–Cold War US grand strategy.[4]

Excerpts from the Pentagon's February 18 draft of the Defense Planning Guidance for the Fiscal Years 1994–1999:

This Defense Planning guidance addresses the fundamentally new situation which has been created by the collapse of the Soviet Union, the disintegration of the internal as well as the external empire, and the discrediting of Communism as an ideology with global pretensions and influence. The new international environment has also been shaped by the victory of the United States and its coalition allies over Iraqi aggression—the first post–Cold War conflict and a defining event in US global leadership. In addition to these two victories, there has been a less visible one, the integration of Germany and Japan into a US-led system of collective security and the creation of a democratic "zone of peace." ...

DEFENSE STRATEGY OBJECTIVES

Our first objective is to prevent the re-emergence of a new rival, either on the territory of the former Soviet Union or elsewhere, that poses a threat on the order of that posed formerly by the Soviet Union. This is a dominant consideration underlying the new regional defense strategy and requires that we endeavor to prevent any hostile power from dominating

---

3   Paul Wolfowitz, "Remembering the Future," *National Interest*, March 1, 2000.

4   Asked by a reporter what he thought when the document leaked, John Lewis Gaddis replied, "I was a little surprised somebody would put this kind of thing down on paper." Cited in Brands, "Choosing Primacy," p. 28. Once the controversy died down, Cheney and Wolfowitz charged I. Lewis Libby with reworking the draft. The final product, released to the public in 1993 as the Pentagon's Regional Defense Strategy, discussed inter-allied collaboration more delicately but did not differ in substance from Khalilzad's blueprint.

a region whose resources would, under consolidated control, be sufficient to generate global power. These regions include Western Europe, East Asia, the territory of the former Soviet Union, and Southwest Asia.

There are three additional aspects to this objective: First, the US must show the leadership necessary to establish and protect a new order that holds the promise of convincing potential competitors that they need not aspire to a greater role or pursue a more aggressive posture to protect their legitimate interests. Second, in the non-defense areas, we must account sufficiently for the interests of the advanced industrial nations to discourage them from challenging our leadership or seeking to overturn the established political and economic order. Finally, we must maintain the mechanisms for deterring potential competitors from even aspiring to a larger regional or global role. An effective reconstitution capability is important here, since it implies that a potential rival could not hope to quickly or easily gain a predominant military position in the world.

The second objective is to address sources of regional conflict and instability in such a way as to promote increasing respect for international law, limit international violence, and encourage the spread of democratic forms of government and open economic systems. These objectives are especially important in deterring conflicts or threats in regions of security importance to the United States because of their proximity (such as Latin America), or where we have treaty obligations or security commitments to other nations. While the US cannot become the world's "policeman," by assuming responsibility for righting every wrong, we will retain the pre-eminent responsibility for addressing selectively those wrongs which threaten not only our interests, but those of our allies or friends, or which could seriously unsettle international relations. Various types of US interests may be involved in such instances: access to vital raw materials, primarily Persian Gulf oil; proliferation of weapons of mass destruction and ballistic missiles, threats to US citizens from terrorism or regional or local conflict, and threats to US society from narcotics trafficking ...

It is improbable that a global conventional challenge to US and Western security will re-emerge from the Eurasian heartland for many years to come. Even in the highly unlikely event that some future leadership in the former Soviet Union adopted strategic aims of recovering the lost empire or otherwise threatened global interests, the loss of Warsaw Pact allies and the subsequent and continuing dissolution of military capability would make any hope of success require several years or more of strategic and doctrinal re-orientation and force regeneration and redeployment, which in turn could only happen after a lengthy political realignment and re-orientation to authoritarian and aggressive political and economic control. Furthermore, any such political upheaval in or among the states of the former USSR would be much more likely to issue in internal or localized hostilities, rather than a concerted strategic effort to marshal capabilities for external expansionism—the ability to project power beyond their borders.

There are other potential nations or coalitions that could, in the further future, develop strategic aims and a defense posture of region-wide or global domination. Our strategy must now refocus on precluding the emergence of any potential future global competitor. But because we no longer face either a global threat or a hostile, non-democratic power dominating a region critical to our interests, we have the opportunity to meet threats at lower levels and lower costs—as long as we are prepared to reconstitute additional forces should the need to counter a global threat re-emerge ...

REGIONAL THREATS AND RISK

With the demise of a global military threat to US interests, regional military threats, including possible conflicts arising in and from the territory of the former Soviet Union, will be of primary concern to the US in the future. These threats are likely to arise in regions critical to the security of the US and its allies, including Europe, East Asia, the Middle East and Southwest Asia, and the territory of the former Soviet Union. We also have important interests at stake in Latin America, Oceania, and Sub-Saharan Africa. In both cases, the US will be concerned with preventing the domination of key regions by a hostile power ...

Former Soviet Union
The former Soviet state achieved global reach and power by consolidating control over the resources in the territory of the former USSR. The best means of assuring that no hostile power is able to consolidate control over the resources within the former Soviet Union is to support its successor states (especially Russia and Ukraine) in their efforts to become peaceful democracies with market-based economies. A democratic partnership

with Russia and the other republics would be the best possible outcome for the United States. At the same time, we must also hedge against the possibility that democracy will fail, with the potential that an authoritarian regime bent on regenerating aggressive military power could emerge in Russia, or that similar regimes in other successor republics could lead to spreading conflict within the former USSR or Eastern Europe ...

For the immediate future, key US concerns will be the ability of Russia and the other republics to demilitarize their societies, convert their military industries to civilian production, eliminate or, in the case of Russia, radically reduce their nuclear weapons inventory, maintain firm command and control over nuclear weapons, and prevent leakage of advanced military technology and expertise to other countries ...

Western Europe
NATO continues to provide the indispensable foundation for a stable security environment in Europe. Therefore, it is of fundamental importance to preserve NATO as the primary instrument of Western defense and security, as well as the channel for US influence and participation in European security affairs. While the United States supports the goal of European integration, we must seek to prevent the emergence of European-only security arrangements which would undermine NATO, particularly the alliance's integrated command structure ...

East-Central Europe
The end of the Warsaw Pact and the dissolution of the Soviet Union have gone a long way toward increasing stability and reducing the military threat to Europe. The ascendancy of democratic reformers in the Russian republic, should this process continue, is likely to create a more benign policy toward Eastern Europe. However, the US must keep in mind the long history of conflict between the states of Eastern Europe, as well as the potential for conflict between the states of Eastern Europe and those of the former Soviet Union ...

The most promising avenues for anchoring the East-Central Europeans into the West and for stabilizing their democratic institutions is their participation in Western political and economic organizations. East-Central European membership in the (European Community) at the earliest opportunity, and expanded NATO liaison ...

The US could also consider extending to the East-Central European states security commitments analogous to those we have extended to Persian Gulf states ...

Should there be a re-emergence of a threat from the Soviet Union's successor state, we should plan to defend against such a threat in Eastern Europe, should there be an alliance decision to do so.

East Asia and Pacific

... Defense of Korea will likely remain one of the most demanding major regional contingencies ... Asia is home to the world's greatest concentration of traditional Communist states, with fundamental values, governance, and policies decidedly at variance with our own and those of our friends and allies.

To buttress the vital political and economic relationships we have along the Pacific rim, we must maintain our status as a military power of the first magnitude in the area. This will enable the US to continue to contribute to regional security and stability by acting as a balancing force and prevent emergence of a vacuum or a regional hegemon ...

Middle East and Southwest Asia

In the Middle East and Southwest Asia, our overall objective is to remain the predominant outside power in the region and preserve US and Western access to the region's oil. We also seek to deter further aggression in the region, foster regional stability, protect US nationals and property, and safeguard our access to international air and seaways. As demonstrated by Iraq's invasion of Kuwait, it remains fundamentally important to prevent a hegemon or alignment of powers from dominating the region. This pertains especially to the Arabian peninsula. Therefore, we must continue to play a strong role through enhanced deterrence and improved cooperative security ...

We will seek to prevent the further development of a nuclear arms race on the Indian subcontinent. In this regard, we should work to have both countries, India and Pakistan, adhere to the Nuclear Non-Proliferation Treaty and to place their nuclear energy facilities under International Atomic Energy Agency safeguards. We should discourage Indian hegemonic aspirations over the other states in South Asia and on the Indian Ocean. With regard to Pakistan, a constructive US–Pakistan military relationship will be an important element in our strategy to promote stable security conditions in Southwest Asia and Central Asia. We should therefore endeavor to rebuild our military relationship given acceptable resolution of our nuclear concerns …

Latin America

Cuba's growing domestic crisis holds out the prospect for positive change, but over the near term, Cuba's tenuous internal situation is likely to generate new challenges to US policy. Consequently, our programs must provide capabilities to meet a variety of Cuban contingencies which could include an attempted repetition of the Mariel boatlift, a military provocation against the US or an American ally, or political instability and internal conflict in Cuba.

4

History, Grand Strategy, and NATO Enlargement

John Lewis Gaddis

Some principles of strategy are so basic that when stated they sound like platitudes: treat former enemies magnanimously; do not take on unnecessary new ones; keep the big picture in view; balance ends and means; avoid emotion and isolation in making decisions; be willing to acknowledge error. All fairly straightforward, one might think. Who could object to them?

And yet—consider the Clinton administration's single most important foreign policy initiative: the decision to expand NATO to include Poland, Hungary and the Czech Republic. NATO enlargement, I believe, manages to violate *every one* of the strategic principles just mentioned.

Perhaps that is why historians—normally so contentious—are in uncharacteristic agreement: with remarkably few exceptions, they see NATO enlargement as ill-conceived, ill-timed, and above all ill-suited to the realities of the post–Cold War world. Indeed I can recall no other moment in my own experience as a practicing historian at which there was less support, within the community of historians, for an announced policy position.

A significant gap has thus opened between those who make grand strategy and those who reflect upon it: on this issue at least, official and accumulated wisdom are pointing in very different directions. This chapter focuses on how this has happened, which leads us back to a list of basic principles for grand strategy.

First, consider *the magnanimous treatment of defeated adversaries*. There are three great points of reference here—1815–18, 1918–19 and 1945–48— and historians are in general accord as to the lessons to be drawn from each. They applaud the settlements of the Napoleonic Wars and of the Second World War because the victorious allies moved as quickly as possible to bring their vanquished adversaries—France in the first case, Germany and Japan in the second—back into the international system as full participants in postwar security structures. Historians tend to criticize (if not condemn) the First World War settlement precisely because it failed to do that for two of the most powerful states in Europe—Germany and Soviet Russia. The resulting instability, they argue, paved the way for yet another conflagration. It was not for nothing that Winston Churchill, having personally witnessed two of these instances and having studied the third, chose as one of the "morals" of his great history of the Second World War: "In Victory: Magnanimity."

That approach would seem all the more relevant to the fourth great case that now confronts us—the post–Cold War settlement. The Soviet Union was never an actual military opponent. Its defeat finally came not on the battlefield but as the result of a change of heart, and then of character, and then ultimately of system. The use of force, very fortunately for everyone, was not even necessary.

The process of rehabilitating our adversary—of transforming it from a revisionist or even revolutionary state to one prepared to accept the existing international order—began, therefore, even before the Cold War ended. It was as if the Germans and the Japanese, say at some point in 1943 or 1944, had suddenly laid down their arms, announced that they had seen the light, and begun for themselves the processes of disarmament, democratization and economic reorganization for which their enemies had been fighting.

It is all the stranger, therefore, that the Clinton administration has chosen to respond to this most fortunate outcome of the Cold War, not by following the successful examples of 1815–18 or 1945–48, but by *appearing*, at least, to emulate the unfortunate precedent of 1918–19: one that preserves, and even expands, a security structure left over from a conflict that has now ended, while excluding the former adversary from it. If the US could afford to be *inclusive* in dealing with its *actual* enemies Germany and Japan after 1945—just as Napoleon's conquerors were in dealing with France after 1815—then why is it now *excluding* a country that, throughout the Cold War, remained only a potential adversary?

The answer most often given is that the Russians have no choice but to accept what NATO has decided to do—that having swallowed the loss of their sphere of influence in Eastern Europe, the reunification of Germany and the eventual breakup of the former Soviet Union itself, their only alternative with respect to enlarging the alliance is to gulp and swallow yet again. We, the victors, are free to impose upon them whatever settlement we choose.

Not only is that view arrogant; it is also short-sighted, for it assumes that defeated adversaries have no choices. And yet, even the Germans in 1945, as thoroughly vanquished an enemy as there has ever been, had alternatives: they could favor either their Eastern or their Western occupiers. The fact that they chose the West had much to do with American and British efforts to make their occupation policies as conciliatory as possible. The Soviet Union's failure to understand that need—its inability to see that wholesale reparations removals and mass rapes were not likely to win it friends among the Germans—did a good deal to determine the robustness of one postwar Germany, and the brittleness of the other. The Germans had a choice, and they made it decisively. If the US could be that accommodating then to the wishes of a country that had produced one of the most loathsome regimes in history but had lost its capacity to inflict injury, it is difficult to understand why Washington now has elected not to accommodate a country that has chosen to democratize itself, but still retains a considerable capacity to do harm. By insisting on NATO enlargement, it seems, we are violating a second great principle of strategy, which is *that one should never take on more enemies than necessary at any given moment.*

For Russia does indeed have a choice: it is in the interesting position of being able to lean one way or another in a strategic triangle that is likely to define the geopolitics of the early twenty-first century. It can continue to align itself, as it has patiently done so far, with the United States and Western Europe. Or it can do what the US itself did a quarter century ago under the guidance of Richard Nixon and Henry Kissinger: it can tilt toward China.

Given the complementarity that exists between Russia's capacity to export military technology and China's ability to produce marketable consumer goods, there is nothing inherently implausible in this scenario. It would not be the first time Russia and China had linked up out of concern, even if misguided, over American aggressiveness: we know from Soviet and Chinese documents that this was precisely the reason behind the 1950 Sino-Soviet alliance.[1] And of course classical balance-of-power theory tells us that this is what we should expect: if country A feels itself threatened by country B, it is apt to align itself with country C. Country C in this case is one less likely even than Russia to see its interests as compatible with our own.

That brings us to a third strategic principle that is being violated here, which is *the need to take a global and not just a regional perspective.* US General George C. Marshall coined the term "theateritis," during the Second World War, to refer to the tendency among some of his military commanders to see only the requirements of their own campaigns, not those of the war as a whole. I am hardly alone in the view that the Clinton administration has succumbed to a kind of geopolitical theateritis: as Richard Haass has pointed out, "in his second term, the first post–Cold War president has focused most of his foreign policy efforts on NATO, a child of the Cold War."[2]

The temptation is certainly understandable. NATO was the West's most impressive institutional success during that conflict, and it is only natural to want to find some purpose for it in the post–Cold War era. But does it fit current needs? Will we really be able to say in years to come—can we say now—that military insecurity in the middle of Europe, the problem NATO was created to solve, was (is) the greatest one that now confronts us?

The sources of insecurity in Europe these days lie more in the economic than the military realm: disparities in living standards divide the continent, not armies or ideologies. But the European Union (EU), the obvious instrument for dealing with these difficulties, has come down with its own form of theateritis, the single-minded push to achieve a single currency among its existing members by the end of this decade. So it has been left to NATO to try to reintegrate and stabilize Europe as a whole, which is roughly comparable to using a monkey wrench to

---

1   See John Lewis Gaddis, *We Now Know: Rethinking Cold War History* (New York: Oxford University Press, 1997), pp. 68–70.

2   Richard N. Haass, "Fatal Distraction: Bill Clinton's Foreign Policy," *Foreign Policy* 108 (Autumn 1997), p. 119.

repair a computer. The results will no doubt be striking, but perhaps not in the ways intended.

Containing Russia, of course, has never been NATO's only role. Its members quickly found it a useful instrument, as well, for restraining the growth of German power (by *including* the Germans, note, not *excluding* them), and for ensuring that the Americans themselves remained in Europe and did not revert to their old habits of isolationism. "Mission creep" was not invented in Mogadishu.

But the likelihood of German aggression today seems about as remote as a US withdrawal from the continent: neither of these old fears from the late 1940s and early 1950s is even remotely credible now. If in the effort to ward off these phantoms we should revive another specter from those years that is a real possibility—a Sino-Russian alignment—then future generations would have a good case for alleging "theateritis" on the part of our own.

Even if we grant, though, for the sake of argument, that NATO enlargement is, or should be, an urgent priority, there is yet another strategic principle that has been bypassed here, which has to do with *providing the means to accomplish selected ends.* The dangers of letting interests outstrip capabilities are well known. One would surely expect, therefore, that on as important a matter as this—the designation of three additional countries in the center of Europe as vital to the defense of the US—those charged with organizing those defenses would have been consulted, and carefully listened to.

Yet it is hard to find evidence that the Department of Defense, or the Joint Chiefs of Staff, played any significant role in making this decision. The fact that US interests have been expanded but their budget has not suggests that quite clearly.[3] It is true that the military were much involved in the now-eclipsed Partnership for Peace (PfP). But that initiative was to have included the Russians in a relationship with NATO as originally constituted. It did not involve enlarging the alliance in such a way as to advertise the Russians' *exclusion*.[4]

One might conclude, from the administration's failure to match military means with political ends, one of two things. Either the countries the US

---

3   See Paul Kennedy, "Let's See the Pentagon's Plan for Defending Poland," *Los Angeles Times*, May 16, 1997.

4   Vojtech Mastny, *Reassuring NATO: Eastern Europe, Russia, and the Western Alliance* (Oslo: Institutt for Forsvarsstudier, 1997), p. 61.

is proposing to bring into NATO are not in danger, in which case one wonders why it is then necessary to include them. Or they are in danger, in which case we have yet to prepare adequately to protect them. Either way, ends and means are misaligned.

So where did the decision to enlarge NATO come from? The most authoritative study so far, that of Professor James Goldgeier of George Washington University, singles out three individuals as having played key roles: President Clinton himself, who became interested in the issue through an impromptu conversation with Václav Havel and Lech Wałęsa at the April 1993 dedication of the Holocaust Museum in Washington, DC; former National Security Advisor Anthony Lake, who kept the idea alive within the administration through the next year and a half; and Richard Holbrooke, assistant secretary of state for European affairs, who insisted at several critical moments in autumn 1994 that NATO enlargement was official policy—thereby, or so it appears, making it so.[5]

With almost no public or congressional debate—and with remarkably little interagency consultation—momentum built up behind something that seemed a good idea at the time to a few critically placed individuals. *Why*, though, did it seem a good idea? This is where things get murky, for although we can trace the process by which the decision was made, the reasoning of the principal decision-makers—since they chose not to articulate it—remains obscure.

To be sure, the Poles, Czechs, and Hungarians badly wanted their role within the "new" Europe recognized, both symbolically and institutionally. How did it happen, though, that the Americans responded so much more favorably and rapidly than EU members did? The most frequent explanation I have heard is that the Clinton administration, recalling the West's abandonment of these countries, first to German and then Soviet domination during the 1930s and 1940s, felt an emotional obligation to them.[6]

If so, the history behind that sentiment is pretty shaky. The US, after all, had no hand at all in the 1938 Munich agreement, and it could have challenged Soviet control of Eastern Europe after the Second World War only at the risk of starting a Third World War, which would hardly have

---

5   James M. Goldgeier, "NATO Expansion: The Anatomy of a Decision," *Washington Quarterly* 21:1 (Winter 1998), pp. 85–102.

6   See, for example, Sherle R. Schwenninger, "The Case against NATO Enlargement: Clinton's Fateful Gamble," *Nation* 265 (October 20, 1997), p. 26.

liberated anybody.[7] Nor is it clear that the Czechs, the Poles, and the Hungarians suffered more during the past half-century than the people we propose to leave out—the Slovaks, Romanians, Bulgarians, Latvians, Lithuanians, Estonians, Ukrainians, and even the Russians themselves— all of whom were, in one way or another, victims of German and/or Soviet oppression.

What we are seeing, then, is a kind of selective sentimentalism. The historic plight of some peoples moves us more than does that of others, despite the fact that they all have compelling claims as victims. Emotionalism, but of a surprisingly elitist character, appears to be at work here.

One of the clearest lessons that has emerged from the new Soviet documentation on Cold War history has to do with *the dangers of making emotionally based decisions in isolation*. Stalin's authorization to Kim Il-Sung to invade South Korea, Khrushchev's placement of missiles in Cuba, and Brezhnev's decision to invade Afghanistan all took place because leaders at the top responded to events emotionally, and then acted without consulting their own subordinate experts.[8] Those who raised doubts were simply told that the decision had been made, and that it was too late to reconsider.

I do not want to be misunderstood here. I am not claiming that decision-making in the Clinton administration replicates that within the former Soviet Union. I *am* suggesting, though, that on NATO enlargement emotions at the top do appear to have combined with a disregard for advice coming up from below—and that given what happened in the Soviet Union when decisions were made in this way, that pattern ought to set off alarm bells in our minds.

Well, people will say, maybe NATO enlargement was not the best model of thoughtful, strategically informed decision-making. But the decision has been made, for better or for worse, and going back on it now— especially having the Senate refuse to approve it—would be a disaster far greater in its scope and consequences than any NATO enlargement itself will bring.

---

7 Michael Mandelbaum, *The Dawn of Peace in Europe* (New York: Twentieth Century Fund Press, 1996), pp. 55–6.

8 Gaddis, *We Now Know*, pp. 290–1; on Afghanistan, see Odd Arne Westad, "The Road to Kabul: Soviet Policy on Afghanistan, 1978–1979," in *The Fall of Détente: Soviet-American Relations during the Carter Years*, ed. Westad (Oslo: Scandinavian University Press, 1997), pp. 132–3.

This sounds to me rather like the refusal of the *Titanic*'s captain to cut his ship's speed when he was informed there were icebergs ahead. And that brings up a final principle of strategy, which is that *consistency is a fine idea most of the time, but there are moments when it is just plain irresponsible.*

Only historians will be able to say with any assurance whether this is such a moment. Their current mood, though, ought not to give the administration much comfort. So is there anything that might yet be done to avoid the damage so many of us see lying ahead if we hold to our present course?

It is not unknown for great nations—even the US—to acknowledge mistakes publicly and change their policies. Ronald Reagan did it in Lebanon: in 1983 that country's security was a vital US interest; in 1984 (after over two hundred Marines had been killed there) it was no longer so. Surely the Nixon-Kissinger opening to China was an acknowledgment that the longtime policy of isolating that country had been misguided. The US certainly reversed course in Vietnam, although only after years of resisting that possibility. John Foster Dulles once threatened an "agonizing reappraisal" of Washington's whole policy toward Europe if the French did not approve the European Defense Community. Paris did not approve, Dulles did not reappraise, and the skies did not fall. And, lest we forget, Washington's entire containment strategy after the Second World War constituted an implicit acknowledgment of error in having believed, as it had during the war, that the Soviet Union under Stalin could be a lasting peacetime ally. Mistakes happen all the time, and governments usually find ways to survive them.

In the case of NATO enlargement, though, an acknowledgment of error—a reversal of course—is not really necessary: the US could resolve most of the problems its policy of selective enlargement has caused by acting upon the implied premises of its own argument, and *enlarging the enlargement process.* We could say that NATO enlargement is such a good idea that we think it unfair just to apply the benefits to the Czechs, Poles, and Hungarians—that we will open the alliance to the other East Europeans, and ultimately to the Russians themselves.

But that would totally change NATO's character, its defenders will protest. Precisely so—NATO *ought* to change to meet the conditions of the new world in which it exists. But there is no precedent for such a dramatic move, NATO's advocates will insist. Precisely not—including Russia now could hardly be as dramatic a step as it was to bring France back into the

Concert of Europe as early as 1818, or to include Germany as a recipient of Marshall Plan aid as early as 1947. But Russia is not yet a predictable, democratic state, NATO's supporters will complain. Precisely beside the point—for neither were Greece and Turkey when they were admitted as NATO members, quite uncontroversially, way back in 1952.

There is here illustrated one more lesson from the past, which is that what people think of as radical innovations often actually exist as historical precedents. People tend to be shocked in rough proportion to the amount of history they have managed to forget.

George F. Kennan, a man who remembers a great deal of history, was one of the earliest and most vocal opponents of NATO enlargement, just as he was of the Vietnam War. Commenting on the Johnson administration's claim that any reversal of course in Southeast Asia would fatally compromise American credibility, Kennan reminded the Senate Foreign Relations Committee in 1966 that "there is more respect to be won in the opinion of this world by a resolute and courageous liquidation of unsound positions than by the most stubborn pursuit of extravagant and unpromising objectives."[9]

Perhaps, as Kennan's biographer, I am slightly biased. But he was obviously right then. I think he is right now.

---

9   US Senate, *Supplemental Foreign Assistance Fiscal Year 1966—Vietnam: Hearings before the Committee on Foreign Relations* (Washington DC: Government Printing Office, 1966), pp. 335–6.

5

The Enlargement of NATO and the EU

Peter Gowan

The end of the Cold War is itself now coming to an end as Europe enters a new phase marked by the redivision of the continent. This is the real significance of the NATO enlargement and the likely significance of the next moves of the EU in the long saga of what is called EU eastward enlargement.

This may seem a perverse view of the process that was launched by the NATO Madrid Summit in July 1997 and by the EU Commission's Agenda 2000 documents. After all, the continent has already been divided between those inside the EU and NATO since 1989, and those outside. And are not the decisions of 1997 going to produce a less divided, more inclusive result?

As far as NATO is concerned this will be true only in an arithmetical and not a political sense, because the main political meaning of the NATO enlargement lies not in Poland's inclusion, but above all in Russia's exclusion from a determined effort to consolidate NATO as Europe's main political institution.

In the case of the EU, the break between the hopes of 1989 and the emerging realities has been more gradual, but the result is turning out to be the same: the European political economy is being fragmented once again, in ways that are different in character from those which existed during the Cold War but which, for a number of countries, are likely to be just as deep.

At the same time, the two parallel processes of new divisions—the one involving NATO and the other involving the EU—must each be seen in the context of the other, the impact of each feeding back on the other.

We will attempt, briefly, to analyze the character, causes and consequences of the emergent divisions.

The Liberal Universalist Promise of 1989–91

The populations of the former Soviet bloc were assured after 1989 that once they became market economies and democracies, the division of Europe would be overcome and they would be included in "the West" and in "Europe." NATO officials touring the former USSR and East-Central Europe assured audiences that European peace and security were now "indivisible" and that all Europeans were now "in the same boat." Provided all the states became "market economies" and "democracies," everybody would be included. With the threat of Communism and of the USSR gone, Europe would, in President Bush's words, become "whole and free" in a system of collective security without alliances against enemies.

More than rhetoric was involved: the Organization for Security and Co-operation in Europe (OSCE) was strengthened as a pan-European security forum, recognized as a UN regional organization and given roles in reducing conflict and promoting the peaceful settlement of disputes. A strong, pan-European conventional arms control treaty, the CFE, was approved, limiting force strengths. And the admittedly unsatisfactory Treaty on the Non-Proliferation of Nuclear Weapons (NPT) was re-endorsed with a supposed commitment on the part of the nuclear powers to move toward deeper disarmament. All these steps were part of a wider framework for what could be described as a liberal vision for building a new kind of security order in Europe, based upon genuine collective security rather than a power politics rivalry such as existed during the Cold War and in the 1930s.

These possibilities seemed all the more realizable because Germany had a political culture very different from the more militarist and nationalist traditions of some other Western states (such as France and Britain): strong constituencies in the Federal Republic desired a multilateral civilian model of European development.

NATO's first moves toward the Central and Eastern European Countries (CEECs) in the 1990s seemed to confirm this commitment to pan-European security: the North Atlantic Cooperation Council, followed by the Partnership for Peace (PfP), were, in principle, all-inclusive bodies for Eurasia as a whole.

The seeds of this liberal order were supposed to be contained within the womb of the NATO alliance itself: the NATO powers claimed that their alliance was based not upon power politics but precisely on what contemporary liberal schools of thought about international relations claim: the internal democratic systems and the shared liberal and democratic values of the Western states. If this was the case, then there was every reason to hope that the transformation of the former Soviet bloc into liberal democracies would generate a similar harmony of shared values across the whole of the continent, thus making real collective security based on common observance of shared norms and rules a reality. Such were the declaratory principles of the NATO powers during the 1990s. And, indeed, such are their declared principles today.

Of course, peace and security depend upon more than the design of security and political institutions. They rest on economic and social preconditions: without prosperity and/or economic development, such values and institutions can come under strain, if not collapse. This was the point at which the role of the EU and the other institutions of the West's political economy raised great hopes in Central and Eastern Europe. As in the case of Western Europe after World War II, the CEECs now hoped that they would be offered a development-oriented insertion in the international division of labor and that the latter would soon be anchored in their accession to the European Community (EC)/European Union (EU). And even if this EU did not stretch as far eastward as Russia (despite John Major's declared aim of including Russia), a regime of free trade would link the EU to a prosperous Commonwealth of Independent States (CIS). The EU, committed precisely to European unity and having always recognized that Europe included Budapest and Sofia even if it was uncertain about Kiev and Moscow, would adapt to accommodate the CEECs.

Against this background, the CEECs have spent the last decade transforming themselves into market economies and liberal democracies. Today both private capitalism and liberal democracy is the norm—though not universal—across the former Soviet bloc region. The transformation to capitalism has been extremely costly in economic, social and health terms. But the peoples of the region have largely accepted these privations for one overriding reason: the goal of entering the club of West European–style prosperity, democracy, and peace offered to them by the leaders of the Western alliance. Of course, neither the capitalism nor the democracy that has emerged is perfect from the standpoint of liberal norms. But that only makes these CEE states similar to their far-from-perfect counterparts in the West. The main thing is that they have passed the test set for them by the West European states: they have been accepted into the Council of Europe. They are on target.

But now the goalposts are being moved.

NATO Enlargement

In 1994 the US administration indicated it was in favor of NATO's eastward enlargement. It then retreated somewhat, giving no date and promoting the Partnership for Peace as perhaps even an alternative. But in 1996, after the Russian presidential elections were out of the way, Washington lifted enlargement to the top of NATO's agenda, and the process of enlarging NATO began at the Madrid Summit in July 1997 in order to be completed by 1999.

The form of the American campaign for enlargement is interesting because of its complete lack of credibility. We are led to believe that picking suitable entrants to NATO has nothing to do with geopolitics but is rather about which states of the region have achieved high enough standards of democracy and market economy to be worthy. Thus, during Secretary General Solana's tour of the CEECs in 1996: "The secretary general will be making it clear that no decisions have been taken yet and that each applicant will be judged on individual merit," a NATO official informed us. "But it is clear that some countries are more ready to join than others and, obviously, they will be the first to join." Although NATO has not yet specified formal criteria for admitting members from the former Warsaw Pact, "it is no secret that countries judged to have made the most progress in democratic and economic reforms will be favored."[1]

---

1   Adrian Bridge, "NATO Chief Tours States Fighting to Join Alliance," *Independent*, April 15, 1996.

This is a brave attempt to pretend that NATO is a norm-based collective security body preoccupied above all by democratic concerns, rather than the strategic interests of its main states. But nobody can seriously believe that. In reality everyone knows the main lines of the division that is planned. Only the details on the exact boundaries are in doubt. The American-German–led Western alliance will be moving into Poland, the Czech Republic and Hungary through incorporating these countries within NATO. At the same time, the Balkans and the former Soviet Union are to be excluded.

Of course, the exact modalities of Polish membership are not yet clear.[2] But these are essentially insignificant details. They do not touch the main issues: namely that Poland will be integrated into NATO's military capacity and Russia will be left outside.

The first consequence is an inevitable and major political blow to Russia which will tend almost certainly to be as permanent as the old division of Europe was. Russia will be excluded from significant legitimate political influence over the major political issues in the affairs of Central and Western Europe whenever the Western powers want it to be excluded. Discussion and decision-making will take place first within NATO, and only afterward will Russia be consulted—or not—as the case may be. This is bound to be as unacceptable to any Russian government as it would be to any British government if the UK were placed in a similar situation by a security alliance stretching from Calais to the Urals. It simply makes a mockery of the notion of respecting Russia's interests as an important European power—never mind a Great Power.

But enlargement into Poland cannot be assumed to be of purely political significance. Even if Poland were not formally integrated into the NATO command and even if there were no permanent stationing of either nuclear weapons or non-Polish NATO troops on Polish territory, the military strategic balance of force would profoundly change for Russia as a result of Polish membership, because NATO would acquire the ability to build the infrastructures and coordination mechanisms to deploy force on Poland's borders with Ukraine very rapidly in a crisis. As a result, the United States and Germany acquire the ability to use a far more potent form of coercive diplomacy against Russia, in the event that Russian and

---

2   The December 1996 NATO ministerial meeting informed the Russian government that NATO does not plan to station nuclear weapons on Polish territory.

US interests clash in the zones around Russia's borders. This again is inherent in any expansion of NATO into Poland. Soothing words about strategic partnerships, consultation, etc. between the US/NATO and Russia will not dispose of this fact.

In this connection it is important to recognize the transformation of the balance of military power that has occurred since 1989. Today NATO has three times the military strength of Russia *and the rest of the CIS combined*. With Poland and the other CEECs joining, NATO's factor of predominance will be four to one. This is also important when considering the rhetoric from Warsaw or from the Republican Right in the United States about the continued "Russian threat": such language as an explanation for NATO expansion is just not credible.

Thus Polish membership of NATO will absolutely, inevitably repolarize European politics. Those who say Russia should welcome this enlargement because NATO is purely defensive and threatens nobody are either ignorant of international politics or mendacious, because they ignore the simple fact that Russia will face a mighty nuclear-armed military alliance on its own border (of the Kaliningrad triangle), an alliance whose leading powers are already engaged in a vigorous competition with Russia for influence over its Asian energy-and-minerals underbelly and over Ukraine.

Russia will, therefore, inevitably do what it can under any leadership to undermine this state of affairs. Of course, some argue that Russia will have to come to realize that it must accept the new realities, give up its ambitions to be a Great Power in European politics and accept that what counts now is strength as a capitalist economy. Along this line of argument, NATO expansion actually helps Russia by making her face these facts. But this is itself just the language of *Machtpolitik* and acknowledges that NATO enlargement is a deliberate assertion of power against Russia designed to make its elites sober up and face defeat. It is also a disingenuous argument because the quest for economic strength cannot be divorced from the quest for political influence, above all in Russia's case, where a close relationship with Ukraine and the Caspian and Asian republics can bring the new Russian capitals very handsome rewards.

Against this background, we can predict an effort by Russian governments to combat NATO's expansion into Poland. This response might take a variety of forms and might develop at a variety of paces over the next decades. Russia could threaten Poland by stuffing Kaliningrad or

Belarus with tactical nuclear weapons;[3] it could repudiate the CFE; scrap its START (Strategic Arms Reduction Treaty) commitments;[4] engage in wrecking tactics in the UN; turn the Baltic states into hostages; turn nasty on the Black Sea Fleet; turn its base on the Dniester into a threat to Moldova; embark upon a more activist policy to destabilize Ukraine or seek to expand its influence in the Balkans. None of this may seriously threaten the security of Western Europe and it might even strengthen the currently very ragged cohesion of the Atlantic alliance and US leadership in Western Europe. But it could cause misery for hundreds of millions of people in Eastern Europe and the former Soviet Union.

Particularly dangerous will be the onset of intense American-Russian rivalry within Ukraine. Russia has powerful levers for pursuing this struggle, not least its economic leverage over the Ukrainian economy, its links within Ukraine's political elites and the crisis of Ukraine's armed forces and state administration (not to speak of its appalling general economic crisis). At the same time, American hopes that it has a strong base of political support in Ukraine may prove unfounded, and a deep internal crisis within that country could ensue.

Along the borders between those definitely in and those definitely out, there lies a gray zone of states which may or may not be included. The French government would like Romania in, while other Western governments disagree. The German government would favor Slovenia's inclusion; others (notably in Italy) are far less enthusiastic. Slovakia is another gray zone country. The states left out will become a field of political rivalry between Russia and the West and, in the Balkans, between Turkey and Greece. Indeed, there are clear signs that such rivalry is already underway in Bulgaria.

In any case, the results of this expansion can only be to increase insecurity for the excluded states by tilting the local balance of forces against Slovakia, Romania, and Bulgaria. The tendency will be for the excluded to fear a new local assertiveness from the included and to devote more

---

3 Russian defense minister Igor Rodionov has warned that NATO's enlargement might force Russia to target nuclear missiles on countries joining the Atlantic alliance. See the *Independent*, November 30, 1996. Belarus president Lukashenko warned that Belarus might still want to keep the nuclear weapons on its territory if Poland joined NATO. See the *Independent*, November 14, 1996.

4 Alexander Lebed, while still Boris Yeltsin's security chief, warned of a change in Russia's attitude toward arms control treaties at his meeting with NATO leaders in Brussels in October. See the *Independent*, October 8, 1996.

of their extremely meager resources to military budgets. Thus already overstretched budgets and poverty-stricken populations will be strained even further.

If Romania is left out of NATO while Hungary is included, the potential for conflict between Romania and Hungary over Transylvania will increase, despite the treaty between left-wing governments in both countries regulating their relations on this issue. Both the Romanian and the Hungarian right are far from reconciled with the treaty in place. The same pattern could occur between Hungary and Slovakia if the latter is excluded from NATO. On the other hand, if Romania is included in NATO, the potential for irredentist projects on the part of a Romanian government toward both Moldova and Ukraine (over North Bukovina) may create a new zone of tension. A foretaste of such future possible rivalries was given in late autumn 1996, when Boris Yeltsin suggested that an alliance with Bulgaria might be built: this exacerbated political tensions within that country in ways that could only further deepen the political (and financial) crisis there. The maneuvers within Bulgaria were directly stimulated by the plans for NATO enlargement. The whole area of the southern Balkans may be pushed back into the role of becoming a cockpit for power rivalries as a result of the NATO expansion.

Of course, Western policymakers are fully alert to these dangers. This is why they are trying to insist that NATO's expansion has nothing whatever to do with US power politics and state interests, but is precisely a continuation of the liberal collective security project: once a state has proved itself to be a consolidated democracy, it will be awarded NATO membership irrespective of geopolitics or geostrategy. In other words, those excluded must be persuaded that their exclusion is the result of failings by their governments to come up to Western standards of freedom, democracy and liberal rights. Insofar as this message is convincing to the electorates of the excluded countries, the division of Europe will not pose too serious a challenge to European stability and security, at least in the short term. Local voters will blame their own state elites rather than the Western powers for their exclusion from the Western club of rich states. The politicians who have been demanding sacrifice after sacrifice in order to "enter Europe" will not be discredited and will be able to call for one more big round of sacrifice to ensure eventual entry into the promised West.

But this public relations exercise carries little weight in a region close

to one of NATO's three or four most important states—Turkey—which
is currently engaged in a war against the Kurds and systematically uses
torture against its own population. They, therefore, like the Russians, ask
themselves what is really going on in Washington: what is the real reason
—as opposed to the news management absurdities—for the new division
of Europe?

The Causes of NATO's Expansion

We can be sure that NATO's expansion has nothing to do with particular current tensions, conflicts or threats in the CEECs today. If potential
Russian threats had been the motive, NATO would not be entering Poland,
it would be opening its doors to the Baltic states. Yet precisely because
Russia would have the capacity to occupy the Baltics, NATO wishes to
steer clear of them! At the same time, by entering Poland, NATO actually
increases the insecurity of the Baltics.

The conclusion is inescapable, that the first and main basis for the move
into Poland is not a Russian threat *but Russia's current extreme weakness.*
Because of the catastrophic social and economic collapse inside Russia and
the fact that its state has, for the moment, been captured by a clan of gangster
capitalists around the West's protégé Boris Yeltsin, the Russian state is in no
position at present to resist the enlargement. This Russian weakness will
almost certainly be temporary. We must assume the Russian economy and
state will revive. It could easily grow tenfold stronger in resource terms
than it is today. NATO is thus exploiting a "window of opportunity" that
will not stay open for very long. It is a case, therefore, of establishing a fait
accompli against Russia swiftly.

The analogy with Germany's fate after the First World War is all too
obvious. The new order then was based upon a temporarily weak Germany,
and when Germany revived it worked to undermine the Versailles order.
After the Second World War, the institutions of Western Europe were
built by the US precisely in order to provide a framework for the revival
of the strength of the defeated power (or at least of its western part). This
time round the defeated power is to be excluded just like the Weimar
Republic in the 1920s.

In other words, NATO's expansion into Poland has little or nothing to
do with strengthening Europe's peace, security and stability. It is a piece

of opportunism, an adventure, gambling with Europe's future security for the sake of something other than security.

The fashionable answer among West European diplomats as to what this something-other-than-security actually is tends to be a variant on Disraeli's remark about the causes of the British Empire: it was done in a fit of collective absence of mind on the part of the American administration: Clinton stumbled into it without much thought in his Detroit speech in October 1996 or he was after the Polish vote in the Midwest; or whatever, but the main thing is that once Clinton has publicly committed himself to it, we are lumbered with it and must make the best of it.[5]

These kinds of explanations cannot be taken seriously, not least because they express unwarranted contempt for the American policymaking system. Whatever the weakness of decision-making in the US executive, no American president would be allowed to gamble with Europe's future for the sake of the Chicago vote.

Since the enlargement decision reshapes Europe's future, we must assume that the US origins of the policy derive from considerations on an equivalent level: namely, considerations about securing the United States' future as the dominant world power after the Soviet bloc collapse.

If we approach the search for causes at this level, we can engage in "backward mapping," from the consequences of NATO expansion into Poland for America's power position in Europe, to the likely motives for that decision.

Four main features of an explanation stand out:

1) Norm-based collective security

By asserting NATO power in ways that weaken Russia, the US is asserting its monocratic dominance in European politics, precisely to defeat decisively European pressures for a norm-based, inclusive collective security order in Europe. To appreciate this, we must distinguish between quite different senses of the notion of norm-based collective security. A genuinely inclusive collective security order involves three core elements:

(a) a collective *decision-making system* on policy and on operations, based upon clear rules.

---

5   Clinton's Detroit speech marked the definitive American commitment to rapid NATO expansion.

(b) clear rules on unacceptable state behavior and on modes of collective action against states that break the rules.
(c) clear mechanisms for joint action to enforce the rules.

Both the Bush and Clinton administrations have consistently opposed such conceptions for the obvious reason that they would undermine US single-power dominance over decisions and operations within NATO. To strengthen the OSCE toward playing these roles would have reduced US power to that of being only *primus inter pares* in European affairs: it would have remained the most influential power because of its military capacity, its military infrastructures in Europe, its leadership of the world economy, the strength of its multinational corporations (MNCs), and its capacity, assisted by its great media strengths, to dominate the international agenda. But during the Cold War, the US had been more than first among equals: it had dominated and controlled the high politics of Western Europe. A European collective security regime would have required the US to have accepted a loss of direct institutional control, through NATO, of the destiny of Europe.

Worse, under a collective security order, the West European states could have developed their own security identity independently of the US. The WEU could have replaced NATO as the primary locus of strategic policy-making and as the primary nexus of military forces among West European states. NATO could, at best, have become a meeting place only between two centers of strategy and two organizations of force—one American, one West European. And the West Europeans could have insisted that US actions in Europe conform strictly to rules laid down in a strengthened OSCE and in other such collective security fora.

And if Russia had been included, there would have been three power poles within pan-European security—the US, a unifying Western Europe (around France and Germany) and Russia—raising the distinct possibility of the US finding itself as one against two.

With the expansion of the EU into the Visegrád countries, this kind of marginalization could have stared the US in the face. Key political issues involving Russia, Central Europe, and the EU could have been discussed first between EU powers and Russia, since NATO would not be involved with Russia or Central Europe. At the same time, if Russia had been drawn into NATO, the issue of the US's monocratic power over decision-making and operational command within NATO could not have been avoided.

In such circumstances, given EU expansion into Visegrád, the US faced a potentially very real loss of control-power if NATO stayed as it was without expansion. And by expansion, the US assures the continuation of its monocratic institutional position: no separate West European security policy or operational frameworks.

The US conceals these issues by using the language of collective security and of a "West European identity" in quite different senses. By "collective" it means something arithmetic—a collection of states (under its command); by "norm-based" it means that *the US* can be relied upon *to decide* matters on the basis of democratic, liberal, human rights, etc. norms; i.e., it will not be *institutionally* bound by any such norms. And as for the "European identity," this can mean a transatlantic division of labor: the troops will be European and the command will be American (as well as the infrastructures).

2) Germany and Russia

Beyond these matters of current institutional design for Europe's security order, there are deeper questions of geopolitical strategy into the twenty-first century for the US. As the Pentagon document leaked in early 1992 made clear, the American government is preoccupied by its long-term position in Eurasia, which in turn governs its capacity to exercise "world leadership."[6] The great danger here for the US is that Germany becomes the hegemonic power in Western and Central Europe and then establishes a condominium with Russia over the bulk of the Eurasian landmass. To prevent that happening, US political ascendancy in the territory between Germany and Russia becomes pivotal. Via NATO expansion into Poland (as well as via US companies acquiring a strong presence in Poland), US influence in that key country can be secured.

3) The Drang Nach Kiev

For American policy planners, Poland is only one part of the necessary geopolitical wedge between Germany and Russia. In many ways, Ukraine is an even more important prize. A combined Polish-Ukrainian corridor under US leadership would decisively split "Europe" from Russia, exclude Russia also from the Balkans, go a long way toward securing the Black Sea for the US, link up with America's Turkish bastion, and

---

6   See the excerpts of the FY 1994–1999 Defense Planning Guidance in Chapter 3 of this volume.

provide a very important base for the "Great Game" for the energy and mineral resources of the Caspian and the Asian republics of the former USSR.

Of course, to move NATO into Ukraine today would cause an explosive confrontation with Moscow. For this reason, US policy toward Ukraine under President Clinton has been marked by considerable subtlety.

Following Bush's notorious "Chicken Kiev" speech in the Ukrainian capital in 1991, when he attacked "unrealistic nationalism" at a time when the US was worried about the consequences of Soviet collapse, Clinton joined a partnership with Moscow to ensure that Kiev became non-nuclear. What was not noticed by Russian politicians was that if Ukraine had decided to maintain its nuclear status, it could have done so in the medium term only by means of rebuilding its security relationship with Moscow. Thus, Ukraine's abandonment of nuclear weapons freed it from such future dependence.

With Kiev's agreement to become non-nuclear, the US government has combined a symbolic emphasis on its special relationship with Moscow with an energetic intensification of its relations with Ukraine. Kiev is now the recipient of the third largest amount of US aid. Washington has been vigorously seeking to strengthen Ukraine's mass media integrity and to strengthen military cooperation under the umbrella of the Partnership for Peace notably through joint exercises and through strengthening military cooperation with Poland. The IMF has been unusually flexible in its approach to Ukraine's socioeconomic problems.

Washington now feels confident that it has a strong policy understanding with the Ukrainian government whereby the latter insists to Moscow on its right to cooperate with the West through the PfP and on its freedom from any security pact with Moscow. After initially expressing strong reservations about NATO's expansion into Poland and stressing its own "neutralist" posture, Kiev has evolved toward supporting NATO expansion while saying it has no interest in joining NATO; and at the end of 1996, President Kuchma went further, indicating that in a very distant future Ukraine might itself eventually seek to become a NATO member.

Once NATO enters Poland, it will have the capacity to project its influence across the border into Ukraine in such a way as to ensure that Ukraine could withstand any Russian pressure to enter a security pact with Moscow. In the event of a crisis between Kiev and Moscow, NATO could offer massive assistance to Ukraine. And in the meantime, via PfP, cooperation and assistance can be steadily increased. Without NATO expansion, all this would be much more difficult.

This motive for NATO expansion into Poland, as a means of projecting US influence into Ukraine, was signaled by Polish president Kwasniewski. Speaking in London at the Royal Institute of International Affairs, he said: "We are confident that Poland's accession to NATO will lead to a projection of stability and security into areas stretching beyond our eastern frontier." This can only refer to the goal of pulling Ukraine away from a security link with Russia.

In short, NATO's expansion into Poland marks the return of power politics to Europe in place of the project of an inclusive and collective new security order. The relationship between liberal universalism and power politics turns out not to be dichotomous: it acquires the complementarity of means and ends: liberal universalism is the rhetorical means toward US power politics ends.

4) The new Russian threat

There is an obvious criticism that could be leveled against this analysis of US power-maximization interests in NATO expansion. This is that it over-emphasizes what might be called the traditional "realist" way of looking at international politics: it exaggerates the military-strategic elements of power over the political-economy elements. Along this line of argument, the key way in which the American state assures its global dominance today is less through its military capacity than through its imposition of its global political-economy regime on states. In other words, American ascendancy is assured through reorganizing the internal structures of states to allow their penetration by American capitalist companies and through requiring these states to maintain their viability through competition on world markets in which US capital predominates.

All this is true in general: for the US in its relations with most states, military power is a reserve power, not the first means of influence. But it is not possible in the Russian case, because Russia is different: it has such vast energy and raw material resources that even with a gangster capitalist elite on an almost Zairian scale of sybaritic corruption, it has not the slightest difficulty in maintaining a healthy trade surplus and in keeping Western capital at bay. And it can do all this without being integrated into the WTO. Moreover, it can offer both energy security and, at least in the medium term, significant credit support to governments looking for alternatives to the IMF. Its big capitals can also already move into other states and establish themselves as influential politicoeconomic rivals to Western MNCs, especially in the crucial energy sector.

During the Cold War, this Russian economic capacity did not constitute a serious challenge because of the ideological divide against Communism. But with the Communist collapse, Russia's potential structural power in the energy sector and the expansionist capacities of its capitals constitute a new kind of threat to US dominance over the international political economy.

Since 1991 the American administration, its MNCs, and the IMF have been involved in a complex double operation to influence developments in Russia. On the one hand, there was the real possibility that the Yegor Gaidar government would actually open Russia's economic assets to American buyers.[7] If American capital had been able to buy up Russia's oil and gas resources as well as the bulk of Russia's other mineral resources, we would not have seen any NATO expansion into Poland excluding Russia. Washington would have adopted a "Russia first" policy. But the Gaidar-Burbulis drive collapsed, despite the West's successful promotion of the idea of a coup d'état by Yeltsin against the constitution in August 1993. The US then found itself backing Chernomyrdin-style Russian corporate capitalism against the Communist challenge. In this cleavage, Washington had to back Yeltsin-Chernomyrdin, but the latter was at the same time a potential challenge to the US drive for a "globalized" capitalism in which all states would have to comply with market institutions designed to favor US MNCs. Thus, as soon as Yeltsin had managed to beat off the Communists, the Clinton administration moved forward with a NATO expansion that will have the effect of containing the expansion of Russian capital abroad.

The Rebuilding of US Leadership through Bosnia

So far we have implied that the US has been able to act more or less as it has pleased in European politics. Yet in reality, despite its assertion of power during the Gulf War of 1991, Washington was in danger of

7   [Gaidar, as minister of finance and then acting prime minister, spearheaded privatization and the lifting of price controls. Together with Yeltsin's consigliere Gennady Burbulis, Gaidar incarnated neoliberal "shock therapy." Controversy over this economic agenda saw both men exit the cabinet at the end of 1992; Gaidar was replaced by Viktor Chernomyrdin.]

political marginalization in a Europe that was peaceful and full of enthusiasm for overcoming the confrontation between the blocs in 1990 and 1991. The expansion of NATO today is conceivable only against the background of Washington's successful rebuilding of its authority over the West European states over the last six years. The first step in this US effort was, of course, ensuring that Germany was unified within NATO. The US reconstruction of NATO's ascendancy in Europe then passed through the Bosnian conflict.

With Germany's success in pushing the other European Community states to recognize Slovenia and Croatia at the end of 1991, the US, which had been against such recognition, found itself threatened with being marginalized on the major political conflict in Europe: that over the crisis of the Yugoslav state. The Bush administration was thus staring in the face the prospect of America's European ascendancy dissolving like a lump of sugar in Chancellor Kohl's coffee cup. In late January 1992, therefore, the Bush administration launched its campaign for an independent Bosnian state. As Susan Woodward explains, the US was "concerned that Germany was 'getting out ahead of the US' (according to Deputy Secretary of State Eagleburger) and that it had lost any leverage on the Yugoslav situation after the EC's December decision." She adds:

> The re-entry of the United States into the Yugoslav debacle as part of a balance of power dynamic already in play in Europe added yet another element to the particular way in which Yugoslavia would unravel. The United States, though in competition with Germany, remained primarily concerned with maintaining the Atlanticist posture of the Kohl government ... In place of the confrontation that could have resulted [with Germany over recognition of Croatia] the United States appeared to move towards a geopolitical division of labor instead, conceding a primary sphere of influence over Croatia to Germany and taking on Bosnia as its responsibility.[8]

As the West European states pointed out at the time, an attempt to create an independent, unified Bosnian state would lead to war, and the war that resulted became the basis for a reassertion of NATO as the primary instrument of force in European politics.

---

8   Susan L. Woodward, *Balkan Tragedy: Chaos and Dissolution after the Cold War* (Washington, DC: Brookings Institution, 1995), pp. 196–7.

On this basis, the Clinton administration launched the plan for NATO's eastward enlargement into Poland in order to ensure that when the Visegrád countries were pulled under the wing of Germany within the framework of the EU, Germany would not, in Eagleburger's phrase, be "getting out ahead of the US" in deciding the great political issues of East-Central Europe together with Russia, leaving the US marginalized.

Conclusion: The Double Division of Europe

The divisions accompanying the NATO expansion and those attending the EU's differentiations between applicants will reinforce each other in dangerous ways, deepening both splits.

The NATO enlargement takes place before that of the EU. Indeed, contrary to the views of politicians in Poland or Hungary, these countries' entry into NATO will not speed up their entry into the EU, but may more probably actually enable the EU member states to delay it. At the same time, the tendency among states excluded from NATO can be to increase insecurities and rivalries, not only in the former Soviet Union but also in the Balkans, thus risking the diversion of budgetary resources to military spending and thus imposing further strains on their crisis-ridden economies. At the same time, the EU signal that some of the associated states can forget accession in the near future will exacerbate internal political strains within them, making them a greater investment risk and raising their costs of borrowing on international financial markets.

Those countries that are offered eventual membership in the EU will probably not join the Union for at least another seven years. And even for them, the prospect of gaining the full current *acquis* can be ruled out. The only question will be whether the systems of transfers will be reformed on the basis of some principle of equity across both new members and old, or whether the arrangements for the new eastern members will be obviously those for a second-class status of membership, as a recent Commission report suggested.

The intellectual key to finding ways to reverse the drift toward a new era of division and conflict in Europe lies in turning current problem definitions on their heads. The current problem-solving agendas in Europe all have one thing in common: all the problems, threats, instabilities, and policy disasters are held to reside in the East. Work toward a solution can begin when we recognize that the main sources of the main problems in fact lie in the West. Among the latter, two are fundamental and interlinked: the first is an unsustainable model of capitalist growth; the second is an unviable—or, at least, destabilizing—model of international political management.

The currently fashionable model for capitalist growth is that of "globalization" plus "shareholder value"—in other words, grabbing market share abroad and putting the interests of rentiers in securities markets first. It is unsustainable because it is economically inefficient on a gigantic scale and it is a systematic breeder of systemic crises. It also ultimately threatens Western leadership of the world economy. The fact that it also currently generates enormous fortunes for very small social groups both in the West and in the East only makes it more dangerous because more difficult to change.

Globalization in the CEECs has been destroying and will continue to destroy vast amounts of productive assets, through subordinating economic life to the logics of financial speculation. In 1996, 11 percent of Bulgaria's GDP was sacrificed on the altar of the preferences of international financial speculation. These kinds of breakdowns are normal and systemic within the globalization model: to explain them by reference to the activities of a finance minister in a Balkan country is to turn reality on its head.

At present this system is staggering from one local blowout to another, avoiding a systemic collapse through frantic and ceaseless state intervention by the G7 states via the IMF. This chaotic financial context is linked to deep sources of stagnation in the West's industrial structures. The lack of profitable outlets for productive investment feeds the global speculative bubble. It also threatens fierce industrial wars between the main Western states as the semi-monopolies of each state try to grab market shares from their rivals. To prevent such conflicts, the Western states seek through globalization to grab extra market shares for their main companies in the East and the South. They also try to open new regions of capital growth within their own economies via privatizations and attempts to turn welfare systems into zones of capital growth for the private financial markets.

Across all these activities the common theme is pauperizing ever-larger groups of the world's population. The weakest regions bear the brunt of the misery.

In these Western-centered processes lie the origins of the most serious problems of the CEECs: the groups of gangster capitalists, the corrupt bureaucrats, the social and inter-ethnic tensions, the malnutrition, disease, and mounting death rates in large parts of the region.

This economically and socially regressive growth model is interacting with a system of international governance in the West which is radically dysfunctional. It is also best understood by situating it within inter-capitalist tensions in the West. At the end of the Cold War, the United States faced the possibility that the main West European states could reorganize the political economy of western Eurasia in the interests of their own strategies for international capital accumulation. This could have been managed either in the framework of a pan-European collective security order, or through a cooperative arrangement between a Western European Union (WEU) and a Moscow-centered Eastern security network, or through some combination of the two. NATO would have declined and withered. For the United States this would have marked a dangerous loss of political and economic influence.

The Clinton administration therefore embarked upon a campaign to ensure its continued "leadership" over Western Europe's relations with the rest of western Eurasia, first through the Bosnian war and then through the enlargement of NATO into the Visegrád states. US concern for continued control over its West European "allies" has been the basic rationale for NATO's enlargement. The consequences of this enlargement in the excluded zone and the possible roles of NATO in the East have been secondary details in this entire process.

The West European states were ready to accept this US campaign because their own interstate system has been gridlocked: only Germany could give a lead but the other main states of the EU devote their energies to preventing German leadership. As a result the only forms of collective action on which the West European states can unite are those where they have a common interest in exporting problems abroad by engaging in collective mercantilism against weaker actors in the international political economy. Gridlock on international political strategy within the EU forms the basis for the return of American leadership in Western Europe as a supposed *pouvoir neutre* above the petty, provincial squabbles over an essentially trivial agenda within the so-called Common Foreign and Security Policy of the EU and the WEU. The US concept of NATO enlargement met Germany's immediate need of securing Poland as a buffer on its eastern flank, while the French and British had no positive alternative to offer.

The result of these Machiavellian power maneuvers among the Western states is a policy toward the excluded European zone that can best be described as unprincipled ad-hocery: the antithesis of a genuinely norm-based, principled approach to security issues. It is entirely unclear what principle, for example, the Western powers stand for in their efforts to reorganize the former Yugoslavia. They are evidently not in favor of ethnic self-determination for the micro-nations of the area. On the other hand, they are also not, it seems, in favor of respecting the territorial integrity of the existing states that have emerged from the Yugoslav collapse. NATO claims the right to launch aggression against a sovereign state—the new Yugoslav state—because it is hostile to the internally repressive policies of that state in Kosovo. But it simultaneously rejects self-determination for the Kosovar Albanians because that would undermine the "principles" applied to Bosnia at Dayton and the "principles" applied to Macedonia. At the same time, NATO's American leadership is determined to ensure that it has the right to do as it pleases, unconstrained by UN principles and resolutions. And there is a yawning gap between NATO's attempt to legitimate its power plays in terms of human rights (rather than the rights of states) and its instrument for supposedly enforcing "human rights"— missile attacks and bombing raids.

There is an overarching strategic concept of sorts in the double enlarge-ment. It is a strategy for Americanizing the social structures of Europe within the NATO security perimeter while Centralamericanizing the hinterland beyond the perimeter. First, the CEECs have become and will continue to be a significant middle-class market for Western multi-nationals grabbing market share there at will, using the Single Market rules embodied in the Europe Agreements to legitimize their market domination. Second, the CEECs will offer a limitless supply of cheap labor for Western multinationals to use for the labor-intensive parts of their production circuits. Third, these attractions will be used by big capital in Western Europe to threaten to exit eastward unless Western Europe Americanizes its labor markets, turns the welfare states into minimal safety nets and allows British- or American-style social inequality, poverty, urban decay, and prison populations. Western Europe will be distinguishable from the US only by the virulence of its internal racist, neo-fascist, and xenophobic movements.

And, increasingly, the Europe within the security perimeter will be unified by fear of the ugly arc of poverty and political turbulence stretching from the Kaliningrad triangle to the Balkan Mountains. This will be the spontaneous result of the current international political-economy regime for the excluded region of South-Eastern and Eastern Europe, and of the current NATO power project's capricious, coercive diplomacy. It is simply utopian to imagine that the current trends in Russia, Ukraine, and South-Eastern Europe can continue much longer without grave and tragic consequences. But this spontaneous drift will not easily be changed: the globalization-cum-neoliberal policy cycle is still on its upward curve in Europe, and there is still a rich vein of resources for capital growth to be dug out of Western welfare states, CEEC debt, and the CEEC privatizations of state enterprises, especially the public utilities. And the political path toward an alternative is firmly blocked by the lack of federal democracy within the EU, the disarray on the European left, and the great power interests of the United States in western Eurasia.

It will therefore take more than persuasion to change course in Europe. Therapies will not be applied until an exogenous shock brings home the truth that the West's interlocking structures of accumulation and governance are not acceptable. The best kind of such shock leading to therapy would be a social movement by the peoples of Europe to demand a New Deal. The worst would be a blowout in the globalized financial system or a full-scale breakdown of order in the big republics of the former Soviet Union.

There is a nevertheless perfectly viable alternative *policy* strategy for the reintegration of Europe on a capitalist basis, but it is one that would require a break with the American-led globalization-neoliberal approach in economics and with the American power politics strategy for the European region. Thus the obstacles to an alternative lie not in policy ideas but in political trends.

The alternative strategy is one centered upon market growth within the Eastern region: a strategy for rapid reindustrialization in the East through very large infrastructure projects and through a serious pan-European campaign for the desperately needed revival of economic development in the CIS, particularly Russia and Ukraine. The main economic obstacle to such market growth in the East lies in severe payments constraints facing states in the region: heavy indebtedness and current account deficits. With the arrival of the euro, these problems could be overcome through a bold, coordinated strategy involving both the European Central Bank and an EU "economic government." The currencies in the East could be underwritten, substantial capital transfers for infrastructure investment in the East could be raised through a large public bond issue at EU level; governments in the East could be encouraged to re-impose controls on their capital accounts; they could be given new flexibility in their trade regimes and industrial policies, and could be given far more generous access to the EU market. Within such a new strategic framework, Western Europe's economy could revive and incomes could be substantially raised in the East. With rising incomes in the East, the new security barriers being erected along NATO's and the EU's borders could be overcome and the European Social Model could be preserved. Such a genuine reconstruction and development effort could be combined with a new, more genuine collective security regime being built across the continent, one that would have the broad authority to mediate and help maintain peace by gaining confidence on the part of both sides in conflicts. And any such new strategy would have to end the dangerous trend toward trying to exclude Russia and Ukraine from European affairs.

There is enormous development potential still in the Eastern region of Europe. Growth rates of 10 percent per annum in many of these states are not unthinkable if a strong, effective framework for financial, monetary and trade relations is put in place. This strategy might involve a delay in the EU's eastward enlargement, but it would meet the real goals of people in the CEECs when they seek to join the EU: a strategy for rapid, sustained economic development in the East; and a genuine commitment on the part of Western Europe to make the societies of the region genuine equals with Western Europe.

But such a new strategy would require three preconditions that are currently lacking. First, a break with the social projects of globalization and neoliberalism. The fate of Oskar Lafontaine shows how far we still are from that.[9] Secondly, it would require a serious international political leadership at the EU level, or at least at the Euroland level. This leadership can come only from Germany and France working together to transform the EU into a genuine political actor capable of acting strategically in the

9   [As minister of finance in Gerhard Schröder's SPD government, elected in September 1998, Lafontaine promoted a Keynesian economic agenda and criticized Bundesbank and ECB orthodoxy. He resigned five months later, having been obstructed in the cabinet and targeted by a venomous, coordinated media campaign.]

pan-European political economy. It would require a genuinely federal institutional development and the building of a real democratic identity within Europe—without these, the responses of significant parts of the EU to this strategy would be to oppose it as being, allegedly, too German-centered.

But there is a third great problem with the strategic reorientation that we have proposed: how to manage the hostility of the Anglo-American state and business elites in Washington and among "Third Way" Labour and its business cronies? This is not necessarily an insuperable problem, but it is one that the social democrats of Western Europe are unlikely, given their past record, to be able to overcome. The line of least resistance is so much easier.

Thus the most likely variant may be back to the future: back to 1920s-style, grossly unequal states in Western Europe with narrow social bases alongside broken-down regimes in the East; rising xenophobia and neo-fascist currents in the West, continuing stagnation and mounting social degradation. Only the forms of democratic deficit may be different. We had thought that interwar capitalist society was a thing of the past, a deviation overcome by postwar social progress. But it turns out that the postwar social gains were the deviation, and the interwar state and society are again the norm. Postwar social progress was, it seems, a tactical, aberrant form of European capitalism made necessary by the challenge of Communism. We know now the second half of that sentence whose first half, so strongly believed in 1989, stated: "Western-style welfare capitalism is better than Eastern Communism." The second half went unnoticed ten years ago. It reads: "... but Western-style welfare capitalism only existed because of Communism." Europe seems to be drifting toward a divided, turbulent and ugly future.

PART TWO
Out of Area

6

The NATO Powers and the Balkan Tragedy

Peter Gowan

Western powers usually legitimize military interventions in terms of a proclaimed commitment to some universalist norm or to some goal embodying such a norm. These declared goals can oscillate, but they are important because a central element of their foreign policy, particularly when it involves starting a war, is maintaining the support of their domestic population. In the Anglo-Saxon countries, people like to think of themselves as the guardians and promoters, through their states, of the most civilized, humane, liberal and democratic values in the world. It is true that they have short attention spans and are generally far more ignorant of the world outside their borders than the populations of many other countries, but at least the elected leaders of their states can run into domestic trouble if the declared norms and goals are not implemented or if implementation is carried through with such barbarity that they contradict other, more basic, norms and goals.

The attack on Yugoslavia is justified as aiming to end the oppression of the Kosovo Albanians and guaranteeing their human rights. The result may be a NATO protectorate, it may be autonomy within Serbia, it may involve a partition of Kosovo, it may even lead to an independent Kosovo, it may be built under Ibrahim Rugova's leadership or that of the Kosovo Liberation Army (KLA). We simply do not know. These aims are only the latest of a whole series enunciated by the NATO powers since the start of the Yugoslav crisis in the late 1980s. It would tire the reader's patience if we were to list all the norms and goals proclaimed by these powers since 1989. A recitation, in any case, would tell us little of the real operational goals of the NATO powers in Yugoslavia over the last decade. Their operations have not been governed by any universalist norms geared to improving the conditions of the peoples of the area, but by their own *state political interests and state political goals*. These real objectives of the Western states have usually had little to do with the human rights of the citizenry. Yugoslavia has, for a long time, been the cockpit of Europe. At the same time, the operations of the Western powers in the Yugoslav theater have been a major—some would say, *the* major—cause of many of the barbarities that have confronted Yugoslav men and women in the past. A balanced judgment on the March 1999 NATO assault on Yugoslavia necessitates a study of the whole tragedy.

The Western Powers and the Collapse of Yugoslavia

The post–Second World War Yugoslav state was, in many respects, a model of how to build a multinational state, though, from the beginning, the incorporation of Kosovo into Serbia was an anomaly.[1] The Federation was constructed against a double background: an interwar Yugoslavia which had been dominated by an oppressive Serbian ruling class; and a wartime slaughter in which the occupying Italian and German forces enlisted Croatian fascism for ferocious massacres and also exploited anti-Serb sentiments among the Kosovo Albanian—and some elements in the Bosnian Muslim—population, to bolster their rule.

The new Yugoslav state pursued economic redistribution and development in the constituent republics. It evolved a self-management model to show its defiance of Stalin. Anti-Stalinist, internationalist socialists from the whole of Western Europe rallied to Tito and special brigades helped to rebuild the railways. The new republican borders ensured that the previously dominant Serb nation—the largest nation in Yugoslavia—would never again dominate the other Yugoslav nations. Both constituent nations

---

1   On the historical background of Kosovo's place in postwar Yugoslav history, see Branka Magaš's prescient article under the name of Michelle Lee, "Kosovo between Yugoslavia and Albania," *New Left Review* I:140 (July–August 1983), pp. 62–91.

and republics were furnished with rights of equal constitutional status; and, finally, the state was anchored in a transnational League of Communists rooted in all the Yugoslav nations (though most weakly in Kosovo). The Communists exercised a monopoly of political power but, despite the oligarchic character of the new state, they enjoyed wide support within the population as the guarantors of all the positive elements in the system and as the people who had led a successful resistance against fascism.

Partly to ease Serb sensitivities over the fact that very large parts of the Serbian population were left outside the Serbian Republic, the Communist leadership allocated Kosovo to the Serb republic as an autonomous province. They viewed this as a temporary measure until their goal, shared by the Bulgarian and Albanian Communists, of a Balkan Federation in which the borders dividing Albanian communities could wither away. The Stalin–Tito split blocked this.

There was one further important structural element in the stability of the postwar Yugoslav state. Both the USSR and the US were committed to maintaining the integrity and neutrality of Yugoslavia as a state on the borders of superpower confrontation in Europe.

The collapse of this state was a result of both internal and external factors. Assigning comparative weight to the external as against the internal in the generalized crisis that shook Yugoslavia in 1990–91 is a complex matter. However, without understanding the role of the Western powers in helping to produce and channel the crisis, it is difficult to comprehend the disintegration of Yugoslavia. Yet this Western role has largely been overlooked in Western literature.[2]

From Debt to Crisis

The fundamental cause of the Yugoslav collapse was an economic crisis. This was then used by social groups in Yugoslavia and in the West to undermine the collectivist core of the economy and push Yugoslavia toward a full capitalist restoration. The economic crisis was the product

---

2 The striking exceptions have been two outstanding and courageous works of scholarship: Susan Woodward's *The Balkan Tragedy: Chaos and Dissolution after the Cold War* (Washington, DC: Brookings Institution, 1995) remains unsurpassed to this day, but see also Catherine Samary, *Yugoslavia Dismembered* (New York: Monthly Review Press, 1995).

of disastrous errors by Yugoslav governments in the 1970s. They borrowed vast amounts of Western capital in order to fund growth through exports. The Western economies entered a recession, blocked Yugoslav exports and created a huge debt problem. The Yugoslav government accepted an IMF plan that shifted the burden of the crisis onto the Yugoslav working class. Simultaneously, strong social groups emerged within the Yugoslav League of Communists, allied to Western business, banking and state interests and began the push toward neoliberalism, to the delight of the US. It was the Reagan administration that, in 1984, had adopted an NSC proposal to push Yugoslavia toward a capitalist restoration.[3]

This, naturally, undermined a central pillar of the old state: the collectivist link between the party and the working class. The effects were varied. In Kosovo, where the links between Yugoslav Communism and the population had always been weak, and where the economic crisis was at its most intense, there was an uprising in 1981 demanding full republican status. The mass mobilizations included separatist tendencies, wanting to unite Kosovo with Albania. Since 1974, Kosovo had been an autonomous province of the Serbian Republic, a status that gave it far more extensive rights and power within Yugoslavia than enjoyed by national minorities in any West European state. However, in response to the separatist agitation, the central state began to reassert its power and harshly to repress those deemed to be unreliable.

In Serbia, there was an attempt by the intelligentsia to reorganize the link between the party and the people on a Serbian nationalist and anti-Kosovar basis. This movement was ultimately joined and led by the Serbian Communist leader Milošević. It mobilized populist Serbian anti-Albanian chauvinism as a new basis for maintaining popular support for the party while actually implementing the Reagan administration's "structural adjustment" program processed through the World Bank.[4]

---

3 Uniquely, in Yugoslavia, the World Bank imposed a savage bankruptcy mechanism on the industrial sector. In 1989–90, the decisive years, this produced, out of a total industrial workforce of 2.7 million, six hundred thousand redundancies without compensation, along with a further half a million workers not receiving pay in the early months of 1990. This social shock hit mainly Serbia, Bosnia, Macedonia and Kosovo. See World Bank, *Industrial Restructuring Study, Overview*, Washington, DC, June 1991; see also, Michel Chossudovsky, "Dismantling the Former Yugoslavia: Recolonising Bosnia," *Economic and Political Weekly* 31:9 (March 1996), pp. 521–5.

4 This involved traumatic social shocks inflicted on the working class.

In Slovenia, the Communist leadership resisted Milošević and sought new legitimacy by agitating for greater autonomy, with the obvious ultimate goal of splitting away from Yugoslavia altogether: thus capitalist restoration would be seen as a means toward Slovenia "joining Europe." Similar nationalist trends emerged in Croatia, though largely outside the Communist Party. All these attempts to replace the collectivist link between leaders and peoples with new ideologies embraced the symbols and discourses of pre-1945 Yugoslav bourgeois nationalisms. This shift toward prewar values on the part of former Communist leaders and others building new pro-capitalist parties was not a peculiarly Yugoslav phenomenon: it occurred right across the Soviet bloc and the rise of such trends was generally welcomed in Western capitals, where attempts by former ruling parties to maintain social links with the working class were seen as the main enemy to be combated.[5]

Preparing the Carve-Up

This was the situation in 1989, when the Soviet bloc started to crumble. As it did so, the US withdrew its earlier commitment to the maintenance of the integrity of the Yugoslav state. This shift by the US signaled the general view in the main Western powers: none of them had a significant stake in Yugoslav unity and all of them were pushing for a rapid switch to capitalism in the region, a switch to be brought about through induced economic slumps destroying the social gains of populations under the previous order. The populations were expected to put up with their loss of social rights and economic security because they had the prospect of later "entering Europe"—a phrase which meant joining the European Community (EC) club of the rich. This package of policies and conditionalities worked, initially, in much of East-Central Europe, uniting the populations around governments taking the shock-therapy road to capitalism. But in two states, it produced splits and political fragmentation: Czechoslovakia was one and Yugoslavia was the other.

In the Yugoslav case, the tactic's destructive role took a particularly virulent form both because of the zeal of Western policymakers in introducing their new paradigm in their first two cases—Yugoslavia and Poland, where

---

5 Milošević, though presented as a unique phenomenon, was part of a regional political genus, which included figures like Iliescu and Mečiar, and should be analyzed as such.

the shocks were launched simultaneously on January 1, 1990—and because some European governments actually wanted the breakup of Yugoslavia. Their pressure thus combined with the general Western drive for capitalism to speed the breakup during 1990. On one side were a number of European states eager to gain independence for Slovenia and Croatia; on the other side was the United States, keen to ensure that Yugoslavia paid its debts to Western banks and "globalized" its political economy through shock therapy in order to guarantee a regime in the country that would be open for Western multinationals.

The forces enthusiastic to see the breakup of Yugoslavia through independence for Slovenia and Croatia consisted of Germany, Austria, Hungary, the Vatican and, more ambivalently, Italy. Since the mid-1980s, the Vatican and Austria had started an active campaign in East-Central and Eastern Europe to rebuild their influence there and, by 1989–90, the Vatican was openly championing independence for Slovenia and Croatia. By 1990, Austria's government was equally explicit. In the words of a study by the International Institute of Strategic Studies, Austria had "a remarkably open and sometimes brazen policy aimed at helping Slovenia and Croatia in their efforts to leave the [Yugoslav] Federation."[6]

The real goal of Austrian policy was to expand Austria's regional influence, since it "saw the Yugoslav crisis as an auspicious moment for self-assertion."[7] In the summer of 1991, the EC was finally prompted to warn Austria that, if it continued its energetic efforts to break up Yugoslavia, it would be excluded from eventual EC membership, but even that threat did not stop Austrian efforts. The Hungarian government of the late József Antall, elected in the spring of 1990, adopted a policy very much in line with that of Austria, but with additional Hungarian goals vis-à-vis Serbia's Vojvodina Province. Thus Hungary secretly supplied automatic assault rifles to Croatia in late 1990. And, in July 1991, at the very height of the crisis between Serbia and Croatia, the Hungarian prime minister declared that the international treaties designating Hungary's southern borders with Serbia and, in particular, with Vojvodina were treaties made only with Yugoslavia. This, he said, was a "historical fact" which "must

---

6   John Zametica, *The Yugoslav Conflict*, Adelphi Papers, no. 270 (London: International Institute for Strategic Studies, 1992), p. 49.

7   Ibid., p. 50. Austria seemed to have hopes for rebuilding a kind of "Habsburg" sphere in Slovenia, Croatia, and Hungary.

be kept in view."[8] Referring to the 1920 Treaty of Trianon, Antal spelt out just why Hungary was so vigorously supporting Croatia's secession: "We gave Vojvodina to Yugoslavia. If there is no more Yugoslavia, then we should get it back."[9]

These maneuvers by Austria and Hungary to break up Yugoslavia were, of course, then overshadowed by the German government's decision to grant recognition to Slovenia and Croatia. The German government's open championing of Yugoslavia's breakup did not occur until the early summer of 1991, but long before that, both Slovenia and Croatia were getting encouragement from Bonn for their efforts.

The US Agenda

This campaign was not, of course, supported by the United States. It championed Yugoslav unity, as did Britain and France. But for the US, unity was not the main goal: its policy was principally governed by its concern to ensure the imposition of shock therapy on the country as a whole via the IMF. In 1989, Jeffrey Sachs was in Yugoslavia helping the federal government under Ante Marković prepare the IMF package, which was then introduced in 1990, just at the time when the crucial parliamentary elections were being held in the various republics. While Marković bears responsibility for giving in to Western pressure, the practical consequences of implementation of the package were to deprive his government of most of its substance. By 1991, it was incapable of paying its soldiers, thus weakening the guarantors of the old state.

This was a critical turning point in the tragedy. Marković, in the spring of 1990, was by far the most popular politician not only in Yugoslavia as a whole but in each of its constituent republics. He should have been able to rally the population for Yugoslavism against the particularist nationalisms of Milošević in Serbia or Tudjman in Croatia, and he should have been able to count on the obedience of the armed forces. He was supported by 83 percent of the population in Croatia, by 81 percent in Serbia, by 59 percent in Slovenia and by 79 percent in Yugoslavia as a whole. This level of support showed how much of the Yugoslav population remained

---

8   Ibid. Zametica cites the Hungarian Ministry of Foreign Affairs, *Newsletter* 398, July 9, 1991.

9   Woodward, *Balkan Tragedy*, p. 219.

strongly committed to the state's preservation. But Marković had agreed to couple his Yugoslavism with the IMF shock therapy program and EC conditionality, and it was this that gave the separatists their opening. Their appeal to their electorates involved offering to repudiate the Marković-IMF austerity measures and, by doing so, help their republics prepare to leave Yugoslavia altogether and "join Europe." The appeals of the nationalists in Slovenia and Croatia worked. As Susan Woodward explains: "In every republic, beginning with Slovenia and Croatia in the spring, governments ignored the monetary restrictions of Marković's stabilization programme in order to win votes."[10] After winning elections, they worked hard to break up the country. If Western policy for Yugoslavia had been a Marshall Plan, which the federal authorities could have used to rebuild the country's economic and cohesion, the whole story would have been different.

This is not a case of being wise after the event. Western policymakers were very well aware of the issue at the time. In 1989–90, the US government faced an acute trade-off in its Yugoslav policy. The State Department was concerned in 1990 about Yugoslav political stability. In 1990, the CIA was warning the Bush administration that Yugoslavia was heading for civil war within eighteen months.[11] The dilemma was well brought out by a journalist at a press conference given by Secretary of State Baker on July 5, 1990, in Washington. The journalist asked:

> I noticed in the remarks that you made today that were distributed to us, you expressed some concerns about the situation in Yugoslavia. Now, how does conditionality apply to the kind of problem that you have described in Yugoslavia, which is less to do with the central government and more to do with the different republics. It is not clear whether Belgrade could deliver some of the things that you want. How will that be judged?

Baker, normally laconic, replied with some feeling but more evasion:

> The question you raised is a very, very good question. There will have to be some serious thought given to the degree to which you look at the republic level as opposed to looking at the central government level.

---

10   Ibid.

11   The CIA report was later leaked. Its contents were explained in the *International Herald Tribune*, November 29, 1990, cited in Zametica, *The Yugoslav Conflict*, p. 58.

And you are quite right. There are some things in some countries with respect to which the central government can deliver on; and in other countries that cannot be done.[12]

But the US government as a whole opted for the priority of the shock therapy program. Thus was the internal dynamic toward the Yugoslav collapse into civil war decisively accelerated. The only European states that did have a strategic interest in the region wanted to break Yugoslavia up.

Specifically Yugoslav structural flaws did, of course, push toward collapse. Many would argue that the decentralized "market socialism" was a disastrous experiment for a state in Yugoslavia's geopolitical situation. The 1974 Constitution, though better for the Kosovars, gave too much to the republics, crippling the institutional and material power of the federal government. Tito's authority substituted for this weakness until his death in 1980, after which it could not be avoided and the state was plunged into crisis. But if the Western powers had been interested in putting the interests of the Yugoslav people first, they had adequate levers to play a decisive role, alongside Yugoslavia's federal government, in maintaining the country's integrity. Instead, the Western powers most interested in Yugoslav developments actually assisted, politically and materially, in bringing about the collapse.

The Western Powers and the Atrocities

In 1990–91, Yugoslavia was heading toward dissolution, despite the fact that the overwhelming majority of its population did not favor such a course. The breakup violated a cardinal principle of the new post–Cold War state system, enshrined in the Conference on Security and Co-operation in Europe (CSCE) and the Treaty of Paris of 1990: that interstate borders in Europe should not be changed. Instead, internal arrangements within states should be put in place to ensure adequate rights for all groups. But the Western powers were not prepared to enforce such principles in the Yugoslav case because Germany did not want to and the other states did

---

12   "Baker Says East Europe Aid for Reform, Not Status Quo." Secretary of State Baker's press briefing following a meeting of the Group of 24, Tracking Number: 145648 Text: TXT404, 3Fm Re (Background for the Houston Economic Summit, US Information Agency, July 5, 1990).

not have any strategic interest in doing so. Norms not relevant to Western state interests were ditched. In the early summer of 1991, German and Austrian efforts to advance the dissolution achieved a triumph by getting the EC to mediate between Slovenia and Croatia and the central Yugoslav authorities. The EC states were eager to enhance their foreign policy role and standing through such mediation. They therefore accepted a function that implied Yugoslavia's destruction: mediation between forces within a state over and above that state's unity implies a repudiation of the state's sovereign authority.

The breakup might have been possible without great bloodshed if clear criteria could have been established for providing security for all the main groups of people within the Yugoslav space. That was the issue that confronted the Western powers once they got involved in "mediation." And the Western role in establishing rights and norms for the protection of Yugoslavia's peoples was crucial, for only the triumphant Western powers could give post-Yugoslav entities the rights of states in the inter-state system.

The problem here was that Yugoslavia's constitutional arrangements, furnishing rights to Yugoslavia's republican territories and its nations and peoples, were premised upon it remaining an integrated state. There were two cardinal structural issues here. The first was a division of the country into republics in such a way that the non-Serb nations would not fear that Yugoslavia would become a Serb-dominated state. To achieve this, as Branka Magas explains, required "winning Serbian acceptance of the new constitutional order which was to divide—more in form than in fact—the Serb nation inside post-revolutionary Yugoslavia."[13] Thus, large parts of the Serb population were placed within other republican terri-tories or within autonomous provinces which enjoyed greater autonomy than, say, the Basque country in today's Spain. The Serbs were thus split up between Serbia proper, Croatia, Bosnia, Vojvodina, and Kosovo. This was, indeed, a question "more in form than in fact" within an integrated Yugoslavia, but it became, of course, a division more of fact than of form in the context of Yugoslavia's breakup. But Yugoslavia's constitutional principles did provide a key to its resolution, for the constitution gave rights to nations of equal force to the rights of republics. Thus, under these criteria, the Serb nationals in, say, Croatia, were the subjects of national

---

13   Branka Magas, *The Destruction of Yugoslavia* (London: Verso, 1993), p. 34.

rights which could not be overridden by the will of the Croatian republic. But how was this issue to be dealt with in a context where the Yugoslav constitution was collapsing?

The second major issue concerned the major non-Slav nation within Yugoslavia, the Kosovo Albanians. While postwar Yugoslavia divided the Serbs within the state, it divided the Albanians both within the state and between Yugoslavia and Albania. As a result, there were always understandable tendencies within the Albanian communities of Kosovo and Macedonia that would have preferred to unite all Albanians in a single Albanian state. With the breakup of Yugoslavia, for many Yugoslav Albanians that became a realistic possibility. How was—and is—that problem to be dealt with?

The Croatian Question

The answers that the Western powers gave to these two cardinal questions contributed directly to the bloody cycles of butchery in the Yugoslav theater during the 1990s. In 1991, the Western powers, led by Germany, gave their answer on the question of the Serb population in Croatia. They declared that Croatia should be entitled to independence on grounds of self-determination and that this should be within the boundaries of republican Croatia established within post–Second World War Yugoslavia. Self-determination was established by the fact that a referendum of the Croatian nation had voted for independence. This was a formula for war between the Croatian nationalist government and Croatia's Serb population because it violated the principles for handling the national question established in the postwar Yugoslav constitution: it denied the Serbs in Croatia their sovereign national rights.

Under that constitution, the will of a republican majority could not override the equally valid will of a constituent nation. Thus, the vote of the Croatian majority for independence could not override the rights of the Serb population, which had to be equally respected. The political leaders of the Serbian population in Croatia accordingly organized a referendum on whether to remain within an independent Croatia, and the result was an overwhelming rejection. According to the Yugoslav principles, Croatian independence should have been dependent upon a prior resolution of that conflict of rights and democratic wills.

But the EC states during 1991 ignored this, rejecting the Yugoslav idea that the Serb nation had rights equal to the Croatian republican will. Instead, the majority of EC states adopted the view that the Serb population of Croatia should accept their status as a national minority within an independent Croatia. This approach should, of course, have implied that CSCE principles for protecting minority rights should be guaranteed before Croatian independence was recognized. But the Croatian government rejected the guarantee of such CSCE standards.

The German government decided to brush this CSCE principle aside and recognized Croatia without any prior commitment by the Croatian government to adequate minority rights for Croatia's Serbian population. The German position thus involved a double betrayal of Croatia's Serbs: a betrayal of the Yugoslav principles concerning their rights; and a parallel betrayal of the CSCE principles concerning their rights. It was bound to drive the Croatian Serb population toward war under the leadership of Serb nationalism. And it led the American mediator Cyrus Vance to call the resulting war "Genscher's war," referring to the German foreign minister. This may be an exaggeration: it was also Tudjman's and Milošević's. But it was Genscher who made it clear to the Croatian Serbs that they had nobody to depend on for their rights but the force of their own arms and those of Serbia.

The reason why the German government took this stand remains obscure. Equally important is why the other EC powers accepted the German line. The bargaining on this issue reached a climax at an all-night meeting of European Political Co-operation on December 15–16, 1991, in Brussels. At that meeting, Chancellor Kohl got the British to support him by offering John Major two big inducements over the Maastricht Treaty: the British opt-out on Monetary Union and a British opt-out on the Social Charter (rights for workers within the EC). And at the same time, Kohl promised that he would not recognize Croatia and Slovenia until they had implemented minority rights—essentially for Croatia's Serbs. But having made that big concession, Kohl then proceeded to renege on it, unilaterally recognizing Croatia and Slovenia on December 23 without any such guarantees.[14]

The question then is, why did the other main Western powers accept this German unilateralism? And the answer is twofold: first, the US did

---

14   For a full account, see Woodward, *Balkan Tragedy*, p. 184.

not accept this German *démarche*—it finally decided to move on the Yugoslav crisis. As far as the other EC powers were concerned, Yugoslavia was simply not an important strategic issue for them: far more important was the Maastricht Treaty (and, for the British, being able to opt out of central parts of it).

The CSCE principles could also have been invoked at this time to draw attention to the oppression of the majority population of Kosovo within the new Yugoslavia. But no Western power had a stake in that issue.

Within the EC, one body, the Badinter Commission, did warn that the unconstitutional breakup of the Yugoslav Federation would lead to appalling intercommunal strife. The Badinter Commission took a view close to earlier Yugoslav jurisprudence: it declared that Bosnian independence should not be accepted unless substantial approval was given to such independence by all three peoples within Bosnia—the Bosnian Serbs, the Bosnian Muslims and the Bosnian Croats. Thus, while the EC took a "historic rights" approach to recognizing borders in the Croatian case (and in the Kosovo case), it took the approach of recognizing the democratic rights of all national groupings in the Bosnian case. Since the Bosnian Serbs were bitterly against a Bosnian independence which would cut them off from the Serbs of Serbia, Badinter's line implied no acceptance of Bosnian independence. This was also the German line in January 1992, and it was largely accepted by the European Community. But at this critical juncture, the United States intervened vigorously in the Yugoslav crisis for the first time.

US Intervention: Playing the Bosnian Card against an Emerging German Sphere of Influence

During 1991, the United States' declared policy was one of supporting Yugoslav unity. But in reality, the US stood back from the Yugoslav crisis, simply watching the chaotic maneuverings of the European powers on the issue.[15] The Bush administration was preoccupied by one overriding

---

15 As it happened, the Bush administration was staffed at the top by longtime Yugoslav experts: Eagleburger, in charge of European policy, was a former ambassador and Scowcroft, head of the National Security Council, had been in the Belgrade Embassy and had written his PhD on Yugoslavia. Woodward claims that one of the reasons for US passivity during 1990–91 was that both men had had business interests in Yugoslavia, and

European policy issue: ensuring that Western Europe remained firmly subordinated to the Atlantic Alliance under US leadership. And it viewed this as a serious problem as a result of fundamental features of the Soviet collapse. First, NATO—the military cornerstone of the alliance—had lost its rationale and there were moves in Western Europe (and Russia) to build a new security order in Europe that would tend to undermine US leadership. Second, newly united Germany seemed to be building a new political bloc with France through the Maastricht Treaty, with its stress on a Common Foreign and Security Policy leading toward "a common defense." This seemed to be more than mere words, since Germany and France were in the process of building a joint military corps, the so-called Euro-Corps outside the NATO framework—a move that profoundly disturbed Washington and London. Third, Germany's drive in relation to Yugoslavia seemed to be geared not simply to domestic German constituencies, but *to the construction of a German sphere of influence* in Central Europe, involving Austria, Hungary, Croatia, and Slovenia and, perhaps later, drawing in Czechoslovakia and, eventually and most crucially, Poland. This seemed to be the only explanation for the extraordinary assertive unilateralism of Genscher and Kohl, riding roughshod over their EC partners in December 1991 and sending a signal to the whole of Europe that Bonn had become the place where the shape of the new Europe was being decided.

This was not acceptable to the Bush administration. As Eagleburger explained, Germany "was getting out ahead of the US" with its Croatian drive. In other words, the US interpretation of Genscher's drive to break up Yugoslavia was far from being that it was just a sop to Catholic domestic constituencies and the editor of the *Frankfurter Allgemeine Zeitung*. In response to this challenge, the US administration decided to take over the political leadership in the Yugoslav crisis.

But just as Germany's various declared universalist norms and goals were in the service not of the Yugoslav people but of German political influence, so the United States was not, of course, entering the Yugoslav theater to calm the storms of war and provide new security for Yugoslavia's terrified peoples. Quite the reverse: it was entering the scene to push Germany and the European Union aside, but it was going to do so, as it turned out, *by laying the basis for a new and much more savage Yugoslav war.*

---

questions were already been raised in the US about the possible influence of these interests on US policy toward the country. See ibid., p. 155.

Washington's chosen instrument for taking the lead was that of encouraging the Bosnian government to press for independence and, therefore, for a Bosnian war. Bosnian independence was opposed by the German government and the EC. They aimed to try to hold the rest of Yugoslavia together. The US administration decided to put a stop to that by launching a drive for Bosnian independence, which got underway in January 1992, just as the EC was following Germany's lead in recognizing Croatia and Slovenia.

Germany had redefined the problem: Europe must defend independent Croatia against Serbian/Yugoslav aggression. Now Washington would provide a new problem definition: Europe and the world must defend an independent Bosnia against Serbian/Yugoslav aggression and, perhaps, if tactically useful, against Croatian aggression as well. Thus did the US enunciate the great norm that would provide it with European leadership: self-determination for the Bosnian nation and defense of its independence against aggression.

Bosnia: A State without a Nation

There was a factual problem with the American line: there was no Bosnian nation in a political sense or in a Yugoslav constitutional sense. There were, instead, three nations in Bosnia, none of which had a majority of the population. As of the 1981 census, Bosnia contained the following main national groups: 1,629,000 Muslims; 1,320,000 Serbs; 758,000 Croatians; 326,000 Yugoslavs. It was evident from voting results that the majority of Bosnia's own population was not going to respect the authority of an independent Bosnian state. And it was equally obvious that large parts of that population would go to war rather than accept the state. The American government knew this perfectly well. So, by pushing the Alija Izetbegović government to launch a drive for independence, the Bush administration was, in fact, pushing for war.

As far as the Izetbegović government itself was concerned, it had been bitterly opposed to the German drive to grant Croatia independence because it had been sure that this would increase pressures within Bosnia for independence and thus for civil war. Izetbegović had made an emotional plea to Genscher in December to draw back in order to save Bosnia, but to no avail. In March 1992 when the US Bosnian independence campaign was in full swing, Izetbegović reached an EC-brokered agreement with Bosnian Croats and Serbs on a three-canton confederal settlement. But a week later, he repudiated his earlier agreement because, according to the *New York Times*, the US government urged him to go all-out for a unitary, sovereign, independent state.[16] This set a course that was certain to produce an atrocious civil war in which both Bosnian Croats and Bosnian Serbs would be sure to gain support from their respective states.

If, at this time, the United States had decided to back the EC and German positions to keep Bosnia within rump Yugoslavia and to shore up its security in that context, the US would have conceded to Germany game, set, and match in the European politics of Yugoslavia's crisis. It was this policy of *the use of Yugoslav developments for wider US European goals* which led the US down a road which trampled underfoot postwar Yugoslav jurisprudence on national rights: a government representing a minority of Bosnia's population was to be encouraged to ignore the expressed democratic will of other large Bosnian communities and attempt to establish a Bosnian state without a Bosnian nation. Quite predictably, Serbian paramilitary groups, some of them en route to the Krajina, were beginning to wipe out Bosnian Muslim villages. An appalling and vicious war was unfolding.

The war was a policy success for the US, which took control of events in the Yugoslav theater and very successfully polarized European politics around those who supported the "Bosnian nation" versus those who supported a drive for "Greater Serbia"—a state uniting all Serbs—and the consequent drive for ethnic cleansing and barbaric massacres. Decisive in the success of the US operation were precisely the barbaric methods employed by one wing of the "Bosnian nation"—the Bosnian Serbs— against the Bosnian Muslims. But also important were the covert supply of weapons to the Bosnian Muslims by the US and the reconciliation between Germany and the US over wider European policy.

Of course, there were other consequences of the US's playing of the Bosnian card, two in particular: First, the biggest nation in the Yugoslav arena, the Serbs, had their national rights trampled underfoot by the Western powers. This meant that they would rally to Milošević's Serbian government as their protector—and it also meant that Western liberal-democratic politics could scarcely triumph in a Serbia whose people were being victimized by Western liberal-democratic states. The second

---

16   See the *New York Times*, June 17, 1993.

consequence was that Yugoslavia's fourth biggest nation, the Kosovo and Macedonia Albanians, with their own national aspirations to freedom and unity, were also to be ignored by the Western powers: or, rather, left in the hands of a Serb nation enraged by Western disregard for their rights, in a Serb state with over six hundred thousand Serb refugees, ethnically cleansed by action under NATO leadership in the last stages of the Bosnian war.

The New German-American Partnership and the Road to Dayton

As the Bosnian war continued through 1993 and 1994, the rivalry and mutual suspicions between Germany and the United States over various broad European issues gave way to a new unity around a new political program for Europe and the Atlantic Alliance. One vital step to this was the Uruguay Round Agreement—embracing a common vision not just for "trade" in the usual sense of that word, but actually for the expansion of Atlantic capitalism across the world through the strategy of "globalizing" national political economies. Another absolutely crucial step was the agreement at the Brussels North Atlantic Council meeting of January 1994 to expand NATO eastward into Poland—the key country for both the US and Germany. This decision, taken essentially by the US and Germany, was actually about how to reorganize European international politics after the end of the Cold War. To understand the significance of this Brussels summit decision, we must look at the broader debates and political battles between the Western powers over the shape of the post–Cold War European order. This debate can be bisected analytically into its political side and its military side.

The Political Concept for Europe

The collapse of the Soviet bloc had reopened the question of how to structure and channel power politics across Europe. There were three "big ideas" in the early 1990s, and two of them were absolutely unacceptable to the US:

Option I: A pan-European collective security system, embracing Russia and the US as well as all the other states of Europe, in an institutionalized framework—a much strengthened and streamlined OSCE—that would be norm-based: clear rules that all should enforce and that would lead all to coerce any state that breached them.

Option II: A two-pillar power structure involving the EU and Western European Union (WEU) in Western Europe and Russia and the CIS in the East. NATO would fade into the background as an ultimate guarantor of its members' security, while the WEU/EU would expand into East-Central Europe—something Russia could have lived with.

Option III: NATO under American leadership would take command of European politics. The OSCE would be marginalized, the WEU/EU would not be allowed to have a policymaking authority and a command structure autonomous from US supervision—exercised through NATO— and NATO would expand eastward but would exclude Russia. So Europe would be re-polarized further east between a US-dominated Western Europe and a weakened Russia. Germany would be expected to discuss Eastern issues first with the US and its Western partners, rather than having the option of discussing with Russia before bargaining with its Western partners.

Options I and II would have undermined the American power position in Europe. But during the early 1990s, there was resistance to Option III, not only from the Russians but also from many European states. It became a vital issue for the US to translate this option into reality.

Yugoslavia may, at first sight, seem to have little to do with these security debates among the Western powers. But what was going on was not just a "debate": it was a political battle over the future political shape of Europe. And such battles between the Western powers are fought not only in words but also by deeds and by creating facts. In this context, Yugoslavia was a central arena for winning arguments by these methods.

Thus, if the EU had successfully handled the Yugoslav crisis in 1990–91, that would have given a great boost to Option II. The fact that, during the Bosnian war, the United States found that it could not do without political help from the Russians meant the formation of the Contact Group and implied an inclusive collective security approach to European affairs—Option I.

But with an agreement between Germany and the United States on making NATO the central pillar of the new European system and on expanding NATO eastward, the way was open for putting that German-American approach into practice in the Yugoslav theater. Success there would then feed back onto the wider European political field with the actual expansion of NATO into Poland.

The Military Concept for a New NATO

NATO as a military structure geared to fighting a war with the Soviet Union became redundant with the collapse of the Soviet bloc. But American leadership of Western Europe depended upon the US being able to supply vital military services to its West European allies. The Yugoslav wars gave the US and the French and British states an argument as to a new role for their military capabilities: the argument that chaos in East-Central Europe would require the Western powers to "project power'" eastward. In other words, to take aggressive military action to defeat forces in the East which were undermining stability or threatening the new political economy of Europe.

This concept greatly favored the US in its battle to rebuild its political leadership of Europe, because the West Europeans lacked key military resources for handling such aggressive "power projection" on their own: they lacked military transport infrastructures and planes, they lacked battlefield satellite intelligence-gathering equipment, and they lacked key new technologies such as cruise missiles and other such "smart" weapons. The US could supply all these. For the West Europeans to supply them would involve big increases in military budgets at a time of fiscal strain—first the European Monetary System, then the Maastricht criteria, against a general background of economic stagnation.

Thus, with this new military concept for eastward power projection outside the NATO area, the US could hope to gain the support not only of the UK—which was already on-side—but also of France, which was eager to use its military capacity abroad to gain political clout in Western Europe. The vital issue though, for the US, was to win over the Germans. In the early 1990s, the German government seemed genuinely interested in a more autonomous European military instrument, built around a Franco-German axis and the Euro-Corps. This was also something that President Mitterrand had favored. But by 1994, Germany was coming round to the idea that the notion of an autonomous West European instrument was impossible: it had to be a US-led NATO instrument.

The Yugoslav Road to the New NATO

During 1994 and 1995, these shifts on the new political and military role of NATO in the New Europe fed back into the Bosnian conflict. There were, at first, acute tensions between the US and the British and French, because the US wanted to demonstrate its enormous air power with strikes against the Bosnian Serbs, but that threatened the safety of the British and French troops on the ground. The tensions reached the point where some thought NATO might even split on the issue. But during 1995, an effective set of tactics emerged.

First, the US adopted the German approach to wrapping up the Bosnian war by building an alliance between the Bosnian government and the Croatian government against the Bosnian Serbs. This was a great success against the Serbs, effectively ethnically cleansing them from both Croatian territory and parts of Bosnian territory. Second, NATO could swing into action vigorously "out of area," with British and French forces as well as US air power and the Croatian and Bosnian Muslim forces driving the Bosnian Serbs back into defeat. The whole operation under US leadership was crowned with a European political triumph for the US in the form of the Dayton Agreement—no one at this time spared any thought for the people of Kosovo. The US tried to argue that the key to victory had been their air strikes, showing how central the US was to "European security" as a result.

The fact that Dayton did not produce the original US-stated goal of a sovereign, unitary Bosnia was a mere detail, largely ignored by Western European electorates. The US had taken command of Yugoslav affairs and of the high politics of Europe through the reorganization of NATO and the new German-American partnership, both of which could be blooded in the Bosnian war.

The US Approach to the New Balkan Backlash

To understand the US decision to launch war against Yugoslavia on March 24, 1999, we must understand how events have "progressed" in both the Balkan theater and in the broader regional European context since Dayton.

The big change in the Balkan region was the Albanian explosion leading to the collapse of an effective Albanian state and the destabilization of both Serbia and Macedonia by the arrival of the KLA—itself assisted by the Albanian collapse.

The real politics of Dayton did not produce a viable independent state: it has been a two-"entity" NATO protectorate unable to collect 80 percent of its tax entitlements and devoting a staggering quarter of its GDP to military procurement two years after Dayton.[17] Its future survival will depend on keeping the two main states in the area, Croatia and Serbia, in line. The Croatian government has not actually stayed in line, since it has integrated the Bosnian Croat population into Croatia. But the Milošević regime did keep in line, though it could not keep the Bosnian Serbs themselves under control since a majority of them viewed him as a traitor to the Serb nation by agreeing to Dayton in the first place. What US policy did not wish to contemplate, however, was an Albanian mass irredentist movement, since this would menace the fragile but pivotal republic of Macedonia, as well as Albania. But decades of lack of concern to produce a solution in Kosovo, coupled with the collapse of the Albanian state in 1996–97, opened the door precisely to such an irredentist movement for a Greater Albania.

The Sali Berisha government of Albania, which lasted until 1996, was a corrupt dictatorship which rigged the elections and imprisoned the leader of the opposition, but he served American policy well because he sealed off the border between Albanian and Yugoslavia and gave no encouragement to the national aspirations of the Albanians in Kosovo and Macedonia. (Berisha seems actually to have been a find of British intelligence, and as a result, the British were very reluctant to see him overthrown.)

With the popular uprising that overthrew Berisha, the Albanian state was completely shattered, its security forces dissolved and their arms were seized by the population—some 750,000 Kalashnikovs were privatized. Despite Italian military intervention, the new Socialist government of Fatos Nano, just out of Berisha's jail, could not impose order on Albania's territory and could not seal the borders with Macedonia and Kosovo. This gave an opening to the KLA, an organization whose leaders had once admired Enver Hoxha but that now opened itself to all those who rejected the reformist and pacifist stance of Ibrahim Rugova. The KLA offensive gained a very receptive response both in Kosovo and in Macedonia,

---

17   See Carlos Westendorp's testimony to the European Parliament in December 1998, reported in *Agence Europe Bulletin*, no. 7355 (December 3, 1998), p. 5.

where the national aspirations of the Albanians had long been repressed. The KLA offensive in Kosovo got under way in February 1998 and was very effective, targeting Serbian officials and security personnel across the province.

Dealing with the KLA

This presented the Clinton administration with an acute dilemma. It had to do something, since a Greater Albania was out of the question. There was, of course, an obvious solution: for the US and NATO to take a firmer grip over developments in Macedonia and Albania while at the same time leaving the KLA in Kosovo to the operations of the Milošević regime. This could be accomplished through a combination of Milošević offering Kosovan autonomy within Serbia, backed by the moderate Kosovan leader Rugova, along with a Turkish- or Colombian-style counter-insurgency operation against the KLA, clearing out villages along the frontier with Albania and crushing the KLA militarily.

It would, in effect, involve an alliance between the US and the person whom the Americans had built up as the Saddam Hussein of the Balkans: Slobodan Milošević. From March to September 1998, the Clinton administration nevertheless pursued this strategy, combining rhetoric and cosmetic actions against Milošević with effective acquiescence in the autonomy plus counter-insurgency approach. This was the line supported by the two Yugoslav experts of the Clinton team: Richard Holbrooke and Christopher Hill. It was also the line supported by many West European governments and by the Russian government.

The signal for this tactic was given when the US ambassador in Yugoslavia publicly branded the KLA a terrorist organization. According to the BBC, this was the specific go-ahead for Milošević to launch his counterinsurgency in March, along with his offer of provincial autonomy.[18] This tactic continued through UN Security Council Resolution 1199 in September, and it was embodied in the October 13 Holbrooke-Milošević agreement introducing American-led OSCE monitors into Kosovo. As far as the EU side of the operation was concerned, it continued right through into January 1999.

---

18   Nened Sebak, "The KLA: Terrorists or Freedom Fighters?," BBC, June 28, 1998.

But sometime in October, Madeleine Albright changed tack. The change involved instructing Hill to produce a new document that would form the basis for peace negotiations between the parties in Kosovo. And this new document contained the key change: Milošević was to have to accept a de facto NATO protectorate over Kosovo. The document did not, of course, use these words: it spoke only of a NATO-led military compliance force to supervise the transformation of Kosovo while it remained, *juridically*, a province of Serbia. But *politically* that meant a NATO protectorate. Albright would have known that no Serbian politician could dare to accept such a diktat from NATO. This new line was supplied to the Yugoslav government in December and was met with outrage from the Serbian side. Why was the new line adopted?

Supporters of the subsequent attack on Yugoslavia tend to assume that the change of American line must have had something to do with a desire to relieve the sufferings of the Kosovo people, perhaps, according to Robin Cook, for example, because between October and Christmas 1998 Milošević started to behave in a new and brutal way in Kosovo. Yet this was not the view of Cook and the other EU foreign ministers at their EU General Affairs Council meeting on December 8 when Albright had already changed strategy. The report of the meeting in the *Agence Europe Bulletin* the following day stated the following: "At the close of its debate on the situation in the Western Balkans, the General Affairs Council mainly expressed its concern for the recent 'intensification of military action' in Kosovo, noting that *'increased activity by the KLA has prompted an increased presence of Serbian security forces in the region.'*"[19] This makes it very clear that the EU's analysis did not suggest any qualitative shift in the basic approach of Milošević: on the contrary, it saw the KLA as the driving force behind the lack of a ceasefire.

Albright's Gamble

This unchanging local Yugoslav context in which the Albright strategy shift took place suggests that the reasons for the shift did not lie within the Yugoslav theater itself at all. As in the case of the US *démarche* of January 1992 leading to the Bosnian war, the source of the shift must therefore be sought in wider US political goals in Europe.

---

19   *Agence Europe Bulletin*, no. 7359, December 9, 1998, p. 4.

A military attack on Yugoslavia by the whole NATO alliance would, of course, have enormous pan-European political consequences, far more important for the state interests of all the great powers than the fate of the Kosovo Albanians. Success would decisively consolidate US leadership in Europe. Success outside the framework of UN Security Council permission would ensure no collective security in Europe by the UN back door of a Russian veto. And it would seal the unity of the alliance against a background where the launch of the euro—an event potentially of global *political* significance—could pull it apart.

On a narrower front, a successful military operation against Milošević before the Washington summit to agree to NATO's new role would have been a stunning political triumph for Madeleine Albright, whose term of office had, hitherto, been marked by a long catalogue of failure, most notably in the Middle East.

There were obvious political problems for Albright in gaining her triumph. First, the Russian problem, but following the rouble collapse in autumn 1998, the Russian state was hopelessly weak. No less difficult was the resistance of the West Europeans. Albright overcame that with three tactics. First, her tactic of preempting meetings of the Contact Group by holding press conferences in advance, staking out her position publicly with extremely bellicose and militarist language against Milošević—she had been pursuing this tactic for many months. Second, these incessant threats from Albright created the conditions in which she could argue that NATO's very credibility was at stake: after all the threats she had made, NATO could not back down "now." And third, the Clinton administration spread two pieces of supposedly insider intelligence information: one was that Milošević actually wanted a NATO attack so that he could sell the NATO compliance force domestically; and the other, that the Yugoslav military would in any case soon overthrow Milošević. Such stories could lull the West Europeans into thinking the NATO attack would swiftly be over. In fact, as we now know, the relevant US agencies, notably the Pentagon and the CIA, were actually providing quite other information: it would be a very long and difficult air campaign; and there could be a huge refugee crisis.[20] But the only specifically Balkan issue that mattered to the administration was the avoidance of any commitment to a Greater Albania through self-determination for the Albanians of Kosovo and Macedonia.

---

20   See the *Washington Post* coverage from April 1 through 7, 1999, for information on these issues, especially April 5, 1999.

Albright had allies in France and, of course, Britain by early January, and they were the co-chairs at Rambouillet. With them on board, the option of Germany standing aside was unthinkable—Germany cannot act without France, for fear of being branded with hegemonist ambitions. As for the rest of the EU states, they could not remotely afford to exclude themselves.

Conclusion

There is a powerful impulse within the electorates of the NATO states for their governments to give a lead to the world and really help the less fortunate overwhelming majority of humanity to improve their lives and strengthen their security and welfare. But we must bear in mind two unfortunate facts: first, the NATO states have been and are hell-bent on exacerbating the inequalities of power and wealth in the world, on destroying all challenges to their overwhelming military and economic power and on subordinating almost all other considerations to these goals; and second, the NATO states are finding it extraordinarily easy to manipulate their domestic electorates into believing that these states are indeed leading the world's population toward a more just and humane future when, in reality, they are doing no such thing.

The fate of Yugoslavia in the 1990s has been a classic case of this general story. NATO electorates thought their states were trying to help in Yugoslavia, even if they were not "doing enough." In reality, Western policies promoted the descent into barbaric wars. There are occasions when advanced capitalist countries will help the populations of other states. But these occasions are rare, namely when the welfare of the populations of these other states is a vital weapon in a struggle against another powerful enemy. This applied to US policy toward Western Europe when it was threatened by Communist triumph in the early postwar years. The welfare of the people of Yugoslavia has been irrelevant to the NATO powers in the 1990s because these powers have faced no effective enemies whatever.

The Bosnian War produced terrible atrocities, reminiscent of those perpetrated in the Spanish Civil War, in Ireland in the 1920s by the Black and Tans, by the Wehrmacht and Einsatzgruppen on the Eastern Front in the Second World War, by the Americans in Vietnam or by the Turkish security forces in eastern Turkey today. These atrocities were not perpetrated only by the Bosnian Serbs, but theirs were the most visible cases.

No doubt, more such massacres have been perpetrated in Kosovo by the Serbian security forces who are, at the time of writing, being targeted for annihilation by the NATO powers.

It is surely right that institutions should be built that can put a stop to such acts of political violence and can punish their perpetrators. But we face an acute dilemma when we confront this task because we know enough about the dynamics of politics to be able to identify not only the perpetrators of atrocities, but the international actors who helped and continue to help create *the conditions in which such perpetrators arise*. And in the Yugoslav case, the Western powers, by their deliberate acts of commission and omission, played a central role in creating the conditions in which barbaric acts were bound to flourish.

There is something deeply disturbing about a system of Western power politics that can casually and costlessly make a major contribution to plunging Yugoslavia into turmoil and wars, can then use these wars to further their geopolitical ends, and can then seek to make political capital out of War Crimes Court judgments of perpetrators of atrocities, while themselves refusing all responsibility.

A Western policy that put the *human security* of the people of East-Central, Eastern, and South-Eastern Europe first would involve a new Marshall Plan for the entire region entailing a development-oriented framework for the region. But that would involve scrapping the whole mercantilist and imperial economic program of the EU and the IMF/World Bank toward the region. There is not the slightest sign of a prepared-ness of the Western powers to change course on these issues. Instead, the successful extermination of the Yugoslav conscripts in Kosovo will, no doubt, be followed by "aid" for gangster mafias of the kind that flourish in the aftermath of any devastating war, as is evident in NATO's Bosnian protectorate today.

A Real Solution

A solution to the plight of the various Albanian and Slav communi-ties in the region also requires an entirely new political framework of a regional kind that breaks with the Western powers' drive in the region in the 1990s, which has, in effect, fragmented the populations into small and often largely non-viable statelets. Bosnia survives only as a paper-state that is, in reality, a NATO protectorate. Macedonia survives through US determination to prevent the Albanian minority there from either separating or gaining a federal state structure. A separate Kosovo would have to be a NATO protectorate, not least to prevent a KLA government from achieving the goal of a Greater Albania. The Serbian population is divided into the Republika Srpska "entity" and what will be a defeated and embattled Serbia. Montenegro's future is at risk. And every one of these statelets must devote desperately meager resources to large military budgets while most of their populations cling to nationalist leaderships in the hope of some minimal safety. The only genuine winner among the states in the Yugoslav theater—apart from Slovenia, which has escaped the scene—is Croatia, thanks to its great-power support. Yet Tudjman's triumphs have only increased his appetite for new conquests, in particular a slice of Bosnia that he has already, de facto, swallowed.[21]

The search for a new regional political framework that can provide all the Albanian and the Slav communities with a new unity and security must involve a new program for Balkan confederation or federation. Such a new project can come only from social and political movements among the peoples of the region. Before the current NATO aggression against the region's largest nation, it was still perhaps conceivable that the Western powers could have gained sufficient trust to have had a semblance of being a *pouvoir neutre* that might encourage such an endogenous popular movement for reconciliation and partial reunification. Now that is impossible in the short or even medium term. Any such endogenous movement of reconciliation will now have to repudiate this NATO aggression to have any credibility.

Some may imagine that the NATO powers may actually take responsibility for the lives of the people of the region and may themselves engineer a new politics and a new start. But this is to completely misunderstand the basic premise of the whole operation of the Western powers in the Yugoslav theater since the late 1980s. That premise is that not a single one of the NATO powers had a vital state interest in ex-Yugoslavia. For the European Union, their only vital interest is containment of conflict, above all containment of refugee movements. The US does not even have that stake in the region's future.

A NATO "victory" in this war could promote the Clinton administration's central objective in waging the war: the winning over of Western Europe's political systems to US leadership of the new, aggressive NATO.

---

21   Brooke Unger has made this point forcefully in "The Balkans: The Two Culprits," *Economist*, January 24, 1998.

After all, the political elites of all the main parties of Western Europe now find themselves justifying, day in and day out, the vital necessity and enormous human value of the new NATO: Western Europe is being won to the idea that attacking damaged sovereign states is legitimate; shattering their military forces, infrastructures and economies is permissible; ignoring the UN Charter and the checks built into the UN Security Council structure is unavoidable; marginalizing and excluding a currently weak Russia is necessary; humiliating and ignoring the interests of the largest nation in former Yugoslavia, the Serbs, is vital. And we Europeans could never have achieved all these things without the generous leadership of the United States.

The story of Western involvement in the region is obscured by a poisonous Western imperial propaganda that turns reality on its head. It says that the Balkans cause the West no end of trouble because of the appalling characters who live there. The reality is that the Western powers have caused the Balkan peoples no end of suffering because they continue to use the region as a theater for their power politics.

7

Afghanistan: Mirage of the Good War

Tariq Ali

Rarely has there been such an enthusiastic display of international unity as that which greeted the invasion of Afghanistan in 2001. Support for the war was universal in the chanceries of the West, even before its aims and parameters had been declared. NATO governments rushed to assert themselves "all for one." Blair jetted round the world, proselytizing the "doctrine of the international community" and the opportunities for peace-keeping and nation-building in the Hindu Kush. Putin welcomed the extension of American bases along Russia's southern borders. Every mainstream Western party endorsed the war; every media network—with BBC World and CNN in the lead—became its megaphone. For the German Greens, as for Laura Bush and Cherie Blair, it was a war for the liberation of the women of Afghanistan.[1] For the White House, a fight for civilization. For Iran, the impending defeat of the Wahhabi enemy.

Three years later, as the chaos in Iraq deepened, Afghanistan became the "good war" by comparison. It had been legitimized by the UN—even if the resolution was not passed until after the bombs had finished falling—and

---

1 In fact, the only period in Afghan history where women were granted equal rights and educated was from 1979–89, the decade it was ruled by the PDPA, backed by Soviet troops. Repressive in many ways, on the health and education fronts real progress was achieved, as in Iraq under Saddam. Hence the nostalgia for the past among poorer sections of society in both countries.

backed by NATO. If tactical differences had sharpened over Iraq, they could be resolved in Afghanistan. First Zapatero, then Prodi, then Rudd compensated for pulling troops out of Iraq by dispatching them to Kabul.[2] France and Germany could extol their peace-keeping or civilizing roles there. As suicide bombings increased in Baghdad, Afghanistan was now— for American Democrats keen to prove their "security" credentials—the "real front" of the war on terror, supported by every US presidential candidate in the run-up to the 2008 elections, with Senator Obama pressuring the White House to violate Pakistani sovereignty whenever necessary. With varying degrees of firmness, the occupation of Afghanistan was also supported by China, Iran, and Russia; though in the case of the latter, there was always a strong element of schadenfreude. Soviet veterans of the Afghan war were amazed to see their mistakes now being repeated by the United States in a war even more inhumane than its predecessor.

Meanwhile, the number of Afghan civilians killed has exceeded many tens of times over the 2,746 who died in Manhattan. Unemployment is around 60 percent, and maternal, infant and child mortality levels are now among the highest in the world. Opium harvests have soared, and the "Neo-Taliban" is growing stronger year by year. By common consent, Karzai's government does not even control its own capital, let alone provide an example of "good governance." Reconstruction funds vanish into cronies' pockets or go to pay short-contract Western consultants. Police are predators rather than protectors. The social crisis is deepening. Increasingly, Western commentators have evoked the specter of failure—usually in order to spur *encore un effort*. A *Guardian* leader summarizes: "Defeat looks possible, with all the terrible consequences that will bring."[3]

Two principal arguments, often overlapping, are put forward as to "what went wrong" in Afghanistan. For liberal imperialists, the answer can be summarized in two words: "not enough." The invasion organized by

---

2   Visiting Madrid after Zapatero's election triumph of March 2008, I was informed by a senior government official that they had considered a total withdrawal from Afghanistan a few months before the polls but had been outmaneuvered by the US promising Spain that the head of its military would be proposed for commander of the NATO forces, and a withdrawal from Kabul would disrupt this possibility. Spain drew back, only to discover it had been tricked.

3   "Failing State," *Guardian*, February 1, 2008; see also "The Good War, Still to Be Won" and "Gates, Truth and Afghanistan," *New York Times*, August 20, 2007, and February 12, 2008; "Must They Be Wars without End?," *Economist*, December 13, 2007; International Crisis Group, "Combating Afghanistan's Insurgency," November 2, 2006.

Bush, Cheney, and Rumsfeld was done on the cheap. The "light footprint" demanded by the Pentagon meant that there were too few troops on the ground in 2001–2. Financial commitment to "state-building" was insufficient. Though it may now be too late, the answer is to pour in more troops, more money—"multiple billions" over "multiple years," according to the US ambassador in Kabul.[4] The second answer—advanced by Karzai and the White House, but propagated by the Western media generally—can be summed up in one word: Pakistan. Neither of these arguments holds water.

Political Failures

True, there was a sense of relief in Kabul when the Taliban's Wahhabite Emirate was overthrown. Though rape and heroin production had been curtailed under their rule, warlords kept at bay and order largely restored in a country that had been racked by foreign and civil wars since 1979, the end result had been a ruthless social dictatorship with a level of control over the everyday lives of ordinary people that made the clerical regime in Iran appear an island of enlightenment. The Taliban government fell without a serious struggle. Islamabad, officially committed to the US cause, forbade any frontal confrontation.[5] Some Taliban zealots crossed the border into Pakistan, while a more independent faction loyal to Mullah Omar decamped to the mountains to fight another day. Kabul was undefended; the BBC war correspondent entered the capital before the Northern Alliance. What many Afghans now expected from a successor government was a similar level of order, minus the repression and social restrictions, and a freeing of the country's spirit. What they were instead presented with was a melancholy spectacle that blasted all their hopes.

The problem was not lack of funds but the Western state-building project itself, by its nature an exogenous process—aiming to construct an army able to suppress its own population but incapable of defending the nation from outside powers; a civil administration with no control over planning or social infrastructure, which are in the hands of Western

---

4   David Rohde and James Risen, "CIA Review Highlights Afghan Leader's Woes," *New York Times*, November 5, 2006.

5   Pakistan's key role in securing this "victory" was underplayed in the Western media at the time. The public was told that it was elite Special Forces units and CIA "specialists" that had liberated Afghanistan; having triumphed here, they could now be sent on to Iraq.

NGOs; and a government whose foreign policy marches in step with Washington's. It bore no relation to the realities on the ground. After the fall of the Taliban government, four major armed groups re-emerged as strong regional players. In the gas-rich and more industrialized north, bordering the Central Asian republics of Uzbekistan and Tajikistan, the Uzbek warlord Rashid Dostum was in charge with his capital in Mazar-i-Sharif. Allied first to the Communists, later the Taliban and most recently NATO, General Dostum had demonstrated his latest loyalty by massacring two to three thousand Taliban and Arab prisoners under the approving gaze of US intelligence personnel in December 2001.

Not too far from Dostum, in the mountainous northeast of the country, a region rich in emeralds, lapis lazuli, and opium, the late Ahmed Shah Masoud had built a fighting organization of Tajiks, who regularly ambushed troops on the Salang Highway that linked Kabul to Tashkent during the Soviet occupation. Masoud had been the leader of the armed wing of Burhanuddin Rabbani's Jamaat-i-Islami, which operated in tandem with an allied Islamist leader, Abd al-Rabb Sayyaf (both men were lecturers in sharia at the law faculty of Kabul University in 1973, where these movements were incubated). Until 1993 they were funded by Saudi Arabia, after which the latter gradually shifted its support to the Taliban. Masoud maintained a semi-independence during the Taliban period, up to his death on September 9, 2001.[6] Masoud's supporters are currently in the government but are not considered 100 percent reliable as far as NATO is concerned.

To the west, sheltered by neighboring Iran, lies the ancient city of Herat, once a center of learning and culture where poets, artists, and scholars flourished. Among the important works illustrated here over the course of three centuries was a fifteenth-century version of the classic *Miraj-nameh*, an early medieval account of the Prophet's ascent to heaven from the Dome of the Rock and the punishments he observed as he passed through hell.[7]

---

6   Masoud had been a favourite pin-up in Paris during the Soviet–Afghan war, usually portrayed as a ruggedly romantic, anti-Communist Che Guevara. His membership in Rabbani's Islamist group and reactionary views on most social issues were barely mentioned. But if he had presented an image of incorruptible masculinity to his supporters in the West, it was not the same at home. Rape and the heroin trade were not uncommon in areas under his control.

7   The stunning illustrations were exquisitely calligraphed by Malik Bakshi in the Uighur script. There are sixty-one paintings in all, created with great love for the Prophet of Islam. He is depicted with Central Asian features and seen flying to heaven on a magical

In modern Herat, the Shia warlord Ismail Khan holds sway. A former army captain inspired by the Islamic Revolution in Iran, Ismail achieved instant fame by leading a garrison revolt against the pro-Moscow regime in 1979. Backed by Tehran, he built up a strong force that united all the Shia groups and was to trouble the Russians throughout their stay. Tens of thousands of refugees from this region (where a Persian dialect is the spoken language) were given work, shelter, and training in Iran. From 1992 to 1995, the province was run on authoritarian lines. It was a harsh regime: Ismail Khan's half-witted effrontery soon began to alienate his allies, while his high-tax and forced conscription policies angered peasant families. By the time the Taliban took power in Kabul in 1996, support had already drained away from the warlord. Herat fell without a struggle, and Ismail was imprisoned by the Taliban, only escaping in March 2000. His supporters meanwhile crossed the border to Iran where they bided their time, to return in October 2001 under NATO cover.

The south was another story again. The Pashtun villages bore the brunt of the fighting during the 1980s and '90s.[8] Rapid population growth, coupled with the disruptions of war and the resulting loss of livestock, hastened the collapse of the subsistence economy. In many districts this was replaced by poppy cultivation and the rule of local bandits and strongmen. By the early 1990s, three militant Sunni groups had acquired dominance in the region: the Taliban, the group led by Ahmed Shah Masoud from the Panjshir province, and the followers of Gulbuddin Hekmatyar, once Pakistan's favorite, who had been groomed by the Saudis as the new leader. The jihad was long over, and now the jihadis were at each other's throats, with control of the drug trade the major stake in a brutal power struggle. Under Benazir Bhutto's second premiership, Pakistan's military backing for the Taliban proved decisive. But the overthrow of the Mullah Omar

---

steed with a woman's head. There are also illustrations of a meeting with Gabriel and Adam, a sighting of houris at the gates of Paradise, and of winebibbers being punished in hell. European scholars have suggested that an early Latin translation of the poem may have been a source of inspiration for Dante.

8   Afghanistan's ethnography has generated a highly politicized statistical debate. The six-year survey carried out by a Norwegian foundation is probably the most accurate. This suggests that Pashtuns make up an estimated 63 percent of the population, along with the mainly Persian-speaking Tajiks (12 percent), Uzbeks (9 percent), and the mainly Shia Hazaras (6 percent): Wak Foundation, Norway 1999. The CIA Factbook, by contrast, gives 42, 27, 9, and 9 percent, respectively. The tiny non-Muslim minority of Hindus and Sikhs, mainly shopkeepers and traders in Kabul, were displaced by the Taliban; some were killed, and thousands fled to India.

government in the winter of 2001 saw the re-emergence of many of the
local gangsters whose predations it had partly checked.

Anointment of Karzai

Washington assigned the task of assembling a new government to
Zalmay Khalilzad, its Afghan-American pro-consul in Kabul. The capital
was occupied by competing militias, united only by opposition to the
toppled Taliban, and their representatives had to be accommodated on
every level. The Northern Alliance candidate for president, Abdul Haq
of Jalalabad, had conveniently been captured and executed in October
2001 by the Taliban when he entered the country with a small group
from Pakistan. (His supporters alleged betrayal by the CIA and the ISI,
who were unhappy about his links to Russia and Iran, and tipped off
Mullah Omar.) Another obvious anti-Taliban candidate was Ahmed Shah
Masoud; but he had also been killed—by a suicide bomber of unknown
provenance—two days before 9/11. Masoud would no doubt have been
the EU choice for Afghan president, had he lived; the French government issued a postage stamp with his portrait, and Kabul airport bears
his name. Whether he would have proved as reliable a client as Khalilzad's
transplanted protégé, Hamid Karzai, must now remain an open question.

Aware that the US could not run the country without the Northern
Alliance and its backers in Tehran and Moscow, Khalilzad toned down
the emancipatory rhetoric and concentrated on the serious business of
occupation. The coalition he constructed resembled a blind octopus, with
mainly Tajik limbs and Karzai as its unseeing eye. The Afghan president
comes from the Durrani tribe of Pashtuns from Kandahar. His father had
served in a junior capacity in Zahir Shah's government. Young Karzai
backed the mujaheddin against Russia and later supported the Taliban,
though he turned down their offer to become Afghanistan's ambassador
to the UN, preferring to relocate and work for UNOCAL. Here he backed
up Khalilzad, who was then representing CentGas in its bid to construct
a pipeline that would take gas from Turkmenistan across Afghanistan to
Pakistan and India.[9]

---

9   The CentGas consortium, incorporated in 1997, included UNOCAL, Gazprom,
Hyundai, and oil companies from Saudi Arabia, Japan, and Pakistan. In late 1997 a Taliban
delegation received full honors when they visited UNOCAL HQ, hoping to sign the £2

After his appointment as interim president, the Saudi daily *Al-Watan* published a revealing profile of Karzai, stating that he had been a CIA pawn since the eighties, with his status on the Afghan chessboard enhanced every few years:

Since then, Karzai's ties with the Americans have not been interrupted. At the same time, he established ties with the British and other European and international sides, especially after he became deputy foreign minister in 1992 in the wake of the Afghan mujaheddin's assumption of power and the overthrow of the pro-Moscow Najibullah regime. Karzai found no contradiction between his ties with the Americans and his support for the Taliban movement as of 1994, when the Americans had—secretly and through the Pakistanis—supported the Taliban's assumption of power to put an end to the civil war and the actual partition of Afghanistan due to the failure of Burhanuddin Rabbani's experience in ruling the country.[10]

Karzai was duly installed in December 2001, but intimacy with US intelligence networks failed to translate into authority or legitimacy at home. Karzai harbored no illusions about his popularity in the country. He knew his biological and political life was heavily dependent on the occupation and demanded a bodyguard of US Marines or American mercenaries, rather than a security detail from his own ethnic Pashtun base.[11] There were at least three coup attempts against him in 2002–3 by his Northern Alliance allies; these were fought off by the International Security Assistance Force (ISAF), which was largely tied down in assuring Karzai's security—while

---

billion pipeline contract. According to the *Sunday Telegraph* ("Oil Barons Court Taliban in Texas," December 14, 1997): "The Islamic warriors appear to have been persuaded to close the deal, not through delicate negotiation but by old-fashioned Texan hospitality. Dressed in traditional *shalwar kameez*, Afghan waistcoats, and loose, black turbans, the high-ranking delegation was given VIP treatment during the four-day stay." The project was suspended in 1998, as the Taliban were split on whom to award the pipeline project to: Mullah Rabbani preferred the offer from the Argentine company Bridas, while Mullah Omar was strongly in favour of the American-led deal. But US-Taliban contacts continued till mid-2001 both in Islamabad and New York, where the Taliban maintained a "diplomatic office" headed by Abdul Hakim Mojahed.

10   BBC Monitoring Service, December 15, 2001.

11   The late Benazir Bhutto made the same request for American protection on her return to Pakistan, but in her case it was vetoed by Islamabad.

also providing a vivid illustration of where his support lay.[12] A quick-fix presidential contest organized at great expense by Western PR firms in October 2004—just in time for the US elections—failed to bolster support for the puppet president inside the country. Karzai's habit of parachuting his relatives and protégés into provincial governor or police chief jobs has driven many local communities into alliance with the Taliban, as the main antigovernment force. In Zabul, Helmand and elsewhere, all the insurgents had to do was "approach the victims of the pro-Karzai strongmen and promise them protection and support. Attempts by local elders to seek protection in Kabul routinely ended nowhere, as the wrongdoers enjoyed either direct US support or Karzai's sympathy."[13]

Nor is it any secret that Karzai's younger brother, Ahmad Wali Karzai, has now become one of the richest drug barons in the country. At a meeting with Pakistan's president in 2005, when Karzai was bleating about Pakistan's inability to stop cross-border smuggling, Musharraf suggested that perhaps Karzai should set an example by bringing his sibling under control. (The hatred for each other of these two close allies of Washington is well known in the region.)

New Inequalities

Also feeding the resentment is the behavior of a new elite clustered around Karzai and the occupying forces, which has specialized in creaming off foreign aid to create its own criminal networks of graft and patronage. The corruptions of this layer grow each month like an untreated tumor. Western funds are siphoned off to build fancy homes for the native enforcers. Housing scandals erupted as early as 2002, when cabinet ministers awarded themselves and favored cronies prime real estate in Kabul, where land prices were rocketing, since the occupiers and their camp followers had to live in the style to which they were accustomed. Karzai's colleagues, protected by ISAF troops, built their large villas in full view of the mud-brick hovels of the poor. The burgeoning slum settlements of

---

12   Barry McCaffrey, "Trip to Afghanistan and Pakistan," US Military Academy Memorandum, West Point, NY, 2006, p. 8.

13   Antonio Giustozzi, *Koran, Kalashnikov and Laptop: The Neo-Taliban Insurgency in Afghanistan* (London: Hurst, 2007), p. 60. The corruption and brutality of the newly established Afghan National Police is also widely credited with turning the population against the Karzai government.

Kabul, where the population has now swollen to an estimated 3 million, are a measure of the social crisis that has engulfed the country.

The ancient city has suffered cruelly over the past thirty years. Jade Maiwand, the modernized "Oxford Street" that cut through the center in the 1970s, was reduced to rubble during the warfare of 1992–96. An American-Afghan architect describes how Kabul has been relentlessly transformed

> from a modern capital, to the military and political headquarters of an invading army, to the besieged seat of power of a puppet regime, to the front lines of factional conflict resulting in the destruction of two-thirds of its urban mass, to the testing fields of religious fanaticism which erased from the city the final layers of urban life, to the target of an international war on terrorism.[14]

Yet never have such gaping inequalities featured on this scale before. Little of the supposed $19 billion "aid and reconstruction" money has reached the majority of Afghans. The mains electricity supply is worse now than five years ago, and while the rich can use private generators to power their air conditioners, hot-water heaters, computers and satellite TVs, average Kabulis "suffered a summer without fans and face a winter without heaters."[15] As a result, hundreds of shelterless Afghans are literally freezing to death each winter.

Then there are the NGOs who descended on the country like locusts after the occupation. As one observer reports:

> A reputed 10,000 NGO staff have turned Kabul into the Klondike during the gold rush, building office blocks, driving up rents, cruising about in armored jeeps, and spending stupefying sums of other people's money, essentially on themselves. They take orders only from some distant agency, but then the same goes for the American army, NATO, the UN, the EU, and the supposedly sovereign Afghan government.[16]

---

14   Ajmal Maiwandi, "Re-Doing Kabul," presented at the London School of Economics, July 11, 2002.

15   Barnett Rubin, "Saving Afghanistan," *Foreign Affairs* 86:1 (January–February 2007), pp. 57–78.

16   Simon Jenkins, "It Takes Inane Optimism to See Victory in Afghanistan," *Guardian*, August 8, 2007.

Even supporters of the occupation have lost patience with these bodies, and some of the most successful candidates in the 2005 National Assembly elections made an attack on them a centerpiece of their campaigns. Worse, according to one US specialist, "their well-funded activities highlighted the poverty and ineffectiveness of the civil administration and discredited its local representatives in the eyes of the local populace."[17] Unsurprisingly, NGO employees began to be targeted by the insurgents, including in the north, and had to hire mercenary protection.

In sum: even in the estimate of the West's own specialists and institutions, "nation-building" in Afghanistan has been flawed in its very conception. It has so far produced a puppet president dependent for his survival on foreign mercenaries, a corrupt and abusive police force, a "non-functioning" judiciary, a thriving criminal layer, and a deepening social and economic crisis. It beggars belief to argue that "more of this" will be the answer to Afghanistan's problems.

An Afghan Surge?

The argument that more NATO troops are the solution is equally unsustainable. All the evidence suggests that the brutality of the occupying forces has been one of the main sources of recruits for the Taliban. American air power, lovingly referred to as "Big Daddy" by frightened US soldiers on unwelcome terrain, is far from paternal when it comes to targeting Pashtun villages. There is widespread fury among Afghans at the number of civilian casualties, many of them children. There have been numerous incidents of rape and rough treatment of women by ISAF soldiers, as well as indiscriminate bombing of villages and house-to-house search-and-arrest missions. The behavior of the foreign mercenaries backing up the NATO forces is just as bad. Even sympathetic observers admit that "their alcohol consumption and patronage of a growing number of brothels in Kabul ... is arousing public anger and resentment."[18] To this

---

17   S. Frederick Starr, "Sovereignty and Legitimacy in Afghan Nation-Building," in *Nation-Building beyond Afghanistan and Iraq*, ed. Francis Fukuyama (Baltimore: Johns Hopkins University Press, 2006), p. 117.

18   Barnett Rubin, "Proposals for Improved Stability in Afghanistan," in *Crescent of Crisis: US-European Strategy for the Greater Middle East*, ed. Ivo Daalder, Nicole Gnesotto, and Philip Gordon (Washington, DC: Brookings, 2006), p. 149.

could be added the deaths by torture at the US-run Bagram prison and the resuscitation of a Soviet-era security law under which detainees are being sentenced to twenty-year jail terms on the basis of summary allegations by US military authorities. All this creates a thirst for dignity that can only be assuaged by genuine independence.

Talk of "victory" sounds increasingly hollow to Afghan ears. Many who detest the Taliban are so angered by the failures of NATO and the behavior of its troops that they are pleased there is some opposition. What was initially viewed by some locals as a necessary police action against al-Qaeda following the 9/11 attacks is now perceived by a growing majority in the region as a fully fledged imperial occupation. Successive recent reports have suggested that the unpopularity of the government and the "disrespectful" behavior of the occupying troops have had the effect of creating nostalgia for the time when the Taliban were in power. The repression leaves people with no option but to back those trying to resist, especially in a part of the world where the culture of revenge is strong. When a whole community feels threatened it reinforces solidarity, regardless of the character or weakness of those who fight back. This does not just apply to the countryside. The mass protests in Kabul, when civilians were killed by an American military vehicle, signaled the obvious targets:

> Rioters chanted slogans against the United States and President Karzai and attacked the Parliament building, the offices of media outlets and nongovernmental organizations, diplomatic residences, brothels, and hotels and restaurants that purportedly served alcohol. The police, many of whom disappeared, proved incompetent, and the vulnerability of the government to mass violence became clear.[19]

As the British and Russians discovered to their cost in the preceding two centuries, Afghans do not like being occupied. If a second-generation Taliban is now growing and creating new alliances, it is not because its sectarian religious practices have become popular, but because it is the only available umbrella for national liberation. Initially, the middle-cadre Taliban who fled across the border in November 2001 and started low-level guerrilla activity the following year attracted only a trickle of new recruits from madrasas and refugee camps. From 2004 onward, increasing

---

19   Rubin, "Saving Afghanistan."

numbers of young Waziris were radicalized by Pakistani military and police incursions in the tribal areas, as well as devastating attacks on villages by unmanned US "drones." At the same time, the movement was starting to win active support from village mullahs in Zabul, Helmand, Ghazni, Paktika, and Kandahar provinces, and then in the towns. By 2006 there were reports of Kabul mullahs who had previously supported Karzai's allies but were now railing against the foreigners and the government; calls for jihad against the occupiers were heard in the northeast border provinces of Takhar and Badakhshan.

The largest pool for new Taliban recruits, according to a well-informed recent estimate, has been "communities antagonized by the local authorities and security forces." In Kandahar, Helmand and Uruzgan, Karzai's cronies—district and provincial governors, security bosses, police chiefs— are quite prepared to tip off US troops against their local rivals, as well as subjecting the latter to harassment and extortion. In these circumstances, the Taliban are the only available defense. (According to the same report, the Taliban themselves have claimed that families driven into refugee camps by indiscriminate US airpower attacks on their villages have been their major source of recruits.) By 2006 the movement was winning the support of traders and businessmen in Kandahar, and led a mini "Tet offensive" there that year. One reason suggested for their increasing support in towns is that the new-model Taliban have relaxed their religious strictures, for males at least—no longer demanding beards or banning music—and improved their propaganda: producing cassette tapes and CDs of popular singers, and DVDs of US and Israeli atrocities in Iraq, Lebanon, and Palestine.[20]

The re-emergence of the Taliban cannot therefore simply be blamed on Islamabad's failure to police the border, or cut "command and control" links, as the Americans claim. While the ISI played a crucial role in bringing the Taliban to power in 1996 and in the retreat of 2001, they no longer have the same degree of control over a more diffuse and widespread movement, for which the occupation itself has been the main recruiting sergeant. It is a traditional colonial ploy to blame "outsiders" for internal problems: Karzai specializes in this approach. If anything, the destabilization functions in the other direction: the war in Afghanistan has created a critical situation in two Pakistani frontier provinces, and the

---

20   Giustozzi, *Koran, Kalashnikov and Laptop*, pp. 42, 69.

use of the Pakistan army by CENTCOM has resulted in suicide terrorism in Lahore, where the Federal Investigation Agency and the Naval War College have been targeted by supporters of the Afghan insurgents. The Pashtun majority in Afghanistan has always had close links to its fellow Pashtuns in Pakistan. The present border was an imposition by the British Empire, but it has always remained porous. It is virtually impossible to build a Texan fence or an Israeli wall across the mountainous and largely unmarked 1,500-mile frontier that separates the two countries.

Older Models

The current occupation of Afghanistan naturally recalls colonial operations in the region, not just to Afghans but to some Western myth-makers—usually British, but with a few subcontinental mimics—who try to draw lessons from the older model; the implication being that the British were "good imperialists" who have a great deal to teach the brutish, impatient Americans. The British administrators were, for the most part, racist to the core, and their self-proclaimed "competence" involved the efficient imposition of social apartheid in every colony they controlled. They could be equally brutal in Africa, the Middle East, and India. Though a promise of civilizational uplift was required as ideological justification, then as now, the facts of the colonial legacy speak for themselves. In 1947, the year the British left India, the overwhelming majority of midnight's children were illiterate, and 85 percent of the economy was rural.[21]

Not bad intentions or botched initiatives, but the imperial presence itself was the problem. Kipling is much quoted today by editorialists urging a bigger Western "footprint" in Afghanistan, but even he was fully aware of the hatred felt by the Pashtuns for the British, and wrote as much in one of his last dispatches from Peshawar in April 1885 to the *Civil and Military Gazette* in Lahore:

---

21 "Per capita income was about one-twentieth of the level then attained in developed countries ... Illiteracy was a high 84 percent and the majority (60 percent) of children in the six to eleven age-group did not attend school; mass communicable diseases (malaria, smallpox and cholera) were widespread and, in the absence of a good public health service and sanitation, mortality rates (27 per 1,000) were very high." Dharma Kumar and Meghnad Desai, eds., *Cambridge Economic History of India*, vol. 2, *c. 1757–c. 1970* (Cambridge: Cambridge University Press, 1983), p. 23.

Pathans, Afridis, Logas, Kohistanis, Turcomans, and a hundred other varieties of the turbulent Afghan race, are gathered in the vast human menagerie between the Edwardes Gate and the Ghor Khutri. As an Englishman passes, they will turn to scowl on him, and in many cases to spit fluently on the ground after he has passed. One burly, big-paunched ruffian, with shaven head and a neck creased and dimpled with rolls of fat, is specially zealous in this religious rite—contenting himself with no perfunctory performance, but with a whole-souled expectoration, that must be as refreshing to his comrades as it is disgusting to the European.[22]

One reason among many for the Pashtuns' historic resentment was the torching of the famous bazaar in Kabul, a triumph of Mughal architecture. Ali Mardan Khan, a renowned governor, architect and engineer, had built the *chahr-chatta* (four-sided) roofed and arcaded central market in the seventeenth century on the model of those in old Euro-Arabian Muslim cities—Cairo, Damascus, Baghdad, Palermo or Córdoba. It was regarded as unique in the region; nothing on the same scale was built in Lahore or Delhi. The bazaar was deliberately destroyed in 1842 by General Pollock's "Army of Retribution," remembered as among the worst killers, looters and marauders ever to arrive in Afghanistan, a contest in which competition remains strong. Defeated in a number of cities and forced to evacuate Kabul, the British punished its citizens by removing the market from the map. What will remain of Kabul when the current occupiers finally withdraw is yet to be seen, but its spreading mass of deeply impoverished squatter settlements suggest that it is set to be one of the major new capitals of the "planet of slums."[23]

The Western occupation of Afghanistan is now confronted with five seemingly intractable, interrelated problems. The systemic failures of its nation-building strategy, the corruption of its local agents, the growing alienation of large sectors of the population, and the strengthening of armed resistance are all compounded by the distortions wrought by the opium-heroin industry on the country's economy. According to UN estimates, narcotics account for 53 percent of the country's gross domestic product, and the poppy fields continue to spread. Some 90 percent of the

---

22   [Rudyard Kipling, "The City of Evil Countenances," republished in *Kipling's India: Uncollected Sketches, 1884–88*, ed. Thomas Pinney (London: Macmillan, 1986), p. 83.]

23   Mike Davis, "Planet of Slums," *New Left Review* II:26 (March–April 2004), p. 13.

world opium supply emanates from Afghanistan. Since 2003 the NATO mission has made no serious attempt to bring about a reduction in this lucrative trade. Karzai's own supporters would rapidly desert if their activities in this sphere were disrupted, and the amount of state help needed over many years to boost agriculture and cottage industries and reduce dependence on poppy farming would require an entirely different set of priorities. Only a surreal utopian could expect NATO countries, busy privatizing and deregulating their own economies, to embark upon full-scale national-development projects abroad.

NATO's Goals

It need hardly be added that the bombardment and occupation of Afghanistan has been a disastrous—and predictable—failure in capturing the perpetrators of 9/11. This could only have been the result of effective police work, not of international war and military occupation. Everything that has happened in Afghanistan since 2001—not to mention Iraq, Palestine, and Lebanon—has had the opposite effect, as the West's own intelligence reports have repeatedly confirmed. According to the official 9/11 Commission report, Mullah Omar's initial response to Washington's demands that Osama bin Laden be handed over and al-Qaeda deprived of a safe haven was "not negative"; he himself had opposed any al-Qaeda attack on US targets.[24] But while the Mullah was playing for time, the White House closed down negotiations. It required a swift war of revenge. Afghanistan had been denominated the first port of call in the "global war on terror," with Iraq already the administration's main target. The shock-and-awe six-week aerial onslaught that followed was merely a drumroll for the forthcoming intervention in Iraq, with no military rationale in Afghanistan. Predictably, it only gave al-Qaeda leaders the chance to vanish into the hills. To portray the invasion as a "war of self-defense" for NATO makes a mockery of international law, which was perverted to twist a flukishly successful attack by a tiny, terrorist Arab groupuscule into an excuse for an open-ended American military thrust into the Middle East and Central Eurasia.

Herein lie the reasons for the near-unanimity among Western opinion-

---

24   *The 9/11 Commission Report* (New York: W. W. Norton, 2004), pp. 333–4, 251–2.

makers that the occupation must not only continue but expand—"many billions over many years." They are to be sought not in the mountain fastnesses of Afghanistan, but in Washington and Brussels. As the *Economist* summarizes, "Defeat would be a body blow not only to the Afghans, but"—and more importantly, of course—"to the NATO alliance."[25] As ever, geopolitics prevails over Afghan interests in the calculus of the big powers. The basing agreement signed by the US with its appointee in Kabul in May 2005 gives the Pentagon the right to maintain a massive military presence in Afghanistan in perpetuity, potentially including nuclear missiles. That Washington is seeking permanent bases in this fraught and inhospitable terrain not simply for the sake of "democratization and good governance" was made clear by NATO's secretary general Jaap de Hoop Scheffer at the Brookings Institution in February this year: a permanent NATO presence in a country that borders the ex-Soviet republics, China, Iran, and Pakistan, was too good to miss.[26]

More strategically, Afghanistan has become a central theater for reconstituting, and extending, the West's power-political grip on the world order. It provides, first, an opportunity for the US to shrug off problems in persuading its allies to play a broader role in Iraq. As Obama and Clinton have stressed, America and its allies "have greater unity of purpose in Afghanistan. The ultimate outcome of NATO's effort to stabilize Afghanistan and US leadership of that effort may well affect the cohesiveness of the alliance and Washington's ability to shape NATO's future."[27] Beyond this, it is the rise of China that has prompted NATO strategists to propose a vastly expanded role for the Western military alliance. Once focused on the Euro-Atlantic area, a recent essay in *NATO Review* suggests, "in the twenty-first century NATO must become an alliance *founded* on the Euro-Atlantic area, designed to project systemic stability beyond its borders":

> The center of gravity of power on this planet is moving inexorably eastward … The Asia-Pacific region brings much that is dynamic and positive to this world, but as yet the rapid change therein is neither stable nor embedded in stable institutions. Until this is achieved, it is the strategic responsibility of Europeans and North Americans, and the

---

25   "Must They Be Wars without End?"

26   "Afghanistan and NATO: Forging the 21st Century Alliance," February 29, 2008; available on the Brookings website.

27   Paul Gallis, "NATO in Afghanistan," CRS Report for Congress, October 23, 2007.

institutions they have built, to lead the way ... Security effectiveness in such a world is impossible without both legitimacy and capability.[28]

The only way to protect the international system the West has built, the author continues, is to "re-energize" the transatlantic relationship: "There can be no systemic security without Asian security, and there will be no Asian security without a strong role for the West therein."

These ambitions have yet to be realized. In Afghanistan there were angry street demonstrations against Karzai's signing of the US bases agreement—a clear indication, if one was still needed, that NATO will have to take Karzai with them if they withdraw. Uzbekistan responded by asking the United States to withdraw its base and personnel from their country. The Russians and Chinese are reported to have protested strongly in private, and subsequently conducted joint military operations on each other's territory for the first time: "concern over apparent US plans for permanent bases in Afghanistan and Central Asia" was an important cause of their rapprochement.[29] More limply, Iran responded by increasing export duties, bringing construction in Herat to a halt.[30]

There are at least two routes out of the Khyber impasse. The first and worst would be to Balkanize the country. This appears to be the dominant pattern of imperial hegemony at the moment, but whereas the Kurds in Iraq and the Kosovars and others in the former Yugoslavia were willing client-nationalists, the likelihood of Tajiks or Hazaras playing this role effectively is more remote in Afghanistan. Some US intelligence officers have been informally discussing the creation of a Pashtun state that unites the tribes and dissolves the Durand Line, but this would destabilize Pakistan and Afghanistan to such a degree that the consequences would be unpredictable. In any event there appear to be no takers in either country at the moment.

The alternative would require a withdrawal of all US forces, either preceded or followed by a regional pact to guarantee Afghan stability for the next ten years. Pakistan, Iran, India, Russia, and, possibly, China

---

28   Julian Lindley-French, "Big World, Big Future, Big NATO," *NATO Review*, Winter 2005.

29   Rubin, "Proposals for Improved Stability in Afghanistan."

30   In response to Karzai's pleas, Tehran proposed a treaty that would prohibit foreign intelligence operations in each country against the other; hard to see how Karzai could have signed this with a straight face.

could guarantee and support a functioning national government, pledged to preserve the ethnic and religious diversity of Afghanistan and create a space in which all its citizens can breathe, think, and eat every day. It would need a serious social and economic plan to rebuild the country and provide the basic necessities for its people. This would not only be in the interests of Afghanistan, it would be seen as such by its people— physically, politically, and morally exhausted by decades of war and two occupations. Violence, arbitrary or deliberate, has been their fate for too long. They want the nightmare to end and not be replaced with horrors of a different kind. Religious extremists would get short shrift from the people if they disrupted an agreed peace and began a jihad to recreate the Taliban Emirate of Mullah Omar.

The US occupation has not made this task easy. Its predictable failures have revived the Taliban, and increasingly the Pashtuns are uniting behind them. But though the Taliban have been entirely conflated with al-Qaeda in the Western media, most of their supporters are driven by local concerns; their political evolution would be more likely to parallel that of Pakistan's domesticated Islamists if the invaders were to leave. A NATO withdrawal could facilitate a serious peace process. It might also benefit Pakistan, provided its military leaders abandoned foolish notions of "strategic depth" and viewed India not as an enemy but as a possible partner in creating a cohesive regional framework within which many contentious issues could be resolved. Are Pakistan's military leaders and politicians capable of grasping the nettle and moving their country forward? Will Washington let them? The solution is political, not military. And it lies in the region, not in Washington or Brussels.

8

A Model Humanitarian Intervention? Reassessing NATO's Libya Campaign

Alan J. Kuperman

On March 17, 2011, the United Nations authorized military intervention in Libya to protect the country's civilians. The Security Council was reacting to violence between Libyan government forces and domestic opponents that had erupted the preceding month. Two days after the authorization, NATO initiated the intervention, including establishing a no-fly zone and launching aerial attacks on government forces. After seven months, Libyan rebel forces conquered the country and killed the former authoritarian ruler, Muammar al-Qaddafi, in October 2011. Western media and politicians praised the intervention as a humanitarian success for averting a bloodbath in Libya's second largest city, Benghazi, and helping replace the dictatorial Qaddafi regime with a transitional council pledged to democracy. Based on this ostensible success, many experts now cite Libya as a model for implementing the humanitarian principle known as the "responsibility to protect" (R2P). Before such conclusions are embraced, however, a more rigorous assessment of the net humanitarian impact of NATO's intervention in Libya is warranted.

The Libya intervention is the latest in a series of international military actions after the Cold War justified on the basis of protecting noncombatants. This renaissance of "humanitarian intervention" started in the early 1990s, with prominent deployments of United Nations–authorized air and ground forces to northern Iraq, Bosnia, and Somalia. After NATO intervened in Kosovo in 1999, US President Bill Clinton declared, "If the world community has the power to stop it, we ought to stop genocide and ethnic cleansing."[1] The Kosovo intervention, however, had not been authorized by the United Nations, thereby calling into question its legality and legitimacy, so an international commission was formed to establish ground rules for future action. In 2001 this collective declared the existence of an international "responsibility to protect" endangered noncombatants.[2] In 2005 the UN General Assembly endorsed a version of R2P that emphasizes the responsibilities of states to protect their own citizens and of the international community to assist those efforts peacefully, while still requiring Security Council authorization prior to military intervention.[3] In 2007 the United Nations appointed a special adviser on the responsibility to protect and another on the prevention of genocide.

Debate on whether and how to intervene to protect noncombatants can be divided into three broad schools. Advocates claim that intervention is beneficial and ethically required, even where outcomes are suboptimal.[4] Opponents argue that intervention at best temporarily postpones the inevitable and, in any case, is an unethical waste of resources on goals outside the national interest.[5] In between are those who believe that intervention

---

1   Bill Clinton, interview, *Late Edition with Wolf Blitzer*, June 20, 1999.

2   International Commission on Intervention and State Sovereignty, *The Responsibility to Protect* (Ottawa: International Development Research Centre, 2001).

3   The UN resolution acknowledges the existence of an international "responsibility to use appropriate diplomatic, humanitarian, and other peaceful means … to help protect populations from genocide, war crimes, ethnic cleansing, and crimes against humanity" and to authorize force "on a case-by-case basis … should peaceful means be inadequate." UN General Assembly, 60th session, *World Summit Outcome*, 2005, resolution adopted by the General Assembly, October 24, 2005, p. 30, par. 139. See also Alan J. Kuperman, "R2P: Catchy Name for a Fading Norm," *Ethnopolitics* 10:1 (March 2011), pp. 127–30.

4   See, for example, Gareth Evans, *The Responsibility to Protect: Ending Mass Atrocity Crimes Once and for All* (Washington, DC: Brookings Institution Press, 2008); and Ivo H. Daalder and Michael E. O'Hanlon, *Winning Ugly: NATO's War to Save Kosovo* (Washington, DC: Brookings Institution Press, 2000).

5   See, for example, Ted Galen Carpenter, ed., *NATO's Empty Victory: A Postmortem on the Balkan War* (Washington, DC: CATO Institute, 2000); Michael Mandelbaum, "A Perfect Failure: NATO's War against Yugoslavia," *Foreign Affairs* 78:5 (September–October

is justified if it can do more good than harm, but that such cases are relatively rare in light of two factors.[6] First, perpetrators of violence often act more quickly than interveners can respond.[7] Second, intervention often rewards militants and thus encourages rebellion, which typically endangers noncombatants, thereby exacerbating the harm that it seeks to alleviate—a dynamic akin to "moral hazard."[8] To mitigate that problem, this school recommends that intervention be reserved for the rare cases where noncombatants are intentionally targeted, as opposed to where they are the collateral damage of counter-insurgency campaigns aimed at rebels.

Fundamentally, the R2P debate is about whether intervention can achieve its explicit humanitarian objective, which is the main focus of this article. Secondarily, however, the debate extends to the impact of humanitarian intervention on other interests, including the security and prosperity of intervening states and the spread of democracy. The Libya case, as demonstrated below, sheds light on all of these aspects of the debate.

The following analysis starts by reciting the widely accepted Western narrative of Libya's 2011 conflict and intervention. Next, it documents two significant errors in this narrative: the nature of violence prior to NATO intervention and the goal of that intervention. Third, it conducts a counterfactual analysis to explore the likely outcome in Libya if NATO had not intervened. Fourth, it documents the actual outcome in Libya in the wake of NATO intervention. Fifth, it explores whether the prospect of NATO intervention in Libya fostered the rebellion that provoked the Libyan government's crackdown, via a moral hazard dynamic. Sixth, it examines the postwar situation in Libya and its neighbors to assess the longer-term costs and benefits of NATO intervention. Finally, it summarizes the net impact of the intervention.

1999), pp. 2–8; and Michael Mandelbaum, "Foreign Policy as Social Work," *Foreign Affairs* 75:1 (January–February 1996), pp. 16–32.

6　This school of thought is summarized in Alan J. Kuperman, "Rethinking the Responsibility to Protect," *Whitehead Journal of Diplomacy and International Relations* 10:1 (Winter–Spring 2009), pp. 33–43.

7　Alan J. Kuperman, "Rwanda in Retrospect," *Foreign Affairs* 79:1 (January–February 2000), pp. 94–118.

8　Alan J. Kuperman, "The Moral Hazard of Humanitarian Intervention: Lessons from the Balkans," *International Studies Quarterly* 52:1 (March 2008), pp. 49–80.

Conventional Wisdom: Success of R2P

The mainstream narrative of the Libya conflict and NATO intervention runs as follows. By early 2011, two successful, nonviolent "Arab
Spring" uprisings in Tunisia and Egypt had lifted the veil of fear in Libya.
Accordingly, in mid-February 2011, the Libyan people rose up in analogous, nationwide, nonviolent protests against their dictator, Muammar
al-Qaddafi, whose oppressive rule they universally detested. Qaddafi
responded by ordering his forces to shoot the peaceful protesters, killing
thousands of innocent civilians in the first three days, especially in the
eastern city of Benghazi. Such brutal government violence compelled the
peaceful protesters to take up arms in self-defense and launch a rebellion.
These freedom fighters made progress for two weeks, gaining control over
half of the country by early March. Qaddafi again retaliated in a criminally disproportionate manner, ordering his ground troops to fire heavy
weapons indiscriminately into residential areas and his air force to bomb
civilians. Over the next ten days, government forces pushed the liberation
movement back to its last stronghold, Benghazi. There, Qaddafi explicitly
threatened to attack civilians, deployed his troops to the gates of the city,
and prepared to engage in a "bloodbath."

On March 17, 2011, the UN Security Council responded by authorizing
a no-fly zone and all necessary means except occupation troops to protect
Libya's civilians from Qaddafi's forces. This protection against criminal violence gradually enabled the freedom fighters, because of their nationwide
support, to turn the tide of the conflict, overthrow Qaddafi, and pave the
way for representative government. Overall, the NATO intervention—by
protecting Benghazi and helping remove Qaddafi from power—averted
a Rwanda-like genocide, restored human rights to the Libyan people,
fostered democracy and the rule of law, and helped sustain momentum for
the Arab Spring.[9] It did so quickly and without deploying ground forces,
thereby establishing a new model for successful implementation of the
emerging norm of the responsibility to protect.[10]

---

9   For evidence that the intervention was motivated by a desire to prevent "another
Rwanda," see Paul D. Miller, "Libya Is Not Rwanda," *Foreign Policy* blog, March 30, 2011.
See also David Jackson, "One Reason for Obama's Decision on Libya: Rwanda," *USA
Today*, March 24, 2011.

10   At the start of the intervention, President Barack Obama stated, "We are not
putting any ground forces into Libya." Barack Obama, "President Obama Says the Mission
in Libya Is Succeeding," weekly address, White House, March 26, 2011. After Qaddafi's

This conventional wisdom has been endorsed in the world's most widely read journal of international affairs by no less than the top US military and civilian representatives to the transatlantic alliance that led the intervention. The US permanent representative to NATO and the Supreme Allied Commander Europe, writing in *Foreign Affairs*, concluded as follows: "NATO's operation in Libya has rightly been hailed as a model intervention. The alliance responded rapidly to a deteriorating situation that threatened hundreds of thousands of civilians rebelling against an oppressive regime. It succeeded in protecting those civilians."[11]

Did Qaddafi Target Peaceful Civilians?

The first problem with the mainstream narrative is that it relies on two demonstrably false premises: that Qaddafi initiated the violence by targeting peaceful protesters and that NATO intervention aimed primarily to protect civilians. Contrary to most contemporaneous Western reporting, many Libyan protesters were armed and violent from the first day of the uprising, February 15, 2011, in Benghazi.[12] Government forces initially responded with nonlethal force: rubber bullets and water cannons. Western media on that first day incorrectly reported that Qaddafi's forces had fired live ammunition at peaceful protesters, citing video posted on the internet. The British Broadcasting Corporation, to its credit, admitted the next day that "subsequent inquiries suggested this was footage originally uploaded more than a year ago," but few other Western media corrected the error or acknowledged that they had fallen victim to anti-government propaganda.[13] Qaddafi's security forces refrained from deadly force until the protesters' violence escalated and spread during the following days.

In Benghazi the protesters used firearms, Molotov cocktails, bulldozers, and bomb-laden vehicles to capture the army garrison in this, the biggest

---

death, he reiterated, "Without putting a single US service member on the ground, we achieved our objectives." Barack Obama, "Bringing Home Our Troops," weekly address, White House, October 22, 2011.

11   Ivo H. Daalder and James G. Stavridis, "NATO's Victory in Libya: The Right Way to Run an Intervention," *Foreign Affairs* 91:2 (March–April 2012), p. 2.

12   "Libya Protests: Second City Benghazi Hit by Violence," bbc.com, February 16, 2011.

13   Ibid.

city in eastern Libya, on February 20, just three days after launching their "Day of Rage" on February 17. Indeed, in all four cities initially consumed by the conflict, large-scale violence was initiated not by government forces but rather by the protesters. In Benghazi, on February 15, protesters threw petrol bombs.[14] In Al Bayda, on February 17, "witnesses told Amnesty International that in the evening they saw police defectors shooting at al-Gaddafi forces. From then on, the protests quickly escalated into violent confrontations."[15] In the capital, Tripoli, on February 20, protesters initiated the violence by burning government buildings, thereby prompting Qaddafi's forces to respond brutally. According to one eyewitness testimony, the protesters "kicked out the pro-Gaddafi people in the Square and burned the internal security center. They entered and burned it all, and I think the general security building overlooking the martyrs square too … [Later], suddenly cars came, the land cruisers, with people. They were far away so I can't tell you if they were Africans or Libyans or from Sirte. They gave us no chance. Heavy fire, like it was a war."[16] In Misurata, on February 21, protesters attacked and seized weapons from police and army bases, triggering a spiral of violence. As the UN reported, "Protests appeared to have escalated rapidly, however, with demonstrators attacking offices of the Revolutionary Committees, police stations and military barracks on February 21 and 22, 2011, and arming themselves with weapons found at these locations. The Qadhafi Government admitted to firing live ammunition at those who, it said, were involved in violent actions."[17]

Likewise, a former high-level Libyan military commander told a UN inquiry that "only after demonstrators acquired arms did the Qadhafi forces begin using live ammunition."[18] Moreover, when government forces initially responded violently, notably on February 17 in Benghazi, they aimed to wound, not to kill. According to a French doctor working in a Benghazi hospital, on that day, "we had dozens of patients with

---

14   Ibid.

15   Amnesty International, *The Battle for Libya: Killings, Disappearances, and Torture* (London: Amnesty International, 2011), p. 37.

16   "They Gave Us No Chance: Heavy Fire, like It Was a War," *Alive in Libya*, February 20, 2011.

17   UN Human Rights Council, 19th session, "Report of the International Commission of Inquiry on Libya," A/HRC/19/68, advance unedited version, March 2, 2012, p. 53.

18   Ibid., p. 52. The report correctly notes that government forces quickly escalated to deadly force.

bullet wounds in the abdominal area or in the legs."[19] He explains that "at first, the security forces shot people in the legs and abdomen," and only "subsequently, in the chest and head."[20] The government's escalation was undoubtedly rapid—from rubber bullets, to wounding shots, to deadly force, in about three days—but the regime was responding to the protesters' escalation of violence. Not all or even most of the protesters in the crowds of this initial uprising were armed, so the government's retaliation unavoidably hit many unarmed protesters, who effectively were "human shields" for the rebels (whether intended as such or not). However, the image created by Western media of Qaddafi's forces initiating violence by attacking purely peaceful protesters was false.

After absorbing the first strike from armed protesters in these cities, government forces subsequently initiated violence in several other cities where protesters had been peaceful. The regime may have suspected, correctly, that the rebels aimed to militarize these protests, too. The government's belated resort to preemptive force, however, failed to stop the spread of rebellion. On February 23, for example, the Libyan army's 32nd Brigade, commanded by Qaddafi's son Khamis, arrived in Zawiya near the capital and shot at protesters who had been conducting sit-ins for four days.[21] Despite this, the city fell to the rebels just three days later.

Although the government did respond forcefully to the rebels, it never targeted civilians or resorted to "indiscriminate" force, as Western media reported. Indeed, early press accounts exaggerated the death toll by a factor of ten. This error can be traced partly to the French physician in Benghazi, who extrapolated wildly from the tiny sample in his hospital. Shortly after returning home on February 21, he was quoted as estimating that "more than 2,000 deaths" had occurred in Benghazi and its surroundings during his stay.[22] In reality, Human Rights Watch has documented only 233 deaths across all of Libya before this doctor left the country.[23] The

---

19   Gérard Buffet, "French Doctor Recounts 'Apocalyptic' Scenes in Libya," interview, Agence France-Presse, February 2011.

20   Quoted in François Malye, "Libye: 'C'etait un carnage absolu,'" *Le Point*, February 23, 2011.

21   UN Human Rights Council, "Report of the International Commission of Inquiry on Libya," p. 55.

22   Gerard Buffet, quoted in Malye, "Libye." The article states that this doctor returned to France on Monday, meaning February 21, so his estimate of more than two thousand deaths is presumably from the preceding day.

23   "Libya: Governments Should Demand End to Unlawful Killings: Death Toll up

international press also reported incorrectly, starting on February 21, that Qaddafi's air force was indiscriminately strafing and bombing civilians in Benghazi and Tripoli.[24] Only after the war ended did a prominent article, by the International Crisis Group's North Africa Project leader, reveal that "the story was untrue."[25]

The best evidence that Qaddafi did not use force indiscriminately, but rather targeted the rebels narrowly, comes from Libya's third-largest city, Misurata, which had become the most intense theater of the civil war by March 2011. During the first seven weeks of fighting, according to Human Rights Watch, 949 people in Misurata were wounded, of whom only 22 were women and 8 children.[26] This means that less than 3 percent of the wounded were female, which is strong evidence that government forces strove to target only combatants. (Violence in Misurata at the time mainly comprised government attacks on buildings and firefights with militants, so the dearth of wounded females cannot be explained by the lack of women at peaceful protests, because those tapered off quickly and were not the major source of casualties.) If government forces had targeted civilian areas indiscriminately, as alleged, the female percentage of wounded should have approached 50 percent, rather than 3 percent.

Moreover, Human Rights Watch reports that during this initial period of fighting, Misurata's medical facilities documented a total of 257 people killed—including rebels and government forces—in a city of 400,000. That means that the proportion of the population killed during nearly two months of fighting in the war's most intense theater was less than 0.0006, which represents indisputable evidence that the government avoided using indiscriminate force. It should be noted that Human Rights Watch's report did accuse the government of "targeting civilians and civilian objects," in violation of international law. The organization's own data,

---

to at Least 233 over Four Days," Human Rights Watch, February 20, 2011; this and other cited reports are available on the Human Rights Watch website.

24   One article quotes a protestor as follows, "Warplanes and helicopters are indis-criminately bombing one area after another. There are many, many dead." "Fresh Violence Rages in Libya," aljazeera.com, February 22, 2011. See also Miret el Naggar, Jonathan S. Landay, and Margaret Talev, "Gadhafi Accused of Genocide against His Own People," McClatchy, February 21, 2011, which reports US officials confirming such attacks.

25   Hugh Roberts, "Who Said Gaddafi Had to Go?," *London Review of Books* 33:22 (November 2011), pp. 8–18.

26   "Libya: Government Attacks in Misrata Kill Civilians: Unlawful Strikes on Medical Clinic," Human Rights Watch, April 4, 2011.

however, demonstrate that any such use of force by the government was the exception, not the rule.

Similar evidence comes from Tripoli, where the government used significant force only during one two-day period prior to NATO intervention, to suppress violent protesters who were burning government buildings. Libyan doctors subsequently told an investigative commission of the UN Human Rights Council that they observed more than two hundred corpses in the city's morgues on February 20–1. According to the UN council's report, however, "almost all of the bodies received were male. [The doctors] could only recall the bodies of two women killed—one shot and one stabbed—during the period of the protests."[27] If women were only 1 percent of the victims in the capital, it again suggests strongly that the government targeted its force narrowly at violent protesters, who were virtually all male, rather than indiscriminately at the civilian populace.

Also contrary to conventional wisdom, Qaddafi's regime never threatened or perpetrated revenge killings against civilians in areas that it recaptured from the rebels. The government did attempt to intimidate the rebels by promising to be relentless in pursuing them. For example, on February 20, Qaddafi's son Saif al-Islam declared that "we will fight to the last man and woman and bullet." Two days later, Qaddafi warned that he would deploy forces to tribal regions to "sanitize Libya an inch at a time" and "clear them of these rats," as he referred to the rebels.[28] This rhetoric, however, never translated into reprisal targeting of civilians. From March 5 to March 15, Libyan government forces retook all but one of the major rebel-held cities, including Ajdabiya, Bani Walid, Brega, Ras Lanuf, Zawiya, and most of Misurata. In none of those cities did the regime target civilians in revenge, let alone commit a bloodbath. When the regime was poised in mid-March to recapture the last rebel-held city, Benghazi, it again threatened ruthless violence against rebels who stayed to fight, as reported. International media, however, either failed to report or downplayed the regime's public reassurances that it would not target civilians, or rebels who laid down their arms, or rebels who fled, as the regime encouraged them to do. On March 17, Qaddafi directly addressed the rebels of Benghazi: "Throw away your weapons, exactly like your

---

27   UN Human Rights Council, "Report of the International Commission of Inquiry on Libya," p. 54.

28   International Criminal Court (ICC), "Situation in the Libyan Arab Jamahiriya," ICC-01/11, ICC, The Hague, June 27, 2011, p. 10.

brothers in Ajdabiya and other places did. They laid down their arms and they are safe. We never pursued them at all."[29]

Was NATO's Primary Goal to Protect Civilians?

NATO's intervention in Libya may have been borne mainly from a desire to protect civilians, consistent with the UN Security Council authorization. But within a few weeks of the operation's launch, the evidence shows that NATO's primary aim had evolved to overthrowing Qaddafi's regime, even at the expense of increasing harm to Libya's civilians.[30] If NATO had prioritized the protection of civilians, in accordance with its authorization, the transatlantic alliance would have enforced the no-fly zone, bombed forces that were threatening civilians, and attempted to forge a ceasefire.

Instead, NATO took actions that were unnecessary or inconsistent with protecting civilians, but which fostered regime change. Less than two weeks into the intervention, for example, NATO began attacking Libyan

---

29   "Qadhafi Promises 'No Mercy with Traitors' in Address to Benghazi, 17 March 2011," BBC Monitoring Service, March 19, 2011. His statement also included the following excerpts: "Whoever joins us, we the people, the liberator; whoever hands over his weapons, stays at home without any weapons, whatever he did previously, he will be pardoned, protected. We will pardon anyone in the streets. Throw away your rifle in the streets. Starting tomorrow, we will collect rifles from the streets—machine guns, ammunition. Anyone who throws away his weapon and stays at home peacefully will be pardoned no matter what he did in the past. He is protected. Throw away your rifle, you my son, and your family who are listening to me. I tell you get rid of your rifle, your automatic rifle and stay at home. But, if you enter any room with weapons, you'll be chased from room to room, and whoever is found with a weapon, it means he is an enemy ... We will search only for Al-Zanadiqah [ancient term for "unbelievers"] and the traitors. We will have no mercy on them. We will remove the walls around them one by one in search of them. [Words indistinct] unless they flee. We have left the way open to them. Escape. Let those who escape go forever. Let the dogs tear up their carcasses. Let them go to Egypt [words indistinct]. The search will be only for the traitors who [words indistinct] working for the United States and Britain, the colonialists."

30   UN Security Council Resolution, No. 1973, March 17, 2011, "authorizes Member States to take all necessary measures to protect civilians"; available on the UN website. Hugh Roberts states that the UN resolution was drafted deliberately to authorize regime change, because NATO had always viewed this as necessary to protect Libya's civilians: "It followed that effective protection required the elimination of the threat, which was Gaddafi himself." Roberts, "Who Said Gaddafi Had to Go?" My argument is slightly different—that soon after the intervention had started, NATO came to view the removal of Qaddafi as an end in itself, not a means, even if it undermined the original goal of protecting civilians.

forces that were retreating and therefore not a threat to civilians, who were far away.[31] At the same time, NATO started bombing forces in Qaddafi's hometown of Sirte, where they represented no threat to civilians because the residents supported the regime.[32] Government officials, the *New York Times* reported, immediately protested that "Western powers were now attacking the Libyan Army in retreat, a far cry from the United Nations mandate to establish a no-fly zone to protect civilians." To support this allegation, a Qaddafi spokesman noted that Libyan forces "were attacked as they were clearly moving westbound."[33]

Rather than pursuing a ceasefire, NATO and its allies aided the rebels who rejected this peaceful path and who instead sought to overthrow Qaddafi. Such assistance to the rebels significantly extended the war and magnified the harm to civilians, contrary to the intent of the UN authorization. For example, on March 4, the United Kingdom announced that it would deploy military experts to advise the rebels in eastern Libya, a step characterized by the press as "a clear intervention on the ground to bolster the anti-Gaddafi uprising."[34] In the middle of that month, President Barack Obama signed an intelligence "finding" approving covert aid to the rebels.[35] When the Security Council authorized the intervention, on March 17, the United States already knew that Egypt was supplying arms to the rebels.[36] By April 6, British military and intelligence officials in Benghazi were helping the rebels establish a command structure and defense ministry.[37] By mid-April, Qatar was shipping French antitank

31   The *New York Times* reported that "government forces were retreating south and west from Adjabiya and, in some cases, had abandoned their vehicles and equipment, presumably to avoid being attacked by allied warplanes." Kareem Fahim and David D. Kirkpatrick, "Airstrikes Clear Way for Libyan Rebels' First Major Advance," *New York Times*, March 27, 2011.

32   Praveen Swami, Rosa Prince, and Toby Harnden, "Coalition Forces Strike Sirte; Leader's Home Town," *Telegraph*, March 28, 2011.

33   David D. Kirkpatrick and Kareem Fahim, "Libyan Rebels March toward Qaddafi Stronghold," *New York Times*, March 28, 2011.

34   Patrick Wintour and Richard Norton-Taylor, "Libyan Opposition Leaders to Get Advice from UK Military," *Guardian*, March 4, 2011.

35   Mark Hosenball, "Obama Authorizes Secret Help for Libya Rebels," Reuters, March 30, 2011.

36   A senior US official confirmed, "This is something we have knowledge of." Charles Levinson and Matthew Rosenberg, "Egypt Said to Arm Libya Rebels," *Wall Street Journal*, March 17, 2011.

37   Mark Urban, "SAS on Ground during Libya Crisis," *BBC Newsnight*, January 18, 2012.

missiles to rebels in eastern Libya,[38] and "the Obama administration secretly gave its blessing" to such arms transfers.[39] Early the next month, France started air-dropping weapons to opposition forces in western Libya, who were being trained by operatives from France, Italy, and the United Kingdom—as these countries later acknowledged to a UN panel.[40]

Qatar, a NATO ally, was the most egregious in pushing the boundaries of the UN authorization, which had been explicit in "excluding a foreign occupation force of any form on any part of Libyan territory."[41] Qatar's military chief of staff subsequently revealed that "the numbers of Qataris on ground were hundreds in every region." Qataris also were "running the training and communication operations" for the rebels, he said. The leader of the Libyan opposition's umbrella National Transitional Council (NTC), Mustafa Abdel Jalil, concurred that Qataris had "planned" and were "a major partner in all the battles we fought."[42]

NATO and its allies kept providing such military aid even as the rebels repeatedly rejected the government's ceasefire offers, which could have ended the violence and thereby spared civilians. As early as March 3, 2011, barely two weeks into the violence, Qaddafi had embraced Venezuela's offer of mediation, but Jalil "totally rejected the concept of talks."[43] On April 11, Qaddafi accepted an African Union proposal for an immediate ceasefire to be followed by a national dialogue, but the rebels said they refused to consider any ceasefire until the Libyan leader left power.[44] On May 26, Libya's government offered not merely a ceasefire, but negotiations toward

---

38   Ian Black, "Libyan Rebels Receiving Anti-Tank Weapons from Qatar," *Guardian*, April 14, 2011.

39   James Risen, Mark Mazzetti, and Michael S. Schmidt, "Militant Forces Got Arms Meant for Libya Rebels," *New York Times*, December 6, 2012.

40   Samnia Nakhoul, "Special Report: The Secret Plan to Take Tripoli," Reuters, September 6, 2011; Colum Lynch, "UN Panel Documents Military Shopping List That Helped Topple Qaddafi," *Foreign Policy* blog, April 4, 2012; and Michael Birnbaum, "France Sent Arms to Libyan Rebels," *Washington Post*, June 29, 2011.

41   UN Security Council Resolution, No. 1973, March 17, 2011. Roberts argues that even Yemen's significant deployment of ground troops did not violate this provision, because "Article 42 of the 1907 Hague Regulations states that 'territory is considered occupied when it is actually placed under the authority of the hostile army.'" Roberts, "Who Said Gaddafi Had to Go?"

42   Quoted in "Qatar Admits It Had Boots on the Ground in Libya," alarabiya.net, October 26, 2011.

43   "Gaddafi Accepts Chavez Talks Offer," alJazeera.com, March 3, 2011.

44   Peter Kenyon, "Libyan Rebels Reject AU Cease-Fire Plan," National Public Radio, April 11, 2011.

a constitutional government and compensation to victims, yet the rebels again demurred in favor of war.[45] It is impossible to know if Qaddafi would have honored a ceasefire or the promise to negotiate a political transition. But if NATO had sought primarily to protect civilians, it would have conditioned its aid to the rebels on their sincerely exploring the regime's offers. There is no evidence that NATO ever sought to use its leverage in this manner. To the contrary, all available evidence indicates that NATO's primary objective, starting early in the intervention, was to help the rebels overthrow Qaddafi, even if this escalated and extended the civil war and thereby magnified the threat to Libya's civilians.

What if NATO Had Not Intervened?

To estimate the likely outcome if NATO had not intervened in Libya, it is essential to review the first month of the conflict, prior to intervention. Contrary to the portrayal by Western media of a nationwide peaceful protest against a dictatorial regime, the conflict started as an armed rebellion by regional, tribal, and Islamist opponents of the regime. The regional aspect is demonstrated by the fact that from February 15 to February 19, 2011, violent uprisings emerged only in eastern Libya—the historic, regional rival to Tripoli—in four cities: Ajdabiya, Al Bayda, Benghazi, and Dama. By contrast, near the capital, the protests originally were nonviolent and confined to one city, Zawiya. The tribal element of the militancy emerged on February 20, when the rebellion spread to the first city beyond eastern Libya, Misurata, where the main "tribe has a rivalry going back generations with" the Warfalla tribe, allied to Qaddafi.[46] Violent protest also erupted that day in the capital; but without

---

45   Martin Chulov, "Libyan Regime Makes Peace Offer That Sidelines Gaddafi," *Guardian*, May 26, 2011.

46   David D. Kirkpatrick, "Libya Results Seen to Break Islamist Wave," *New York Times*, July 9, 2012. This tribal aspect is further illustrated by subsequent events. A *USA Today* article reports that, after the war, Misurata's "militia used artillery to hammer" Bani Walid, a "city whose tribal chiefs have long been rivals of those in Misrata." The article adds, "The Warfallas, the people of Bani Walid, viewed the attack as revenge for their support of Gadhafi." Mathieu Galtier, "Militias Are Taking Over in Post-Gadhafi Libya," *USA Today*, January 3, 2013. But tribal rivalry was likely not the only cause of rebellion in Misurata, given that tribal affiliations in Libyan cities are typically weaker than in the periphery.

Table 1. No Bloodbaths by Qaddafi Forces

Ranking by Size	City	Population	Date Captured by Rebels	Date Retaken by Government	Bloodbath When Retaken?
1	Tripoli	1,150,989	—	—	—
2	Benghazi	650,629	February 20	—	—
3	Misurata	386,120	February 23	March 20	no
4	Tarhuna	210,697	—	—	—
5	Al Bayda	206,180	February 23	—	—
6	Al Khums	201,943	—	—	—
7	Zawiyah	186,123	February 26	March 9	no
8	Zuwara	180,310	February 23	March 14	no
9	Ajdabiya	134,358	February 26	March 16	no

KEY: "—" means city not captured by rebels or retaken by government prior to significant NATO intervention.
POPULATION SOURCES: http://www.worldcities.us/libya_cities/; and http://population. mongabay.com/population/libya.
NOTE: In Misurata, government forces entered the center on March 20 but failed to control the entire city before retreating after NATO intervened.

regional or tribal rivalry to sustain the Tripoli uprising, security forces crushed it in two days.

Initially benefiting from surprise, the rebels made rapid progress over the next two weeks. In the east, they captured Libya's entire coastline, from Egypt to Ras Lanuf, the port used for most oil exports. On the central coast, they gained control of Misurata and its surrounding towns. Just west of the capital, they took the cities of Zawiya and Zuwara. As a result, they briefly controlled six of Libya's nine biggest cities (see table 1). Moreover, in the Nafusa Mountains southwest of the capital, they claimed Gharyan, Yafran, and Nalut. By March 5, the high point of the initial violent uprising, the rebels thus controlled at least half of the country's populated areas.

The rebels' progress was short-lived, however, as Qaddafi's forces commenced a massive counter-offensive on March 7. Within two days, government troops had retaken Ras Lanuf in the east, the biggest mountain town of Gharyan in the west, and Zawiya near the capital. Just one week later, Qaddafi had recaptured virtually all significantly populated areas west of the rebels' final stronghold of Benghazi. A small part of Misurata remained contested, but the rebels there were doomed because they had no access to supplies, given that Qaddafi now controlled both the sea and land lines of communication to the city.

With the rebels in abject retreat, and the government poised to attack their last stronghold of Benghazi, Qaddafi's son Saif al-Islam declared on

March 16: "Everything will be over in 48 hours."[47] Had the UN not authorized intervention the following day, enabling NATO to start bombing Libyan forces on March 19, his prediction likely would have proved correct—except for a slight exaggeration on timing. In the preceding week, the rebels had not put up any real defense; they possessed only the rudimentary equipment and training needed to start a rebellion, not to win a war. They retreated, typically within two days, from each successive town that the army targeted on its eastward march: Ras Lanuf, Brega, and Ajdabiya. Based on this progression, government forces probably would have captured Benghazi by March 20. The remaining small towns farther east along the coast almost surely would have fallen the following week, prompting the rebels to flee to Egypt for refuge. Without NATO intervention, therefore, Libya's rebellion and civil war—and resulting endangerment of civilians—likely would have ended by late March 2011, less than six weeks after the conflict had started.

Although it is impossible to know precisely how many Libyans would have perished from the violence if NATO had not intervened, estimates should be based on the conflict's progression and trajectory. Starting with this evidence, the analysis below concludes that approximately 1,100 Libyans—including government forces, rebels, and noncombatants—likely would have died without NATO intervention. Conflict-related deaths prior to the intervention were confined mainly to five areas of Libya, and likely would have remained so in the absence of NATO action. The bloodiest region was Benghazi and its surroundings in eastern Libya. In early March, a medical committee in the city reported, apparently based on counting corpses, that at least 228 residents had been killed since the start of the conflict.[48] From that moment until NATO intervened, however, the city remained under rebel control and thus suffered few if any additional casualties. In all of eastern Libya, including Benghazi, medics estimated that at least four hundred people had been killed by March 9, though the basis of this estimate is unknown.[49] Additional war-related deaths, perhaps a dozen or two, likely occurred when Ajdabiya was retaken by the

---

47   Quoted in "Libyan Army Calls for Benghazi to Surrender as Saif Gaddafi Says Town Will Fall within 48 Hours," *Telegraph*, March 16, 2011.

48   The count included "30 unidentified bodies," and 1,932 were reported wounded. See "Gaddafi Forces Retake Towns Near Capital," *Sydney Morning Herald*, March 2, 2011.

49   Antoine Lambroschini, "Kadhafi Says West after Libya's Oil as Rebels Pounded," *Sydney Morning Herald*, March 9, 2011.

government in mid-March. Similarly, if not for the intervention, Benghazi and towns to the east probably would have suffered dozens of additional deaths when government forces recaptured them in late March. There is no reason to believe, however, that a bloodbath would have occurred in Benghazi, considering that Qaddafi had not threatened to attack civilians there and had not perpetrated such violence in any of the other cities that his forces recaptured from rebels (see table 1). Accordingly, the best estimate is that without NATO intervention, about five hundred Libyans in Benghazi and surrounding areas of eastern Libya would have died as the result of a six-week conflict.

Three other Libyan cities reportedly suffered significant casualties prior to NATO intervention. In Misurata, as noted, 257 conflict-related deaths had been documented by April 10, after seven weeks of fighting that included three weeks of NATO intervention.[50] Interpolation suggests that if the war had ended earlier, in late March without NATO intervention, Misurata's death toll would have been somewhat lower, around two hundred, depending on when and how the rebels ceased fighting. In Tripoli, as noted, major violence during the early months of the conflict was confined to two days—February 20–1—when the government attacked violent protesters for burning government buildings, leaving at least two hundred dead, according to doctors at city morgues.[51] If the war had ended in late March, without intervention, the toll in Tripoli probably would have remained at that level, given that the capital was firmly under government control. In Zawiya, after the rebels were defeated in mid-March, doctors in the town's hospital were reported to have "counted 175 people killed in battle."[52]

The only other area that likely suffered a substantial number of conflict-related deaths prior to NATO intervention was Libya's central coast, where the cities of Brega and Ras Lanuf changed hands several times, between the government and rebels, from late February through mid-March. With

---

50   "Libya: Government Attacks in Misrata Kill Civilians," Human Rights Watch.

51   UN Human Rights Council, "Report of the International Commission of Inquiry on Libya," pp. 7, 54. Regarding the violence in Tripoli, the International Criminal Court prosecutor claimed a somewhat higher death toll for those two days, plus smaller-scale killing on the three preceding days. See ICC, "Situation in the Libyan Arab Jamahiriya," pp. 15–18.

52   Vivienne Walt, "Gaddafi Gets His Revenge: The Price of Rebellion," *Time*, March 17, 2011.

each attack, the cities were subject to fire from artillery, mortars, rocket-propelled grenades, and additional small arms. Neither side, however, appears to have put up a strong defense, instead retreating when faced with superior firepower. This would explain why control initially switched frequently and why no large-scale casualties were reported. Nevertheless, dozens of deaths probably resulted from such fighting before NATO intervened. By mid-March, however, the government controlled these central-coast cities, so without intervention the death toll there likely would have been capped at this relatively low level.

In its June 2011 explanation of arrest warrants for Qaddafi and his inner circle, the International Criminal Court (ICC) alleged that the regime had targeted noncombatants, but only during a brief period that ended at least two weeks prior to NATO intervention. It stated, "There are reasonable grounds to believe that, as of February 15, 2011 and within a period of less than two weeks in February 2011, (i) hundreds of civilians were killed by the Security Forces."[53] The court separately cites more precise estimates, which it characterizes as credible, "that as the result of the shootings 500 to 700 persons died, only in February."[54] The ICC allegations are consistent with the numerical estimates in this article, although the prosecutor downplays the fact that many among the victims were armed and violent.

If NATO had not intervened in Libya, the above evidence suggests that the conflict would have lasted approximately six weeks and inflicted about 1,100 deaths. This toll includes 500 in Benghazi and the rest of eastern Libya; 200 in Misurata; 200 in Tripoli; 170 in Zawiya; and a few dozen along the central coast. Any such retrospective prediction necessarily has some margin of error. It should be noted, however, that none of the sources for casualty estimates cited in this article was sympathetic to Qaddafi's regime or had any other obvious reason to underestimate the death toll prior to intervention. Of course, it is impossible to rule out the possibility that Qaddafi, if permitted to quash the uprising, subsequently would have rounded up and summarily executed large numbers of suspected rebels. That scenario is unlikely, however, given that he had avoided such widespread retribution after previous rebellions.

---

53   ICC, "Situation in the Libyan Arab Jamahiriya," p. 13.

54   ICC, "First Report of the Prosecutor of the International Criminal Court to the UN Security Council Pursuant to UNSCR 1970," ICC, The Hague, May 4, 2011, p. 4.

The Outcome with NATO Intervention

When the UN authorized the intervention on March 17, 2011, and NATO started bombing two days later, Libyan government forces quickly halted their eastward offensive. As a result, Benghazi was not retaken by the government, the rebels did not flee to Egypt, and the war did not end in late March. Instead, the rebels in Benghazi reversed their retreat and launched a second westward offensive. Within barely a week, benefiting from NATO bombing of government forces, the rebels recaptured Brega and Ras Lanuf. In so doing, however, the ragtag rebels outran their supply lines, so the government again was able to retake the cities two days later. Over the next four months, such cities on the central coast changed hands several more times as the region became a primary theater of the war. Repeatedly, NATO would bomb Libyan forces, enabling the rebels to advance on populated areas, until the government counterattacked—with each round of combat inflicting casualties on both fighters and noncombatants.

In Misurata, too, intervention prolonged and escalated the fighting. On March 19, government forces were just retaking the city's center from the rebels who, without resupply routes, were doomed to fall within days, roughly one month after the fighting had started there. But when NATO attacked both the government's ground forces near the city and its naval vessels off the coast, the rebels gained breathing room and reopened their supply lines. As a result, fighting in Misurata continued for another four months until the rebels eventually prevailed in late July, by which time the city's death toll had grown substantially, as detailed below.

In Libya's western mountains, the rebellion also revived, fostered by an influx of weapons and trainers from NATO member states. Accordingly, by late August 2011, rebels had converged on Tripoli in a pincer from east and west. Not surprisingly, government forces staged a fierce defense of the capital—magnifying severalfold the death toll of soldiers, rebels, and civilians in an area that had been quiescent during the preceding five months—until the rebels captured it on August 28. Qaddafi and some loyalists retreated southward to pro-government areas, where they continued the battle for nearly two more months. On October 20, rebels discovered Qaddafi, and then tortured and summarily executed him. Three days later, on October 23, the regime's last remnants were defeated and the war ended.

As the result of NATO intervention, Libya's war lasted thirty-six weeks, rather than ending in about six weeks, as estimated above. There is no reliable count of the number killed, and claims have varied wildly.[55] At a closed-door conference in November 2011, one US government official reportedly characterized the final death toll as "around 8,000."[56] By contrast, the rebels' interim health minister asserted in September 2011, before the war even had ended, that 30,000 Libyans already had died.[57] In January 2013, however, that figure was sharply reduced by Libya's Ministry of Martyrs and Missing Persons. The revised Libyan estimate is that 4,700 civilians and rebels (grouped together as "revolutionaries") were killed, while the number of government forces killed "may be about the same as among revolutionaries, if not indeed less"[58]—meaning at most another 4,700—in addition to 2,100 missing from both sides combined. Thus, in total, the Libyan government's high-end estimate of the conflict's death toll, as of January 2013, is 11,500.

These two estimates of 8,000 and 11,500—by the US and Libyan governments, respectively—conceivably bound the actual number killed in the conflict. If so, and if the counterfactual analysis above is correct, then NATO intervention magnified the death toll in Libya by about seven to ten times. This would be consistent both with city-level data provided by the rebels, indicating that the intervention multiplied the number of deaths in Tripoli and Misurata, and with NATO's broadening of the geographic scope of fighting within the country. It also would confirm the speculation

---

55 Human Rights Watch has made no estimate. Fred Abrahams, email to author, April 15, 2012.

56 Clara M. O'Donnell and Justin Vaïsse, "Is Libya NATO's Final Bow?," Brookings Institution, December 2, 2011; available on the Brookings website.

57 "At least 30,000 Killed, 50,000 Wounded in Libyan Conflict," Tripoli Post, September 8, 2011. The report characterized this as the "first detailed estimate of the high cost in lives of ousting former Libyan leader Muammar Al Qaddafi from power ... based in part on reports from hospitals, local officials and former rebel commanders." The minister estimated that half of the dead were Qaddafi forces, while the rest were rebels and civilians. He reported that in Misurata at least 2,000 rebels and civilians had been killed, in addition to government forces, a toll roughly ten times higher than if NATO had not intervened, according to the analysis above. The minister estimated that the intense one-week battle for Tripoli in late August 2011 by itself killed 1,700 rebels and 100 civilians, in addition to government troops—making the death toll in the capital also about ten times higher than estimated without intervention. Given that the rebels' estimate of the overall death toll was later reduced by about two-thirds, the estimates for these cities may also have been exaggerated.

58 Umar Khan, "Casualty Figures Exaggerated, Says Ministry," Libya Herald, January 7, 2013.

of knowledgeable observers, such as Seumas Milne, who opined at the war's end that "while the death toll in Libya when NATO intervened was perhaps around 1,000–2,000 (judging by UN estimates), eight months later it is probably more than ten times that figure."[59]

Did NATO Foster the Rebellion?

To measure the humanitarian impact of NATO intervention, the two most obvious metrics are those already discussed: the war's duration and death toll. It is also important, however, to consider whether the expectation of such intervention prompted or initially sustained the Libyan rebellion, which provoked government retaliation and thereby endangered civilians in the first place. That potential dynamic is known as the "moral hazard of humanitarian intervention."[60]

It is not yet known whether the expectation of intervention triggered the rebellion, because the main agitators have yet to write or tell their story. A few weeks into the uprising, however, the rebel leaders clearly viewed prospective NATO intervention as vital, in light of the government's superior military resources. During a television interview on February 28, for example, the head of the rebels' political wing, Mustafa Abdul-Jalil, appealed for international imposition of a no-fly zone: "What we want is an air embargo to stop Gaddafi bringing in mercenaries."[61]

The rebels also had strong reason to believe that such intervention would be forthcoming. As early as February 22, 2011, former UK foreign minister Lord David Owen, while speaking to Al Jazeera, called for a no-fly zone.[62] On March 2, the rebels' military commander spoke by telephone to Britain's foreign secretary "about planning for a No-Fly Zone," according to the UK government.[63] The next day, March 3, British Special Forces and

---

59 Seumas Milne, "If the Libyan War Was about Saving Lives, It Was a Catastrophic Failure," *Guardian*, October 26, 2011.

60 See, for example, Kuperman, "The Moral Hazard of Humanitarian Intervention"; and Timothy W. Crawford and Alan J. Kuperman, eds., *Gambling on Humanitarian Intervention: Moral Hazard, Rebellion, and Civil War* (New York: Routledge, 2006).

61 Quoted in Alex Rossi, "Libya: Rebels 'May Use Force to Take Tripoli,'" Sky News, February 28, 2011.

62 See "Live Blog-Libya Feb 22," *Africa* (Al Jazeera blog), February 22, 2011. He repeated the call on the BBC the next day. See Michael White, "Libya Crisis: Too Late for UN Military Intervention?," *Guardian*, February 23, 2011.

63 "Foreign Secretary Speaks to General Abdul Fattah Younis al Obidi," Foreign

intelligence agents clandestinely attempted to meet with rebels in eastern Libya.[64] On March 5, France formally praised the rebels' establishment of the National Transitional Council. Just five days later, France's president, Nicolas Sarkozy, agreed to recognize the rebel council as Libya's legitimate government during a meeting at his office with the rebels' top diplomat, Mahmoud Jibril.[65] This was remarkable considering that the rebellion was barely three weeks old, and the rebels already had lost most of their initial territorial gains. On the same day, March 10, while the rebels were in abject retreat, their political leader appeared on CNN to plead again desperately for a no-fly zone: "It has to be immediate action."[66]

This evidence demonstrates that, by the third week of the rebellion (if not sooner), the strategy of the rebels depended on forthcoming NATO intervention—which they had grounds to expect. Indeed, the early and significant signals of support from NATO countries help explain why the otherwise feeble rebels continued fighting the government's vastly superior forces. The remaining counterfactual question is whether these Libyan militants would have dared to challenge Qaddafi in the first place without the expectation of NATO support. If not, then NATO's willingness to intervene not only prolonged and escalated Libya's civil war and resultant civilian suffering, but triggered the initial rebellion that provoked Qaddafi's retaliation. To answer this question definitively, however, would require evidence not yet available.

Postwar Libya

Although NATO intervention was explicitly predicated on the short-term goal of protecting civilians, and apparently backfired in this regard, it is worth exploring whether the intervention produced any longer-term net benefit for Libyans. The most positive development in postwar Libya undoubtedly has been the democratic election of July 2012, which brought

and Commonwealth Office, London, United Kingdom, March 2, 2011; available on the FCO website.

64 Martin Chulov, Polly Curtis, and Amy Fallon, "'SAS Unit' Captured in Libya," *Guardian*, March 6, 2011. On March 3, some rebels initially captured the British officials, misunderstanding their intent.

65 Steven Erlanger, "By His Own Reckoning, One Man Made Libya a French Cause," *New York Times*, April 1, 2011.

66 "Rebel Leader Calls for 'Immediate Action' on No-Fly Zone," CNN, March 10, 2011

to power a moderate, secular coalition government—a stark change from Qaddafi's four decades of dictatorship.[67] Less encouraging, the country's first democratically elected prime minister failed to last even one month in office before being removed by a vote of no confidence, attributed to regional rivalries.[68] Other developments have been even more discouraging. In the immediate wake of victory, the rebels perpetrated scores of reprisal killings, in addition to torturing, beating, and arbitrarily detaining thousands of suspected Qaddafi supporters.[69] A Human Rights Watch official characterized this behavior as "a trend of killings, looting and other abuses committed by armed anti-Gaddafi fighters who consider themselves above the law."[70] Rebels also expelled thirty thousand (mostly black) residents from Tawerga, and burned or looted their homes and shops, on grounds that some of them allegedly had been "mercenaries" in the government's attacks on nearby Misurata.[71] The ramification of this racial violence has been nationwide: "For the more than one million African guest workers who came to oil-rich Libya seeking their fortunes, it has meant terror … These innocent migrant laborers now find themselves singled out by ordinary Libyans and rebels who believe they are the enemy."[72] Six months after the war, in April 2012, Human Rights Watch reported that abuses around Misurata still persisted and "appear to be so widespread and systematic that they may amount to crimes against humanity."[73] Ironically, such racial or ethnic violence had never occurred in Qaddafi's Libya.

67   Kirkpatrick, "Libya Results Seen to Break Islamist Wave."

68   David D. Kirkpatrick, "Libya Dismisses Prime Minister, Widening a Power Vacuum," *New York Times*, October 8, 2012.

69   Maggie Michael, "Rights Group: Libyan Rebels Executed Gaddafi Loyalists," *Washington Post*, October 18, 2012.

70   John Lyons, "Libya's Rebels Take Revenge," *Weekend Australian*, November 5, 2011. See also UN Human Rights Council, "Report of the International Commission of Inquiry on Libya," pp. 76, 196–7; and Colum Lynch, "Report: Human Rights Abuses Continue in Libya," *Washington Post*, March 3, 2012, which summarizes the UN report as follows: "Anti-Gaddafi militias carried out reprisal killings of suspected regime loyalists and mercenaries, as well as the wide-scale torture of detainees … Serious abuses continue to be carried out by militias aligned with Libya's new government."

71   Kareem Fahim, "Accused of Fighting for Qaddafi, a Libyan Town's Residents Face Reprisals," *New York Times*, September 24, 2011.

72   William Wheeler and Ayman Oghanna, "After Liberation, Nowhere to Run," *New York Times*, October 30, 2011.

73   "Libya: Wake-Up Call to Misrata's Leaders: Torture, Killings May Amount to Crimes against Humanity," Human Rights Watch, April 8, 2012.

Indeed, during his final decade in power, Qaddafi had significantly improved his overall human rights performance. Amnesty International's 2010 annual report refers to major abuses only prior to 2000. Although the report acknowledges that the "Internal Security Agency (ISA), implicated in those [earlier] violations, continued to operate with impunity," it does not allege any large-scale offenses in the decade of the 2000s.[74]

Beyond humanitarian and human rights concerns, postwar Libya also has a weak record on security and democratization. The new government has failed to disarm or bring under its control the dozens of militias that arose during the revolution. This failure has resulted in deadly turf battles between rival tribes and commanders, as well as a growing threat from radical Islamists. In small signs of progress, the government has succeeded in removing most militia checkpoints in major cities, and has retaken control of seaports, airports, and border crossings. These steps, however, have not halted violence in the periphery or even in the capital. For example, in the southern city of Sabha, in March 2012, skirmishes between rival tribes left 147 dead. In April 2012, the *Washington Post* reported that "rival militiamen, some of them intoxicated and most of them unemployed, battle over turf in the capital."[75] According to the June 2012 edition of the *Middle East Report*, "In the provinces, the *thuwwar* [former rebels] largely rule the roost. Many a militia can outgun the army ... Even in Tripoli, where the government's grasp on security is most advanced, rogue militias continue to occupy key military installations in defiance of NTC demands that they leave."[76] Indeed, in November 2012, militia rivalries in the capital exploded into violence entailing "machine-gun fire and rocket-propelled grenades."[77]

In oil-rich eastern Libya, also known as Cyrenaica or Barqa, persistent regional rivalry has prompted demands for secession and independence,

74 As Amnesty International reports, "Hundreds of cases of enforced disappearance and other serious human rights violations committed in the 1970s, 1980s and 1990s remained unresolved." *Libya: Amnesty International Report 2010* (London: Amnesty International, 2010); available on the Amnesty website.

75 Steve Hendrix, "Free from Gaddafi's Uniting Grip, Libya Confronts Its Diversity," *Washington Post*, April 1, 2012.

76 Nicolas Pelham, "Libya's Restive Revolutionaries," Middle East Research and Information Project, June 1, 2012; available on the MERIP website. See also International Crisis Group, "Divided We Stand: Libya's Enduring Conflicts," Middle East/North Africa Report, no. 130, September 14, 2012; available on the ICG website.

77 Abigail Hauslohner, "Clashes in Capital Highlight Libya's Security Challenges," *Washington Post*, November 5, 2012.

or at least substantial autonomy within a federal system. Militants have attacked electoral offices on grounds that the region is underrepresented in the new government.[78] In September 2012, the *Washington Post* reported that "in many cases, including in Benghazi and in the western mountain town of Zintan ... the militias hold considerably more sway—and arms—than the Interior Ministry's police force." At that time, the chief of security in Benghazi conceded that "there has been no strategy to contain these [militias] and to move them into either the police or the army."[79]

Radical Islamist groups, suppressed under Qaddafi, emerged during the revolution as some of the most competent rebels. They obtained weapons during the war from other countries (especially Qatar) and ever since have refused to disarm.[80] Their persistent threat was highlighted by the September 2012 attack on the US consulate in Benghazi—reportedly by the Ansar al-Sharia militia—that killed Ambassador Christopher Stevens and three of his colleagues. Even prior to the consulate attack, the growing threat from Libya's radical Islamists had compelled many Western diplomats and nongovernmental organizations to evacuate the country.[81] According to a *New York Times* report on the attack, the militia "holds that democracy is incompatible with Islam. It has paraded the streets with weapons calling for an Islamic state, and a few months ago its leader boasted publicly that its fighters could flatten a foreign consulate."[82] Despite subsequent Libyan government pledges to address this threat, the *Washington Post* reported in October 2012 that "armed Islamist extremists are terrorizing the eastern Libyan city of Darna."[83] In Benghazi itself, as of February 2013,

78   David D. Kirkpatrick, "Election Commission Offices in Eastern Libya Are Sacked," *New York Times*, July 2, 2012. See also Hendrix, "Free from Gaddafi's Uniting Grip," which reports that "on March 6, a group of tribal leaders called for a return to the federal structure that governed Libya's three regions in the 1950s: Tripolitania in the west, Fezzan in the south and Barqa in the east."

79   Abigail Hauslohner, "Libya's Weak Government Leaves Perilous Void in East," *Washington Post*, September 20, 2012.

80   Risen, Mazzetti, and Schmidt, "Militant Forces Got Arms Meant for Libya Rebels." For a brief summary of the various factions, see Daniel Wagner and Giorgio Cafiero, "Implications of the Rise of Radical Muslim Groups in Libya," Institute for Near East and Gulf Military Analysis, January 23, 2013; available on the INEGMA website.

81   Abigail Hauslohner and Ernesto Londono, "Security at Libya Outpost Faulted," *Washington Post*, September 30, 2012.

82   David D. Kirkpatrick, Suliman Ali Zway, and Kareem Fahim, "Attack by Fringe Group Highlights the Problem of Libya's Militias," *New York Times*, September 16, 2012.

83   Abigail Hauslohner, "Islamists Hold Sway in Eastern Libyan City," *Washington Post*, October 27, 2012.

Islamist militias had resumed control of the city's entrance and two main hospitals.[84] In Tripoli, in April 2013, a bomb-laden vehicle destroyed half of the French embassy.[85]

In light of this ongoing instability and insecurity, it is perhaps understandable that many Libyans are nostalgic for a strong leader such as Qaddafi, who at minimum maintained order and provided basic social services. The country's first national survey after the war, conducted in late December 2011, reported that 54 percent of respondents "strongly agree" the country needs "a (single) strong Libyan leader."[86] Even when respondents were asked what kind of government Libya would need in the future—after one year, or after five years—this response remained the most popular.[87] These statistics may even underestimate Libyan support for a Qaddafi-like strong man, given that some respondents presumably were inhibited from expressing such an opinion in a country now controlled by the victorious rebels, and to interviewers perceived as pro-revolution. Indeed, the British organizations that conducted the survey downplayed these findings in their executive summary and presented the full survey results only on paper at a small public event, rather than posting them on the internet.[88]

Regional Spillover

Other consequences that must be factored into any assessment of NATO intervention in Libya concern the effects on neighboring states and the

---

84   Abigail Hauslohner, "Islamist Militia Is Edging Back into Benghazi," *Washington Post*, February 17, 2013.

85   David D. Kirkpatrick, "Blast Strikes French Embassy in Rare Attack in Libyan Capital," *New York Times*, April 24, 2013.

86   "First National Survey of Libya," Oxford Research International, in association with the Institute of Human Sciences, University of Oxford, and the University of Benghazi, based on fieldwork from December 13, 2011, to January 1, 2012, Q31A (parentheses in the original).

87   Ibid., Q31B, Q31C.

88   The executive summary released at the public presentation on February 15, 2012, states that "in 12 months' time 42% say they want a strong man (or men)." This statistic was widely reported six weeks later in David D. Kirkpatrick, "Libyan Militias Turn to Politics, a Volatile Mix," *New York Times*, April 3, 2012. Although the statistic is correct, it overshadows the 54 percent who strongly agreed that Libya needed a single strong man immediately. I obtained a copy of the executive summary and full survey results from someone who attended the public presentation, which was held exactly one year after the start of the rebellion, at the Human Sciences Institute, the Pauling Centre, Oxford, UK.

wider region. The most obvious negative impact has been in Mali, which previously was viewed by many diplomats and scholars as the region's exceptional example of peace and democracy. When Qaddafi was defeated, however, Malian ethnic Tuareg fighters in his security forces fled home with their weapons and launched a rebellion in their country's north, where they rapidly inflicted a series of defeats on government forces.[89] Malian army officers, frustrated by these losses, staged a coup on grounds that the government had underequipped them. Making matters worse, the rebellion in the north was quickly hijacked by local Islamist forces (Ansar Dine) and elements of al-Qaeda in the Islamic Maghreb, who defeated the Tuareg, imposed sharia, and declared the northern half of the country independent.[90] All of this fighting, and the imposition of strict Islamic law, spurred a massive displacement of hundreds of thousands of Malian civilians, creating a humanitarian emergency.[91] Indeed, Amnesty International characterized it as "Mali's worst human rights situation in 50 years."[92] In February 2013, a UN official reported that two hundred thousand children had missed school for more than a year, and nearly six hundred thousand people were "in need of immediate food assistance."[93]

Beyond the humanitarian costs, NATO's intervention has exacerbated terrorist activity and other forms of violence in the region. By December 2012, the northern half of Mali had become "the largest territory controlled by Islamic extremists in the world," according to the chairman of the US Senate subcommittee on Africa.[94] The regional US military commander warned that "Al Qaeda's affiliate in North Africa is operating terrorist

89   Adam Nossiter, "Qaddafi's Weapons, Taken by Old Allies, Reinvigorate an Insurgent Army in Mali," New York Times, February 6, 2012; Abigail Hauslohner, "Weapons, Fighters from Libyan War May Be at Root of Regional Unrest," Washington Post, January 19, 2013; and C. J. Chivers, "Looted Libyan Arms in Mali May Have Shifted Conflict's Path," New York Times, February 8, 2013.

90   Ross Douthat, "Libya's Unintended Consequences," New York Times, July 8, 2012.

91   Adam Nossiter, "Jihadists' Fierce Justice Drives Thousands to Flee Mali," New York Times, July 18, 2012.

92   "Mali's Worst Human Rights Situation in 50 Years, Warns Amnesty," Amnesty International, May 16, 2012.

93   Quoted in Rick Gladstone, "UN Official Sees Desperation, Hunger, and Fear on Visit to Mali," New York Times, February 27, 2013.

94   Edward Cody, "Restive Mali Is Ripe for al-Qaeda," Washington Post, June 8, 2012; Greg Miller and Craig Whitlock, "Al-Qaeda in Africa Is under Scrutiny," Washington Post, October 2, 2012; and Craig Whitlock, "Pentagon Helping Organize Multinational Operation in Mali," Washington Post, December 6, 2012.

training camps in northern Mali and providing arms, explosives and financing to a militant Islamist organization in northern Nigeria."[95] Mali's chaos also spread to other neighbors, spurring deadly ethnic conflict in Burkina Faso and the growth of radical Islamism in Niger.[96]

In early 2013, Mali's Islamist forces launched an offensive southward, apparently intent on capturing the capital, Bamako. France responded by intervening militarily on January 11.[97] By early February, four thousand French troops—assisted by French air power, African soldiers mainly from Chad, and US airlift—had dislodged the Islamists from the main cities in northern Mali and started attacking them in rural hideouts.[98] The long-term prognosis, however, is problematic. By mid-February 2013, the militants had reinfiltrated the ostensibly liberated cities of northern Mali,[99] and France had signaled that it planned to withdraw its troops and transfer responsibility to UN peacekeepers.[100] Two months later, the UN Security Council authorized such a mission, but it is unlikely to possess the military capacity to hunt down all of the armed elements or to control large swaths of the country.[101] Accordingly, northern Mali is likely to persist as a base, if not a haven, for radical Islamists.[102]

Yet another negative regional impact has been the flow of weapons, liberated from Qaddafi's arsenal, to arms markets and radical Islamists

95   Eric Schmitt, "American Commander Details Al Qaeda's Strength in Mali," New York Times, December 4, 2012.

96   "Burkina Faso: Deaths Reported in Clash," Associated Press, May 25, 2012. See also Yahia H. Zoubir, "Qaddafi's Spawn: What the Dictator's Demise Unleashed in the Middle East," Foreign Affairs, July 24, 2012; and Sudarsan Raghavan, "Niger Becomes Crossroads in Battle against Militants," Washington Post, August 17, 2012.

97   Edward Cody, "France's Hollande Intervenes in Mali," Washington Post, January 12, 2013.

98   Lydia Polgreen and Scott Sayare, "Militants Pulling Back from French in Mali Fight," New York Times, January 31, 2013; and Cheikh Diouara, "Mali Fight Moves to Saharan Scrubland," Washington Post, February 7, 2013.

99   Peter Tinti and Adam Nossiter, "Militants Infiltrate Towns in Freed Areas of Mali, Raising Peril of Guerrilla War," New York Times, February 17, 2013.

100   Angela Charlton and Baba Ahmed, "France May Begin Troop Pullout from Mali in March," Washington Post, February 6, 2013; and Scott Sayare and Alan Cowell, "As Mali Fighting Persists, France Vows to Exit in Weeks," New York Times, February 7, 2013.

101   Neil MacFarquhar, "UN Votes to Establish Peacekeeping Force for Mali," New York Times, April 26, 2013.

102   According to General Carter F. Ham, head of the Pentagon's Africa Command, "Realistically, probably the best you can get is containment and disruption so that Al Qaeda is no longer able to control territory." Adam Nossiter and Peter Tinti, "Mali War Shifts as Rebels Hide in High Sahara," New York Times, February 10, 2013.

beyond Mali, as documented in a 2013 UN Security Council report.[103] Of greatest concern are man-portable surface-to-air missiles, also known as MANPADs, which in capable hands can readily shoot down civilian airliners and military aircraft.[104] As many as fifteen thousand such missiles were still unaccounted for as of February 2012, according to a US State Department official cited in the *Washington Post*, because a $40 million buyback effort had secured only five thousand of them. Western intelligence sources say that hundreds are loose in the region, including in Niger, where some have been obtained by Boko Haram, the radical Islamic group based in northern Nigeria.[105] A few dozen missiles also have been found in Algeria and Egypt.[106] Al-Qaeda's North African branch is said to be using its "money to stock up on weapons that have flowed out of Libya after dictator Moammar Gaddafi was overthrown."[107] In October 2012, militants in the Gaza Strip fired one such missile for the first time, reportedly aiming at an Israeli army helicopter, and "Israel believes that the weapons originated in Libya."[108] Illustrating the scope of the problem, Libyan MANPADs and sea mines have even surfaced in West African arms markets, where they reportedly have been snapped up by Somali buyers for use by Islamist rebels and pirates in northeast Africa.[109]

It is also possible that Western intervention in Libya exacerbated civil conflict in Syria. When NATO started bombing Libyan forces, in March 2011, Syria's uprising was mainly nonviolent and its government's

---

103   UN Security Council, "Final Report of the Panel of Experts Established Pursuant to Resolution 1973 (2011) Concerning Libya," S/2013/99, February 15, 2013. See also Edith M. Lederer, "UN Panel: Libyan Weapons Spread at Alarming Rate," Associated Press, April 9, 2013, which reports that the illicit transfers "involve more than 12 countries and include heavy and light weapons such as portable air defense systems, explosives, mines, and small arms and ammunition."

104   Rod Nordland and C. J. Chivers, "Heat-Seeking Missiles Are Missing from Libyan Arms Stockpile," *New York Times*, September 8, 2011.

105   David Ignatius, "Libyan Missiles on the Loose," *Washington Post*, May 9, 2012.

106   Scott Stewart, "The Continuing Threat of Libyan Missiles," *Stratfor*, May 3, 2012.

107   Greg Miller, "Assessing al-Qaeda a Year after bin Laden," *Washington Post*, April 29, 2012.

108   "Antiaircraft Missile Is Fired from Gaza, Israeli Officials Say," *New York Times*, October 17, 2012.

109   "Analyst Says Somali Pirates Have New Weapons from Libya," Reuters, April 13, 2012. The report quotes Judith van der Merwe of the Algiers-based African Centre for the Study and Research on Terrorism as follows, "We found that Libyan weapons are being sold in what is the world's biggest black market for illegal gun smugglers, and Somali pirates are among those buying from sellers in Sierra Leone, Liberia and other countries."

response—although criminally disproportionate—was relatively circum-scribed, killing fewer than one hundred Syrians per week. But after NATO intervention helped Libya's rebels turn the tide against Qaddafi in the summer of 2011, Syria's uprising turned violent, escalating that conflict and leading to at least 1,500 deaths per week by early 2013 (a fifteenfold increase in the killing rate).[110] It is unknown whether NATO actions in the spring of 2011—intervening on behalf of rebels in Libya while ignor-ing nonviolent protesters in Syria—were decisive in transforming Syria's uprising from peaceful to violent, and thereby magnifying its death toll.[111] The counterfactual, however, is illuminating: if NATO had not intervened in Libya, and instead had permitted Qaddafi to defeat the Libyan rebels in just six weeks, would Syria's peaceful protesters have been so eager to take up arms? At the least, NATO intervention in Libya encouraged the militarization of Syria's uprising. Therefore, a significant portion of Syria's death toll may be a consequence of NATO intervention in Libya. Ironi-cally, advocates of intervention in Libya had claimed that such action was essential to sustain the momentum of the relatively peaceful Arab Spring revolutions in Tunisia and Egypt. In practice, NATO intervention not only failed to spread peaceful revolution, but it encouraged the militarization of Syria's uprising, which has exacerbated humanitarian suffering, sectar-ianism, and radical Islam in that country and its neighbors.

Some proponents of the Libya intervention claim that simply removing Qaddafi benefited the region and the world. This is questionable, however, because the former Libyan leader had evolved into a relatively benign

---

110   An article in *Times of Israel* includes a chart illustrating the acceleration of killing after Syria's uprising turned violent. For example, in mid-2011, during the first twenty-two weeks of the uprising, when it was mainly nonviolent, about two thousand were killed, or fewer than one hundred per week. But in mid-2012, during the final nine weeks of their data collection period and after the uprising had turned overwhelmingly violent, about six thousand were killed, or nearly seven hundred per week. Tamar Pileggi and Elihu D. Richter, "Butchers and Bystanders in Syria," *Times of Israel*, July 26, 2012. See also Edith M. Lederer, "Syria Death Toll: UN Human Rights Chief Says Casualties 'Probably Approaching' 70,000," Associated Press, February 12, 2013, which reports that, by early 2013, the death rate had climbed further—to about 1,500 per week.

111   Some might argue that the NATO intervention in Libya helped to deter Syria's regime from perpetrating even greater brutality. That cannot be disproved, but most inter-national observers characterize the Syrian regime's violence as excessive, not restrained. Moreover, during the spring of 2011, Syrian security forces killed many more nonviolent protesters than had Libya's security forces prior to the NATO intervention. Accordingly, there is little evidence that Syria's government was attempting to stay beneath some threshold of violence that it expected to trigger foreign intervention.

figure during his last decade. He switched from supporting terrorists to providing intelligence against them following the September 11, 2001, al-Qaeda attacks on the United States. He reduced aid to foreign rebels and instead sponsored peace initiatives, including for the Darfur region of Sudan. He dismantled and surrendered his weapons of mass destruction program after the US invasion of Iraq in 2003. Indeed, NATO intervention against Qaddafi after he had voluntarily disarmed is likely to hinder future nonproliferation efforts elsewhere. Accordingly, it is difficult to identify any obvious benefit for the region or beyond from NATO's intervention in Libya.

Net Impact

Overall, NATO intervention significantly exacerbated humanitarian suffering in Libya and Mali, as well as security threats throughout the region. The only apparent benefit is that Libyans have been able to vote in democratic elections, but the elected government has little authority in a country now controlled by dozens of tribal and Islamist militias accountable to no one.[112] NATO intervention increased the duration of Libya's civil war by approximately six times, and its death toll by seven to ten times. Human rights conditions in postintervention Libya, which include abuses "so widespread and systematic that they may amount to crimes against humanity,"[113] are considerably worse than in the decade preceding the war.[114] Beyond Libya, NATO intervention destabilized the previously peaceful and democratic Mali—giving rise to civil war, a coup, secession, massive human displacement, a humanitarian emergency, the strengthening of radical Islamists, and "Mali's worst human rights situation in 50 years."[115] Violence and Islamic radicalism have also spread to Niger and Burkina Faso, and thousands of weapons ideal for shooting down civilian airliners either have gone missing or are in the hands of rebels and terrorists. Syria's peaceful protesters were encouraged to militarize, in hopes of attracting similar intervention, and that militant transformation has dramatically escalated Syria's death toll.

---

112   Hauslohner, "Libya's Weak Government Leaves Perilous Void in East."

113   "Libya: Wake-Up Call to Misrata's Leaders," Human Rights Watch.

114   Libya: Amnesty International Report 2010.

115   Amnesty International, "Mali's Worst Human Rights Situation in 50 Years, Warns Amnesty."

Based on the humanitarian grounds originally invoked to justify it, NATO intervention in Libya has proved a disaster. It is possible that, in the long run, the intervention will turn out to have contributed indirectly to some beneficial consequences for Libya or its neighbors that cannot now be predicted. To date, however, the observable impacts on other interests—including human rights in Libya and its neighbors, regional stability, and international security—also have been decidedly negative. If this is a "model intervention," as US officials claim, it is a model of failure.

9

Why France Should Leave NATO

Régis Debray

A 2012 report by former foreign minister Hubert Védrine claimed that French influence would not be improved by reversing Nicolas Sarkozy's decision to return to NATO's integrated command structure. In an open letter, former government adviser Régis Debray disagreed.

Dear Hubert,

It is worth taking seriously the views of someone as skilled as you at cutting through waffle, and that especially applies to your report, commissioned last year by President Hollande, on France's return to the NATO fold. With media interest in inverse proportion to a subject's importance, it's unsurprising your report received little attention. Public opinion isn't interested in defense or France's place in the world, except when national pride is boosted by a victory, such as the recent advance through the desert in Mali, which sent the jihadis fleeing to the mountains with minimal bloodshed.

I learned a great deal from your report, but it left me puzzled. You indirectly exonerate (with a "yes, but ...") President Sarkozy for a return to NATO. You wouldn't have supported that decision when he was in power, but now it seems more awkward to challenge than back it. You hold that no one in the EU would follow our lead, and that France should take the initiative decisively to avoid being sidelined. So I want to pursue a dialogue we began in May 1981, in our adjacent offices at the Élysée.[1]

You contend that NATO's pyramidal structure has now become just a forum without great significance, where each member has the chance to be heard, if it can shout loud enough: NATO is now weaker and doesn't deserve the opprobrium of the past. I believe it is in better health than that. Its membership has more than doubled, from twelve countries in 1949 to twenty-eight in 2013 (with a total population of 910 million). It was originally Atlantic-based, but is now present in Iraq, the Gulf, off the coast of Somalia, in Central Asia, and in Libya, where it took charge of air strikes. It was originally military but has now also become political. It was originally defensive, but is now offensive, though it has no enemy. You believe the "benign neglect" of the US has altered the situation. The US has changed course and is now oriented toward the Pacific, with China rather than the USSR as its adversary/partner. So this causes a change of orientation and creates a situation in which Europe gazes longingly at America, which is enthralled by Asia.

Europe doesn't seem bothered by this infidelity as long as it gets some respect. France has to make do with honorific or technical posts in the command structure in Norfolk (US) or Mons (Belgium), vague hopes of contracts, a few hundred desk jobs, and meetings and cocktail parties. The relative decline of US power in the international system is obvious, but French power seems to have ebbed even more quickly. NATO may have changed since 1966, but so has France.[2]

France is gloomy enough as it is, so I shall skip an analysis of its diminished power, international influence, and independence of action ("independence," yesterday's watchword, has been supplanted by "democracy"). Let's pass over the well-known statistics for jobs, public services, armed forces, industry, use of the French language, and number of prestige projects.

The US is convinced of its exceptionalism: it remains a nation where the flag is raised in schools every morning and proudly worn as a lapel badge, and its president's unambiguous aim is to re-establish US world

---

1   In 1981 Régis Debray became François Mitterrand's representative for international relations. In the same year, Hubert Védrine was appointed as diplomatic adviser to the Élysée [notes to this chapter supplied by *Le Monde diplomatique*].

2   In 1966 France announced its withdrawal from NATO's integrated command.

leadership. The US is not about to lower its sights, especially as the nation has been boosted by the computer revolution, which is US-based, speaks its language and has companies that have put the country at the heart of the digital ecosystem. With its Latino and Asian communities, the US can be seen as a post-European country in a post-occidental world; although no longer the only contender for world leadership, it still spends half the world's military budget and can hold its head high—and implement its new doctrine of leading from behind.

Crowning Glories Lost

France has lost its distinctiveness, and its crowning glories—state, republic, justice, armed forces, education—have been hollowed out from within, like those noble buildings whose facades alone are preserved; neoliberal deregulation has eaten away at the foundations of public power, which was France's strength; the president unrolls the red carpet for the CEO of Google, a private citizen who would once have been received by a junior minister. It's a staggering *capitis diminutio*. We have been fortunate to save our cinema. But as for the rest ...

In 1963 the average left-wing French citizen hoped for a rosy future; his right-wing counterpart had reason to believe that France was key to the European project, and had cultural institutions, and nuclear bombs, too.[3] In 2013 the average French citizen believes in nothing and no one, is frightened of the neighbors, is anxious about the future and regards the past with shame. Despite the gloom, this average person has a surprising resilience.

Maintaining a capacity for reflection and foresight is vital. When the defense minister talks about "the fight against international terrorism"—an absurd expression that no longer has currency even in the US—to explain the intervention in Mali, we must accept that this is an advanced, and late, case of ideological takeover. When France categorizes Salafists, whom it hunts down in Mali, courts in Saudi Arabia and helps in Syria, within the catchall of "terrorism," it is speaking the American language, and may well end up gibbering.

---

3   In 1963 General de Gaulle opposed the UK's admission to the European Economic Community (EEC) on the grounds that it was too close to the US (and underlined the autonomy of France's nuclear deterrent).

Vigilant and Influential

Your challenge—to act within NATO—demands certain abilities, and also willpower:

1) To be "demanding, vigilant and influential," France needs funding, competitive think tanks, and original minds with other sources of inspiration than the Center for Strategic and International Studies (CSIS) in Washington or the International Institute for Strategic Studies (IISS) in London. Where are the equivalents of the architects of France's nuclear strategy? If there are independent strategists out there, they're invisible.

2) It needs willpower, too. This can sometimes take useful advantage of public indifference: from the mid-fifties, indifference allowed Prime Minister Pierre Mendès France and his successors to launch and covertly pursue a nuclear military program. The current "democracy of public opinion" has brought to power weather-vane politicians of all parties, with a greater-than-average sensitivity to the public mood. Government policy keeps changing, with the latest opinion poll as a guide. All our presidents since Pompidou have been seduced into fighting stateless renegades who then melt into their backgrounds, and this has guaranteed a boost to presidential ratings. But it has not been the presidential house style to confront the US, the world's first economic, financial, military, and media superpower. Belief in the rule of law and human goodness does not lead to *virtù* but to obedience to the law of the strongest. The Socialist of 2013 makes connections with the US State Department as readily as his 1936 counterpart did with the British Foreign Office. WikiLeaks revealed that, soon after the 2003 Iraq war, the current finance minister, Pierre Moscovici, then responsible for the Socialist Party's international relations, reassured NATO representatives about his party's goodwill toward the US: he promised that, if his party won the election, it wouldn't behave as Jacques Chirac had done.[4]

There is both a colonial and an Atlanticist gene in the Socialist DNA (nobody's perfect). It is possible to escape genetic determinism but harder to avoid the influence of one's generation, and the values shaped by its

---

4   In October 2005 the former Socialist prime minister Michel Rocard had expressed anger to the US ambassador in Paris over the 2003 speech to the UN by Dominique de Villepin (then foreign minister), and made clear that if he had been president, he would have kept quiet. See *Le Monde*, December 2, 2010.

experiences. François Mitterrand's generation had been through the war, the Resistance and Algeria. People remembered Amgot, Robert Murphy in Vichy, and Roosevelt's wartime manipulations of France, as well as D-Day and the Liberation. The present generation of politicians have short memories and have never had a hard time. They grew up inside a bubble, and they stay within it. They accept that they must be nice. Deliberately difficult people are never nice. Every time France made difficulties internationally, it antagonized vested interests at home: big bosses, powerful institutions and the media.

The shift you propose would need both to galvanize the apparatus of the state and the habits of dissenters (who will be accused of madness or betrayal). It clashes with the elaborate diplomacy needed in a milieu where, if you're not for the US, you must be against it. The more so since, as de Gaulle remarked, "the Americans take it as an insult that we don't agree to be their satellite," and especially when these power relations are mixed up with casual backslapping.

Useless and Harmful

You write about "clarifying the French conception of the Alliance," and I agree, since what is well conceived can be clearly expressed; you are clear and have the facts and figures. But waffle and euphemisms predominate, such as an "integrated command," when it's the leader who does the integrating while retaining complete autonomy. NATO's integration is not reciprocal. The US can spy on (bribe, intercept, listen in on, misinform) its allies, but not vice versa; US soldiers and officers don't expect to be held to account before international tribunals; the world's airlines are obliged to hand over detailed passenger lists to the US authorities, who would not dream of reciprocating.

Every formulaic NATO phrase needs to be translated. "Make your contribution to the common cause" means providing auxiliaries in theaters of war chosen by the US; "eliminate useless duplication in equipment programs" means buying US weapons and equipment, not developing them independently; and "burden sharing" means finance, communication, and control systems designed and made in the US. "The EU, a strategic partner with a unique place in the eyes of the US administration," means that Europe is not a partner but a client and instrument of the hyperpower. There is only one chain of command in NATO: the Supreme Allied Commander Europe (SACEUR) is American, as is the president of the Strategic Concept Expert Group (Madeleine Albright, former US secretary of state).

For France, being a "non-aligned ally" means recovering its language, values, and path. "Security" yoked to "defense," a fetish for technology and a (theologically inspired) desire to dominate the world clash with France's secular, republican character. So why should the left support in power what it condemned in opposition?

I subscribe to the view of Gabriel Robin, French ambassador and permanent representative to NATO and the North Atlantic Council from 1987 to 1993. He said:

> NATO pollutes every dimension of the international landscape. It complicates the building of Europe. It complicates relations with the Organization for Security and Co-operation in Europe (OSCE). It complicates relations with Russia ... It even complicates the operation of the international system because NATO does not conform to international law as it is unable to sign a convention renouncing the right to use force. Not resorting to force is impossible for NATO, because its very purpose is to use force when it sees fit. Nor has it abstained from using force without consulting the Security Council. As a result, I really do not see what a country such as France can hope for from NATO, a useless, harmful organization, except that it will disappear.[5]

NATO is useless because it is anachronistic. At a time when every major nation is playing its own hand (as can be seen in climate conferences), when religious pride or cultural identities are being asserted or reinforced, signing up to NATO is not building for the future. What matters now is ad hoc coalitions, bilateral cooperation, and practical arrangements, not a simplistically dualistic worldview. NATO is a survivor from a bygone age. Traditional interstate wars are disappearing and being replaced by non-conventional conflicts without declarations of war or front lines. The powers of the South (Brazil, South Africa, Argentina, China, India) are freeing themselves from the intellectual and strategic hegemony of the North, yet we ignore the way the world is changing.

---

5 "Sécurité européenne: OTAN, OSCE, Pacte de Sécurité," lecture given to the Res Publica Foundation, March 30, 2009.

NATO Harms the UN

NATO, by removing responsibility and acting as an anesthetic, is harmful to the UN and to respect for international law, because it either bends to its own ends or bypasses Security Council resolutions. It is harmful to France, whose hard-won comparative advantages it cancels out: it automatically makes enemies out of those who aren't hostile to France, by reducing France's ability to engage in dialogue freely, and by destroying goodwill toward France in many countries of the South. France is proud of having obtained favorable declarations on the maintenance of the nuclear deterrent and antiballistic missile defense: in reality, and the long term, deploying these can only marginalize weak-to-strong deterrence. But perhaps Paris, London, and Berlin are living under a terrible threat from Tehran and Pyongyang?

And NATO is harmful to any project of Europe as a power. If Europe wants a destiny, it will have to take a different path from the NATO route that keeps it to the status of a dominion (an independent state whose foreign policy and defense are determined by a foreign power). This may be a good thing for Central and Eastern European nations, because it means they will not face Russia alone. Each state's policies are shaped by geography, and we do not share our allies' geography.

The big idea of the previous French administration, which was to return to the NATO ranks to facilitate a European defense, was squaring the circle. For most Europeans, the strategy is to have no strategy. The money has run out, nobody wants to risk their necks when they've lost everything else, and that's the reason for the sham of a "European bulwark" or a "European general staff within NATO." The UK, the only state capable of defense agreements on a par with France, fashions them to meet US approval, and has recently abandoned plans to share an aircraft carrier. The Atlantic Alliance does not compensate for the weakness of the EU (in its "security and common defense policy"); it fosters and accentuates it. Meanwhile, brilliant young French diplomats flock to a "European diplomatic service" which may be lavishly funded but faces a superhuman task: taking on the external actions of a union that lacks common policies, armed forces, ambitions, or ideals.

Undeclared Foot Soldiers

The language of "influence" sounds like the Fourth Republic: "Those who willingly become foot soldiers hate admitting they are foot soldiers" (de Gaulle again). Advocates of French membership swear they have influence now and will still have influence tomorrow, but believing in effects without having the means is magical thinking. Influence means counting in decision-making, and when has France counted in a US decision? I'm not aware of Barack Obama ever consulting our national authorities before deciding to change strategy or tactics in Afghanistan. He decides; we get on with it.

NATO's second place is naturally occupied by the UK; Germany, though it doesn't have a permanent seat on the Security Council, comes third; France ranks only fourth (in Afghanistan, it was the fourth largest contributor). To talk of "top-level influence within the Alliance" is nonsense.

You might say that France has been sliding in this direction for a long time, and Sarkozy merely completed a process begun under his predecessors. Its culmination came when he said: "We are rejoining our Western family." Today NATO is a system of domination disguised as a family, a rhetorical cliché once confined to "the big family of Socialist states." There is an argument in favor of having several families, natural and elective, to counterbalance each other. I belong to the family of French-speaking nations and feel as much affinity, if not more, with an Algerian, Moroccan, Vietnamese, or Malagasy than with an Albanian, Dane, or Turk (all NATO family members). Culturally, I belong to the Latin family (Mediterranean and South American). Philosophically, I belong to the human family. Why should I limit myself to a single family? And why revive an ultraconservative idea (rejoining the Western family) that is not in the 1949 North Atlantic Treaty, seldom appears in de Gaulle's writing, and was never spoken of by Mitterrand?

Another View of the West

If the world identifies the West with the US empire, the West will encounter more hatred than love, more rejection than respect. France had the responsibility to provide another view of the West, different from

Guantanamo, drone strikes on villages, the death penalty, and arrogance. Giving up on that compromises the future of the best of the West, and betrays its past.

Is this worth outrage and effort? It may well be that our transformation from "great nation" to "beautiful province" best serves happiness and prosperity. What is there to complain about? Isn't it enough to satisfy the national pride of a very average country (1 percent of the world's population and 3 percent of its GDP) for us to intervene militarily in Mali without significant European help, just some US technical support? What more can we ask other than a rapid withdrawal before our troops get bogged down?

From a wider perspective (after Hegel), it may be that the Americanization of lifestyles and thought patterns (which will continue irrespective of NATO) is just the onward march of the individual under a different name. It is an extension of the domain of empathy, good news for minorities and non-conformists—sexual, religious, ethnic, and cultural. A further stage in the progress of civilization, like the transition from unrefined to refined, from scarcity to abundance, from the group to the individual. It might be a good thing to end the epic vision of history quickly if we want to live happily in the twenty-first century rather than the nineteenth. Verdun, Stalingrad, Hiroshima. Algiers, Hanoi: millions of dead, terrible suffering, and all for what? I sometimes think that the indifference to collective destiny, the recourse to the private sphere, France's slow exit from the stage are not simply cowardice, but a manifestation of Saint-Just's prophecy: "Happiness is a new idea in Europe." There is more sense and dignity in fighting for air quality, equal rights between homo- and heterosexuals, the preservation of green spaces and cancer research.

So peace after war, Venus after Mars. Or even Venus superior to Mars? If woman is the future of man, the feminization of values and mores is good, and will exemplify the best of contemporary Europe to future historians. Besides fine victories for feminism and equality, there has been the decline in paternal surnames, and the replacement of the military by the humanitarian, of the hero by the victim, of conviction by compassion, of the surgeon by the nurse, of cure by care.

"It's not school or sport we have a problem with, it's love," said President Sarkozy in May 2007. Nietzsche would have howled, but the philosopher Ibn Khaldoun (1332–1406), in his *Discourse on Universal History*, observed that states come into existence thanks to virile virtues and disappear when they abandon them. This was politically incorrect Bedouin puritanism, but an interesting description of the entropy of civilizations: "As the worm spins its silk then meets its end in becoming entangled in its threads."

Delaying the End

He would perhaps have admired the US talent for slowing the process and delaying the end. The US, while pushing beyond the perimeter with technologies and illustrations of the joys of hyper-individualism and celebratory self-sufficiency, retains both the torments and advantages of virility: the cult of weapons, a vast military budget, school massacres, exaggerated patriotism. Americans are phallocratic and politically independent in what concerns them, but support the "feminization" of frameworks and values elsewhere: oil rigs for the US, wind turbines for everyone else. From this stems a more ecological, peaceful Europe, less traditionalist than the US. European literature and cinema cultivate intimacy, Hollywood focuses on the broad social and historical canvas: Steven Spielberg raises a statue to *Lincoln*, CIA agents bring a tear to the eye in *Argo*. But Jean Dujardin in his spy comedy *OSS 117* makes Europeans cry with laughter.

If the problem is a Hegelian conception of history, and the solution is Buddhist-inspired values, my objections disappear. I'm delighted to know you are ready to serve the Republic and happy, as a casual observer, to go back to my studies. Having no connection to current affairs, they save me from ill humor. We all have our defense mechanisms.

With my best wishes,

Régis Debray

Translated by George Miller

PART THREE
Drang nach Kiev

10

Nyet Means Nyet: Russia's NATO Enlargement Red Lines

William J. Burns

CIA Director William J. Burns occupied a central role in US–Russian diplomacy over the months leading up to the Russian invasion of Ukraine. A career diplomat, he served as ambassador to Russia during George W. Bush's second term. From Moscow, Burns warned that continued NATO aggrandizement and the deployment of American ballistic missiles to Eastern Europe threatened to envenom relations between Russia and the United States. As the prospect of formal Membership Action Plan (MAP) proposals to Ukraine and Georgia hove into view, skippered with special vim by Vice President Cheney with an eye to the April 2008 NATO summit in Bucharest, Burns delivered a series of forceful cables on the subject.[1] In an email that February to Secretary of State Condoleezza Rice, reproduced in his 2019 memoir, Burns reiterated his concerns:

> *Ukrainian entry into NATO is the brightest of all redlines for the Russian elite (not just Putin). In more than two and a half years of conversations*

---

1   Many of these cables, including the one reproduced here, have since been made publicly available by WikiLeaks. For an overview with relevant links, see Branko Marcetic, "Diplomatic Cables Show Russia Saw NATO Expansion as a Red Line," *ACURA View-Point*, January 16, 2023; available at usrussiaaccord.org.

with key Russian players, from knuckle-draggers in the dark recesses of
the Kremlin to Putin's sharpest liberal critics, I have yet to find anyone
who views Ukraine in NATO as anything other than a direct challenge to
Russian interests. At this stage, a MAP offer would be seen not as a tech-
nical step along a long road toward membership, but as throwing down
the strategic gauntlet. Today's Russia will respond. Russian–Ukrainian
relations will go into a deep freeze … It will create fertile soil for Russian
meddling in Crimea and eastern Ukraine.[2]

These worries proved prescient. Months after NATO pledged in Bucharest that Ukraine and Georgia "will become members," Tbilisi launched
and promptly lost a two-week war with Russia. "In many ways," Burns
mused not long before Biden nominated him to head the CIA, "Bucharest left us with the worst of both worlds—indulging the Ukrainians and
Georgians in hopes of NATO membership on which we were unlikely to
deliver, while reinforcing Putin's sense that we were determined to pursue
a course he saw as an existential threat."

2008 February 1, 14:25   08MOSCOW265
B. MOSCOW 182
Classified By: Ambassador William J. Burns. Reasons 1.4 (b) and (d).

1. (C) Summary. Following a muted first reaction to Ukraine's intent to
seek a NATO Membership Action Plan (MAP) at the Bucharest summit
(ref A), Foreign Minister Lavrov and other senior officials have reiterated strong opposition, stressing that Russia would view further eastward
expansion as a potential military threat. NATO enlargement, particularly
to Ukraine, remains "an emotional and neuralgic" issue for Russia, but
strategic policy considerations also underlie strong opposition to NATO
membership for Ukraine and Georgia. In Ukraine, these include fears
that the issue could potentially split the country in two, leading to violence or even, some claim, civil war, which would force Russia to decide
whether to intervene. Additionally, the GOR [Government of Russia] and
experts continue to claim that Ukrainian NATO membership would have
a major impact on Russia's defense industry, Russian–Ukrainian family
connections, and bilateral relations generally. In Georgia, the GOR fears

---

2   William J. Burns, *The Back Channel: American Diplomacy in a Disordered World*
(London: C. Hurst & Co., 2019), p. 233.

continued instability and "provocative acts" in the separatist regions. End summary.

MFA: NATO Enlargement "Potential Military Threat to Russia"

----

2. (U) During his annual review of Russia's foreign policy January 22–23, Foreign Minister Lavrov stressed that Russia had to view continued eastward expansion of NATO, particularly to Ukraine and Georgia, as a potential military threat. While Russia might believe statements from the West that NATO was not directed against Russia, when one looked at recent military activities in NATO countries (establishment of US forward operating locations, etc.) they had to be evaluated not by stated intentions but by potential. Lavrov stressed that maintaining Russia's "sphere of influence" in the neighborhood was anachronistic, and acknowledged that the US and Europe had "legitimate interests" in the region. But, he argued, while countries were free to make their own decisions about their security and which political-military structures to join, they needed to keep in mind the impact on their neighbors.

3. (U) Lavrov emphasized that Russia was convinced that enlargement was not based on security reasons, but was a legacy of the Cold War. He disputed arguments that NATO was an appropriate mechanism for helping to strengthen democratic governments. He said that Russia understood that NATO was in search of a new mission, but there was a growing tendency for new members to do and say whatever they wanted simply because they were under the NATO umbrella (e.g. attempts of some new member countries to "rewrite history and glorify fascists").

4. (U) During a press briefing January 22 in response to a question about Ukraine's request for a MAP, the MFA [Ministry of Foreign Affairs] said "a radical new expansion of NATO may bring about a serious political-military shift that will inevitably affect the security interests of Russia." The spokesman went on to stress that Russia was bound with Ukraine by bilateral obligations set forth in the 1997 Treaty on Friendship, Cooperation and Partnership in which both parties undertook to "refrain from participation in or support of any actions capable of prejudicing the security of the other Side." The spokesman noted that Ukraine's "likely integration into NATO would seriously complicate the many-sided Russian–Ukrainian

relations," and that Russia would "have to take appropriate measures." The spokesman added that "one has the impression that the present Ukrainian leadership regards rapprochement with NATO largely as an alternative to good-neighborly ties with the Russian Federation."

Russian Opposition Neuralgic and Concrete

----

5. (C) Ukraine and Georgia's NATO aspirations not only touch a raw nerve in Russia, they engender serious concerns about the consequences for stability in the region. Not only does Russia perceive encirclement, and efforts to undermine Russia's influence in the region, but it also fears unpredictable and uncontrolled consequences which would seriously affect Russian security interests. Experts tell us that Russia is particularly worried that the strong divisions in Ukraine over NATO membership, with much of the ethnic-Russian community against membership, could lead to a major split, involving violence or at worst, civil war. In that eventuality, Russia would have to decide whether to intervene; a decision Russia does not want to have to face.

6. (C) Dmitriy Trenin, Deputy Director of the Carnegie Moscow Center, expressed concern that Ukraine was, in the long-term, the most potentially destabilizing factor in US–Russian relations, given the level of emotion and neuralgia triggered by its quest for NATO membership. The letter requesting MAP consideration had come as a "bad surprise" to Russian officials, who calculated that Ukraine's NATO aspirations were safely on the backburner. With its public letter, the issue had been "sharpened." Because membership remained divisive in Ukrainian domestic politics, it created an opening for Russian intervention. Trenin expressed concern that elements within the Russian establishment would be encouraged to meddle, stimulating US overt encouragement of opposing political forces, and leaving the US and Russia in a classic confrontational posture. The irony, Trenin professed, was that Ukraine's membership would defang NATO, but neither the Russian public nor elite opinion was ready for that argument. Ukraine's gradual shift towards the West was one thing, its preemptive status as a de jure US military ally another. Trenin cautioned strongly against letting an internal Ukrainian fight for power, where MAP was merely a lever in domestic politics, further complicate US–Russian relations now.

7. (C) Another issue driving Russian opposition to Ukrainian membership is the significant defense industry cooperation the two countries share, including a number of plants where Russian weapons are made. While efforts are underway to shut down or move most of these plants to Russia, and to move the Black Sea fleet from Sevastopol to Novorossiysk earlier than the 2017 deadline, the GOR has made clear that Ukraine's joining NATO would require Russia to make major (costly) changes to its defense industrial cooperation.

8. (C) Similarly, the GOR and experts note that there would also be a significant impact on Russian–Ukrainian economic and labor relations, including the effect on thousands of Ukrainians living and working in Russia and vice versa, due to the necessity of imposing a new visa regime. This, Aleksandr Konovalov, Director of the Institute for Strategic Assessment, argued, would become a boiling cauldron of anger and resentment among the local population.

9. (C) With respect to Georgia, most experts said that while not as neuralgic to Russia as Ukraine, the GOR viewed the situation there as too unstable to withstand the divisiveness NATO membership could cause. Aleksey Arbatov, Deputy Director of the Carnegie Moscow Center, argued that Georgia's NATO aspirations were simply a way to solve its problems in Abkhazia and South Ossetia, and warned that Russia would be put in a difficult situation were that to ensue.

Russia's Response

----

10. (C) The GOR has made it clear that it would have to "seriously review" its entire relationship with Ukraine and Georgia in the event of NATO inviting them to join. This could include major impacts on energy, economic, and political-military engagement, with possible repercussions throughout the region and into Central and Western Europe. Russia would also likely revisit its own relationship with the Alliance and activities in the NATO-Russia Council, and consider further actions in the arms control arena, including the possibility of complete withdrawal from the CFE and INF Treaties, and more direct threats against US missile defense plans.

11. (C) Isabelle Francois, Director of the NATO Information Office in Moscow (protect), said she believed that Russia had accepted that Ukraine and Georgia would eventually join NATO and was engaged in long-term planning to reconfigure its relations with both countries, and with the Alliance. However, Russia was not yet ready to deal with the consequences of further NATO enlargement to its south. She added that while Russia liked the cooperation with NATO in the NATO-Russia Council, Russia would feel it necessary to insist on recasting the NATO-Russia relationship, if not withdraw completely from the NRC, in the event of Ukraine and Georgia joining NATO.

Comment

----

12. (C) Russia's opposition to NATO membership for Ukraine and Georgia is both emotional and based on perceived strategic concerns about the impact on Russia's interests in the region. It is also politically popular to paint the US and NATO as Russia's adversaries and to use NATO's outreach to Ukraine and Georgia as a means of generating support from Russian nationalists. While Russian opposition to the first round of NATO enlargement in the mid-1990s was strong, Russia now feels itself able to respond more forcefully to what it perceives as actions contrary to its national interests.

BURNS

11

Why the Ukraine Crisis Is the West's Fault: The Liberal Delusions That Provoked Putin

John J. Mearsheimer

According to the prevailing wisdom in the West, the Ukraine crisis can be blamed almost entirely on Russian aggression. Russian president Vladimir Putin, the argument goes, annexed Crimea out of a long-standing desire to resuscitate the Soviet empire, and he may eventually go after the rest of Ukraine, as well as other countries in Eastern Europe. In this view, the ouster of Ukrainian president Viktor Yanukovych in February 2014 merely provided a pretext for Putin's decision to order Russian forces to seize part of Ukraine.

But this account is wrong: the United States and its European allies share most of the responsibility for the crisis. The taproot of the trouble is NATO enlargement, the central element of a larger strategy to move Ukraine out of Russia's orbit and integrate it into the West. At the same time, the EU's expansion eastward and the West's backing of the pro-democracy movement in Ukraine—beginning with the Orange Revolution in 2004—were critical elements, too. Since the mid-1990s, Russian leaders have adamantly opposed NATO enlargement, and in recent years, they have made it clear that they would not stand by while their strategically important neighbor turned into a Western bastion. For Putin, the illegal overthrow of Ukraine's democratically elected and pro-Russian president—which he rightly labeled a "coup"—was the final straw. He responded by taking Crimea, a peninsula he feared would host a NATO naval base, and working to destabilize Ukraine until it abandoned its efforts to join the West.

Putin's pushback should have come as no surprise. After all, the West had been moving into Russia's backyard and threatening its core strategic interests, a point Putin made emphatically and repeatedly. Elites in the United States and Europe have been blindsided by events only because they subscribe to a flawed view of international politics. They tend to believe that the logic of realism holds little relevance in the twenty-first century and that Europe can be kept whole and free on the basis of such liberal principles as the rule of law, economic interdependence, and democracy.[1]

But this grand scheme went awry in Ukraine. The crisis there shows that Realpolitik remains relevant—and states that ignore it do so at their own peril. US and European leaders blundered in attempting to turn Ukraine into a Western stronghold on Russia's border. Now that the consequences have been laid bare, it would be an even greater mistake to continue this misbegotten policy.

The Western Affront

As the Cold War came to a close, Soviet leaders preferred that US forces remain in Europe and NATO stay intact, an arrangement they thought would keep a reunified Germany pacified. But they and their Russian successors did not want NATO to grow any larger and assumed that Western diplomats understood their concerns. The Clinton administration evidently thought otherwise, and in the mid-1990s, it began pushing for NATO to expand.

The first round of enlargement took place in 1999 and brought in the Czech Republic, Hungary, and Poland. The second occurred in 2004; it included Bulgaria, Estonia, Latvia, Lithuania, Romania, Slovakia, and Slovenia. Moscow complained bitterly from the start. During NATO's 1995 bombing campaign against the Bosnian Serbs, for example, Russian president Boris Yeltsin said, "This is the first sign of what could happen

---

1   [For complete references to this chapter, see John J. Mearsheimer, *The Great Delusion: Liberal Dreams and International Realities* (New Haven, CT: Yale University Press, 2018).]

when NATO comes right up to the Russian Federation's borders ... The flame of war could burst out across the whole of Europe."[2] But the Russians were too weak at the time to derail NATO's eastward movement—which, at any rate, did not look so threatening, since none of the new members shared a border with Russia, save for the tiny Baltic countries.

Then NATO began looking further east. At its April 2008 summit in Bucharest, the alliance considered admitting Georgia and Ukraine. The George W. Bush administration supported doing so, but France and Germany opposed the move for fear that it would unduly antagonize Russia. In the end, NATO's members reached a compromise: the alliance did not begin the formal process leading to membership, but it issued a statement endorsing the aspirations of Georgia and Ukraine and boldly declaring, "These countries will become members of NATO."[3]

Moscow, however, did not see the outcome as much of a compromise. Alexander Grushko, then Russia's deputy foreign minister, said, "Georgia's and Ukraine's membership in the alliance is a huge strategic mistake which would have most serious consequences for pan-European security." Putin maintained that admitting those two countries to NATO would represent a "direct threat" to Russia. One Russian newspaper reported that Putin, while speaking with Bush, "very transparently hinted that if Ukraine was accepted into NATO, it would cease to exist."[4]

Russia's invasion of Georgia in August 2008 should have dispelled any remaining doubts about Putin's determination to prevent Georgia and Ukraine from joining NATO. Georgian president Mikheil Saakashvili, who was deeply committed to bringing his country into NATO, had decided in the summer of 2008 to reincorporate two separatist regions, Abkhazia and South Ossetia. But Putin sought to keep Georgia weak and divided—and out of NATO. After fighting broke out between the Georgian government and South Ossetian separatists, Russian forces took control

---

2 "Yeltsin Sees War Threat in NATO Enlargement," Jamestown Foundation *Monitor* 1:91 (September 1995); Steven Erlanger, "In New Attack against NATO, Yeltsin Talks of a 'Conflagration of War,'" *New York Times*, September 9, 1995.

3 "Bucharest Summit Declaration Issued by the Heads of State and Government Participating in the Meeting of the North Atlantic Council in Bucharest on 3 April 2008"; available on the NATO website.

4 "NATO Denies Georgia and Ukraine," bbc.co.uk, April 3, 2008; Adrian Blomfield and James Kirkup, "Stay Away, Vladimir Putin Tells NATO," *Telegraph*, April 5, 2008; International Crisis Group, "Ukraine: Running Out of Time," Europe Report, no. 231, May 14, 2014.

of Abkhazia and South Ossetia. Moscow had made its point.[5] Yet despite this clear warning, NATO never publicly abandoned its goal of bringing Georgia and Ukraine into the alliance. And NATO expansion continued marching forward, with Albania and Croatia becoming members in 2009.

The EU, too, has been marching eastward. In May 2008, it unveiled its Eastern Partnership initiative, a program to foster prosperity in such countries as Ukraine and integrate them into the EU economy. Not surprisingly, Russian leaders view the plan as hostile to their country's interests. This past February, before Yanukovych was forced from office, Russian foreign minister Sergey Lavrov accused the EU of trying to create a "sphere of influence" in Eastern Europe.[6] In the eyes of Russian leaders, EU expansion is a stalking horse for NATO expansion.

The West's final tool for peeling Kiev away from Moscow has been its efforts to spread Western values and promote democracy in Ukraine and other post-Soviet states, a plan that often entails funding pro-Western individuals and organizations. Victoria Nuland, the US assistant secretary of state for European and Eurasian affairs, estimated in December 2013 that the United States had invested more than $5 billion since 1991 to help Ukraine achieve "the future it deserves."[7] As part of that effort, the US government has bankrolled the National Endowment for Democracy. The nonprofit foundation has funded more than sixty projects aimed at promoting civil society in Ukraine, and NED's president, Carl Gershman, has called that country "the biggest prize." After Yanukovych won Ukraine's presidential election in February 2010, NED decided he was undermining its goals, and so it stepped up its efforts to support the opposition and strengthen the country's democratic institutions.

When Russian leaders look at Western social engineering in Ukraine, they worry that their country might be next. And such fears are hardly groundless. In September 2013, Gershman wrote in the *Washington Post*, "Ukraine's choice to join Europe will accelerate the demise of the ideology of Russian imperialism that Putin represents."[8] He added: "Russians, too,

---

5   Ronald D. Asmus, *A Little War That Shook the World* (New York: Palgrave, 2009).

6   Valentina Pop, "EU Expanding Its 'Sphere of Influence,' Russia Says," *EUobserver*, March 21, 2009.

7   Victoria Nuland, "Remarks at the US-Ukraine Foundation Conference," Washington, DC, December 13, 2013.

8   "Former Soviet States Stand Up to Russia. Will the US?," *Washington Post*, September 26, 2013.

face a choice, and Putin may find himself on the losing end not just in the near abroad but within Russia itself."

Creating a Crisis

The West's triple package of policies—NATO enlargement, EU expansion, and democracy promotion—added fuel to a fire waiting to ignite. The spark came in November 2013, when Yanukovych rejected a major economic deal he had been negotiating with the EU and decided to accept a $15 billion Russian counteroffer instead. That decision gave rise to antigovernment demonstrations that escalated over the following three months and that by mid-February had led to the deaths of some one hundred protesters. Western emissaries hurriedly flew to Kiev to resolve the crisis. On February 21, the government and the opposition struck a deal that allowed Yanukovych to stay in power until new elections were held. But it immediately fell apart, and Yanukovych fled to Russia the next day.[9] The new government in Kiev was pro-Western and anti-Russian to the core, and it contained four high-ranking members who could legitimately be labeled neofascists.

Although the full extent of US involvement has not yet come to light, it is clear that Washington backed the coup. Nuland and Republican senator John McCain participated in antigovernment demonstrations, and Geoffrey Pyatt, the US ambassador to Ukraine, proclaimed after Yanukovych's toppling that it was "a day for the history books." As a leaked telephone recording revealed, Nuland had advocated regime change and wanted the Ukrainian politician Arseniy Yatsenyuk to become prime minister in the new government, which he did.[10] No wonder Russians of all persuasions think the West played a role in Yanukovych's ouster.

For Putin, the time to act against Ukraine and the West had arrived. Shortly after February 22, he ordered Russian forces to take Crimea from Ukraine, and soon after that, he incorporated it into Russia. The task proved relatively easy, thanks to the thousands of Russian troops already stationed at a naval base in the Crimean port of Sevastopol. Crimea also

---

9   For a detailed account of the lead-up to the February coup, see Richard Sakwa, *Frontline Ukraine: Crisis in the Borderlands* (London: I. B. Tauris, 2015).

10   See Chapter 13 in this volume, "Nuland–Pyatt Transcript."

made for an easy target since ethnic Russians compose roughly 60 percent of its population. Most of them wanted out of Ukraine.

Next, Putin put massive pressure on the new government in Kiev to discourage it from siding with the West against Moscow, making it clear that he would wreck Ukraine as a functioning state before he would allow it to become a Western stronghold on Russia's doorstep. Toward that end, he has provided advisers, arms, and diplomatic support to the Russian separatists in eastern Ukraine, who are pushing the country toward civil war. He has massed a large army on the Ukrainian border, threatening to invade if the government cracks down on the rebels. And he has sharply raised the price of the natural gas Russia sells to Ukraine and demanded payment for past exports. Putin is playing hardball.

The Diagnosis

Putin's actions should be easy to comprehend. A huge expanse of flat land that Napoleonic France, imperial Germany, and Nazi Germany all crossed to strike at Russia itself, Ukraine serves as a buffer state of enormous strategic importance to Russia. No Russian leader would tolerate a military alliance that was Moscow's mortal enemy until recently moving into Ukraine. Nor would any Russian leader stand idly by while the West helped install a government there that was determined to integrate Ukraine into the West.

Washington may not like Moscow's position, but it should understand the logic behind it. This is Geopolitics 101: great powers are always sensitive to potential threats near their home territory. After all, the United States does not tolerate distant great powers deploying military forces anywhere in the Western Hemisphere, much less on its borders. Imagine the outrage in Washington if China built an impressive military alliance and tried to include Canada and Mexico in it. Logic aside, Russian leaders have told their Western counterparts on many occasions that they consider NATO expansion into Georgia and Ukraine unacceptable, along with any effort to turn those countries against Russia—a message that the 2008 Russian–Georgian war also made crystal clear.

Officials from the United States and its European allies contend that they tried hard to assuage Russian fears and that Moscow should understand that NATO has no designs on Russia. In addition to continually denying that its expansion was aimed at containing Russia, the alliance has never permanently deployed military forces in its new member states. In 2002, it even created a body called the NATO-Russia Council in an effort to foster cooperation. To mollify Russia further, the United States announced in 2009 that it would deploy its new missile defense system on warships in European waters, at least initially, rather than on Czech or Polish territory. But none of these measures worked; the Russians remained steadfastly opposed to NATO enlargement, especially into Georgia and Ukraine. And it is the Russians, not the West, who ultimately get to decide what counts as a threat to them.

To understand why the West, especially the United States, failed to understand that its Ukraine policy was laying the groundwork for a major clash with Russia, one must go back to the mid-1990s, when the Clinton administration began advocating NATO expansion. Pundits advanced a variety of arguments for and against enlargement, but there was no consensus on what to do. Most Eastern European émigrés in the United States and their relatives, for example, strongly supported expansion, because they wanted NATO to protect such countries as Hungary and Poland. A few realists also favored the policy because they thought Russia still needed to be contained.

But most realists opposed expansion, in the belief that a declining great power with an aging population and a one-dimensional economy did not in fact need to be contained. And they feared that enlargement would only give Moscow an incentive to cause trouble in Eastern Europe. The US diplomat George Kennan articulated this perspective in a 1998 interview, shortly after the US Senate approved the first round of NATO expansion. "I think the Russians will gradually react quite adversely and it will affect their policies," he said. "I think it is a tragic mistake. There was no reason for this whatsoever. No one was threatening anyone else."[11] Most liberals, on the other hand, favored enlargement, including many key members of the Clinton administration. They believed that the end of the Cold War had fundamentally transformed international politics and that a new, postnational order had replaced the realist logic that used to govern Europe. The United States was not only the "indispensable nation," as Secretary of State Madeleine Albright put it; it was also a benign hegemon and thus

---

11   Quoted in Thomas L. Friedman, "Foreign Affairs: And Now a Word from X," *New York Times*, May 2, 1998.

unlikely to be viewed as a threat in Moscow. The aim, in essence, was to make the entire continent look like Western Europe.

And so the United States and its allies sought to promote democracy in the countries of Eastern Europe, increase economic interdependence among them, and embed them in international institutions. Having won the debate in the United States, liberals had little difficulty convincing their European allies to support NATO enlargement. After all, given the EU's past achievements, Europeans were even more wedded than Americans to the idea that geopolitics no longer mattered and that an all-inclusive liberal order could maintain peace in Europe.

So thoroughly did liberals come to dominate the discourse about European security during the first decade of this century that even as the alliance adopted an open-door policy of growth, NATO expansion faced little realist opposition. The liberal worldview is now accepted dogma among US officials. In March, for example, President Barack Obama delivered a speech about Ukraine in which he talked repeatedly about "the ideals" that motivate Western policy and how those ideals "have often been threatened by an older, more traditional view of power."[12] Secretary of State John Kerry's response to the Crimea crisis reflected this same perspective: "You just don't in the twenty-first century behave in nineteenth-century fashion by invading another country on completely trumped-up pretext."[13]

In essence, the two sides have been operating with different playbooks: Putin and his compatriots have been thinking and acting according to realist dictates, whereas their Western counterparts have been adhering to liberal ideas about international politics. The result is that the United States and its allies unknowingly provoked a major crisis over Ukraine.

Blame Game

In that same 1998 interview, Kennan predicted that NATO expansion would provoke a crisis, after which the proponents of expansion would "say that we always told you that is how the Russians are." As if on cue, most Western officials have portrayed Putin as the real culprit in the Ukraine predicament. In March 2014, according to the *New York*

---

12   "Full Transcript: President Obama Gives Speech Addressing Europe, Russia on March 26," *Washington Post*, March 26, 2014.

13   CBS News, March 2, 2014.

Times, German chancellor Angela Merkel implied that Putin was irrational, telling Obama that he was "in another world."[14] Although Putin no doubt has autocratic tendencies, no evidence supports the charge that he is mentally unbalanced. On the contrary: he is a first-class strategist who should be feared and respected by anyone challenging him on foreign policy.

Other analysts allege, more plausibly, that Putin regrets the demise of the Soviet Union and is determined to reverse it by expanding Russia's borders. According to this interpretation, Putin, having taken Crimea, is now testing the waters to see if the time is right to conquer Ukraine, or at least its eastern part, and he will eventually behave aggressively toward other countries in Russia's neighborhood. For some in this camp, Putin represents a modern-day Adolf Hitler, and striking any kind of deal with him would repeat the mistake of Munich. Thus, NATO must admit Georgia and Ukraine to contain Russia before it dominates its neighbors and threatens Western Europe.

This argument falls apart on close inspection. If Putin were committed to creating a greater Russia, signs of his intentions would almost certainly have arisen before February 22. But there is virtually no evidence that he was bent on taking Crimea, much less any other territory in Ukraine, before that date. Even Western leaders who supported NATO expansion were not doing so out of a fear that Russia was about to use military force. Putin's actions in Crimea took them by complete surprise and appear to have been a spontaneous reaction to Yanukovych's ouster. Right afterward, even Putin said he opposed Crimean secession, before quickly changing his mind.

Besides, even if it wanted to, Russia lacks the capability to easily conquer and annex eastern Ukraine, much less the entire country. Roughly 15 million people—one-third of Ukraine's population—live between the Dnieper River, which bisects the country, and the Russian border. An overwhelming majority of those people want to remain part of Ukraine and would surely resist a Russian occupation. Furthermore, Russia's mediocre army, which shows few signs of turning into a modern Wehrmacht, would have little chance of pacifying all of Ukraine. Moscow is also poorly positioned to pay for a costly occupation; its weak economy would suffer even more in the face of the resulting sanctions.

---

14 Alison Smale, "Ukraine Crisis Limits Merkel's Rapport with Putin," *New York Times*, March 14, 2014.

But even if Russia did boast a powerful military machine and an impressive economy, it would still probably prove unable to successfully occupy Ukraine. One need only consider the Soviet and US experiences in Afghanistan, the US experiences in Vietnam and Iraq, and the Russian experience in Chechnya to be reminded that military occupations usually end badly. Putin surely understands that trying to subdue Ukraine would be like swallowing a porcupine. His response to events there has been defensive, not offensive.

A Way Out

Given that most Western leaders continue to deny that Putin's behavior might be motivated by legitimate security concerns, it is unsurprising that they have tried to modify it by doubling down on their existing policies and have punished Russia to deter further aggression. Although Kerry has maintained that "all options are on the table," neither the United States nor its NATO allies are prepared to use force to defend Ukraine. The West is relying instead on economic sanctions to coerce Russia into ending its support for the insurrection in eastern Ukraine. In July 2014, the United States and the EU put in place their third round of limited sanctions, targeting mainly high-level individuals closely tied to the Russian government and some high-profile banks, energy companies, and defense firms. They also threatened to unleash another, tougher round of sanctions, aimed at whole sectors of the Russian economy.

Such measures will have little effect. Harsh sanctions are likely off the table anyway; Western European countries, especially Germany, have resisted imposing them for fear that Russia might retaliate and cause serious economic damage within the EU. But even if the United States could convince its allies to enact tough measures, Putin would probably not alter his decision-making. History shows that countries will absorb enormous amounts of punishment in order to protect their core strategic interests. There is no reason to think Russia represents an exception to this rule.

Western leaders have also clung to the provocative policies that precipitated the crisis in the first place. In April, US vice president Joseph Biden met with Ukrainian legislators and told them, "This is a second opportunity to make good on the original promise made by the Orange

Revolution."[15] John Brennan, the director of the CIA, did not help things when, that same month, he visited Kiev on a trip the White House said was aimed at improving security cooperation with the Ukrainian government.

The EU, meanwhile, has continued to push its Eastern Partnership. In March, José Manuel Barroso, the president of the European Commission, summarized EU thinking on Ukraine, saying, "We have a debt, a duty of solidarity with that country, and we will work to have them as close as possible to us." And sure enough, on June 27, the EU and Ukraine signed the economic agreement that Yanukovych had fatefully rejected seven months earlier. Also in June, at a meeting of NATO members' foreign ministers, it was agreed that the alliance would remain open to new members, although the foreign ministers refrained from mentioning Ukraine by name. "No third country has a veto over NATO enlargement," announced Anders Fogh Rasmussen, NATO's secretary general.[16] The foreign ministers also agreed to support various measures to improve Ukraine's military capabilities in such areas as command and control, logistics, and cyberdefense. Russian leaders have naturally recoiled at these actions; the West's response to the crisis will only make a bad situation worse.

There is a solution to the crisis in Ukraine, however—although it would require the West to think about the country in a fundamentally new way. The United States and its allies should abandon their plan to Westernize Ukraine and instead aim to make it a neutral buffer between NATO and Russia, akin to Austria's position during the Cold War. Western leaders should acknowledge that Ukraine matters so much to Putin that they cannot support an anti-Russian regime there. This would not mean that a future Ukrainian government would have to be pro-Russian or anti-NATO. On the contrary, the goal should be a sovereign Ukraine that falls in neither the Russian nor the Western camp.

To achieve this end, the United States and its allies should publicly rule out NATO's expansion into both Georgia and Ukraine. The West should also help fashion an economic rescue plan for Ukraine funded jointly by the EU, the International Monetary Fund, Russia, and the United States—a proposal that Moscow should welcome, given its interest in having a prosperous and stable Ukraine on its western flank. And the West should

---

15   Remarks by Vice President Joe Biden at a Meeting with Ukrainian Legislators, Kiev, April 22, 2014.

16   "NATO Says No Third Country Can Veto Membership," Reuters, September 5, 2014.

considerably limit its social-engineering efforts inside Ukraine. It is time to put an end to Western support for another Orange Revolution. Nevertheless, US and European leaders should encourage Ukraine to respect minority rights, especially the language rights of its Russian speakers.

Some may argue that changing policy toward Ukraine at this late date would seriously damage US credibility around the world. There would undoubtedly be certain costs, but the costs of continuing a misguided strategy would be much greater. Furthermore, other countries are likely to respect a state that learns from its mistakes and ultimately devises a policy that deals effectively with the problem at hand. That option is clearly open to the United States.

One also hears the claim that Ukraine has the right to determine whom it wants to ally with and the Russians have no right to prevent Kiev from joining the West. This is a dangerous way for Ukraine to think about its foreign policy choices. The sad truth is that might often makes right when great-power politics are at play. Abstract rights such as self-determination are largely meaningless when powerful states get into brawls with weaker states. Did Cuba have the right to form a military alliance with the Soviet Union during the Cold War? The United States certainly did not think so, and the Russians think the same way about Ukraine joining the West. It is in Ukraine's interest to understand these facts of life and tread carefully when dealing with its more powerful neighbor.

Even if one rejects this analysis, however, and believes that Ukraine has the right to petition to join the EU and NATO, the fact remains that the United States and its European allies have the right to reject these requests. There is no reason that the West has to accommodate Ukraine if it is bent on pursuing a wrong-headed foreign policy, especially if its defense is not a vital interest. Indulging the dreams of some Ukrainians is not worth the animosity and strife it will cause, especially for the Ukrainian people.

Of course, some analysts might concede that NATO handled relations with Ukraine poorly and yet still maintain that Russia constitutes an enemy that will only grow more formidable over time—and that the West therefore has no choice but to continue its present policy. But this viewpoint is badly mistaken. Russia is a declining power, and it will only get weaker with time. Even if Russia were a rising power, moreover, it would still make no sense to incorporate Ukraine into NATO. The reason is simple: the United States and its European allies do not consider Ukraine to be a core strategic interest, as their unwillingness to use military force to come to its aid has proved. It would therefore be the height of folly to create a new NATO member that the other members have no intention of defending. NATO has expanded in the past because liberals assumed the alliance would never have to honor its new security guarantees, but Russia's recent power play shows that granting Ukraine NATO membership could put Russia and the West on a collision course.

Sticking with the current policy would also complicate Western relations with Moscow on other issues. The United States needs Russia's assistance to withdraw US equipment from Afghanistan through Russian territory, reach a nuclear agreement with Iran, and stabilize the situation in Syria. In fact, Moscow has helped Washington on all three of these issues in the past; in the summer of 2013, it was Putin who pulled Obama's chestnuts out of the fire by forging the deal under which Syria agreed to relinquish its chemical weapons, thereby avoiding the US military strike that Obama had threatened. The United States will also someday need Russia's help containing a rising China. Current US policy, however, is only driving Moscow and Beijing closer together.

The United States and its European allies now face a choice on Ukraine. They can continue their current policy, which will exacerbate hostilities with Russia and devastate Ukraine in the process—a scenario in which everyone would come out a loser. Or they can switch gears and work to create a prosperous but neutral Ukraine, one that does not threaten Russia and allows the West to repair its relations with Moscow. With that approach, all sides would win.

12

Annexations

Susan Watkins

Few Western leaders failed to pronounce on the importance of sovereignty, territorial integrity, and the rule of law as Russia moved to annex the Crimea on March 18, 2014. Issues of sovereignty had to be addressed through constitutional means and international law, Obama told his NATO allies in Brussels, so that big states could not simply bully the small. Cameron was adamant that countries could not flout international rules without incurring consequences, and vowed to stand up to aggression. Merkel deplored the fact that the principle of "might makes right" was taking precedence over the strength of law. The G7 leaders recalled, in chorus, that international law prohibits the acquisition of another state's territory through the use of force. When Schröder mused that, as chancellor, he had joined the rest of NATO in bombing a sovereign country, Yugoslavia, without any UN Security Council backing, he was scolded —"shameful"—by his successor; the European Parliament's Greens tried to pass a resolution banning him from speaking on the matter.[1]

So much for the proclamations. What is the historical record?

---

1 Obama: Speech at the Palais des Beaux-Arts, Brussels, March 26, 2014; Cameron: Statement to Parliament, March 10, 2014; Merkel: Statement, March 13, 2014; G7 (UK, US, Canada, France, Germany, Italy, Japan, accompanied by the EU's two presidents): Declaration at The Hague, March 24, 2014; Schröder, "ZEIT-Matinee mit Gerhard Schröder vom 09.03.2014," YouTube; Greens: Gregor Peter Schmitz, "Pipe it, Gerhard,"

1

Western Sahara: an area of one hundred thousand square miles, home to the Sahrawi people, annexed by Morocco in 1975. The Sahrawis' struggle for independence had already won the promise of a referendum on self-rule from Madrid during the final stages of the Franco dictatorship. In October 1975 the International Court of Justice (ICJ) knocked down the claim of Morocco's ruler, King Hassan, to the territory, ruling that the Sahrawis had a right to self-determination. Hassan's response was a propagandistic "Green March" into the Spanish Sahara, backed by a military assault on the Sahrawis' guerrilla organization, the Polisario Front. Ignoring the ICJ's judgment, the Ford administration and the UN helped to broker an agreement between Spain, Morocco, and Mauritania, excluding Sahrawi representatives; Juan Carlos, Spain's acting head of state, ceded the territory to these two powers in November 1975.[2] Hassan's occupation forces bombed population centers, strafed refugee columns and seized the phosphate mines, imposing a police dictatorship that is still in place today. Far from facing diplomatic or economic isolation, Rabat was visited by Israeli leaders in 1977 and hosted meetings for the Carter administration to set the scene for Sadat's trip to Jerusalem in 1979. That year, Hassan was rewarded with large-scale military aid from the United States, France and Saudi Arabia, which turned the tide against the Polisario guerrillas, who had been regaining ground. Hassan seeded the desert with landmines and built a militarized wall of sand, a thousand miles long, to keep the Sahrawis off their land. When he had finished, the UN offered to negotiate a ceasefire, winning the Polisario's agreement in 1991 by once again promising a referendum, which Rabat has stymied ever since by querying voter lists. Hassan, meanwhile, was showered with honors at Buckingham Palace and the Élysée, and given a lavish reception by the Clintons at the White House.

East Timor: seized by Indonesia in 1975. This former Portuguese colony, half an island in the far south of the archipelago, saw a brief moment of independence after the fall of the Lisbon dictatorship, offering a model of self-determination that was in stark contrast to the reign of terror

---

Spiegel, March 13, 2014; Nikolaus Blome, "Round Two: EU Grooming Klitschko to Lead Ukraine," *Spiegel*, December 10, 2013.

    2   Jacob Mundy, "How the US and Morocco Seized the Spanish Sahara," *Le Monde diplomatique* (January 2006).

Suharto had imposed across Indonesia since 1965. The US, his major international backer, knew of the invasion plan and did nothing to stop it. On the contrary: Ford and Kissinger were in Jakarta on a state visit the day before the invasion of East Timor; according to a declassified State Department telegram, they advised Suharto, "It's important that whatever you do succeeds quickly." The use of US-supplied weaponry could be a problem, but Washington would hope to "construe" the attack as self-defense. The thirty-five-thousand-strong Indonesian invasion force embarked on a series of killing sprees and mass executions, on the model of the massacre of communists ten years before.[3] Tens of thousands of Timorese were herded into resettlement camps; Amnesty would estimate that around two hundred thousand people, a third of the population, died from disease, starvation, or as a result of military action in the years that followed. Indonesia benefited from some $250 million in US military aid between 1974 and '79. When Fretilin guerrillas were still holding out against Jakarta's rule, two years after annexation, Carter sent a dozen counter-insurgency aircraft to help finish them off. Suharto was fêted on every visit to Washington, by presidents from Reagan to Clinton. In both East Timor and Western Sahara, as Ford's ambassador to the UN famously noted, "the US wished things to turn out as they did, and worked to bring this about"; the State Department wanted the UN to be "utterly ineffective" in these cases, and he made sure it was.[4]

Palestine: 2,324 square miles seized; East Jerusalem and an additional twenty-seven square miles around it annexed.[5] Israel's 1948–49 land grab had already expanded its territory from 1,554 square miles under the Yishuv in 1937 to over 8,000 square miles in 1949—30 percent more than the UN Partition Plan's allocation of 5,500 square miles, already tilted in the settlers' favor; some seven hundred thousand Palestinians saw their lands expropriated and were blocked from return. The response was not sanctions, but international recognition and admission to the UN, followed by Western help in obtaining nuclear weapons. When Israel annexed East Jerusalem and its environs in 1967 and seized control of the

---

3 Benedict Anderson, "Exit Suharto: Obituary for a Mediocre Tyrant," *New Left Review* II:50 (March–April 2008), pp. 27–59.

4 Daniel Patrick Moynihan, *A Dangerous Place* (New York: Berkley Books, 1980), p. 279.

5 Yoni Mendel, "New Jerusalem?," *New Left Review* II:81 (May–June 2013), pp. 35–56.

West Bank and Gaza, including the central mountain aquifer, Washington once again made sure the UN would do nothing: at the last count, the US has wielded its Security Council veto forty-two times to shield Israeli actions from opprobrium, while blocking Palestinian efforts even to join anodyne international agencies. Micro-annexations, by means of West Bank settlements now housing 350,000 citizens—subject not to Palestinian Authority but to Israeli law—and the Separation Wall, have proceeded unabated under cover of US-sponsored peace talks. Israel remains the world's largest recipient of US military aid and EU research funds.

Cyprus: 1,295 square miles annexed by Turkey in 1974. The Turkish invasion—tanks, jets, warships, artillery—left 4,000 dead, expelled 180,000 Greek Cypriots from their homes, and set up a puppet state, still garrisoned by 35,000 troops. Britain, controlling a large military base on the island, with assorted treaty obligations, did nothing to halt it. A short-lived congressional arms embargo on Ankara was lifted by Carter. Turkey has since been granted lavish US military aid, special favors from the IMF and sustained support from Washington and Brussels for its EU membership bid. When Cyprus itself was due to enter the EU, the US and UK sought to legitimate the Turkish land grab by wringing consent to it with a UN-sponsored plan, which would have ratified Ankara's ethnic cleansing and kept the Turkish troops in place. In a referendum, the "Annan Plan" was rejected by a solid majority of Cypriots. Military occupation by a foreign power persists to this day, inside the EU itself, without a word from Brussels.

2

Few tenets have been more cherished by the "international community" since the end of the Cold War than the notion that rights should trump state sovereignty; typically omitted from the list is the right of national self-determination. It was this principle that was trampled on by the invading power in Western Sahara, East Timor, Palestine and Cyprus— met, in each instance, by sustained popular resistance: armed, in the Sahara and Timor; both unarmed and armed, in Palestine; and plebiscitary in Cyprus, with the rejection of the Annan diktat at the ballot box. In each case, aggression with much loss of life was rewarded with lavish aid and the warmest friendship by the West.

This is what distinguishes the case of the Crimea, where scarcely anyone contests the fact that a majority have been in favor of joining Russia, seen as enjoying higher living standards; and where the annexation was forced through with scarcely a shot being fired—one soldier killed, compared with thousands of civilian deaths in the cases above. It is well known that Khrushchev re-allocated administration of the peninsula from the Russian SFSR to the Ukrainian SSR in 1954 in a typically high-handed manner, naturally without any popular consultation. There was sustained agitation for Crimean secession during the breakup of the Soviet Union. In a January 1991 referendum, seven months before Ukraine's declaration of independence, the Crimea voted in favor of becoming an autonomous republic. In 1992 the Crimean parliament scheduled a referendum on independence, annulled by Kiev, which instead offered autonomous-republic status. In 1994 the first president of the Crimean AR, who had been elected on a platform of union with Russia, called again for a referendum, whereupon Leonid Kuchma—the assassin ruler of Ukraine at the time—abolished his post and put the Crimea under direct presidential rule.

It was the buildup of Russian forces stationed by agreement in Crimea that allowed a referendum to be held along the lines of that thwarted twenty years before. Troop numbers increased from the scheduled 12,500 to 20,000. The Crimean parliament and other key buildings were secured by unmarked forces on February 27. A new parliamentary leadership was sworn in during an emergency session and scheduled the referendum first for May, then, a week later, for March 16. The official returns—95 percent in favor of union with Russia on an 83 percent turnout—cannot correspond to the real distribution of opinion in the Crimea, where 24 percent of the population describes itself as Ukrainian and 10 percent as Tatar. But though NATO leaders have singled out the referendum for attack—"held under the barrel of a gun," as if the elections they themselves organized in Afghanistan or Iraq were not overseen by tens of thousands of troops, armed to the teeth—none have suggested that the majority of the population in Crimea wants to remain in Ukraine. That force was needed to stage the referendum at all is plain. But this was not Chechnya, where Yeltsin and Putin rivaled Hassan and Suharto in the brutality with which they drowned a movement for national independence in blood. To that the West had no objection.[6] On the contrary: as Russian tanks

---

6   Tariq Ali, "How Vladimir Putin Became Evil," *Guardian*, March 28, 2014.

entered an obliterated city, Clinton congratulated them on the "liberation of Grozny."

To qualify is not to condone. The retrograde logic of Moscow's interventions has been to strengthen Ukraine's far right and to help shore up the transitional government in Kiev, even as it implements savage IMF cuts. Putin has become NATO's best recruiting sergeant. The fact remains that Russia is reacting, clumsily and defensively, to a continuous eastward thrust by NATO, loosely but systematically correlated with the EU's social-engineering projects. The Atlantic Alliance penetrated ex-Soviet borders in 2004, with the accession of Lithuania, Latvia and Estonia (along with Slovakia, Slovenia, Bulgaria and Romania). By 2008, Washington had put Ukraine and Georgia's memberships on the table.

III

The return of the Crimea to Russia was a by-blow of the crisis in Ukraine, but the two are analytically distinct. Since the breakup of the Soviet Union, Ukraine has come to constitute a latent version of a classic power vacuum, a result of the cultural and economic disaggregation of the country into two roughly equal halves. Under the Soviet system the Ukrainian SSR never functioned as a homogeneous state, in part because its key cities were so important to the Soviet Union as a whole: Donetsk for coal and engineering, Dnepropetrovsk for missiles, Kharkov for satellites and tanks—all had closer links with Moscow than with Kiev, itself a vital center for the USSR's high-tech industry. Today, most of the migrant flow to the EU comes from the less populated western regions—Lviv is only thirty miles from the Polish border—where much of the agricultural land has been leased to multinationals and the factories closed down. The fragmentation of the country has made possible a political system more open and pluralist than Russia's, as different power blocs re-combine against each other. But it has also prevented the Ukrainian state from achieving much coherence or stability.[7] It is not only weaker than its counterpart in Russia but still more corrupt, captured by competing billionaires, whose oscillation in power has become the hallmark of its recent history. Thus Poroshenko, the confectionery magnate, and

---

7 For a comparison of post-Soviet trajectories, see Dmitri Furman, "Imitation Democracies," *New Left Review* II:54 (November–December 2008), pp. 29–47.

Pinchuk, Kuchma's son-in-law, can aim to take control of the government apparatus in Kiev in a way that Moscow tycoons like Prokhorov or Khodorkovsky can now only dream of.

The congenital weakness of the Ukrainian state, rooted in these conditions, has drawn the West and Russia into rival bids to fill the strategic vacuum. Both sides' room for maneuver is limited by their mutual involvement elsewhere: the US needs Moscow's assistance on Afghanistan and Iran, a greater prize than Ukraine; Russia confronts Washington's hold over the international banking system. In Ukraine, the priorities for Moscow are twofold: to hold off any further penetration of NATO or the EU inside the ex-USSR, and to prevent political contagion from the less regimented Ukrainian political arena into Russia itself. On the Western side, the EU is constitutively enmeshed in the logic and rhetoric of enlargement: if Turkey is to be invited in, on what grounds should Ukraine be excluded? Costs—per capita GDP in Ukraine is now a third of Turkey's—and caution about provoking Russia, its major gas supplier, have long inhibited the EU from too forward a policy. Germany in particular has held back, halting Ukraine and Georgia at the entrance ramp to NATO in 2008. But other EU states—notably Poland and Sweden, the powers that invaded Russia in the seventeenth and eighteenth centuries—have become much more aggressive in pressing for an eastward thrust. For Washington, meanwhile, there is simply the imperial automatism of the global hegemon: if there is a power vacuum in a medium-sized country, the State Department's reflex response is to move in and take charge. In Ukraine, the US has much less to lose than the EU, though also much less to gain than Russia. But once the crisis broke in Kiev, Washington could not resist the opportunity to construct a regime to its liking.

13

Nuland–Pyatt Transcript

The recording of this discussion between State Department operative Victoria Nuland and Ambassador Geoffrey Pyatt was released on February 7, 2014, and is available on the BBC website. It offers a vivid glimpse into the process of imperial interference overseas—"personality management" —as these functionaries plan the composition of the new Ukrainian government. Germany had been grooming the former boxer, Vitali Klitschko, with Merkel's chief of staff, Ronald Pofalla, advising on his marital problems.[1] Nuland is determined to exclude Klitschko in favor of Arseniy Yatsenyuk, former banker and head of the US-backed Open Ukraine Foundation, who has "the economic experience." Meanwhile UN officials are summoned to "help glue this thing"—Jeff Feltman, an American UN undersecretary general, producing UN envoy and former Netherlands ambassador to Ukraine Robert Serry. Events since the tape was released have corresponded closely to the scenario Nuland and Pyatt designed: on February 23, Yatsenyuk was appointed prime minister of the provisional Ukrainian government; on March 29, Klitschko renounced his candidacy for the May presidential elections.

---

1   Nikolaus Blome, "Round Two: EU Grooming Klitschko to Lead Ukraine," *Spiegel*, December 10, 2013.

Nuland: What do you think?

Pyatt: I think we're in play. The Klitschko piece is obviously the complicated electron here. Especially the announcement of him as deputy
prime minister, and you've seen some of my notes on the troubles in
the marriage right now, so we're trying to get a read really fast on where
he is on this stuff. But I think your argument to him, which you'll need
to make, I think that's the next phone call you want to set up, is exactly
the one you made to Yats [Yatsenyuk]. And I'm glad you sort of put him
on the spot on where he fits in this scenario. And I'm very glad that he
said what he said in response.

Nuland: Good. I don't think Klitsch should go into the government. I don't
think it's necessary, I don't think it's a good idea.

Pyatt: Yeah. I guess … in terms of him not going into the government,
just let him stay out and do his political homework and stuff. I'm just
thinking in terms of the process moving ahead, we want to keep the
moderate democrats together. The problem is going to be Tyahnybok
and his guys, and I'm sure that's part of what Yanukovych is calculating
on all this.

Nuland: I think Yats is the guy who's got the economic experience, the
governing experience. He's the … what he needs is Klitsch and Tyahnybok on the outside. He needs to be talking to them four times a week,
you know. I just think Klitsch going in … he's going to be at that level
working for Yatsenyuk, it's just not going to work.

Pyatt: Yeah, no, I think that's right. OK. Good. Do you want us to set up a
call with him as the next step?

Nuland: My understanding from that call—but you tell me—was that the
big three were going into their own meeting and that Yats was going to
offer in that context a … three-plus-one conversation or three-plus-two
with you. Is that not how you understood it?

Pyatt: No. I think … I mean that's what he proposed but I think, just
knowing the dynamic that's been with them where Klitschko has been
the top dog, he's going to take a while to show up for whatever meeting
they've got, and he's probably talking to his guys at this point, so I think
you reaching out directly to him helps with the personality management
among the three, and it gives you also a chance to move fast on all this
stuff and put us behind it before they all sit down and he explains why
he doesn't like it.

Nuland: OK, good. I'm happy. Why don't you reach out to him and see if he wants to talk before or after.

Pyatt: OK, will do. Thanks.

Nuland: OK. One more wrinkle for you Geoff. I can't remember if I told you this, or if I only told Washington this, that when I talked to Jeff Feltman this morning, he had a new name for the UN, that guy Robert Serry. Did I write you that this morning?

Pyatt: Yeah, I saw that.

Nuland: OK. He's now gotten both Serry and Ban Ki-moon to agree that Serry could come in Monday or Tuesday. So that would be great, I think, to help glue this thing and to have the UN help glue it and, you know, fuck the EU.

Pyatt: No, exactly. And I think we've got to do something to make it stick together because you can be pretty sure that if it does start to gain altitude, that the Russians will be working behind the scenes to try to torpedo it. And again the fact that this is out there right now, I'm still trying to figure out in my mind why Yanukovych [garbled] that. In the meantime there's a Party of Regions faction meeting going on right now and I'm sure there's a lively argument going on in that group at this point. But anyway we could land jelly side up on this one if we move fast. So let me work on Klitschko and if you can just keep … we want to try to get somebody with an international personality to come out here and help to midwife this thing. The other issue is some kind of outreach to Yanukovych, but we probably regroup on that tomorrow as we see how things start to fall into place.

Nuland: So on that piece Geoff, when I wrote the note Sullivan's come back to me VFR saying you need Biden, and I said probably tomorrow for an atta-boy and to get the deets [details] to stick. So Biden's willing.

Pyatt: OK. Great. Thanks.

14

Sleepwalking into a Big War

Michael T. Klare

As the 2016 US presidential race approaches its climax and European officials ponder the implications of the UK's Brexit vote, public discussion of security affairs is largely confined to strategies for combating international terrorism. Both Hillary Clinton and Donald Trump are trying to persuade voters of their superior qualifications to lead this battle, while European leaders scramble to bolster their countries' defenses against homegrown extremists. But though talk of terrorism fills the news media and the political space, it is secondary in the conversations of generals, admirals, and defense ministers: it's not low-level conflict that commands their attention but rather what they call "big wars"—large-scale, high-level conflict with great-power adversaries like Russia and China. Such major conflicts, long considered most unlikely, are now deemed "plausible" by Western military strategists, who claim that urgent steps are needed to deter and, if necessary, prevail in such engagements.

This development, overlooked by the media, has serious consequences, starting with heightened tension between Russia and the West, each eyeing the other in the expectation of a confrontation. More worrying is the fact that many politicians believe that war is not only possible but may break out at any moment—a view that historically has tended to precipitate military responses where diplomatic solutions might have been possible.

The origins of this thinking can be found in the reports and comments of senior military officials (typically at professional meetings and conferences). "In both Brussels and Washington, it has been many years since Russia was a focus of defense planning," but that "has now changed for the foreseeable future," states one such report, summarizing the views at a workshop organized in 2015 by the Institute of National Strategic Studies (INSS), a branch of the US National Defense University. The report says that as a result of Russian aggression in Crimea and eastern Ukraine, many defense experts "can now envision a plausible pathway to war," and this, in turn, "has led defense planners to recognize the need for renewed focus of the possibility of confrontation and conflict with Moscow."[1]

"A Return to Great Power Competition"

Such a conflict would be most likely to occur on NATO's eastern front, encompassing Poland and the Baltic states, and would be fought with high-tech conventional weapons. But these planners also postulate that it could encompass Scandinavia and the Black Sea region and might escalate into the nuclear realm. So US and European strategists are calling for a buildup of Western military capabilities in all of these regions and for moves to enhance the credibility of NATO's tactical nuclear options.[2] A recent article in the *NATO Review* calls for the increased inclusion of nuclear-capable aircraft in future NATO military exercises, to create uncertainty in Russian minds about the point at which NATO commanders might order nuclear strikes to counter any Russian breakthrough on the eastern front (and presumably deter such an assault).[3]

This way of thinking, though confined until recently to military academies and think tanks, has begun to shape government policy in significant and alarming ways. We see this in the new US defense budget, in decisions adopted at the NATO summit in July 2016, and in the UK's decision to renew the Trident nuclear missile program.

---

1   Paul Bernstein, "Putin's Russia and US Defense Strategy," Workshop Report, Institute for National Strategic Studies (INSS), National Defense University (NDU), August 19–20, 2015.

2   See Alexander Mattelaer, "The NATO Warsaw Summit: How to Strengthen Alliance Cohesion," Strategic Forum, INSS/NDU, June 2016.

3   Camille Grand, "Nuclear Deterrence and the Alliance in the 21st Century," *NATO Review*, July 4, 2016.

US defense secretary Ash Carter said the new budget "marks a major inflection point for the Department of Defense." Whereas the department had been focused in recent years "on large-scale counter-insurgency operations," it must now prepare for "a return to great power competition," possibly involving all-out conflict with a "high-end enemy" such as Russia or China. These countries, Carter declared, "are our most stressing competitors," possessing advanced weapons that could neutralize some US advantages. To overcome this challenge, "we must have—and be seen to have—the ability to impose unacceptable costs on an advanced aggressor that will either dissuade them from taking provocative action or make them deeply regret it if they do."[4]

In the short term, this will require urgent action to bolster US capacity to counter a potential Russian assault on NATO positions in Eastern Europe. Under its European Reassurance Initiative, the Pentagon will spend $3.4 billion in fiscal 2017 to deploy an extra armored combat brigade in Europe and to pre-position the arms and equipment for yet another brigade. To bolster US strength over the long term, there would be greater US spending on high-tech conventional weapons needed to defeat a high-end enemy, such as advanced combat aircraft, surface ships and submarines. Carter noted that, on top of this, "the budget also invests in modernizing our nuclear deterrent."[5] It's hard not to be struck by echoes of the Cold War.

The final communiqué adopted by the NATO heads of state and government in Warsaw on July 9, 2016, is also reminiscent of this era.[6] Coming just a few days after the Brexit vote, the NATO summit drowned out any concerns over disarray in Europe with a stentorian anti-Russian attitude. "Russia's recent activities and policies have reduced stability and security, increased unpredictability and changed the security environment," says the communiqué. As a result, NATO remains "open to political dialogue"; however, it must not only suspend "all practical civilian and military cooperation" with Russia but also take steps to enhance its "deterrence and defense posture."

Of the steps taken at the summit to implement this commitment, the most important is to deploy, in rotation, multinational combat battalions

---

4   US Department of Defense, Remarks by Secretary Carter on the Budget at the Economic Club of Washington, DC, February 2, 2016.

5   Secretary of Defense Ash Carter, Submitted Statement—Senate Appropriations Committee–Defense (FY 2017 Budget Request), April 27, 2016.

6   NATO, Warsaw Summit Communiqué, Warsaw, July 9, 2016.

in Poland and the three Baltic republics, with the US, UK, Canada, and Germany each assuming leadership of one unit. These deployments are notable because they represent the first semi-permanent garrison of NATO forces on the territory of the former Soviet Union and imply that any skirmish with Russian forces in the Baltic region could trigger a full-scale (possibly nuclear) war.

It became clear that nuclear escalation is still a very real consideration in the minds of Western leaders soon after the NATO summit, when Britain's new prime minister Theresa May, in her first major parliamentary appearance after assuming office, won a vote on July 18 to preserve and enhance the Trident nuclear missile program. "The nuclear threat has not gone away," she told Parliament. "If anything, it has increased."[7] On this basis, she asked British lawmakers to approve a multiyear £41 billion ($53 billion) plan to maintain and modernize the UK's fleet of missile-carrying submarines.

Analyzing the Other's Moves

When explaining the need to prepare for a major war against a high-end enemy, US and European analysts usually point to Russian aggression in Ukraine and Chinese adventurism in the South China Sea.[8] Western military moves, it is claimed, are an undesired but necessary reaction to provocations by others. But probe more deeply into the thinking of senior leaders and a different picture emerges. Running throughout this discussion is a pervasive anxiety that the world has changed in significant ways, and that the strategic advantages once possessed by the West are slipping away as other powers gain increased military and geopolitical leverage. In this new era—"a time of renewed great power competition," as Carter put it—the US's military might no longer appears as formidable as it once did, while the military capabilities of rival powers appear increasingly potent.

When speaking of Russia's moves in Crimea and eastern Ukraine, Western analysts highlight what they view as the illegal nature of the Russian intervention. But their real concern is over evidence that Russian

---

7   Quoted in Stephen Castle, "Britain's New Leader Votes to Renew Nuclear Program," *New York Times*, July 19, 2016.

8   See Didier Cormorand, "For a Fistful of Rocks," *Le Monde diplomatique* (July 2016).

investment in enhanced military capabilities over the past decade is beginning to bear fruit. Whereas Western observers largely dismissed the Russian forces in the wars in Chechnya and South Ossetia as substandard, those deployed in Crimea and Syria are believed to be well equipped and high quality. "Russia has made significant strides in developing the capability to use force effectively," noted the INSS report.

Western observers have also been impressed by the growing strength and effectiveness of the Chinese military. China's ability to convert low-lying reefs and atolls in the South China Sea into islands capable of housing substantial military installations has surprised and alarmed US military officials, who had long viewed the area as an American lake. Although the US still enjoys air and naval superiority in the region, these bold moves suggest that China has become a significant military competitor and a growing future challenge.

Under these circumstances, strategists see no option but to acquire capabilities that will enable the US to retain a significant military advantage over all potential rivals for decades and prevent them from imposing their will on the international system and undermining vital US interests. And this means emphasizing the big-war threats that justify lavish spending on the super-sophisticated weapons needed to defeat a high-end enemy.

Of the $583 billion in Carter's February US defense budget, $71.4 billion will be allocated to research and development on new, advanced weapons—an amount greater than the entire defense budget of all but a few other countries. "We have to do this," Carter said, "to stay ahead of future threats in a changing world, as other nations try to catch on to the advantages that we have enjoyed for decades, in areas like precision-guided munitions, stealth, cyber and space."[9]

Expenditure on Advanced Arms

Besides these research efforts, mammoth sums will be spent on the acquisition of advanced weapons intended to overcome Russian and Chinese defensive systems and bolster US military capabilities in potential areas of conflict, such as the Baltic and the western Pacific. Some $12 billion will be spent over the next five years on preliminary development of

9   US Department of Defense, remarks by Secretary Carter on the budget.

the B-21 Long-Range Strike Bomber, a stealth aircraft capable of carrying thermonuclear weapons and designed to penetrate Russia's heavily defended airspace. To counter Chinese gains in the Pacific, the Pentagon will acquire additional *Virginia*-class submarines and *Burke*-class guided missile destroyers, and begin deployment of the Terminal High-Altitude Area Defense (THAAD) system in South Korea—an antimissile system meant to defend against attacks from North Korea, but which could also bring down Chinese missiles.

A President Clinton or Trump would put their own stamp on military policy. But it is highly unlikely that the current emphasis on planning for a major conflict with Russia and/or China will disappear, no matter who wins the election. Clinton already has the support of many neocons, who consider her more trustworthy than Trump and more hawkish than Obama. Trump has repeatedly stated his determination to rebuild the US's "depleted" military capability, and has chosen former generals as key foreign policy advisers. He has largely focused on the fight against ISIS, and said that "if our country got along with Russia, that would be a great thing." But he has also expressed concern that China is "building a ... fortress in the South China Sea" and has emphasized the need to invest in new weapons systems more than Obama has done, or Clinton during her time in government.[10]

So should we expect military posturing and muscle flexing in highly contested areas like Eastern Europe and the South China Sea to become the new normal, with a risk of accident, miscalculation and unintended escalation? The US, Russia, and China have all signaled that they will deploy more forces in these areas, in more frequent and elaborate military exercises. Any of these could produce an accidental clash between the major powers, precipitating an uncontrolled chain of events culminating in full-scale war.

An equally dangerous outcome is the growing militarization of international relations, with the major powers more inclined to threaten military action than to resolve disputes at the negotiation table. This is not unprecedented: Christopher Clark's *The Sleepwalkers* and other accounts of 1914 describe how European leaders were induced by military officers to favor armed over diplomatic responses to perceived affronts, hastening the onset of mass slaughter.

---

10   Maggie Haberman and David E. Sanger, "Donald Trump Expounds on His Foreign Policy Views," *New York Times*, March 26, 2016.

Although military thinkers in the West have embraced the big-war approach with particular enthusiasm, this outlook has powerful advocates in Russia and China—actions on both sides tend to reinforce the arguments made by their military thinkers. It is clear that the problem is not East or West, but rather the shared assumption that a full-scale war between the major powers is entirely possible and requires urgent military preparations. Only by repudiating this assumption—by demonstrating how such preparations more often precipitate than discourage the outbreak of conflict—will it be possible to eliminate the risk of unintended escalation and improve the chances for success in overcoming other urgent dangers.

PART FOUR
Battlefield Ukraine

15

An Avoidable War?

Susan Watkins

The remorseless shelling of the cities; the bodies unburied in the streets; the terrified refugees, atrocities, grief; the blackened, smoldering ruins; in Ukraine, after two months of fighting, the UN reports nearly two thousand verified civilian deaths, a number certain to rise, perhaps tenfold or more. The horrors of the Russian invasion have dominated the news for weeks, galvanizing an international upsurge of solidarity, at once antiwar—to halt and reverse Moscow's murderous advance—and pro-escalation: calls to quicken the stream of Javelins, drones, and Stinger missiles into a torrent of bombers and fighter jets; at the limit, for the US Air Force to bomb Russian airfields and impose a no-fly zone. Twitter is alight with blue and yellow flags. Hundreds of millions in charitable donations are flowing to help the refugees, matched by the unending columns of trucks heading east with fresh munitions.

It's worth pausing here to register the proportionality of scale and response. Even as Russian forces bombard Ukrainian cities, the Ethiopian army is shelling Tigray, under military blockade for a year, cut off from electricity, food and medical supplies, with an estimated 50,000–100,000 deaths from direct killings, plus 150,000–200,000 more from starvation. So, too, in Yemen, children are dying of cholera in ruined towns after seven years of near-perpetual air strikes and shelling by the Saudi-UAE coalition, with US–UK support. Casualties are estimated at around 260,000 direct and indirect deaths. That world responses have been in inverse proportion to fatalities scarcely needs saying. Yemen gets hand-wringing UN reports, the odd inside-page headline of a short-lived ceasefire; Tigray and its surrounding regions are cast in outer darkness.

If Russia's invasion looms larger in Western consciousness, one reason is the scale of media coverage. In the Ukraine war's first month, the major US networks devoted 562 minutes of airtime to the conflict, over a third of their news coverage. This compared to 306 minutes for the first month of the US invasion of Afghanistan, 414 minutes for the US–UK invasion of Iraq, and 345 minutes for the US exit from Kabul in August 2021.[1] Density of coverage has combined with empathy of viewpoint. For once, this is not a NATO war, but—metonymically speaking—a Russian war against NATO. For the first time since the 1990s, the Western media is embedded on the side of the victims, the defenders. It provides a global platform for Zelensky as their leader, an eloquent emblem of the Ukrainian resistance. Few in the West can summon up the image, engraved in local memory, of an Afghan wedding blasted to carnage by US bombs, or picture the gruesome reprisals by Anglo-American troops in their siege and subjugation of Fallujah. The bodies on Bucha's streets remain imprinted on the screen.

A single narrative, implicit in news reports and explicit in editorial comment, drives the media coverage. This is an unprovoked Russian attack in which, contrary to Putin's declarations, NATO's eastward enlargement played no part. For the *New York Times*, it is "an unprovoked invasion," for the *Financial Times*, a case of "naked and unprovoked aggression," for the *Guardian*, "an unprovoked assault." "Russia's president has launched an unprovoked assault on his neighbor," agreed the *Economist*. "He has come to believe that NATO threatens Russia and its people"—"he is obsessed with the defensive alliance to his west."[2]

Sustaining the argument that NATO expansionism played no part in the crisis required some casuistic contortions on the part of the broadsheet

---

1   Jim Lobe, "Networks Covered the War in Ukraine More Than the US Invasion of Iraq," *Responsible Statecraft*, April 8, 2022.

2   Editorial Board, "No Justification for a Brazen Invasion," *New York Times*, February 23, 2022; Editorial Board, "Putin Opens a Dark New Chapter in Europe," *Financial Times*, February 24, 2022; "The *Guardian* View on Putin's War in Ukraine: A Bleak New Beginning," *Guardian*, February 24, 2022; "History Will Judge Putin Harshly for His War," *Economist*, February 26, 2022.

press. "Analysts and historians will long debate whether Mr. Putin's griev-ances had bases in fact, whether the United States and its allies were too cavalier in expanding NATO, whether Russia was justified in believing that its security was compromised. There will also be heated questioning over whether Mr. Biden and other Western leaders could have done more to assuage Mr. Putin," admitted the *New_York Times*. "The wisdom of NATO's post–Cold War enlargement to the east will be debated in years to come," the *Financial Times* agreed, while insisting that, contrary to Kremlin claims, the West had never given any guarantees that this would not happen; that enlargement anyway responded to requests from the ex–Warsaw Pact countries; and that in any case, despite the fact that NATO had announced Ukraine's forthcoming membership in 2008, it was not on a path to join, even if the Western powers had encouraged the country "to integrate more closely with their institutions."[3]

Here a second line of argument blends with the first. On the hallowed principle of sovereign national self-determination, Ukraine has every right to elect to join NATO, taking its place within a defensive alliance of liberal democracies. That Putin disagrees merely demonstrates his autocratic hatred for democracy. Opinions diverge on Biden's policy of staying out of the war, while arming Ukraine and pressing Europe to join in punitive sanctions on Russia. If none have gone so far as the *New York Times*, which has acclaimed Biden as "the resolute face of the world's premier democracy and most powerful nation," managing the crisis "with toughness, patience, resolve and dignity," no major Western news outlet is pressing for an immediate ceasefire and a negotiated settlement.[4] The only question is how far to escalate.

Armed for Victory

Putin's lurch to war, disastrous for Russia as well as for Ukraine, is unjustifiable. But it was not unprovoked. NATO enlargement has been an aggressive operation and Moscow has always been in its sights. In calling for a stable settlement of military borders, the Kremlin has a good case. From its foundation in 1949, NATO was always an offensive, not a

---

3 "No Justification for a Brazen Invasion," *New York Times*; "Putin Opens a Dark New Chapter," *Financial Times*.

4 Ibid.

defensive, enterprise, whose ultimate objective in American eyes was the restoration of a normal capitalism in the Soviet bloc.

After the Second World War, if two colossi faced off against each other, as Isaac Deutscher put it, the US had emerged strengthened from the global conflict, "in full-blooded vigor," while the Soviet Union lay almost prostrate, bled white, with over 20 million dead; its army rapidly demobilized from 11 million troops to under 3 million, and struggled to remobilize in 1949. The initial moves to rearmament came from the West—as did the initial purge of elected Communist deputies from the postwar governments in Italy and France; Stalin was following suit when he ejected anticommunists from the coalition governments in Eastern Europe and instituted one-party rule.[5] But NATO was always a political and hegemonic project as well as a military alliance. While West Germany, America's chief trophy of the War, lay defenseless and disarmed, Britain and France, faced with the loss of their empires, were concluding their own security alliances in the treaties of Dunkirk and Brussels. This was the context for Washington's move to turn the North Atlantic Treaty signatories into an "Organization," a multinational military structure that would arm Western Europe against communism and, at the same stroke, bring it under American supreme command. The armies of the member states did not add much to US firepower, but their territories offered forward emplacements for US planes and missiles, four thousand miles to its east, and NATO command-and-control systems penetrated deep into their military structures. The European lefts opposed this remilitarization from the start. Social democratic Sweden balked at joining. The Spanish left fought hard for a No vote in the NATO referendum after Franco's death. In the early eighties, a pan-European movement of movements mobilized against Reagan's cruise and Pershing missiles in the final spurt of the Cold War arms race that accelerated the Soviet Union's demise.

---

5   Isaac Deutscher, "Myths of the Cold War," in *Containment and Revolution: Western Policy towards Social Revolution, 1917 to Vietnam*, ed. David Horowitz (London: Blond, 1967), pp. 13–25. The shooting war against Communism had already begun in Greece—Churchill and Truman slaughtering the anti-Nazi partisans of EAM-ELAS from 1945—and the political campaign to remove elected Communist deputies from postwar governments in Italy and France was completed in 1947. It was only after this that Stalin evicted the anticommunists from coalition governments in Eastern Europe—often posited as the aggressive move to which NATO was the defensive response—and instituted single-party police states, executing independent-minded socialists in spectacles such as the Slánský trial and putting an end to the Bolsheviks' hopes that socialist societies in Europe would be able to develop on a higher plane than backward Russia.

If, as the claim goes, NATO won the Cold War without firing a single shot, this indicates the plethora of military, political, and economic instruments which the US had—and still has—to hand, rather than the pacific nature of the alliance. The Cold War was fought on the American side by sustained support for West European capital, covert operations, ideological offensives, and a ferocious arms race, as well as proxy and overt wars in the Third World, political and military backing for dictatorships to crush local left forces, and the diplomatic coup of Nixon's China policy.[6] Although NATO was primed for a hot war in Europe, it never had to be put to use.

After the Cold War, NATO's political and hegemonic drive came to the fore; its targeting of Moscow was more residual. In principle, the liberalization of Russia should have made it fittable into the "common European home." But Russia is not a conventional nation-state.[7] The largest country in the world, with a population nearly twice that of Germany, it dwarfed the other EU members, while its nuclear capacity towered over that of France and Britain. Besides, the prospect of a united, sovereign Europe risked marginalizing Washington. With the collapse of Communism, the menace from the east that had justified US command over the continent disappeared, and the possibility emerged of Western Europe forging independent relations with its eastern half; and of a newly powerful Germany reordering the region according to its own designs, as Kohl would immediately begin to do in Yugoslavia.

Sovereign Self-Determination?

It was in part to maintain its strategic hegemony over Berlin that Washington engineered the expansion of NATO from 1990, first into the GDR, then the Visegrád states, the Balkans, and the Baltics. For the US to command Europe still involved dividing it against Russia, and in the countries subjugated under the Warsaw Pact it found eager recruits. Brussels would also admit these countries into the European Union, but this was not just a slower and more expensive process; crucially, it

6 The NATO nuclear strategy known as "massive retaliation" in fact envisaged massive anticipatory and pre-emptive strikes: Richard Betts, *American Force: Dangers, Delusions, and Dilemmas in National Security* (New York: Columbia University Press, 2012), p. 43.

7 Perry Anderson, "Incommensurate Russia," *New Left Review* II:94 (July–August 2015), p. 42.

did not include the US. NATO was a vehicle for extending American power deep into Europe, creating a corridor of Atlanticist powers in between Germany and Russia. Enlarging NATO was cheap and easy, as the ex-Comecon countries were suing for admission, and Clinton and Bush could discount the Article Five commitment to defend them, given Russia's post-Soviet *écrasement*.

Here began the myth of NATO as a political club for democracies, which a country like Ukraine might freely elect to join on the principle of self-determination. But on several counts, this is wishful thinking. First, democracy has proved dispensable for NATO, where the governing logic remains that of a hegemon's military instrument. NATO's long-standing southeastern pillars, Greece and Turkey, remained in place under ferocious military dictatorships—and in Ankara's case, despite its extinction of democratic will in Cyprus. Second, to join NATO is precisely to surrender sovereign self-determination to external military command—the reason de Gaulle pulled France from NATO integration. There may be a case for small countries, knowing themselves to be prey, to surrender their sovereignty to a greater power in exchange for protection; the weak do what they must. But those proposing it for Ukraine should be frank about what is entailed: not the exercise of sovereign self-determination but its abrogation, and a willingness to see Ukrainian territory become a militarized front line against its giant neighbor. Third, the era of cost-free NATO enlargement has come to an end. Whatever the outcome of the 2022 war for Ukraine, its price tag will be unignorable.

Nor was NATO ever a merely political project. Even as it expanded in the new unipolar world, it was repurposed as a military posse for the global sheriff, fighting hot wars in Yugoslavia, Afghanistan, and Libya, with upgraded munitions, logistics, and command structures. Neither NATO's vast real-estate footprint—its "dignified" component, the sprawling glass palace outside Brussels; its "efficient" military HQ in Norfolk, Virginia, and forty-odd major bases—nor the third-rate European politicians (Stoltenberg, etc.) who serve as civilian figureheads for its burgeoning bureaucracy, or the pomp of the US Supreme Allied Command Europe—should be hypostasized. NATO remains one of many American instruments, and not the fastest or most flexible. It serves as multilateral cover for some US operations, but has been dispensable in others, like the invasion of Iraq.

Yet post-Soviet Moscow remained a constant NATO target. The Kremlin's grand strategy was to offer Washington significant if not invariable assistance—logistics for the occupation of Afghanistan, pressure on Iran to forgo nuclear arms, collaboration with Israel to keep Syrian Islamists out of power—and expect in return due respect for it as a great power, with its own version of the kind of regional sensitivity the US has historically displayed in the Caribbean. But as Atlanticist commentators were quick to point out, this was not just a presumptuous overestimate of its standing in the world, but an outdated conception of the interstate order. The self-evident principle of the "international community" obtaining since 1991 was the leadership of a single superpower, not a collection of equals. To claim a say in determining where NATO's advance should stop was as good as trying to give orders to Washington. Hence the contemptuous responses to Putin at Munich in 2007 and Bucharest in 2008—where Putin, naively, was offering transport for what would become Obama's surge in Afghanistan—at which Ukraine and Georgia were slated for entry into NATO.[8]

The Kremlin's response to these humiliations became an increasingly unstable compound of a rationalist defensive sovereignty, the case put to stronger powers, and a tyrannical expansionism, threatened for weaker ones—expressive of what Lenin denounced as Great Russian chauvinism.[9] This had been on full display in Putin's subjugation of Chechnya as he

---

8   The Russian paper *Kommersant* published an insider report of the Bucharest summit in its edition of April 7, 2008, speculating on the links between Moscow's assistance in transporting NATO cargo to Afghanistan and the NATO Membership Action Plans for Georgia and Ukraine.

9   Lenin's account of class-conscious national feeling remains the best antidote to chauvinisms great and small. "Is a sense of national pride alien to us?" he asked of Russia's revolutionary socialists in the opening months of the First World War. "Certainly not! We love our language and our country, and we are doing our very utmost to raise *her* toiling masses (i.e., nine-tenths of *her* population) to the level of a democratic and socialist consciousness. To us it is most painful to see and feel the outrages, the oppression and the humiliation that our fair country suffers at the hands of the tsar's butchers, the nobles and the capitalists ... We are full of a sense of national pride, and for that very reason we *particularly* hate *our* slavish past (when the landed nobility led the peasants into war to stifle the freedom of Hungary, Poland, Persia and China), and our slavish present, when these selfsame landed proprietors, aided by the capitalists, are loading us into a war in order to throttle Poland and the Ukraine, crush the democratic movement in Persia and China, and strengthen the gang of Romanovs, Bobrinskys and Purishkeviches, who are a disgrace to our Great-Russian national dignity. Nobody is to be blamed for being born a slave; but a slave who not only eschews a striving for freedom but justifies and eulogizes his slavery (e.g., calls the throttling of Poland and the Ukraine, etc., a 'defense of the fatherland' of the Great Russians)—such a slave is a lickspittle and a boor, who arouses a legitimate feeling of indignation, contempt and loathing": V. I. Lenin, "On the National Pride of the Great

ascended to the presidency in 2000.[10] In 2008 a massive show of firepower to defend the micro-states on Georgia's borders against Saakashvili's incursions left Tbilisi limping away.

This volatile combination of defensive and aggressive postures runs through Putin's political writings, which contain a weird admixture of conventional attempts to strike a partner's deal with the United States and neo-tsarist bullying of small states. The thuggery—in Chechnya, his generals deployed *kontraktniki* soldiers, recruited from Russia's prisons—speaks to the Petersburg milieu in which Putin rose up, while the expansionist motif has historically been a constitutive feature of the Russian state.[11] But the Frankensteins who colluded with the fraudulent 1993 referendum that implanted a hyper-presidential constitution in the heart of post-Soviet Russia, and who oversaw the shock therapy and crash privatizations which set it beating, hail from Clinton's State Department, Rubin's Treasury and Harvard Square.

Streets of Kiev

The catalyst of the present crisis was the 2014 Maidan uprising in Ukraine. The overthrow of Yanukovych, after sniper fire against peaceful protesters galvanized an uprising against him, saw US State Department officials in Kiev actively choosing members of the new government. Putin's reaction was to annex Crimea.[12] That was not a Chechnya *redux*. Lacking bloodshed and probably enjoying majority support, it was visibly unlike the

Russians," *Sotsial-Demokrat* 35 (December 12, 1914), in *Collected Works*, vol. 21 (Moscow: Progress Publishers, 1974), pp. 102–3.

10   See Tony Wood's incisive account in "The Case for Chechnya," *New Left Review* II:30 (November–December 2004), at a time when many of those now baying for Putin's blood studiously looked away, or merely tut-tutted, Clinton actually celebrating the "liberation of Grozny," and Blair rushing to Moscow to congratulate Putin on his election victory.

11   Georgi Derluguian, "Recasting Russia," *New Left Review* II:12 (November–December 2001), and "A Small World War," *New Left Review* II:128 (March–April 2021).

12   The general belief has been that Yanukovych's security forces opened fire on the protesters, even though the gatherings were starting to wind down. Yet what to date seems to be the only extensive examination of witness testimony, video footage, forensic examinations and ballistic evidence argues the sniper fire of February 20, 2014, came from buildings held by the far right. See Ivan Katchanovski, "The Maidan Massacre in Ukraine: Revelations from Trials and Investigation," paper presented at the International Council for Central and East European Studies, Concordia University, Montreal, August 2021; and

famously ruthless annexations of East Timor, Northern Cyprus, Western Sahara, and East Jerusalem, all condoned without tremor by the "international community." But for Obama, the loss of Crimea was a direct blow to the authority of the regime installed in Kiev and hence the will of the West. Sanctions were imposed on Putin's associates and Russian businesses, costing the country some $170 billion by mid-2016, with another $400 billion lost in a precipitate fall of oil and gas prices after 2014, sometimes held to have been engineered by Washington through Riyadh.

Covert fomenting and arming by Moscow of breakaway "republics" in the Donbas, following its takeover of Crimea, was from the start another matter, leading to a bloody civil war within Ukraine. In military terms, it would in due course be outmatched by a concerted US military training and armament program. In 2016 Obama redoubled American military aid and appointed John Abizaid, the commanding general in Iraq during the early years of its occupation, as senior adviser to Ukraine's minister of defense in a planned five-year partnership. Abizaid's executive officer, a veteran of special-forces operations in Kosovo, Afghanistan, and Iraq, has described the American makeover of a "decrepit" Ukrainian military into a professionalized Western army, with US-organized command-and-control systems, operations planning, IT, and logistical infrastructures, plus significant antiaircraft capability. As Stephen Kotkin would rejoice in the *Times Literary Supplement*, Ukraine might not be in NATO, but NATO was in Ukraine.[13]

Since 2013, every move Russia has made on the Ukrainian front has been jujitsued by the combination of Kiev's radicalized ruling bloc—the amalgam of Westernizing liberals with radical nationalists, both powering the country in the same direction—and the growing flood of US money, arms, and military training.[14] The 2015 Minsk peace accords, representing an advance for Russia in the Donbas but also a possible exit from militarization, were undermined by the Obama "surge." Neither Obama nor Trump had any interest in the accords; absent American will, France and

---

"The Hidden Origin of the Escalating Ukraine–Russia Conflict," *Canadian Dimension*, January 22, 2022, which have yet to be rebutted.

13 Stephen Kotkin, "Freedom at Stake: How Did Russia and the West Fall Out?," *Times Literary Supplement*, March 11, 2022. See also the interview with Col. Liam Collins, Radio Free Europe/Radio Liberty, March 23, 2022; "Who Are you, General John Abizaid?," *Ukrinform*, September 14, 2016.

14 Volodymyr Ishchenko, "Towards the Abyss," *New Left Review* II:133/134 (January–April 2022).

Germany failed to push them forward. Putin's grandstanding mobilization on Ukraine's borders from November 2021 was dismissed by Biden, who could no doubt have prevented an invasion had he been willing to negotiate a serious agreement on military frontiers. According to the latest US intelligence accounts, Putin only made the final decision on the invasion at the start of February—throwing the dice on a "small victorious war," as Nicholas II's minister said of the 1904 Russo-Japanese debacle—six weeks after Blinken had metaphorically torn up his negotiating drafts.[15]

The result has been an explosive lurch into a vengeful adventurism, proclaiming war aims that are a grim satire of Washington's justifications in Kosovo and Bush-Blair's in Iraq—stopping genocide, demilitarizing, and saving the population from despotism with regime change. The Kremlin's catastrophically misjudged invasion has generalized the bad-jujitsu logic. Moscow has succeeded in uniting Ukraine on a pro-West, nationalist basis and tightening Washington's hold over Berlin. Fukuyama sees new light on world history's liberal horizon, as regime change in Russia comes into view.

America's Proxy War

In Ukraine, Obama's erstwhile director of the CIA has candidly explained, the US is fighting a proxy war with Russia.[16] In such a conflict, the war aims of the great power and those of its proxy may not coincide. For the Ukrainian leadership, the goal is to expand the war in order to end it faster—with the imposition by the US or NATO of a no-fly zone, knocking out Russian jets and air defenses to relieve the pressure on Ukrainian fighters and citizens. Already NATO steel and popular courage have altered the course of the war in Kiev's favor, at a price of high devastation and mounting Ukrainian casualty rates.

For the Biden administration, on the other hand, the strategic logic could be to keep the Russians pinned down as long as possible, or at least until Putin is ousted from the Kremlin. Putin has blundered into a bear trap, and for the time being it suits the US to keep him there. Brave

---

15   James Risen, "US Intelligence Says Putin Made a Last-Minute Decision to Invade Ukraine," *Intercept*, March 11, 2022.

16   Leon Panetta on Bloomberg TV: "It's a proxy war with Russia, whether we say so or not." March 17, 2022. See also Jeremy Scahill, "The US Has Its Own Agenda against Russia," *Intercept*, April 1, 2022.

Ukrainians make perfect proxy forces, and every Russian atrocity broadens the case for regime change in Moscow. While Zelensky has suggested that saving lives is more important than land—"ultimately it's just territory"— North Atlantic war-gamers like Lawrence Freedman speak of the need to take back the Donbas, if not Crimea.[17] In Europe, the price of a longer war has been lowered for the time being, thanks to Biden's deal with Scholz to keep Russia's oil and gas flowing to German homes and plants. In the US, higher wheat prices will benefit the politically sensitive Midwest. Russian cyber operations have so far failed to materialize.

Putin's war aims demonstrate the same compound of the rational and the delusional that drove him forward. Had he wanted simply to reinforce the need for serious negotiations on a forward boundary for US arms, an Israeli-style blitz on the military infrastructure the NATO powers have been constructing in Ukraine would have sufficed to send the message, avoiding civilian casualties. Instead, his initial move—premised on a lightning-strike regime change, backed by a display of infantry shock-and-awe—was fatally based on FSB fantasies of a non-existent Ukraine. Russia now appears to be trying to regroup and dig in, besieging, one by one, the grimy Ukrainian-held cities of the Donbas. In doing so, it continues to play into Washington's hands.

The most thoughtful critical writing on the war—by Anatol Lieven and Keith Gessen, for example; as well as some of the powerful experiential work published by Gessen and his colleagues in the online *n+1*—is most alive to the tragedy that this onslaught of Great Russian chauvinism is inflicting on the breadth and richness of Russian culture itself. To bomb Kharkov or, if it comes to that, Odessa in the name of gathering Russian lands makes a nihilistic mockery of the battles fought here in the Second World War—all the more terrible because the missiles are aimed at cultural kith and kin. Lieven has gone further than some of his colleagues at the Quincy Institute in calling for a ceasefire and negotiated settlement, in which sanctions would be lifted and neutrality status for Ukraine agreed. There is no sign that Biden is ready for that.

---

17   Zelensky interview in the *Economist*, March 28, 2022; Lawrence Freedman, "Peace in Ukraine Will Be Elusive Unless One Side Makes a Breakthrough," *Financial Times*, April 1, 2022.

16

Matrix of War

Tony Wood

The Russian invasion of Ukraine on February 24, 2022, launched by the Kremlin after months of rising tensions, quickly generated a flood of casualties and several million refugees, as well as bringing the senseless destruction of cities and towns. A negotiated peace may yet bring it to an end. But amid the continued bombardment of Ukrainian cities by Russian artillery and the ramping up of Western military aid to Ukraine, the possibility remains that the war will continue. With that, the odds of a wider conflagration involving several nuclear-armed states would shorten alarmingly. While it is not yet clear how the war will unfold, the world stands at the threshold of a troubled new period. What follows is an attempt to sketch out the historical matrix from which the present conflict developed, and to identify the possible scenarios that lie ahead.

1

The Kremlin bears the responsibility for unleashing this war and regardless of the outcome will carry a heavy moral burden for the destruction it has already caused. Amid a broad surge of sympathy for Ukraine and condemnation of Putin—briefly expressed in Russia too, by a burst of spontaneous antiwar demonstrations—the drive by the US and its allies to punish and ostracize the current regime has gathered pace. But justifiable outrage and the immediate demands of solidarity with Ukrainians should not be allowed to shut out larger questions of historical responsibility. As the most powerful bloc in a decades-long geopolitical contest over Ukraine, the US and its NATO allies necessarily played a role in shaping the context for the invasion, just as inter-imperial rivalries in the Belle Epoque set the stage for the descent into war in August 1914. Any analysis that confines itself to Russia's actions alone, or that looks no further than the inside of Putin's head, is at best a one-sided delusion, and at worst willfully distorts the facts.

A clear understanding requires us to keep in view three interwoven strands of analysis: first, Ukraine's own internal development and priorities since 1991; second, the advance of NATO and the EU into the strategic vacuum left in Eastern Europe after the end of the Cold War; and third, Russia's trajectory from post-Soviet decline to national reassertion. The clashes and confluences of these three dynamics produced the broader context in which Russia then committed its act of aggression.

2

The war of 2022 is at once the expression and the outcome of longer-term dynamics that have placed Ukraine at the center of rival geopolitical and geo-economic projects: on the one hand a Western-driven tandem of NATO and the EU, seeking to extend the US's strategic dominion and to fold Ukraine into the EU's liberal capitalist architecture; on the other Russian attempts to re-establish a sphere of influence in its "near abroad." The balance of power—military, economic, ideological—between these two projects has been lopsided, to say the least. For much of the 1990s and 2000s, one of them was able to advance unopposed while the other remained little more than a compensatory fantasy, amid Russia's post-Soviet disarray. Yet since the mid-2000s, with Russia's economy revived by natural-resource revenues, these two rival projects have been on a collision course, their fundamental incompatibility increasingly plain.

Since gaining sovereignty in 1991, Ukraine has undergone simultaneous, accelerated processes of state-formation and nation-building, all while attempting to advance its own interests, autonomous of both the West and

Russia. But having tried to balance between Russia and the West in the 1990s and early 2000s, it was thereafter faced with a zero-sum choice. Since 2014—after the annexation of Crimea and especially the ongoing war in the Donbas—the confrontation of the two projects has only intensified, producing a kind of tectonic shearing that has reshaped the Ukrainian polity, its leaders tilting the country firmly in a westward direction even as its eastern territories remained mired in a Russian-sponsored separatist conflict. Putin's invasion of 2022 was designed to shatter this pre-existing political and strategic pattern, to then reshape it to Moscow's specifications. Yet it may only confirm the underlying historical trend, in which Russia's post-Soviet neighbors accelerate away from it, producing precisely the fortified ring of pro-Western states Russian policy has spent years trying to forestall.

3

The consolidation of a fervently pro-Western Ukrainian polity, its stance defined in large measure by the need to resist Russian hostility, is all the more stunning a historical outcome given the country's plural inheritance and its considerable degree of closeness with Russia. In its territorial composition, culture, and demographic profile, the Ukraine that gained independence with the disintegration of the USSR was quite different from, say, the Baltic states, whose territorial outlines had been established after the First World War, and which remained culturally distinct from the rest of the Union. Ukraine's modern-day boundaries, stretching from the historical heartland of Ukrainian nationalism in the west to that of Soviet industrial modernity in the east—from the Baroque cupolas of Lviv to the Constructivist Palace of Industry in Kharkov—are the legacy of both imperial and Soviet pasts.[1] It was the Bolsheviks who, in the wake of the Civil War, defined the contours of the Ukrainian SSR in 1922, bringing together Kiev and the core of medieval Rus' with steppe lands originally conquered by the Romanov Empire in the eighteenth century and the industrializing Donbas. At the beginning and end of the Second World War, further Ukrainian-speaking provinces in the west that had been Hapsburg and then Polish lands were added. In 1954, Crimea—from

---

1   For a balanced historical overview of these epochs, see Orest Subtelny, *Ukraine: A History*, 4th ed. (Toronto: University of Toronto Press, 2009), pp. 201–335 and 348–537.

1921 an autonomous unit within the Russian component of the USSR, its entire Crimean Tatar population deported en masse in 1944—was transferred to the Ukrainian SSR.

Early Soviet policies, in line with Leninist principles on self-determination, had encouraged the use of the Ukrainian language and "indigenization" of state structures; the 1920s also brought a literary and cultural flowering, as nationalist networks previously separated by imperial borders received state sanction. But at the end of the decade, Moscow reversed course and adopted a punitive approach; Ukraine's nationalist intelligentsia was decimated.[2] Thereafter, though the ruling echelons of Communist Ukraine would be Ukrainians, the room for expression of even a Sovietized Ukrainian national identity narrowed considerably. Demographically, while Russian protestations that Ukrainians are their "brother people" have always been both patronizing and self-serving, since tsarist times there has been considerable migration and intermarriage between the two, at all levels of society. If the industrialization of the Ukrainian east involved an influx of Russian speakers, conversely, the colonization of Siberia's agrarian frontier was to a significant extent carried out by Ukrainian peasants. Anatol Lieven has likened Ukrainians' role in the Russian empire to that of the Scots rather than the Irish—except that, in the legal and economic domains, it was "impossible to tell who were the 'colonizers' and who were the 'colonized.'"[3] In this Ukraine differed from the Central Asian and Caucasian Soviet republics, where something closer to a colonial relationship obtained. Across the USSR, Russian had in most cases been the language of high politics, education and social advancement—the medium of Soviet modernization, as Lieven put it—and the bilingualism expected of non-Russians was rarely reciprocated.[4] Here, too, Ukraine differed: by the end of the Soviet era most of Ukraine was genuinely bilingual, with Russian the lingua franca or mother tongue in several of the major cities, and people in Kiev and the central provinces speaking dialects that merged the two.

What Ukraine shared with most other former Soviet republics was

---

2   On both phases see Terry Martin, *The Affirmative Action Empire: Nations and Nationalism in the Soviet Union, 1923–1939* (Ithaca, NY: Cornell University Press, 2001), especially chaps. 2, 3, 6 and 7. Thanks also to Kyle Shybunko for his insights on this period.

3   Anatol Lieven, *Ukraine and Russia: A Fraternal Rivalry* (Washington, DC: United States Institute of Peace Press, 1999), p. 27.

4   Lieven, *Ukraine and Russia*, p. 50.

an economic structure that had been fundamentally geared to be part of an all-union system—and hence one that would be dramatically unbalanced when it became a sovereign unit. Alongside a large agricultural sector, Ukraine possessed the mines and heavy industry of the Donbas, as well as a sizable military sector. Already stagnating by the 1980s, these would be cut adrift by the Soviet collapse, leaving Ukraine scrambling to find new export markets even as it attempted to rebalance its economy, amid a slump still more profound than those besetting other post-Soviet states: GDP contracted by more than 60 percent between 1990 and 1999, and even in 2020 remained at barely half its late Soviet level (in constant prices).[5] Ukraine was also the last of the former Soviet republics to create a permanent currency: the temporary *karbovanets* coupon, introduced in 1992 and then ravaged by hyperinflation, was replaced by the *hryvnia* only in 1996.

These specificities—territorial diversity, a sui generis relationship with Russia, legacies of Soviet economic interdependence—made Ukraine an intrinsically diverse and potentially more divided country than many of its post-Soviet peers. They would place marked constraints on its development during the 1990s.

4

Nationalist movements—above all the Rukh Party—played a prominent role in the Ukrainian drive for sovereignty at the end of the Soviet era, though this was in practice led by a section of the former *nomenklatura*. The December 1991 referendum on independence produced a 91 percent "Yes" vote.[6] Yet this overwhelming mandate had also been premised on the arrival of greater prosperity, and when this failed to materialize, discontent with President Leonid Kravchuk grew. In 1994 it was Leonid Kuchma—a Russian-speaker from Chernihiv, subsequently based in Dnipropetrovsk—who won the presidency by campaigning on a platform of improved ties with Russia and promises of decentralization. However, his margin of victory was narrow—52 percent to Kravchuk's 45—and

---

5   World Bank national accounts data, "GDP (constant 2015 US$)—Ukraine."

6   Figure from Ella Zadorozhniuk and Dmitri Furman, "Ukrainskie regiony i ukrainskaia politika," in *Ukraina i Rossiia: obshchestva i gosudarstva*, ed. Furman (Moscow: Prava cheloveka, 1997), p. 104, table V.

the national totals concealed profound regional imbalances: Kravchuk, a native of Rivne, had scored over 90 percent in some western provinces, while Kuchma almost reversed those figures in the east and south; the center was divided.[7] After the election, decentralization was dropped, and while the institutional momentum of "Ukrainianization" stalled, Kuchma made a point of learning Ukrainian himself.

Kuchma's decade in office, from 1994 to 2005, brought a strategic balancing that both reflected and enshrined the country's internal disparities. As Orest Subtelny put it, "Since the various political forces in the country could not agree on which geopolitical orientation to adopt, all accepted that neutrality, for the time being, was the best option"—codifying Ukraine's "non-bloc status" in legislation and adopting a "multi-vector foreign policy."[8] On the one hand, Kuchma concluded several key treaties with Yeltsin, including a crucial 1997 accord that guaranteed Ukraine's sovereignty and agreed on a division of the Black Sea fleet. In 2000–1 he made deals with Putin on gas pipelines that, among other things, redounded to the benefit of a handful of oligarchic clans, creating a layer of tycoons with a material stake in improved ties with Russia.[9] On the other hand, Kuchma also made many overtures to the West, seeking closer economic links with the EU as well as pursuing cooperation with NATO.[10] It was also Kuchma who dispatched 1,700 Ukrainian troops to take part in the post-invasion "stabilization" of Iraq in 2003.[11]

More than a matter of short-term political expediency, this balancing act was ultimately rooted in the geopolitical and economic dilemmas facing post-Soviet Ukraine: should it seek to integrate with the West, at the risk of semi-permanent demotion to peripheral status, or re-establish links with Russia, at the price of diminished sovereignty or even reincorporation into a refurbished USSR? Ukraine's ambivalent attitude to the Commonwealth of Independent States, jointly created by Yeltsin, Kravchuk, and Stanislav Shushkevich of Belarus in 1991, stemmed largely from fears of the second

---

7   Figures from Zadorozhniuk and Furman, "Ukrainskie regiony i ukrainskaia politika," p. 104.

8   Subtelny, *Ukraine*, p. 598.

9   Yuliya Yurchenko, *Ukraine and the Empire of Capital* (London: Pluto Press, 2018), pp. 75–8.

10   This included a highly provocative joint exercise with US forces off the coast of Crimea in 1997, which prompted anti-NATO protests in the peninsula: Lieven, *Ukraine and Russia*, p. 120.

11   "Kuchma Asks Parliament to Send Troops to Iraq," *Kyiv Post*, June 3, 2003.

of these scenarios. Concerns about the first, meanwhile, drove Kuchma's interest in reviving Ukraine's high-value manufacturing sectors, in order to integrate into the world economy on better terms as well as creating a strong national capitalist class. While the first component of this project was thwarted by continuing economic disaster, the second was realized in the perverse form of oligarchic clans that were the state-designated recipients of a privatization bonanza in the early 2000s.[12]

Nevertheless, Ukraine's trade patterns did rapidly diversify after 1991. While 53 percent of Ukraine's exports went to Russia in 1995, by 2009 only 25 percent did; conversely, Russia went from accounting for 43 percent of Ukraine's imports to only 20 percent over the same period.[13] A portion of the slack was taken up by EU countries: in 1996 these accounted for only 11 percent of Ukrainian exports, but by 2009 their share had risen to 24 percent.[14] These shifts exemplify a broader centrifugal tendency among former Soviet states, each of which forged new trade ties, in many cases virtually from scratch, and correspondingly loosened their economic interdependence with Russia, without yet severing it completely. But the underlying dynamic of dwindling Russian economic influence was clear.

5

Russia's precipitous collapse as a great power in the 1990s was not only the cause of social and economic disaster on the domestic front. It was also the enabling condition for a wholesale strategic realignment of Eastern Europe. The dismantling of the Warsaw Pact was not matched, as the Soviet leadership had naively hoped, by a symmetrical winding down of NATO.[15] On the contrary, the withdrawal of Soviet military power

---

12   Marko Bojcun, *Towards a Political Economy of Ukraine: Selected Essays, 1990–2015* (Stuttgart: Ibidem, 2020), p. 211; and Yurchenko, *Ukraine and the Empire of Capital*, pp. 83–6.

13   Sergei Kulik et al., *Ekonomicheskie interesy i zadachi Rossii v SNG* (Moscow: Institute of Contemporary Development, 2010), p. 97, Prilozhenie 11.

14   Figures from Harvard Atlas of Economic Complexity.

15   "Let's disband both NATO and the Warsaw Pact. Let's release your allies and ours," Soviet foreign minister Eduard Shevardnadze suggested to US secretary of state James Baker in September 1989; quoted in Mary Elise Sarotte, *Not One Inch: America, Russia, and the Making of Post-Cold War Stalemate* (New Haven, CT: Yale University Press, 2021), p. 29.

provided an opportunity that Washington was determined not to pass up. When the US threatened to torpedo the process of German reunification unless it took place within NATO, the Soviets did not insist on neutrality.[16] With Soviet retreat leaving the sole superpower in command of the field, Eastern European leaders were quick to press their cases for NATO membership, the Visegrád Group—the Czech Republic, Hungary, Poland—jointly declaring it their goal in 1992. By 1994 Clinton was announcing on a visit to Poland that the admission of new members to the alliance was "no longer a question of whether, but when and how."[17] The few voices of opposition to NATO expansion in Washington—including George Kennan, architect of containment—were ignored, their concerns over provoking Russia and the hesitation of the US's NATO allies dismissed. Military considerations were set aside on the grounds that "the possibility that Poland or the Czech Republic would actually need defending seemed remote."[18] Indeed the main reason NATO expansion could gather such momentum was precisely because Russia was not a threat. That momentum was sustained into the 2000s: after the Divide as Vise-grád? Group joined in 1999, seven more countries—the Baltic states plus Bulgaria, Romania, Slovakia, and Slovenia—did so in 2004, followed by Albania and Croatia in 2009.

Yet while the expansion was fundamentally premised on Russia's weakness, it also initially required a shield of ambiguity to soften the blow for Moscow, and in particular to avoid harming Yeltsin's 1996 reelection bid. The US pursued a two-track policy in which Russian collaboration with NATO was encouraged but aspirations to actual membership deflected. For Russian strategists, however, the question of NATO's ultimate purpose lingered: if the alliance was not directed against Russia, why shouldn't Russia join it? The aspiration itself stemmed from the prevalence in the foreign-policy thinking of the time of a "Westernizing" line, seeking closer integration with the West and the creation of a common security architecture, "from Vancouver to Vladivostok" in the phrase used in 1991 by the US and German foreign ministers, and echoed by their Russian peer Andrei Kozyrev.[19] This line continued to predominate well into Putin's

---

16   Sarotte, *Not One Inch*, chaps. 2 and 3.
17   Ibid., p. 191; see also James Goldgeier, *Not Whether but When: The US Decision to Enlarge NATO* (Washington, DC: Brookings Institution Press, 1999).
18   Goldgeier, *Not Whether but When*, p. 142.
19   Sarotte, *Not One Inch*, p. 128.

reign. In 2000 he even proposed Russian membership in NATO and reaf-
firmed Russia's place as "part of European culture."[20] Western approval for
his war on Chechnya in 1999 was matched by Russian support for Bush's
"War on Terror" after 9/11. But Russian hopes for a deeper partnership,
let alone a redrawing of the global security architecture, were confounded.
In the second half of the 2000s, indeed, evidence mounted that Russian
and Western interests were fundamentally incompatible—and events in
Ukraine would play a central role both in revealing and in deepening that
incompatibility.

6

The "Orange Revolution" of 2004–5, in which popular protests brought
to power the pro-Western Viktor Yushchenko in place of the Russian-
backed Viktor Yanukovych, set the country on a political path that now
diverged decisively from that of most of its post-Soviet peers. Dmitri
Furman identified a family resemblance between the regimes that came
to power in the early 1990s, labeling them "imitation democracies."[21]
The term referred to a gap between democratic form and antidemocratic
substance, a facade of elections covering the continued hold of a single
"party of power." Yet while Ukraine conformed to this pattern in the
1990s—Kuchma too, like Yeltsin and Kazakhstan's Nazarbaev, faced
down his parliament and managed to impose a new constitution—its
very internal heterogeneity made the maintenance of an undivided ruling
clique impossible. Political life was more varied and contestatory than in
most other parts of the former USSR; Ukraine also experienced a more
polycentric version of the oligarchic enrichment that had taken place
in Russia, producing inter-clan strife with regional overtones that was
readily transferred to the political sphere.[22] The three-way rivalry between
Yushchenko, Yanukovych, and Yulia Tymoshenko—from Sumy, Donetsk
province, and Dnipropetrovsk, respectively—that unfolded in the second
half of the 2000s swiftly dulled the initial euphoria of the Orange Revolution. But oligarchic intrigues aside, genuine political competition became

20   "Putin Says 'Why Not?' to Russia Joining NATO," *Washington Post*, March 6, 2000.
21   Dmitri Furman, *Imitation Democracy: The Development of Russia's Post-Soviet
Political System* (London: Verso, 2022).
22   Bojcun, *Towards a Political Economy of Ukraine*, pp. 137–8.

the norm of civic life in a way that simply did not apply in Russia. This created spaces in which mass mobilizations could potentially tilt the balance at moments of crisis—without, however, fundamentally altering the broader parameters of Ukraine's post-Soviet political economy.

Yushchenko's victory also brought an intensification in the struggle between Western and Russian interests over Ukraine, matched by a heightening of Ukraine's internal political differences. Veering away from Kuchma's strategy of navigating between Russia and the West, Yushchenko enacted a westward lurch, both economically and geopolitically. In 2008, the Ukrainian government began discussions with the EU over what would eventually become an Association Agreement, and joined the EU's Eastern Partnership in 2009. Betting firmly on economic ties with the West, Yushchenko liberalized Ukraine's financial markets and presided over an influx of foreign investment, the total climbing from a net $1.7 billion inflow in 2004 to one of $10.2 billion in 2007 (though this was still modest by regional standards: the equivalent 2007 figure for Poland was $25 billion). But rather than reinvigorating Ukraine's industrial plant, much of the investment flowed into finance and real estate. The share of foreign capital in Ukrainian banking rose from 13 percent in 2004 to over 50 percent in 2009; three-fifths of that share was held by interests from six EU countries, with Russian finance accounting for another fifth.[23]

While GDP growth averaged more than 6 percent between 2004 and 2008, the fruits were unevenly distributed in social and geographical terms. The western provinces, historically impoverished when part of Austria-Hungary and Poland, continued to lag furthest behind: the weight of agriculture in their economies and unemployment levels left them worse off than the center and east, the latter buoyed by demand for coal, coke, and steel.[24] Their prolonged misery was among the preconditions for the nationalist mobilizations of 2014; pro-EU sentiment was in many cases underpinned by a frustrated desire for the better opportunities offered by even the lower rungs of EU labor markets. But while the pro-Western orientation of the government was certainly shared by a large portion of the populace, the eastern provinces remained economically linked as

23 Figures from World Bank national accounts data, "Foreign Direct Investment, Net Inflows (BoP, current US$)"; and Bojcun, *Towards a Political Economy of Ukraine*, pp. 200–1.

24 Bojcun, *Towards a Political Economy of Ukraine*, p. 201; Volodymyr Ishchenko, "Ukraine's Fractures," *New Left Review* II:87 (May–June 2014), pp. 27–35.

well as culturally close to Russia. They remained a sufficiently strong base for Yanukovych to challenge successfully for power in 2010—a reminder both that Ukraine's choice between the rival blocs to east and west had not been definitively decided, and that the choice itself was a dividing factor in Ukrainian domestic politics.

7

Alongside moves to integrate more closely with the EU, Yushchenko stepped up Ukraine's push for full NATO membership. At the time, there was no popular mandate for such a course, and the Ukrainian constitution barred foreign military bases.[25] But the Ukrainian government's aspiration was approved at NATO's Bucharest summit in April 2008, together with that of Georgia. The official communiqué stated flatly that "these countries will become members of NATO."[26] But the process was shorn of an explicit timeline in the face of objections to Ukrainian or Georgian membership from Putin. This was a key turning point, and one where the historically culpable role of the US in driving NATO expansion needs to be emphasized. Sufficiently aware of Russian concerns to hold back from offering Ukraine and Georgia an immediate path to membership, the Bush administration overrode French and German misgivings to insist that the process would advance all the same. This left the two aspirant states in a waiting room, with none of the supposed benefits of membership, while continuing to amplify Russian concerns. Imposed by Washington from the safe distance of five thousand miles, this policy course knowingly placed the populations of Georgia and Ukraine in danger, a shameful strategic calculation for which only non-NATO members have so far been made to pay the price.

NATO's assumption may well have been that Russia would simply have to swallow the next round of expansion as it had previous ones. But Russia's temporary powerlessness to oppose the alliance's growth in the 1990s was not the same as permanent acquiescence, and NATO planners surely foresaw that a reaction of some kind would sooner or later take place. It came barely four months after the Bucharest gathering, in the

25   Rajan Menon and Eugene Rumer, *Conflict in Ukraine: The Unwinding of the Post–Cold War Order* (Cambridge, MA: MIT Press, 2015), p. 39.

26   "Bucharest Summit Declaration," April 3, 2008.

form of the Russo-Georgian War. Though it lasted a matter of days, the August 2008 war set a pattern that would be followed in Ukraine in 2014. Justified by the Kremlin in terms of a humanitarian "responsibility to protect"—turning previous Western rhetoric against it—Russia's intervention effectively solidified internal divisions into "frozen" separatist conflicts that were clearly intended to serve as a block on full NATO membership. At the same time, the Russo-Georgian war highlighted the Kremlin's lack of means of persuasion other than force, which thereafter increasingly became one tool of foreign policy among others—a dangerous lowering of the threshold for the use of military power. Yet while Russia's stance had visibly altered, the broader parameters of US policy remained the same, rendering further clashes all but inevitable.

8

The Maidan protests of 2013–14 and their aftermath crystallized a powerful set of polarizations within Ukrainian politics, in which external economic and geopolitical forces appeared as stark binary choices of an existential kind: the West or Russia, NATO or Putin, the EU versus the Russian-led Eurasian Union, even civilization or barbarism. These oppositions were overlaid onto the country's uneven political, social, and demographic map, amid economic stagnation. After contracting drastically with the onset of the global economic crisis—GDP shrank by 15 percent in 2009—and then briefly rallying, by 2013 growth was flatlining. Economic frustrations were aggravated by the corruption and authoritarian tenor of Yanukovych's rule. The former governor of Donetsk and his associated clan were clearly inclined to favor Russian material interests—and of course to profit from them personally—but negotiations with the EU on an Association Agreement accelerated under Yanukovych, maintaining the country's westward momentum. Yet it was also apparent that many of Ukraine's domestic industries would be greatly damaged by the terms of the Association Agreement, and even some of its oligarchs had reservations, in particular about the incompatibility of closer enmeshment with the EU and continued trade with Russia.[27]

It was Yanukovych's U-turn on signing the agreement in December 2013, followed by harsh repression of the initial Euromaidan protests, that

---

27   Yurchenko, *Ukraine and the Empire of Capital*, pp. 155–6.

sparked the wider revolt that led to his ouster the following February. The Maidan laid bare many of the dysfunctions of the previous system, and at the same time demonstrated how brittle the support for pro-Russian politicians was. With Yanukovych and his ilk in profound discredit, the political stage was soon dominated by pro-Western figures who maneuvered to gain the approval of the Maidan. Yet the apparent consensus on display in the streets of Kiev was far from a nationwide phenomenon, and political developments in the capital opened up a rift with the Russian-speaking east, which the Kremlin then assiduously widened by annexing Crimea and arming separatist forces in the Donbas. These actions did much to confirm Ukrainian nationalists' long-standing claims that Russia posed a threat to their country's territorial integrity. The war in the Donbas and the Crimean annexation also ultimately helped to produce the very outcome they were supposed to avert: the consolidation of a firmly pro-Western Ukraine with growing ties to the EU and NATO.

9

The Ukraine crisis of 2013–14 also marked a watershed for Russia, both in terms of its domestic politics and its international orientation. Externally, its upshot was undoubtedly a geopolitical defeat for the Kremlin, cementing Ukraine's pro-Western orientation and sharpening hostilities with the US and Europe. Internally, however, the annexation of Crimea was trumpeted by the Kremlin as a triumph, returning to the national fold territory it considered "an inseparable part of Russia," as Putin termed it in his March 2014 speech announcing Crimea's incorporation into the Russian Federation.[28] Widely popular at the time, the annexation generated a "Crimean consensus" that enabled Putin easily to weather the ensuing confrontation with the West, the sanctions regime depicted as simply another facet of a broader Western assault on Russia. But the successful establishment of this consensus itself pointed to another crucial development: the new prominence within official ideology and practice of Russian great-power nationalism.

For much of the 1990s, Russian nationalism was the dog that did not bark, confounding predictions that a revanchist politics would emerge

---

28   "Address by President of the Russian Federation," March 18, 2014.

from the humiliations of the USSR's collapse. Part of the reason for this was disarray at the level of the state and profound anomie in society, which made full-blown nationalist mobilizations as unlikely to succeed as any other form of mass politics. But another reason for the initial weakness of Russian nationalism lay in Russia's own status as a multinational federation, in which Russians formed the vast majority—80 percent according to the first post-Soviet census of 2002—alongside scores of other ethnic groups, many of them the "titular nationalities" of autonomous republics or regions. In such a structure, an overtly ethnicized Russian nationalism would be destabilizing. Hence the recourse to distinct terms to refer to ethnic Russians—*russkie*—and citizens of the Russian Federation—*rossiane*—with official statements generally careful to deploy the latter. Putin's colonial war in Chechnya was fought not in the name of ethnic Russian dominance, but of "antiterrorism," a catchall that soon came to connote a broader counter-insurgency across the Muslim North Caucasus, but which was never translated into explicitly national terms.

From 2012 onward, however, and with Putin's return to the presidency, elements of nationalist thinking came increasingly to the fore in Kremlin pronouncements, couched in "civilizational" terms that granted Russia a leading role in the defense of "traditional values" against a liberal onslaught.[29] The crackdown on dissent after the 2011–12 protests often took the form of an internal culture war against antinational elements. It was also a wounded Russian nationalism that was mobilized in the Ukraine crisis of 2013–14, deployed to justify Russian intervention on the side of Russian speakers in the Donbas. The conflation of language and civic belonging this involved was indicative either of a deliberate instrumentalization or a profound misunderstanding: many of Ukraine's Russian speakers considered themselves Ukrainians who happened to speak Russian, rather than essentialized but somehow misplaced Russians. The Donbas war also opened up a more alarming set of possibilities: if Russia was willing to place Ukraine's borders in question in the name of defending "Russians," which other frontiers might be subject to revision, and on what basis?

The new prominence of nationalist motivations in the Kremlin's outlook in itself betokened a broader shift, which the Ukraine crisis of 2013–14

---

29   See Ilya Budraitskis, "Putin Lives in the World That Huntington Built," in *Dissidents among Dissidents: Ideology, Politics and the Left in Post-Soviet Russia* (London: Verso, 2022), pp. 7–11.

both rendered apparent and exacerbated: a decoupling of the economic and territorial logics of Russian power.[30] During the natural-resource boom years of the 2000s, Russia's geopolitical priorities and the interests of its capitalists had been broadly aligned, the projection of power in its "near abroad" compatible with an overseas investment drive by Russian corporations; symptomatic of this close overlap was a 2003 manifesto by Anatoly Chubais, orchestrator of Yeltsin's privatization, calling for Russia to forge a "liberal empire," as "the only, unique and natural" power in the former Soviet lands. In Ukraine, these two logics were intertwined to an unusual extent, notably due to the role of its pipelines in conveying Russian gas to European markets. After 2014, however, the two logics were sundered: the Donbas war brought the physical destruction of many Russian-owned industrial assets, while the Crimean annexation led to Western sanctions that hobbled both inward and outward investment. That the Kremlin deemed these penalties worth enduring indicates the underlying shift in the nature of Russian power.

10

The Maidan protests had been a symptom of a long-running crisis of political representation in Ukraine—a crisis common to all post-Soviet states, but given a particularly polarizing twist in the case of Ukraine by the internal repercussions of the country's status as geopolitical object of external contention.[31] Far from resolving this crisis, however, the course of Ukrainian politics after the Maidan only deepened it, and the country's internal rifts widened still further even as its governments stepped up the country's parallel geopolitical and geo-economic integrations with Washington and Brussels.

Petro Poroshenko, elected in 2014, signed a Deep and Comprehensive Free Trade Agreement with the EU that entered into force in 2016, while the US unlocked massive inflows of aid, some $4 billion between 2014 and

---

30   My analysis here draws on Ilya Matveev, "Between Political and Economic Imperialism: Russia's Shifting Global Strategy," *Journal of Labour and Society* 25:2 (May 2022), pp. 198–219.

31   Here I draw on Volodymyr Ishchenko and Oleg Zhuravlev's analysis of the Maidan and its aftermath as a "deficient revolution": "How Maidan Revolutions Reproduce and Intensify the Post-Soviet Crisis of Political Representation," PONARS *Eurasia Policy Memo* No. 714, October 2021.

2021, of which around $2.5 billion was military aid.[32] US diplomats were closely involved in negotiations over the first post-Maidan transitional governments, and thereafter worked tightly with the Ukrainian military and intelligence apparatus. With GDP shrinking rapidly and the country's debt mounting, Poroshenko also began a drastic neoliberal restructuring through IMF-recommended austerity measures—"It would be sad to waste this crisis," in the words of his Lithuanian-born minister of economy and trade, Aivaras Abromavičius.[33]

But if in these respects the post-Maidan order brought an intensification of pre-existing dynamics, in other areas it represented a clear break with what went before. One of the distinguishing features of post-Maidan political life was the abrupt empowerment of right-wing nationalist movements. Having been the most prominent organized force in the Maidan itself, in its wake they retained a far greater mobilizing capacity than any other tendency. Pro-Western liberals, though solidly anchored in policy circles and NGOs, had no such numerical weight. The latter's weakness was compounded by the lack, as Volodymyr Ishchenko puts it, of an institutionalized political and ideological boundary between the liberal wing of civil society and the far right.[34] This enabled the right to gain a degree of ideological influence and institutional sway out of proportion to their actual numbers and, crucially, to their electoral performance: while parties such as Svoboda slumped at the ballot box, far-right slogans became normalized in public discourse and hard-right paramilitary formations were integrated into the state security apparatus by Interior Minister Arsen Avakov during his seven-year tenure (2014–21). It is this contrast between limited electoral reach and extensive state support, as well as its access to actual weaponry, that has marked the Ukrainian right out from rising neo-fascist tendencies elsewhere.

In the context of the ongoing Donbas war, moreover, the nationalist right's depiction of Ukraine as under permanent assault by its antagonistic neighbor had an obvious resonance. The conflict in the Donbas created a surge of fatalities and mass displacement in its first six months—some

---

32 Congressional Research Service, "Ukraine: Background, Conflict with Russia, and US Policy," October 5, 2021, p. 33; and 2014–21 data from ForeignAssistance.gov.

33 "The American Woman Who Stands between Putin and Ukraine," *Bloomberg Businessweek*, March 5, 2015.

34 See the interview with Volodymyr Ishchenko, "Towards the Abyss," in *New Left Review* II:133/134 (January–April 2022).

four thousand dead on both sides by October 2014, with as many as half a million registered as internally displaced persons in Ukraine and tens of thousands more having fled to Russia—and continued to generate a steady stream of casualties thereafter.[35] By May 2018, civilian casualties totaled some three thousand dead and at least seven thousand injured, though reliable figures were hard to come by; according to one estimate, some two-thirds of the casualties were in the more densely populated separatist-held territories.[36]

The ceasefire agreed at Minsk in February 2015 was notional at best, and was deeply resented by a newly empowered nationalism that saw any accord with Russia as an intolerable imposition at best, treason at worst. At key moments, a significant bloc of public opinion, ranging from liberals to the far right, would mobilize to block moves seen as signaling concessions to Russia. This dynamic in part explains why the constitutional changes stipulated under the Second Minsk Protocol of 2015—decentralizing power and according Donetsk and Luhansk provinces special status— were not enacted either under Poroshenko or his successor, Volodymyr Zelensky, both of whom were elected with sizable mandates for peace.

Zelensky's victory in 2019 exemplified the crisis of representation noted above. His thumping margin in the April runoff—73 percent to Poroshenko's 24—was matched by an avalanche in the legislature in July, where his "Servant of the People" party, named after his hit TV show and only a few months old, won 43 percent of the vote and 254 out of a total 450 seats. Antiestablishment sentiment was a core element of Zelensky's appeal, born of frustration with continuing economic stagnation and oligarchic corruption. But his vows to forge peace in the Donbas and his more conciliatory line toward Russian speakers—Poroshenko had cut off pensions and imposed a ban on trade with the separatist-held areas, as well as restricting the use of Russian in the public sphere—were also central, especially in eastern provinces where he outpolled Poroshenko by even higher margins.

The demise of this platform after Zelensky took office testifies to the powerful combined weight of nationalist and pro-Western impulses within the Ukrainian political system. The lack of boundaries between

---

35   International Crisis Group, "Peace in Ukraine: The Costs of War in Donbas," Report No. 261, September 3, 2020.

36   International Crisis Group, "Nobody Wants Us: The Alienated Civilians of Eastern Ukraine," Report No. 252, October 1, 2018.

liberals and the far right made accusations of "selling out" to Russia an especially effective weapon in internal political battles; though often deployed opportunistically by rival oligarchic clans, it had a nationalist ratchet effect, heightening polarization while shrinking the government's room for maneuver. In October 2019, for example, Zelensky announced his government's acceptance of the "Steinmeier Formula," the technical means previously agreed at Minsk for implementing special status for the separatist entities. Yet this was immediately greeted with protests under the slogan "No to Capitulation" and far-right roadblocks to prevent disengagement at the front line.[37]

If the tenor of politics in Ukraine imposed clear constraints on moves to implement the Minsk accords, conversely it only increased the momentum of the country's westward strategic reorientation. In February 2019, Ukraine's constitution was amended to overturn its "non-bloc" status and assert the "irreversibility of the European and Euro-Atlantic course of Ukraine" and to enshrine a commitment to future NATO membership. At the time, surveys suggested that only around 45 percent of the Ukrainian population supported joining NATO.[38]

The rolling state of militarized crisis after 2014 was a powerful accelerant for the consolidation of a Ukrainian national sense of self that was increasingly defined by the antagonism with its larger neighbor. As in so many previous historical conjunctures, from 2014 onward the processes of Ukrainian nation-building and state-formation were overtaken by external forces and distorted by war.

11

Putin's televised speech of February 21, 2022, intended to legitimate the coming invasion, displayed a characteristic blend of attitudes toward Ukraine. Each played a role in the Kremlin's decision to attack its neighbor; none of them is confined to Putin alone. Conflated in policy and

---

37   Katharine Quinn-Judge, "Peace in Ukraine: A Promise Yet to Be Kept," *ISPI Online*, April 17, 2020.

38   The figure is based on polls taken on either side of the constitutional amendment: 44 percent in December 2018 and 49 percent in May 2019. The numbers are especially striking given that the poll was conducted under the auspices of USAID: "Public Opinion Survey of Residents of Ukraine," Center for Insights in Survey Research, November 6–15, 2021.

practice but analytically distinct, these attitudes are rooted in different layers of thinking within Russia's elite, and their sudden superposition in part explains the mix of rational calculation and imperial overreach behind the invasion.

One layer of thinking is strictly geopolitical, seeing Ukraine as a vital strategic emplacement that no Russian government should willingly cede to NATO. A second layer, drawing on both Soviet-era assumptions and the wellsprings of Russian nationalism, retains the conviction that Ukraine is "not a real country," as Putin supposedly told George W. Bush in 2008. This basic perception of modern-day Ukraine as at best a contingent historical construct is widely shared in Russia, articulated by figures ranging from Gorbachev to Solzhenitsyn, themselves drawing on long imperial precedent.[39] A third set of preconceptions about Ukraine is of more recent vintage, and concerns its status as precisely a related but distinct country that is moving along a different political trajectory from Russia. Where Russia has maintained the system of "imitation democracy," Ukraine has repeatedly overturned it through popular uprisings—the Maidan conjuring the specter of a political disorder that poses a direct threat to the Kremlin's rule. Fourthly, there is the geo-economic status of Ukraine: not only the site of the pipelines ferrying Russian gas to its key European markets, but also the largest potential market for any Russian-led regional economic project.

All of these motivations were collapsed together in the decision to invade. Putin's February 21 speech offered a familiar recapitulation of charges against NATO expansion and Western double standards, as well as a critique of post-Maidan Ukraine's "aggressive nationalism and neo-Nazism," amplifying a pet theme of Russian government-run media. But the bulk was devoted to a lengthy history lesson intended to prove the artificial nature of Ukraine's current frontiers. Putin directed particular fury at Lenin and at the Bolsheviks' policies on the national question: "Why was it necessary to make such generous gifts, beyond the wildest dreams of the most zealous nationalists?" Turning to the present, Putin

---

39   In October 1991, Gorbachev told George Bush that "Ukraine in its current borders would be an unstable construct if it broke away," and that "it had come into existence only because local Bolsheviks had at one point gerrymandered it that way to ensure their own power": Sarotte, *Not One Inch*, p. 127. Solzhenitsyn, for his part, assailed Ukrainian nationalists for "eagerly accepting the false Leninist borders of Ukraine": Lieven, *Ukraine and Russia*, p. 150.

asserted that if what Ukrainian nationalists really wanted was "decommunization"—referring mainly to 2015 Rada legislation that banned "communist" organizations and symbols and called for the wholesale renaming of streets—"that suits us fine"; the implication being that the Ukrainians should be prepared to lose territories the Communists had "given" to Ukraine. Recognizing the independence of the Donetsk and Luhansk People's Republics was a first move toward this. The historical fantasy in play here was not a restoration of the Soviet Union and hence reincorporation of a subordinate, semi-sovereign Ukraine; it was rather the unraveling of the Soviet inheritance and a reversion to imperial boundaries, raising the specter of Ukraine's dismemberment.

Has this, in fact, been the goal of Russian policy all along—a revanchist neo-imperialism bent on subjugating its periphery, concealed for a time behind objections to NATO expansion but now finally revealed in the destruction unleashed on Ukraine? For many liberal commentators, the Russian invasion proved that NATO expansion was not in fact the issue, but rather the alibi for Russia's inability to accept a sovereign Ukraine, or else its opposition to the EU.[40] While the US and European establishment's interest in removing NATO expansion from the picture is obvious, some on the left have also taken up a version of this argument, criticizing both themselves and their peers for buying into the narrative of NATO's role.[41] Others have reflected that insufficient attention was paid to the autonomous weight of nationalism within Kremlin calculations, and its dangerous capacity to outstrip any rational consideration of economic or political interests, as well as to Russia's active role in exerting neo-imperial pressure on its environs, rather than merely reacting to Western moves.[42]

Yet the apparent dichotomy now developing between two explanatory schemas—one emphasizing NATO expansion, the other the long-hidden force of Russian nationalism; one supposedly exculpating Russia, the other muting the role of NATO—is ultimately false. There is no real world in which NATO expansion did not occur, and the emergence of an increasingly assertive and militarized Russian nationalism is inextricable from

---

40   For Sam Greene, "despite all the rhetoric about NATO, Moscow's beef is fundamentally with the European Union": "Here's Looking at EU," *TL;DRussia*, February 10, 2022, tldrussia.substack.com.

41   Greg Afinogenov, "The Seeds of War," *Dissent*, March 2, 2022.

42   Volodymyr Artiukh, "US-plaining Is Not Enough: To the Western Left, on Your and Our Mistakes," *e-flux*, March 1, 2022.

that process, because it was in large part propelled and reinforced by it. With regard to Ukraine, Russian nationalist fantasies have persistently been enmeshed with geostrategic calculations, the advancement of oligarchic interests with the self-preservation of the "imitation democratic" system. What weight we assign to these factors can be debated; but that they simultaneously exist should not. Recognition of their existence, moreover, in no way diminishes Russia's responsibility for invading Ukraine. Rather, it helps to clarify it, by enabling us to identify the different links in the causal chain that have brought us to this moment, and to distinguish each actor's degree of culpability. A consequential anti-imperialist politics requires not only condemnation of criminal wars as they unfold, but also an understanding of the field of great-power contention that repeatedly produces them.

12

Russia's decision to invade Ukraine took by surprise even those who had spent months announcing its imminence. Some of the more lucid observers had expected Russian recognition of the Donbas statelets to be followed by a limited military operation to expand their terrain. The initial shock at the much larger-scale invasion that instead ensued was compounded by the apparently delusional nature of the Kremlin's declared war aims: demilitarization and "denazification" of Ukraine, implying not only moves to permanently cripple the Ukrainian military but also to install a new political regime. Did this point to a deeper irrationality on the Kremlin's part—a decoupling of decision-making from basic strategic reasoning? The idea that Russia could, in 2022, impose a puppet government on a country where it could not even help rig an election in 2004 defied plausibility. Yet the initial military strategy, involving rapid attempts to seize Kiev and decapitate the government, reflected this ambition. Within days this approach had visibly failed, prompting a recalibration, and a turn to the artillery bombardment and siege methods seen in Chechnya. Reports of atrocities by Russian forces in occupied areas provided further echoes of that grim precedent.

The appalling paradox of Russian military strategy is that the greatest destruction has so far been visited on the east and south of Ukraine—that is, on the more "Russian" areas that the Kremlin claimed to be "liberating."

Although Putin's February 21 speech might have presaged a "gathering of the Russian lands," the war's first result has been the devastation of Ukraine's Russian-speaking areas, the likely consequence of which will be repulsion of a population the Kremlin long considered a blocking minority within Ukraine. The disregard for their well-being suggests either an improbable intelligence failure—did anyone at the summits of power really believe Russian soldiers would be welcomed as liberators?—or a more fundamental understanding, on some level, that this is a distinct population from that of Russia itself. The very fact that Russian strategists even considered waging this war ultimately attests to their awareness that Ukraine is indeed a separate, sovereign entity on an accelerating course away from Russia's orbit. By physically destroying the shared Soviet inheritance that once bound Russia and Ukraine, the war only confirms the underlying political reality.

13

Five weeks in, it remains to be seen what the future course of the war will be. The worst possible scenario, involving full-scale war between the NATO powers and Russia, has not yet materialized. But the longer the war continues, the higher the possibility of an escalation with potentially catastrophic consequences. Biden's belligerent assertion on a visit to Poland in late March that Putin "cannot remain in power" increased the prospects of such an outcome. Already plainly implied by the West's coordinated economic warfare, unprecedented in its scale, regime change has now been explicitly, if unofficially, posited as the goal of US policy.

A second scenario would be a military defeat for Russia, with a combination of sanctions and US and European weapons shipments helping not just to stem the Russian advance but to force a retreat without any peace agreement. This seems unlikely in itself—the sheer size of the Russian military means they can continue to fight for some time given the political will—and in the absence of a peace settlement would amount to no more than a temporary respite for Ukraine.

A third possibility, and the most disastrous for Ukraine, is the indefinite prolongation of the conflict, with the vastly larger Russian army facing off against Ukrainian forces being constantly rearmed by the US and European powers. The result would be to make Ukraine the site of a relentless proxy war, aid from the US and its allies helping to obstruct without neutralizing the destructive power of Russian arms. This is where the concerted policy of Western governments currently points, and the implications make a mockery of their apparent concerns for Ukrainians' welfare. On February 28, Hillary Clinton on MSNBC described Afghanistan in the 1980s as "the model that people are now looking toward," though "the similarities are not ones you should bank on." The example of Syria seems no less chillingly relevant.

A fourth, less pessimistic scenario involves the swift agreement of a peace. By mid-March 2022 a new set of Russian demands had surfaced in talks between Ukrainian and Russian envoys: Ukrainian neutrality, recognition of Russian sovereignty in Crimea and of the independence of the Donetsk and Luhansk provinces. In late March Ukrainian negotiators put forward a ten-point plan proposing the country adopt non-aligned and non-nuclear status, subject to a referendum, and that its security be guaranteed by a consortium of other states. Discussion of Crimea would be hived off into a separate bilateral process, and the Donbas was not mentioned. Whatever the contours of an eventual peace settlement, and for all the posturing by Washington and its allies, there seems to be broad agreement that NATO membership for Ukraine should be foreclosed. Given how little protection the possibility of NATO membership has given Ukraine, and how much NATO itself did to make the conflict more likely in the first place, the Ukrainian populace may find that an acceptable condition for peace. But with Russian forces seemingly stalled in their advance, and US and European weapons continuing to flood in, the Ukrainian government may have diminishing incentives to accept a settlement at gunpoint, especially if they are being encouraged by their allies to believe those guns will eventually be forced to retreat. If further atrocities after those uncovered at Bucha in early April come to light, the moral case for negotiating a peace with Russia will also become even harder to make.

A fifth possibility, somewhere between the two preceding scenarios, is that a military stalemate leads not to a peace settlement but to an armed truce. On one side, Russian occupying troops may end up in control of enough territory to enforce a de facto partition, while on the other Ukrainian forces, with NATO backing, would stand emplaced behind front lines stretching over hundreds of miles. Russian moves, as of late March, to refocus military efforts on the Donbas distinctly signaled such a possibility. This would be a much larger-scale version of the fortified armistice line between North and South Korea, and would involve a permanent militarization not just of the polities on either side, but across much of Europe.

14

The war has already taken an unacceptable toll on Ukraine, and in any scenario its future looks difficult, if not bleak. Repairing the physical damage and returning refugees to their homes after an eventual peace will be no small task; reinstating its sovereignty will be an undertaking of another order, dependent on the designs and pressures of external forces. A Russian withdrawal, to be hoped for as soon as possible, would allow the work of reconstruction at least to begin. But the invasion has sown an enmity that will linger.

In Russia itself, the war has already led to a more nakedly authoritarian turn. The eruption of protests against the invasion prompted a domestic crackdown, with thousands of arrests in dozens of cities. While popular appetite for the war remains low, the overall increase in Western pressure on the regime and the broader European militarization that will ensue from the conflict may well encourage a rallying around the flag, rather than mass desertions or rebellion. Short of such a political earthquake, the regime would also be little inclined to establish positive relations with Ukraine. In the longer run, if the sanctions-based punishment of Russia becomes institutionalized, it will face a choice between armored autarchy and closer economic integration with China. Either way its dependence on natural-resource exports, and the vast inequalities of the current economic model, will likely deepen even as military spending consumes a mounting share of Russia's diminishing national income.

Europe, too, is likely to militarize further, Germany's announcement in late February that it would boost military spending to over 2 percent of GDP a dark token of things to come. If the reigning political-economic order remains in place, it is difficult to see this ramping up of military expenditures not coming at the cost of what little remains of social safety nets. Neoliberal security states will trade growth for still more missiles and razor wire. It is hard not to see parallels here with the twilight of the Belle Epoque. Then as now, inter-imperial tensions fed a headlong arms race. Then as now, too, public opinion readily rallied behind national governments. In 1914 the parliamentary parties of the left followed suit, voting for war credits in their national legislatures and thus enabling the bloodbath they had pledged to avert two years earlier. This is, of course, another century, and the left is in a far weaker position, with far less influence on the course of events. By the same token, it is much more vulnerable to being swept along or swept aside by a militarized great-power confrontation it played no role in creating. Some of the old tools—internationalism, class solidarity, a fierce and uncompromising analytical clarity—will be needed to rearm the left against this new round of inter-imperial contention: against the powerful, against both their wars and their peace.

17

NATO through Ukrainian Eyes

Volodymyr Ishchenko

Did Russia invade Ukraine to prevent further NATO encroachment on its western marches? Or was such agita merely a pretext? For those who take Vladimir Putin's "legitimate security concerns" at face value, NATO is itself culpable for the war, by holding out the promise of Ukrainian membership while engaging in increasingly intensive military coordination with Kiev. By contrast, Atlanticist consensus rejects the issue altogether, on the grounds that every state has the right to determine its own foreign policy, not least accession to a purely "defensive" alliance. Concerns voiced by two generations of Soviet and Russian leaders can thus be dismissed as a ploy, contrived to dissemble deep-seated imperialistic designs.

Whatever role NATO expansion played in bringing about war, Ukrainians' attitudes counted for little. The grim irony is not only that NATO was far from extending formal membership to Ukraine, but that there was not even evidence of a stable pro-NATO majority in the country. In a typically colonial style, commentators on all sides tended to homogenize Ukrainians, without regard for political diversity in a nation of 40 million people. Contrary to the Kremlin's inclination to resolve Ukraine's geopolitical orientation within a small circle of Great Powers, Ukrainian officials have insisted on the principle "nothing about Ukraine without

Ukraine." However, the problem is not only deciding "without Ukraine" but also deciding "for" a very diverse population as if all held identical opinions on the critical issues in question.

Beyond the global rivalry between the US and Russia, on the one hand, and regional Russo-Ukrainian relations, on the other, the conflict in Ukraine has always also been about internal political and cultural heterogeneity, which necessarily has a class dimension. NATO occupies a peculiar place in this history. For a middle-class civil society, joining the alliance is a necessary step toward "Western integration," catchphrase for an ersatz modernization drive that entails adjustment not only to the demands of capitalist development but to the "civilized world" itself. Other Ukrainians, less well positioned to benefit from this prospective *Gleich-schaltung*, have been progressively stigmatized, silenced, and repressed. The failure to achieve a pluralistic nation-building project for Ukraine has been disastrous, with consequences reaching far beyond its borders.

Did Ukrainians Want to Join NATO?

Non-alignment, ruling out entry into any military pact, was inscribed in the foundational documents of the state of Ukraine, the Declaration of Sovereignty (adopted July 16, 1990) and the Constitution (June 28, 1996), following independence. And up until the tumultuous events of 2014, only a minority of Ukrainians favored NATO membership. Surveys at the time show that support extended to no more than 20–30 percent of the population, irrespective of how the issue was framed. By comparison, support for joining a supranational Union State alongside Russia and Belarus consistently hovered around 50–60 percent (exceeding support for membership in the European Union, although some Ukrainians did not see this as an either-or choice).[1]

Typical explanations of this muted enthusiasm point to ignorance of the alliance's post–Cold War mission and the persistence of negative stereotypes inherited from the Communist era, coupled with the relatively low saliency of the issue insofar as accession was not on the agenda in

---

1   Natalia Panina, ed., *Ukrainske Suspilstvo 1994–2004: Sotsiolohichnyi Monitorynh* (Kiev: Zapovit, 2004), p. 16; "Stavlennia Hromadian Do Integratsiinykh Proektiv," Kiev International Institute of Sociology, March 20, 2012. All KIIS polls cited in this chapter are available at kiis.com.ua.

the near feature.[2] But why should the legacy of Communism weigh so heavily in this matter but not in others?[3] It was certainly not Communist propaganda that caused support for NATO membership to plunge after the 2003 assault on Iraq to below 20 percent in some continuous surveys.[4] That the US, not NATO, led the charge has little bearing; nobody was surprised when support for joining the Russia-led Collective Security Treaty Organization (CSTO) dropped in 2014 after the annexation of Crimea and the outbreak of hostilities in Donbas, despite the fact that the CSTO itself was not involved.

One thing that is clear, however, is that Ukrainian attitudes toward NATO reflected broader class divisions, in addition to preexisting cleavages over regional and national identity. The more affluent and educated the person, the more they were likely to be pro-NATO.[5] In the years following independence, a post-Soviet professional middle class looked to "Euro-Atlantic integration" for career opportunities, payoffs, and political influence, while viewing the less affluent majority as incapable of making informed judgments on issues of foreign policy. Such a project of Westernization, undertaken by this privileged comprador elite, inevitably entailed a break with the "backward" plebeian masses. As the latter clung to what stability they could in the chaotic aftermath of the collapse of the USSR, the former moved to counterfeit their particular interests as the national interest in toto.

Ukraine's cooperation with NATO began almost immediately after independence and deepened over time—although not without hesitation as to the end goal of acquiring membership, a project sometimes included and sometimes excluded from official national security statements. Oscillation

---

2   For example, F. Stephen Larrabee, "Ukraine at the Crossroads," *Washington Quarterly* 30:4 (September 2007), p. 49.

3   Studies show no correlation between support for NATO membership and perceived level of knowledge about the organization. See Valerii Khmelko, "Stavlennia Hromadian Ukrainy Do Yii Vstupu Do Yevrosoiuzu i NATO Ta Yikhni Otsinky Svoyei Obiznanosti Stosovno Tsykh Orhanizatsii," *Sotsiolohiia: Teoriia, Metody, Marketynh*, no. 1 (2006), pp. 71–87.

4   Panina, *Ukrainske Suspilstvo 1994–2004: Sotsiolohichnyi Monitorynh*, p. 16; Andrii Bychenko, "Hromadska Dumka Pro NATO i Pryiednannia Do Nioho Ukrainy," *Natsionalna Bezpeka i Oborona*, 2006, p. 21.

5   Ibid., p. 36; Khmelko, "Stavlennia Hromadian Ukrainy Do Yii Vstupu Do Yevrosoiuzu i NATO Ta Yikhni Otsinky Svoyei Obiznanosti Stosovno Tsykh Orhanizatsii." Although the alliance enjoyed somewhat higher approval in the western regions than in the east, no pro-NATO majority existed there prior to 2014.

was a leitmotif of the so-called "multi-vector" strategy of balancing between Russia and the West. Rivals in Russia posed a threat to the ruling class of independent Ukraine, as tycoons in both countries vied to despoil what remained of Soviet-era infrastructure and state-owned enterprises. At the same time, like their Russian counterparts, Ukrainian political capitalists could not rejoin the Western elite without renouncing the selective benefits they obtained from the state—their major competitive advantage vis-à-vis transnational capital. The upshot was a cautious, opportunistic approach to security arrangements.[6]

More ardent NATO fans were to be found among the pro-Western, moderately nationalist neoliberals and neoconservatives organized politically into various "national-democratic" parties. This camp, which also peopled the small but growing (thanks to Western donors) ranks of Ukraine's NGO-ized civil society, seized its chance after the Orange Revolution of 2004, which brought Viktor Yushchenko to power. It was Yushchenko, encouraged by George W. Bush, who pushed forward Ukraine's application for a NATO Membership Action Plan (MAP). Consulting the electorate was out of the question. On the eve of the April 2008 Bucharest Summit, at which it was declared that Ukraine and Georgia "will become members of NATO," fewer than 20 percent of Ukrainian citizens aspired to do so.[7] The rest were split between those who preferred an alliance with Russia and those attached to the non-aligned status quo; in late May and early June the previous year, the joint Ukraine-NATO "Sea Breeze" naval exercise in Crimea had encountered significant protest, as locals greeted disembarking US Marines with cries of "No to NATO in Ukraine!"[8]

Nor did the Ukrainian elite consolidate behind the membership bid. The issue envenomed Yushchenko's conflict with Yuliia Tymoshenko and Viktor Yanukovych, who represented different fractions of Ukraine's political capitalists.[9] In 2007, then prime minister Yanukovych's refusal

---

6   Political capitalists, in the sense I employ the term here, represent the fraction of the capitalist class whose main competitive advantage derives from selective benefits bestowed by the state, unlike capitalists who look to exploit technological innovations or a particularly cheap labor force. See Volodymyr Ishchenko, "Behind Russia's War Is Thirty Years of Post-Soviet Class Conflict," *Jacobin*, October 3, 2022.

7   Oleksii V. Haran and Mariia Zolkina, "The Demise of Ukraine's 'Eurasian Vector' and the Rise of Pro-NATO Sentiment," PONARS *Eurasia Policy Memo*, February 16, 2017.

8   Stephen F. Cohen, *Soviet Fates and Lost Alternatives: From Stalinism to the New Cold War* (New York: Columbia University Press, 2011), p. 191.

9   Serhii Leshchenko, "Yuliia Tymoshenko: het vid Aliansu!," *Ukrainska pravda*, February 11, 2009.

to sign off on the MAP precipitated a full-blown governmental crisis, resolved only by snap parliamentary elections that September.[10] Even the Russia–Georgia war in 2008 did not substantially affect Ukrainian public opinion.[11] On winning the presidency in 2010, Yanukovych froze further rapprochement with NATO, all while persisting in negotiations over the European Union association agreement that would prove to be his undoing. The EU, and with it the promise of higher living standards, was significantly more attractive in the eyes of Ukrainians than was NATO. In 2012–13, NATO polling numbers ran as low as 13 percent, while upward of 40 percent hoped to join the EU.[12] The same polls showed non-alignment to be the most popular security option, and the Union with Russia and Belarus the most desirable mechanism of economic integration, neck and neck with the EU.

It was not until 2014, with Russia's annexation of Crimea and the war in Donbas, that support for the NATO option increased dramatically, although it still was not embraced by a majority of Ukrainians.[13] Two factors contributed to the change in public opinion. Some previously skeptical Ukrainians now began to see NATO as a bulwark against Russian aggression. But no less importantly, the surveys did not include the most pro-Russian Ukrainian citizens concentrated in the territories no longer under Ukrainian government control—Crimea and parts of the Donetsk and Luhansk regions. Millions of citizens were thereby de facto excluded from the Ukrainian public sphere.[14] In the rest of Ukraine, backing for a military alliance with Russia (as well as economic integration) dropped

---

10   Igor Guzhva, Olesia Medvedeva, and Maksim Minin, "Na grani voiny. Timoshenko snova premier, gibel 106 shakhterov. Chem zhila strana v 2007 godu," *Strana News*, August 11, 2021.

11   Dominique Arel, "Ukraine since the War in Georgia," *Survival* 50:6 (December 2008), pp. 18–19.

12   Haran and Zolkina, "The Demise of Ukraine's 'Eurasian Vector' and the Rise of Pro-NATO Sentiment."

13   Ibid.

14   There were no doubt technical and methodological hurdles to polling in these areas. However, nationalist outcry over the "treasonous" findings of the periodic surveys that were carried out in Crimea and parts of Donbas not controlled by the Ukrainian government raises the question of whether *political* considerations were no less decisive in the choice to omit the opinions of a significant part of the population (never officially deducted from national tallies). See Andrii Gladun, "Sotsiolohiia ta Ideolohiia: Dyskusiia Shchodo Opytuvan pro Nastroi Krymchan," *Commons: Journal of Social Criticism*, April 28, 2015; Gwendolyn Sasse, "The Donbas—Two Parts, or Still One? The Experience of War through the Eyes of the Regional Population," *ZOiS*, May 2, 2017. This is all the more peculiar in light of the regular polling conducted in parts of southeastern Ukraine

sharply from 2014. However, most of those who once inclined toward Russia did not transfer their allegiance to NATO. Rather, they switched to a non-aligned position, in the spirit of "a plague on both your houses."

Support for NATO in Ukraine has continued to vary geographically.[15] Before the 2022 invasion, a solid majority existed only in the western regions. There was, perhaps, a pro-NATO plurality in central Ukraine. But non-alignment prevailed in the east and south: the areas of Ukraine that would take the heaviest blow in the event of a clash with Russia. The correlation between Ukrainians' views on NATO and their different visions of Ukrainian national identity made the issue especially divisive. If many Ukrainians saw in NATO protection from a bellicose neighbor, many others worried that membership in the alliance would forfeit yet more sovereignty to the West,[16] increase tensions with Russia, aggravate internal divisions, and potentially drag Ukraine into one of the US's "forever" wars.[17] Had Bush not defended opening the door to Kiev, over French and German objections, with reference to Ukrainian valor in Kosovo, Afghanistan, and Iraq?[18]

Some evidence did indicate growing support for NATO membership in the wake of the election of Volodymyr Zelensky.[19] To start with, the new president—a Euro-Atlantic partisan, inaccurately besmirched as "pro-Russian" by Ukrainian nationalists and international "friends of Ukraine"[20]—somewhat "de-toxified" the issue among eastern Ukrainian voters, and

occupied by Russia in 2022, despite even more serious concerns about reliability as a result of population dislocations and a moving front line.

15   Gerard Toal, John O'Loughlin, and Kristin M. Bakke, "Is Ukraine Caught between Europe and Russia? We Asked Ukrainians This Important Question," *Washington Post*, February 26, 2020, "Suspilno-Politychni Oriientatsii Naselennia Ukrainy," KIIS, April 2020.

16   "Dumky ta pohliady naselennia Ukrainy: Lypen 2020," Social Monitoring Center, July 21, 2020.

17   "Suspilna Pidtrymka Yevroatlantychnoho Kursu Ukrainy: Otsinky Ta Rekomen-datsii," Razumkov Center, 2021; available at razumkov.org.ua.

18   "Ukraine is the only non-NATO country supporting every NATO mission," the president declaimed ahead of the Bucharest Summit. Steven Lee Myers, "Bush Backs Ukraine's Bid to Join NATO," *New York Times*, April 1, 2008.

19   "Heopolitychni Oriientatsii Zhytelliv Ukrainy: Cherven 2021 Roku," Kiev International Institute of Sociology, July 18, 2021; Olga Onuch and Javier Perez Sandoval, "A Majority of Ukrainians Support Joining NATO. Does This Matter?," *Washington Post*, February 4, 2022.

20   For example, Alexander J. Motyl, "Ukraine's TV President Is Dangerously Pro-Russian," *Foreign Policy*, April 1, 2019.

even more importantly, the Russian military buildup from the spring of 2021 raised alarm. All the same, it is doubtful whether a stable majority, as distinct from fleeting, conjunctural upticks in polling, existed even in the run-up to the invasion. As late as December 2021, polls suggested that non-alignment commanded a plurality of around 45 percent.[21] NATO supporters probably would have prevailed in a referendum; however, even setting aside the limits of a "yes" or "no" response in dictating national security strategy, a vote under these conditions would not have included the millions of Ukrainian citizens in the Donbas and Crimea. If their opinions are taken into account (Ukraine has never formally abandoned the ambition to bring them back), the notion of a stable pro-NATO majority in Ukraine before the full-scale invasion is flawed.

East–West Asymmetries

Skepticism toward NATO can be effaced only by downplaying or delegitimizing the internal diversity of Ukraine. Here, explanations that assume some roughly symmetrical "East/West" political cleavage—whether based on ethnicity and language, national identity, or historically constituted political cultures—mislead insofar as they overlook the profound *asymmetry* between the two main political blocs that emerged in independent Ukraine. The "Western" camp rested on an alliance between the professional middle class and transnational capital, organized and ideologically articulated in the national-liberal civil society of NGOs and militant nationalist parties, and electorally represented by some fractions of Ukrainian political capitalists ("oligarchs") who rather opportunistically joined the camp.[22] The "Eastern" camp—most political capitalists arrayed uneasily behind it—relied on the passive electoral support of industrial workers and public-sector employees, absent any genuine activist mobilization. The mediating civil society layer between the oligarchic "leaders" and their rather apolitical voters was remarkably weaker within the "Eastern" camp.[23]

---

21 Serhii Kudelia, "NATO or Bust: Why Do Ukraine's Leaders Dismiss Neutrality as a Security Strategy?," *Russia Matters*, February 9, 2022.

22 Volodymyr Ishchenko and Małgorzata Kulbaczewska-Figat, "Why Russia's Political Capitalists Went to War—and How the War Could End Their Rule," *Cross-Border Talks*, July 29, 2022.

23 Especially after the repression and marginalization of the left parties that did have

This discrepancy explains why even though the "Eastern" camp comprised a large minority or sometimes even the majority of Ukrainian citizens, its political and organizational resources paled in comparison with those available to Western-oriented nationalists and neoliberals, however unpopular the agendas they sought to impose. The constitutional amendment enshrining Ukraine's intention to join NATO and the EU, enacted in February 2019 by Zelensky's predecessor, Petro Poroshenko, must be understood in this light. Unsurprisingly, plaudits from national-liberal civil society did not prevent the incumbent president's devastating defeat only months later.

Once installed as president, however, Zelensky did not reverse the exclusionary nationalist drift of Poroshenko's rule, despite the expectations of a large part of his voters. Zelensky's civic nationalism remained shallow, paying lip service to diversity in the place of meaningful action. Beginning in 2021, the president increasingly targeted political opponents with threats and sanctions, went after their financial backers, and banned most of the major opposition media. Squawks of disapproval from human rights organizations aside, these measures elicited no significant reaction from "the West," in striking contrast to the repression of opposition elements in Russia and Belarus.[24] Few observers questioned the idea that persecution of so-called pro-Russian forces is inevitable or even legitimate in a country under the foreign threat. Fewer still considered whether depriving a large segment of the population of political and public representation made Ukraine weaker, rather than stronger, vis-à-vis Russia.

After the Invasion

For adepts of the "Western" nation-building project, Russia's invasion of Ukraine turned into an opportunity to transform the country in their own image. Of course, a full-scale invasion can be expected to have more profound effects than the eventful months of Euromaidan, the almost

---

some ability to mobilize their supporters. See Volodymyr Ishchenko, "The Ukrainian Left during and after the Maidan Protests," Study for the Left in the European Parliament, January 2016.

24   "Civic Space and Fundamental Freedoms in Ukraine, 1 November 2019–31 October 2021," United Nations Human Rights, Office of the High Commissioner, Ukraine, 2021.

bloodless annexation of Crimea, and localized combat in Donbas. It would be a bitter irony if Russian arms unified a NATO-oriented Ukrainian nation-state, something that pro-Western elites were unable to accomplish in the three decades after the dissolution of the USSR. But a closer look into the nature of this apparent unity invites doubt as to whether it will outlast the end of the conflict.

If anything could have been expected to follow from the Russian invasion, it was an embrace of NATO. A survey conducted in May 2022 duly found that 73 percent of respondents wanted to see Ukraine to become an alliance member by 2030, although a significant minority of 27 percent still preferred for Ukraine to be non-aligned.[25] An August sample returned comparable figures.[26]

However, wartime polling suffers from a host of challenges. At the time of writing, surveys exclude not only the inhabitants of areas that the government in Kiev did not control before the invasion, but millions of refugees now living abroad. Among those forced to flee their homes, the majority come from the regions in southeastern Ukraine, again skewing the balance of reported opinion.[27] Canvassers struggle to reach the residents of Russian-occupied areas in the south of the country, while the wartime mobilization inescapably amplifies "spiral of silence" effects, discouraging the expression of views that may be considered unpatriotic.[28] One poll that did include Ukrainians relocated abroad—a continuous panel survey via mobile applications, carried out by Gradus in April 2022—turned up remarkable results. Slightly fewer than half of those polled countenanced Ukraine joining NATO, in response to an either/or choice; finer-grained questioning found that 24 percent favored NATO membership, as against 27 percent for non-alignment (with security

25   In the wording of the survey, the two options were not mutually exclusive. "Mozhlyvosti Ta Pereshkody Na Shliakhu Demokratychnoho Perekhodu Ukrainy," KIIS, May 2–11, 2022.

26   "Opytuvannia NDI: Mozhlyvosti Ta Pereshkody Na Shliakhu Demokratychnoho Perekhodu Ukrainy," KIIS, September 20, 2022.

27   "Nastroi ta otsinky ukrainskykh bizhentsiv (lypen-serpen 2022 r.)," Razumkov Center, August 30, 2022.

28   On the basis of an experiment conducted in May 2022, researchers at the Kiev International Institute of Sociology estimate that the spiral of silence contributed an additional 4–6 percent to pro-Western positions. "Pryiniatnist Vidmovy Vid Vstupu Do NATO Pry Otrymanni Harantii Bezpeky Vid Okremykh Krain: Rezultaty Telefonnoho Opytuvannia, Provedenoho 13-18 Travnia 2022 Roku," KIIS, May 24, 2022.

guarantees) and another third undecided.[29] Asked to reflect on the future, only 20 percent mentioned accession to NATO as an "inspiring thing," dwarfed by those who hoped for an end to the war, political and economic transformation, and improvement of their own material well-being, as well as EU member status for Ukraine (39 percent).

Once reductive binary choices are dispensed with, superficial unity on foreign policy and security arrangements conceals a good deal of diversity. Another poll from May 2022 found 42 percent endorsed neutrality for Ukraine on the condition of guarantees from the Western powers, while a roughly equivalent number (39 percent) insisted on entering NATO no matter what.[30] Results like these suggest that only a minority see enrollment in the alliance as a matter of identity, whereas for many others their support is conditional and open to change, especially as a function of NATO's evolving role in the war. As demonstrated by a December 2022 poll, when provided a range of alternatives to choose from as the "best option to guarantee the national security of Ukraine after the Russian aggression"—including strategic cooperation with the US or other allied states, development of Ukraine's own armed forces, and non-aligned status with international security guarantees—joining NATO is the most popular option, but it still falls short of a majority (49 percent).[31] In stark contrast with prevailing orthodoxy in both the US and Western Europe concerning war guilt, Ukrainians deliver more nuanced appraisals. A June 2022 survey commissioned by the *Wall Street Journal* discovered that although 85 percent attributed "a great deal" or at least "some" responsibility for the "ongoing conflict" to Russia, majorities also assign blame to the US (58 percent), NATO (55 percent), and the Ukrainian government (70 percent).[32] Many no doubt reprove the Western powers for not admitting Ukraine to the alliance, sending weapons even earlier, and preparing

---

29   The Gradus poll has its limitations: it was restricted to city dwellers with access to smartphones, and slightly skewed to the more urbanized southeast of the country; however, it did not include people over the age of sixty, who are generally less supportive of NATO. "The Attitudes, Emotions, and Actions of Ukrainians during the Full-Scale War between Russia and Ukraine," Gradus, April 2022; available at gradus.app.

30   "Pryiniatnist Vidmovy Vid Vstupu Do NATO Pry Otrymanni Harantii Bezpeky Vid Okremykh Krain: Rezultaty Telefonnoho Opytuvannia, Provedenoho 13-18 Travnia 2022 Roku," KIIS, May 24, 2022.

31   "Results-2022: Under the Blue-Yellow Flag of Freedom!," Democratic Initiatives Foundation, January 5, 2023; available at dif.org.

32   WSJ/NORC Ukraine Poll June 2022; available at norc.org.

properly for the invasion. However, these were presumably not the chief concerns of the 35 percent who assigned responsibility for the war to "Ukraine's ultra-right nationalists." Startingly, a small but not insignificant minority of the Ukrainians polled (9 percent) did not blame Russia at all.

Aside from doubts over the reliability of survey data, one must also take into account the intense cathexis of wartime patriotism, which does not necessarily promise more lasting, durable national unity. The enormous suffering and deadly risk the invasion imposed on practically every resident of Ukraine inevitably leads many to reject any premise that may be contaminated by enemy "narratives," irrespective of the facts on the ground.[33] Initial success in resisting and repulsing the Russian military in large parts of the occupied territories fed hopes of total victory. Affective responses to the extraordinary stress of the war are evident in connection to not only complex issues of international politics, but also the simple facts of everyday life. Despite a 30 percent fall in GDP, surging unemployment, and regular power cuts due to the Russian attacks on the energy infrastructure, half as many Ukrainians despaired of the economic situation in December 2022 (28 percent) as in pre-invasion polls a year prior (58 percent in November 2021).[34] The percentage of those who report that living conditions are satisfactory for the majority of the population has likewise almost doubled over the same period.

The overall picture looks less like an expression of newfound unity under the leadership of pro-Western elites than a negative coalition against an external foe—a precarious, volatile solidarity, rather than a fundamental shift in political beliefs. Deeper divisions may be subsumed temporarily, but they threaten to return to the fore when the fighting ceases. This will be amplified by new cleavages between those who stayed in Ukraine, those who found refuge abroad, and those who remained in territories annexed by Russia and therefore in one way or another had to collaborate with the occupying authorities. Whatever the outcome on the battlefield, Ukrainian attitudes toward a postwar geostrategic settlement cannot be foretold. If recent history is any guide, they are unlikely to weigh too heavily in the calculations of political elites, whether at home or abroad.

---

33   "Perception Index of the Russian-Ukrainian War: Results of a Telephone Survey Conducted on May 19–24, 2022," KIIS, May 27, 2022.

34   "Hromadska dumka v Ukraini pislia 10 misiatsiv viiny," KIIS, January 15, 2023.

PART FIVE

Atlanticology

18

The Belligerati

Richard Seymour

The defenestration of dignity and common sense may be among the lesser tragedies of war. But in late capitalism the cynical, the sinister and the stupid tend to be enfolded in the same apocalyptic drive. Consider, for a moment, recent gestures of solidarity with the people of Ukraine, currently suffering under Russia's increasingly brutal assault. As Western states have imposed vigorous sanctions on Russia, though not as severe as those imposed on Iran or Iraq, others have taken their own initiatives. In the United Kingdom, some supermarkets have taken Russian vodka off the shelves.[1] Netflix has put its adaptation of Tolstoy's *Anna Karenina*, among other Russian-language dramas, on hold.[2] Throwing its own small yet heroic spanner into the wheels of Russian militarism, the *Journal of Molecular Structures* has banned papers from Russian academic institutions.[3] Finally, a string of multinationals like Coca-Cola and McDonald's have suspended commercial operations in Russia. McDonald's cited "our values" in justification.[4]

---

1 "Supermarkets Remove Russian Vodka from Shelves," bbc.com, March 4, 2022.

2 Jacqui Goddard, "War in Ukraine: Netflix Shelves Tolstoy Adaptation after Criticism," *The Times* (London), March 4, 2022.

3 "Journal Editor Explains Ban on Manuscripts from Russian Institutions," *Retraction Watch*, March 4, 2022.

4 Sarah Butler and Edward Helmore, "McDonald's, Starbucks, Coca-Cola, and Pepsi Suspend Russian Operations," *Guardian*, March 8, 2022.

Like the sanctions themselves, a form of economic warfare that hurts ordinary Russians, these actions make little material difference to Putin's ability to wage war.[5] Rather, they are expressions of a kind of identity formation. On the one hand, we have heard from the *Wall Street Journal* that Russia under Putin is returning to its "Asian past," even though its methods of urban assault turn out to be comparable to those deployed by the United States and its allies in Fallujah and Tal Afar.[6] And, similarly, from Joe Biden and neoconservatives like Niall Ferguson that Putin is trying to restore the Soviet Union, even though he declares "decommunization" to be among his aims in Ukraine.[7] Though most politicians and journalists would be too sensible to make this logic overt, hysteria about all things Russian entered warp speed on day one of the invasion, especially in the UK. Labour MP Chris Bryant set the tone by demanding, in a tweet he has now deleted, that UK-Russian dual nationals should be forced to choose nationalities. Tory MP Tom Tugendhat suggested that "we can expel Russian citizens, all of them."[8] He later claimed to mean only Russian diplomats and oligarchs, but that isn't what he said.

On the other hand, the Ukrainian leadership is conveniently airbrushed and lionized, so that it can be identified as an outpost of an idealized "Europe." Daniel Hannan, writing in the *Telegraph*, declared: "They seem so like us. That is what makes it so shocking."[9] Charlie D'Agata of CBS, reporting from Ukraine's capital, was struck by the same cognitive dissonance: "This isn't a place, with all due respect, like Iraq or Afghanistan that has seen conflict raging for decades. This is a relatively civilized, relatively European city."[10] On ITV News, a journalist underlined that "this is not a developing, Third World nation. This is Europe." Tabloid journalist Matthew Wright, on ITV's *This Morning*, lamented Putin's alleged use of

5   Sylvanus Kwaku Afesorgbor and Peter A. G. van Bergeijk, "Economic Sanctions Will Hurt Russians Long before They Stop Putin's War in Ukraine," *The Conversation*, March 1, 2022.

6   Yaroslav Trofimov, "Russia's Turn to Its Asian Past," *Wall Street Journal*, July 6, 2018.

7   Niall Ferguson, "Vlad the Invader: Putin Is Looking to Rebuild Russia's Empire," *Spectator*, February 26, 2022.

8   Nadine Batchelor-Hunt, "Britain Could Expel All Russian Citizens from the UK, Senior Conservative MP Says," *Yahoo News*, February 24, 2022.

9   Daniel Hannan, "Vladimir Putin's Monstrous Invasion Is an Attack on Civilization Itself," *Telegraph*, February 26, 2022.

10   "Western Media Criticized for Racist 'Blonde Hair Blue Eyes' Coverage of Invasion," *Middle East Eye*, February 27, 2022.

thermobaric weapons in Ukraine. "To be fair," he acknowledged, the US had used it before in Afghanistan. "But the idea of it being used in Europe is stomach churning."

This provincializes sympathy with Ukrainians under siege, reducing what might have become a dangerously universalist impulse—raising standards that could apply in Palestine or Cameroon—to narcissistic solidarity with "people like us." The attachment to Europe is meanwhile libidinized through the figure of Ukrainian prime minister Volodymyr Zelensky, ubiquitously declared a "hero" on the front pages as he channels the Churchill myth. Caitlin Moran of *The Times* confesses a "crush" on Zelensky. The *New York Post* reports that women on TikTok are going "wild" for the Ukrainian premiere. In the *Washington Post*, Kathleen Parker eulogizes him as a modern "warrior-artist."[11]

There has been scarcely any realistic reflection on Zelensky's record as a leader. One of the puzzles about Ukraine's president is the counterintuitive relationship between his funding source and his election promises. His major donor was the brutal oligarch Ihor Kolomoisky, who owns the 1+1 Media Group that broadcast Zelensky's popular comedy vehicle, *Servant of the People*. Kolomoisky was an active proponent of war with Russia in Donbas who bankrolled the neo-Nazi Azov Battalion and other militias responsible for war crimes.[12] Yet Zelensky was elected on a platform of opposing oligarch corruption, ending the war in Donbas and making peace with Russia.

Since 2019, the president has made little progress on this agenda. Although he talked up his commitment to de-oligarchization, in practice this has meant pursuing those with alleged connections to Russia: sanctioning opposition politician Viktor Medvedchuk—accused of having financial ties to Donbas separatists—and abruptly shutting down three TV stations for broadcasting Russian "misinformation." Zelensky's predecessor, Petro Poroshenko, had his assets seized on as yet unevidenced claims that he funded separatist rebels in Donetsk and Luhansk; and in mid-March Zelensky banned eleven Russia-aligned political parties.[13]

---

11 *The Times*, March 3, 2022; *New York Post*, March 1, 2022; *Washington Post*, March 15, 2022.

12 Damien Sharkov, "Ukrainian Nationalist Volunteers Committing 'ISIS-Style' War Crimes," *Newsweek*, September 10, 2014.

13 Grayson Quay, "Zelensky Nationalizes TV News and Restricts Opposition Parties," *The Week*, March 20, 2022.

Indeed, anticorruption activities appear to have been assiduously recast as an effort to root out Russian influence, consolidating Zelensky's grip on power while protecting Kolomoisky. In early 2020, the president sacked prosecutor-general Ruslan Ryaboshapka, who had launched an anticorruption drive whose targets included Kolomoisky. He was replaced by a former Zelensky adviser. Zelensky also appointed his old school friend, Ivan Bakanov, to head the Security Service of Ukraine; hired Kolomoisky's lawyer as his administration's chief of staff; and embarked on a sweeping reform of the security services that Human Rights Watch condemned as a power grab.[14] Zelensky has also beefed up his alliances within the state by appointing dozens of former colleagues from his TV production company to prominent positions.

What became of peace with Russia? The basis for this would have been Minsk II, signed in February 2015 after the collapse of the initial Minsk Protocol. The accords reflected the armed leverage that separatists in Donetsk and Luhansk achieved with Russian military backing. As a result, Ukrainian governments have always resented their terms while claiming to respect them. Whereas Russia insisted on upholding Minsk II's commitment to "local self-governance" and elections in the Donetsk and Luhansk oblasts, Ukraine sought to delay the implementation of such provisions, at least until the withdrawal of Russian forces. To negotiate a peace with his larger neighbor, Zelensky would have needed to accommodate the latter's priorities, which would have been extremely difficult given the disposition of Ukraine's parliament. (He faced fierce criticism for simply agreeing to negotiate with Russia while its forces continued to occupy Crimea.) Thus, caving to both domestic and international pressure, Zelensky stuck to Ukraine's traditional position—refusing to negotiate with Donbas leaders, rejecting federalization and opposing the Russian occupation of Crimea. Not only that; he also increased military cooperation with the US and UK, building new naval bases near the Black Sea, which Russia viewed as hostile Western outposts.[15]

In all likelihood, neither Russia nor Ukraine wanted to implement Minsk II fully. Russia could temporize over withdrawing its forces while

---

14   Luke Harding, "Revealed: 'Anti-oligarch' Ukrainian President's Offshore Connections," *Guardian*, October 3, 2021; Human Rights Watch, Letter to the Members of the Verkhovna Rada of Ukraine, June 3, 2021; available at hrw.org.

15   "Ukraine to Construct Two Naval Bases in Black Sea, Says Zelensky," TASS, October 20, 2020.

increasing its influence in Donetsk and Luhansk, converting them into ever more surreally authoritarian enclaves. Ukraine was reluctant to pass the political provisions for as long as Russian military and political power in the region would turn "local self-governance" into de facto autonomy. More fundamentally, as Volodymyr Ishchenko has argued, the Minsk dilemma reflected the broader failure of nationalist projects in post-Soviet Ukraine.[16] In part because of the fragmentation of the capitalist class, no single project has been able to secure the assent of more than half the population. The liberal-nationalist wing that took power after Maidan, with the involvement of a small but influential far right, was never accepted by the majority in Donetsk and Luhansk, historically the most prosperous, industrially advanced and pro-Russian areas. While Russia's actions since 2014 have drained support for it within Ukraine, and the invasion has likely destroyed it for good, this doesn't mean that Zelensky ever had a chance of mediating the contradictions even if he wanted to. This failure caused his popularity to tank. Though elected with an extraordinary 73 percent of the vote, by June 2021 over half of the electorate didn't want him to run again, and only 21 percent said they would vote for him.[17]

Liberated from informed thinking by official forgetting, however, journalists may still partake of the romance of resistance. The lay priest of liberalism Ian Dunt suggests that passionate Europeanists should send money to the Ukrainian army, while hymning Ukraine as "the ideals of Europe, made flesh and blood."[18] That being the fantasy, there is considerable sympathy for those volunteers who, beseeched by Ukrainian foreign secretary Dmytro Kuleba and egged on by his UK counterpart Liz Truss, have gone to fight Vlad.[19] ITV News treats us to an uncritical interview with British volunteers training with the "Georgian Legion" in Ukraine, initially set up by ethnic Georgians to fight the Russians before being integrated into the Ukrainian army, to fight "a war of the West."[20]

16   Volodymyr Ishchenko, "Contradictions of Post-Soviet Ukraine and Failure of Ukraine's New Left," *Europe Solidaire Sans Frontières*, January 9, 2020.

17   "KIIS Poll: Every Fifth Ukrainian Ready to Vote for Zelensky in Presidential Elections," *Kyiv Post*, June 8, 2021.

18   Ian Dunt, "Ukraine Shows Us the Radicalism of the European Dream of Peace and Democracy," inews.co.uk, March 4, 2022.

19   "Ukraine Conflict: Liz Truss Backs People from UK Who Want to Fight," bbc. com, February 27, 2022.

20   ITV News, March 8, 2022.

Such sentiments have been canalized into demands for a "no-fly zone"—that is, aerial warfare—in Ukraine, as well as increased military expenditures. The usual journalistic galaxy-brains complain that opposition to a no-fly zone is "appeasement," raising folk memories of the Second World War as though they were the first to think of it, or demanding that Western powers call Russia's nuclear bluff. It is clear, though, that the bureaucracies responsible for waging war in NATO do not currently want a no-fly zone, because it implies direct confrontation with a nuclear-armed power. The Pentagon even vetoed a Polish proposal to send Soviet-made MiG-29s to Ukraine on the grounds that it would be close to an act of war. Not for the first time, the punditry, in out-hawking the Pentagon, has become more royalist than the king. The only military assistance that NATO countries plan to offer Ukraine is intended to stimulate a protracted insurgency. As Hillary Clinton gleefully suggested, citing the example of Afghanistan in the 1980s without any hint of regret for the over 2 million lives lost and the birthing of a violent global jihadist movement, this would bleed Russia. It would also destroy Ukraine.

The belligerati have a surer bet with the demand for more military spending. In the UK, both Conservatives and Labour front-benchers are on board. In *The Times*, John Kampfner celebrates Germany's hard turn to armament as bad news for Putin.[21] In Sweden, where public opinion has for the moment swung behind NATO membership, the Social Democratic government has announced a surge in the military budget. The *Economist* notes, with some cheer, that European armament is driving European defense stocks sky-high.[22]

This has little to do with rescuing the people of Ukraine from Russian incursions. The most likely endgame is, of course, a negotiated settlement. Zelensky, who may not welcome the devastation of an Afghanistan-style insurgency, is currently giving himself room for a diplomatic retreat, while Russia's negotiating position is far from maximalist. It seems likely that Putin will have to acknowledge a diminished Ukrainian sovereignty, while Zelensky will have to accept that Crimea belongs to Russia and concede some special status for the eastern "republics" of Luhansk and Donetsk. Given that Ukraine can't win, that NATO won't directly intervene, and

---

21   John Kampfner, "To the Kremlin's Chagrin, Germany Is Back in the Game," *The Times* (London), March 6, 2022.

22   "Russia's Attack on Ukraine Means More Military Spending," *Economist*, March 5, 2022.

that Russia can only triumph at great cost to its own position (and Putin's standing with a spooked military leadership), there is no advantage to prolonging the war.

Though the current cultural ferment will not deliver Ukraine from Russian cluster bombs and shelling, it has in part been harnessed to Britain's culture war. A typical example is provided by Nick Cohen, who appears to write the same three or four columns on repeat. In the *Observer*, he claims that a new vital center has seen off a historically pro-Putin far left and far right.[23] This is, naturally, politically illiterate. Putin's champions in the early days when he was pulverizing Chechnya were those paragons of nineties centrism, Clinton and Blair. Putin was an active participant in the war on terror, of which Cohen was an especially mindless enthusiast. As late as 2014, Blair was calling for common cause with Putin.[24] But the claim that the antiwar left is pro-Putin has been integral to recent moves at the top of British politics, particularly Starmer's attempt to witch-hunt the Stop the War Coalition and crack down on Young Labour for criticizing NATO.[25] The *Telegraph*, taking the gambit a step further, accuses the RMT union of being the "enemy underground" and "Putin apologists" for launching strike action on the London Underground.[26]

To this extent, the culture war over Russia and Ukraine is more about the moral rearmament of "the West" after Iraq and Afghanistan under the ensign of a new Cold War that declares Putin a legatee of Stalin, the resuscitation of a dying Atlanticism, the revitalization of a moralistic Europeanism after the collapse of the Remain cause, and the stigmatization of the left after the shock of Corbyn's leadership of the Labour Party, than it is about Russia or Ukraine. More broadly, it revives in a new landscape the apocalyptic civilizational identities that were such a motivating force during the "war on terror," and which have lately fallen into disarray.

---

23   Nick Cohen, "Far Right and Far Left Alike Admired Putin. Now We've All Turned against Strongmen," *Guardian*, March 5, 2022.

24   Francis Elliott, "Blair Calls on West to Make Common Cause with Putin," *The Times* (London), April 23, 2014.

25   Keir Starmer, "Under My Leadership, Labour's Commitment to NATO Is Unshakable," *Guardian*, February 10, 2022; Rachel Wearmouth, "Keir Starmer Slashes Young Labour Funds and Axes Conference in Fresh Clash with Left," *Mirror*, February 25, 2022.

26   Gordon Rayner, "How Close Is the RMT Union to Vladimir Putin's Russia?," *Telegraph*, March 2, 2022.

19

A Normal War

Alexander Zevin

Russian bombs are falling on Ukraine, not American ones. On this level, the moral aspects of the war are clear. But acknowledging this is not the same as a policy response, nor does one flow automatically from it. By refusing to reflect on either the deeper causes of the war or possible ways out of it, the liberal commentariat in the US falls into its usual patterns, in which America figures as the innocent abroad, a do-gooder, for whom each crisis is something external to be acted on, never something it could be responsible for. "You can't blame the innocent, they are always guilt-less," wrote Graham Greene in *The Quiet American*. For the narrator, a jaded British journalist in Saigon, this is a kind of insanity, embodied in the character of the title: CIA agent Alden Pyle, freshly arrived in Indo-china from Harvard in the early 1950s. "I never knew a man who had better motives for all the trouble he caused."

Such is the tone underlying mainstream reactions in the press, where moral outrage is easily spent in a blaze of condemnation of a foreign country that leaves little to spare for its own. Now was not the time to argue about whether Putin's "grievances had bases in fact," insisted the *New York Times* as the invasion began. Putin bore sole responsibility for the new Cold War, a "potentially more dangerous one because his claims and demands offer no grounds for negotiations." Most of its op-ed writers concurred, from David Brooks to Paul Krugman and Michelle Goldberg, onto not-so-odd couple Bret Stephens and Gail Collins—the US must show Putin that "he will never, ever win this war." This line carried over to editorials in the *New Republic, Atlantic, New Yorker.* For Timothy Snyder in *Foreign Policy*, it was 1939 again, and Putin—as heir to both Hitler and Stalin—had made a Nazi–Soviet pact with himself. At White House press briefings, reporters urged the administration forward: had Biden erred in saying he wanted to avoid the Third World War, asked ABC's correspondent, "emboldening" Putin by ruling out "direct military intervention" too early?

The business press has proven nearly as incendiary. Each issue of the *Financial Times, Economist*, and *Wall Street Journal* bristles with calls for further, harsher sanctions that leapfrog the last. Banning Russian banks from SWIFT is now old hat, financial warfare for the faint-hearted. More radical measures aim at provoking overlapping debt, currency and banking crises: a block on Russian banks from dollar clearing and settlement, a ban on trading in its debt on secondary markets, and seizure of two-thirds of its dollar reserves. These joined embargoes on advanced technology, by businesses and governments, including Boeing and Airbus equipment to service commercial aircraft; and growing calls to end all oil and gas imports not just to the US but Europe too—winter weather, high fuel prices, and freezing pensioners be damned. The financial journalist Matthew Klein has gone from diagnosing trade wars as class wars to promoting them, with calls for a "financial NATO," endowed with "permanent mechanisms" of coercion and a "freedom fund" to compensate investors for the loss of the Russian market—and "(hypothetically) the Chinese one."[1]

Economic escalation has begun building toward military involvement, rather than acting as an alternative to it. The *FT*'s Martin Wolf concluded by mid-March that World War III might be a risk worth taking.[2] Enthusiastic about economic weapons, the media has been positively gung-ho on the physical sort. After two weeks, seventeen thousand antitank weapons had made it to Ukraine, according to the *New York Times*, while US "cybermission teams" had been set up to aid them in unspecified acts of "interference" against Russia—in ways that are testing the legal definitions

---

1   Matthew C. Klein, Jordan Schneider, and David Talbot, "Only a Financial NATO Can Win the Economic War," *Foreign Policy*, March 23, 2022.

2   "Columnists Exchange: Should NATO Become Engaged in the War in Ukraine?," *Financial Times*, March 24, 2022.

of the US as "co-combatant."[3] Only fighter jets and a "no-fly zone"—i.e., bombing Russian airfields—have so far caused any hesitation in these quarters. But there is growing pressure to concede both. The *Wall Street Journal* demands enough airborne matériel to make a no-fly zone redundant: 28 MiG-29s, alongside Su-25s, S-200s, S-300s, and switchblade drones.[4] From this perspective, $800 million in new aid announced on March 15 was a kind of capitulation, "as if Mr. Biden is so wary of provoking Mr. Putin that he's afraid what might happen if Ukraine *won* the war."

This bravado extends to the culture industry at large, where signs abound of a moment akin to that which followed 9/11, when renaming French fries occupied the dead time between Operations Enduring and Iraqi Freedom. Then as now, to set the attack in context was to excuse it; and there is the rush to *do* something, which takes a certain pride in not having thought through the consequences. What has changed is not just the erosion of the unipolar moment, but the multiplication of pathways for virtual war, for participating in it, and being manipulated by it: crowd-funding urban militias on Twitter, posting videos of captured tanks or "army cats," to Instagram and TikTok. The result is somewhere between war as the health of the state and war as self-care—with ballerinas, pianists, painters, and scientists disinvited from fellowships or shows, against blue-and-yellow banners and emojis, at no cost to Americans doing it. Warner Brothers will deny Russian teenagers Batman, Twitch will stop paying them to play video games online, Facebook will allow some users to call for their deaths.

Yet if the *pitch* of hysteria is as high as anything after 9/11—the free world, civilization, good and evil, all hang in the balance once again—there is less unanimity of opinion behind it. Some of the same outlets demanding punitive sanctions, cultural boycotts and unlimited military aid have also carried dissenting voices. So far, these have been politically eclectic, as likely to be on the right as the left: the IR realist John Mearsheimer; Branko Milanovic, the scholar of inequality; former editor of the *New Republic* Peter Beinart; the conservative Catholic Ross Douthat, who urged caution in the *New York Times*, going further than his colleague Thomas Friedman in pointing out that "America and NATO are not just innocent bystanders"; the *sanderista* Elizabeth Bruenig, now at the *Atlantic*; and on

---

3   David E. Sanger et al., "Arming Ukraine: 17,000 Anti-Tank Weapons in 6 Days and a Clandestine Cybercorps," *New York Times*, March 6, 2022.

4   Editorial Board, "Why Not Victory in Ukraine?," *Wall Street Journal*, March 16, 2022.

to Tulsi Gabbard and Tucker Carlson, called traitors or worse, as outliers on the left and right in Congress or TV.

Beyond these cases, how has the American left—defined broadly as critical of capitalism, to one degree or another—reacted to the war? A small group has resisted jingoism in all its forms. The *Nation*'s publisher, Katrina vanden Heuvel, condemned the invasion but also the "rank irrationality" and "arrogance" of US officials whose drive to extend a military alliance to Russia's borders provided the context for it. She called on Biden to press for an immediate ceasefire and Russian withdrawal in exchange for Ukraine's neutrality. Keith Gessen, a founding editor of *n+1*, offered a powerful account of the origins of the war, eschewing pop psychology in favor of history and reportage to question its inevitability.[5] At the other end of the spectrum, some have eagerly joined a liberal smear campaign against alleged *putinistas*, among them George Monbiot in the *Guardian* and Paul Mason in the *New Statesman*, the latter calling for a massive military stimulus to prepare for the coming global conflagration. In the US, this role has gone directly to "culture vultures" at *New York Magazine* or *Vice*.

The largest cohort—the DSA and Squad left; writers for *Jacobin*, *Dissent*, *Jewish Currents*, the *Intercept*, and other smaller publications—lies somewhere in between. Their positions differ only by degree and nuance from the State Department line: against broad sanctions, most also object to pouring arms into Ukraine. But their stance is basically defensive, trumpeting their condemnation of Russia rather than criticizing Biden or NATO, in part to preempt accusations of "tankiness." DSA's initial statement was meandering and vague, though Democrats lined up to disavow it anyway. AOC, whose star it helped to launch, issued a communiqué a few days later, topping off a denunciation of "Putin and his oligarchs" by insisting that "any military action must take place with Congressional approval." As a rallying cry, this one—in effect, "no war of annihilation without congressional approval"—leaves something to be desired. In *Jacobin*, Branko Marcetic sounded just as tough, if more concerned about nuclear war. Thanks to Jeremy Scahill, the *Intercept* continues to document the sheer scale of weapons transfers, but it too has tried to distance itself from a "tankie left" that "makes excuses" for Putin.[6]

---

5   Keith Gessen, "Was It Inevitable? A Short History of Russia's War on Ukraine," *Guardian*, March 11, 2022.

6   Roane Carey, "Don't Be a Tankie: How the Left Should Respond to Russia's Invasion of Ukraine," *Intercept*, March 1, 2022.

This cohort tends to support the "good sanctions" advocated by Thomas Piketty—wielded against "the thin social layer of multi-millionaires on which the regime relies" rather than ordinary Russians.[7] Comparatively humane in spirit, sadly naive in practice, these proposals misunderstood the motives of the power they sought to guide. Within days, Washington rolled out measures to induce a socioeconomic crisis of ordinary savers and earners, while leaving the rich relatively unscathed. "We are going to cause the collapse of the Russian economy," explained France's finance minister, matter-of-factly. Closer readings of books by two architects of the modern sanctions regime, Juan Zarate under Bush and Richard Nephew under Obama, might have cleared up some illusions about their purpose. Iranification is the order of the day, not sanctions with a social democratic twist.

In this sense, a significant section of the left has failed to think beyond a liberal interventionist framework, even if it disagrees with aspects of Biden's response. In *Jewish Currents*, David Klion outlined NATO's expansion and the fears of encirclement this aroused, only to dismiss it as irrelevant: the sole explanation is that "something fundamental has changed in Putin's own mind." In *Dissent*, Greg Afinogenov kept up the attack on those "obsessing" over NATO—blaming a provincialism on the US left that blinded it to greater Russian nationalism, even as he rejected deeper involvement. For Eric Levitz in *New York Magazine*, many socialists were simply "too ideologically rigid to see the conflict through clear eyes." There was "no basis for believing Western imperialism was the chief obstacle to a diplomatic resolution." In fact, wasn't the left morally bound to defend "a democratic government struggling against domination by a far-right autocracy," with arms, sanctions, and the protection of NATO, if that's what it took? Setting out to complicate the "pat ideological answers" of the left, Levitz reproduced the standard justifications for US intervention from the liberal and neoconservative right—without trying to characterize US foreign policy in general, or situate its specific response here in any longer historical continuum.

Neither the respectable left nor the hardline liberals can explain how spiraling "punishments" are meant to bring a quick end to the war, still less a lasting peace. Could it be they are not designed to, and that the US and its allies see a chance to settle their own strategic interests in the

7   Thomas Piketty, "Sanction the Oligarchs, Not the People," *Le Monde* blog, February 15, 2022.

"geopolitical pivot" of Eurasia—in which Ukrainian sovereignty, to say nothing of Ukrainian lives, figures at most incidentally? "On NATO territory, we should be the Pakistan," declared NSA alumnus Douglas Lute. Condoleezza Rice had the same message of support for "throwing the book" at Russia on the grounds that—expressed without a hint of irony —"when you invade a sovereign nation, that is a war crime." Hillary Clinton was even more explicit: the Russian debacle in Afghanistan in the 1980s ought to be the "model" for Ukraine. Plans to turn Ukraine into a new Afghanistan, from the people who just released the old one into the grip of famine, ought to give pause to anyone concerned about Ukrainians.

Even more striking than the hypocrisy of the imperial core is its continuity of outlook: regime change is the unofficial order of the day. If Biden finally said as much in Poland on March 26, this simply underscores how little need he feels to compromise with a government in Moscow that Washington views as illegitimate: loser of the Cold War, weaker in all ways that matter, lacking a liberal or democratic fig leaf to cover its domestic predations, the regime is now a pariah of the "international community" too, and no doubt this looks to many in the security "blob" like the best chance they may ever have to be rid of it. It is worth sparing a moment, however, to recall the ineptitude of our rulers, whose previous efforts at regime change have ended in disaster. Even if the blithest assumptions of the US counter-offensive are borne out, it is not clear what would be gained by returning Russia to the state of economic and political collapse of the 1990s that gave rise to Putin. Ukraine would remain an issue, however pliant his replacement.

Here the narrow focus of the "non-tankie left" runs into an explanatory impasse. The idea that NATO is incidental to this crisis is belied not so much by "Putin's narrative" as the available American sources. In 2008, ambassador William Burns, now CIA chief, cabled that Ukraine and Georgia's aspirations to join the alliance were "neuralgic points" for Russia, which could lead it to intervene militarily.[8] Yet the US continued to hold out the prospect of long-term membership to Ukraine, even as it withdrew from major arms control treaties with Russia and pressed forward with a $1 trillion "modernization" of its nuclear arsenal. In January, Biden rejected two draft security agreements submitted by Russia as the basis for talks in Geneva, including proposals to limit military drills on its border

---

8   See Chapter 10.

and exclude Ukraine. "NATO's door is open," was Blinken's dismissive response.

But the real turning point came earlier, as Mary Elise Sarotte's new history of NATO expansion, *Not One Inch*, makes clear. Taking its title from the agreement that Secretary of State James Baker proposed to Gorbachev in 1990, that if he assented to German reunification NATO would "not shift one inch eastward from its current position," the book details how the exact opposite came to pass—with the US pursuing swift incorporation of all former Warsaw Pact countries, starting with East Germany, the moment Soviet collapse looked imminent. For those who think the issue of Ukraine begins and ends with Putin, Sarotte relates how the pacifistic Gorbachev furiously insisted to Bush that "Ukraine in its current borders would be an unstable construct," had "come into existence only because local Bolsheviks had at one point gerrymandered it that way" by adding Kharkov and Donbas, and Khrushchev later "passed the Crimea from Russia to the Ukraine as a fraternal gesture."[9] No overtures of any kind from NATO should be made directly to it. When Baker pressed a Russian negotiator over nuclear weapons in Ukraine, and what would happen to them in the event of a war with Kiev, the naive reply reads as a tragic signpost en route to the present crisis. He "responded that there were 12 million Russians in Ukraine, with 'many mixed marriages,' so 'what sort of war could that be?' Baker answered simply: 'A normal war.'"

If much of the left is subdued, there seem to be two main reasons. The first stems from its relationship to the Democratic Party since 2016, which has effectively neutralized it as a caucus and activist base. Absent any movement on social reform legislation, progressives have gone along with the quest to link Trump to Putin, to the point that Russophobia increasingly defines the party as such. On this issue, most of the Squad hardly differ from the chair of the House Intelligence Committee. The second is moral sententiousness, underpinned by a powerfully selective memory. Months after the retreat from Afghanistan and theft of its reserves—and during the US-backed Saudi bombing of Yemen—this country is not in a position to dispense moral lessons. As an upholder of the principle of national sovereignty, its credibility is nil. And the moral vacuity of its position matters, not because it absolves Russia of wrongdoing in a warm bath of reciprocal turpitude, but because it points to the urgent need to proceed

---

9   Mary E. Sarotte, *Not One Inch: America, Russia, and the Making of Post–Cold War Stalemate* (New Haven, CT: Yale University Press, 2021), p. 127.

on some other basis if the aim is to find a peaceful solution. Crowd-funding bombs to fuel fighting in Kiev is not that. Nor are indiscriminate sanctions in pursuit of regime change in Moscow. At a minimum, the US left should summon what modest reserves of independence and strength it has to call on its own government to deescalate, pursue direct and indirect talks, to trade guarantees of neutrality for a ceasefire and troop withdrawal. A refusal to contemplate any alteration to a post–Cold War order forged in hubris by the victors is not toughness. It is warmongering.

20

Joining the West

Lily Lynch

A famous quote from Desmond Tutu—"if you are neutral in situations of injustice then you are choosing the side of the oppressor"—has been widely used and abused since Russia's invasion of Ukraine. In numerous fora, it has been deployed to harangue countries into abandoning their neutrality and lining up behind NATO. Never mind that the oppressor to which Tutu referred was apartheid South Africa, a regime actively supported by the Atlantic military alliance. In both Russia and the West, the current moment is characterized by a constantly replenished amnesia.

1

In mid-May 2022, Finland and Sweden opted to repeal their long-standing neutrality policies. Both countries submitted applications to join NATO, in a move that was rightly described as historic. Finland has been neutral since it was defeated by the Soviet Union during the Second World War—signing a Treaty of Friendship, Cooperation and Mutual Assistance with the Soviets in 1948. Sweden, meanwhile, fought numerous wars with Russia between the sixteenth and eighteenth centuries but managed to stay out of any further conflict after 1814. Joining NATO discards a centuries-old tradition that has come to define the country's national identity.

Press coverage of the push for NATO membership has been euphoric. While Sweden has witnessed a limited but still lively debate, in Finland there has been little space for public dissent. On May 17, the cover of Finland's most-read newspaper, *Helsingin Sanomat*, featured an illustration of two blue-and-white figures (the colors of the Finnish flag) rowing a Viking longship toward an illuminated horizon where the four-pointed NATO star is seen rising like the sun. The wooden ship is depicted leaving behind a dark, hulking structure decorated with a red star. The symbolism couldn't be clearer. Or perhaps it could. Several weeks prior, the online version of Sweden's *Dagens Nyheter* featured a pop-up animation of the NATO emblem morphing into a peace sign.

In this media environment, it is perhaps unsurprising that support for NATO membership is high: about 60 percent in Sweden and 75 percent in Finland, at the time of writing. But a closer look at the demographics reveals some cracks in the pro-NATO narrative. For the Atlanticist press, "the NATO question" represents a generational shift, with young people supposedly eager to join against the wishes of their parents, who, we are told, are hopelessly wedded to an outmoded position of Cold War non-alignment. "Having been firmly opposed to any NATO move only weeks ago," wrote former Swedish prime minister turned liberal think tank groupie Carl Bildt, the political class "will now face a contest between an older generation and younger ones looking at the world with fresh eyes."

In reality, though, the opposite is true: the demographic most opposed to NATO membership in Sweden is young men aged eighteen to twenty-nine.[1] And little wonder. They are the segment of the population that would be called upon to join any future military excursion. Contrary to the assumption that Russian aggression has shocked Swedes into unanimous support for the alliance, opposition appears to be on the rise. On March 23, 44 percent of young people surveyed were for NATO and 21 percent against. Two months later, 43 percent of them were for NATO and 32 percent against: a double-digit leap. Support for membership rises with each age bracket, with the elderly most staunchly in favor. The latest polls from Finland tell a similar story. Polling by *Helsingin Sanomat* describes

---

1   "Novus: Unga män mest kritiska till Nato," *SVT Nyheter*, May 11, 2022.

the typical NATO supporter as educated, middle-aged or older, male, working in a management-level position, earning at least €85,000 a year and politically on the right, while the typical NATO skeptic is under the age of thirty, a worker or a student, earning less than €20,000 a year and politically on the left.[2]

Some of the most ardent supporters of NATO membership can be found among Sweden and Finland's business leaders. In June 2022, Finnish president Sauli Niinistö hosted a "secret NATO meeting" in Helsinki. Among those in attendance were Swedish minister of finance Mikael Damberg, top-ranking military officials and powerful figures in the Swedish and Finnish business communities. Chief among them was the billionaire Swedish industrialist Jacob Wallenberg, whose family holdings add up to one-third of the Stockholm Stock Exchange. Wallenberg has been NATO's most enthusiastic cheerleader among Swedish executives. He is a regular participant in the Bilderberg Meeting, an elite group dedicated to spreading the gospel of Atlanticism and free markets. In the weeks leading up to Sweden's decision to apply for NATO membership, the *Financial Times* predicted that the Wallenberg dynasty's stance on Swedish accession would "weigh heavily" on the ruling Social Democrats, over whom he is thought to hold considerable sway.

At the Helsinki summit, Swedish government officials were warned that their country would become less attractive for foreign capital if it remained "the only state in Northern Europe outside of NATO."[3] This, along with significant cajoling from Finland, was one of the decisive factors that led Minister of Defense Peter Hultqvist to change tack and swing behind the alliance. Sweden's *Expressen* reported that the meeting suggested the business community holds far greater power over foreign policy decisions than previously thought. It's not hard to see why business is so invested. Swedish defense industry giant Saab is expecting major profits from NATO membership. The company, whose majority shareholder is the Wallenberg family, has seen its share price nearly double since the Russian invasion. Chief Executive Micael Johansson has said that Sweden's NATO membership will open new possibilities for Saab in the areas of missile defense and surveillance. The company is expecting

---

2   Jarmo Huhtanen, "Nato-kannatus nousi ennätykselliseen 73 prosenttiin," *Helsingin Sanomat*, May 11, 2022.

3   Tomas Nordenskiöld, "Regeringen i hemligt Nato-möte i Finland," *Expressen*, April 11, 2022.

dramatic gains as European countries raise their defense spending, and first quarter reports reveal that operating profits have already risen 10 percent over last year, to $32 million.

The considerable influence of business leaders on the NATO question contrasts with that of the general public. Though Sweden has held referenda on every major decision in recent history—EU membership, the adoption of the euro—it will not consult its citizens on NATO. The most prominent politician to call for a vote is Left Party leader Nooshi Dadgostar, but her requests have been flatly rejected. The government, fearing that NATO membership could be voted down once wartime hysteria wears off, has instead taken a "shock doctrine" approach, ramming the policy through while Ukraine is still in the headlines and the public is afraid. They have also said that a referendum would require extensive organization and could not be held for some months. This means the issue of NATO membership would feature in the September election campaign: a scenario the Social Democrats are determined to avoid.

In Finland, however, there is little mainstream opposition to NATO. The issue has been tinged by nationalist sentiment, and opponents of membership are accused of not caring about their country's security. Parliament voted overwhelmingly in favor of membership in May 2022, with 188 for and only eight against. Of those eight, one was from the right-populist Finns Party, another was a former member of the same outfit, and the remaining six were from the Left Alliance. The other ten Left Alliance MPs, though, voted in favor. One of the party's representatives went so far as to propose new legislation that would criminalize attempts to influence public opinion on behalf of a foreign power: a precedent that could in theory leave NATO critics exposed to prosecution.[4] Recep Tayyip Erdoğan has slowed some of this breakneck momentum. Calling Finland and Sweden "incubators" for Kurdish terror, the Turkish president has vowed to block the two Nordic countries' accession to NATO until they meet his demands. (The alliance requires unanimous approval from all member states for a new country to join.) Erdoğan has blasted Finland and Sweden over their refusal to extradite thirty-three members of the PKK and Gülenist movement, blaming the latter for a bloody coup attempt in 2016. He has also demanded that Sweden lift an arms embargo that it imposed in response to Turkey's incursions in Syria in 2019.

---

4   Lakialoite LA 26/2022 vp, eduskunta.fi, May 23, 2022.

Kurdish issues have recently had an outsize presence in Swedish politics. When the Social Democrats lost their parliamentary majority in 2021, Prime Minister Magdalena Andersson was forced to negotiate directly with a Kurdish MP and ex-Peshmerga fighter named Amineh Kakabaveh, whose vote would decide the fortunes of the government. In exchange for keeping it afloat, Kakabaveh demanded that Sweden lend its support to the YPG in Syria, and the Social Democrats acceded. Since then, Kakabaveh has chided Andersson for "giving in" to Erdoğan and threatened to withdraw her support for the government. The Social Democrats may have avoided making the autumn elections an unofficial referendum on NATO membership, but their government remains extremely weak, and will face intense scrutiny in the months ahead. Many fear that it will strike a private deal with Erdoğan to sacrifice Kurdish activists and Turkish dissidents if he agrees to wave through its NATO bid. Meanwhile, Croatia's increasingly audacious president, Zoran Milanović, has erected another, smaller obstacle: promising to block Sweden and Finland's membership unless Bosnia and Herzegovina's election law is changed so that Bosnian Croats are better represented.

The media, both foreign and domestic, have frequently described Finland and Sweden's accession as "joining the West"—picking a side in the Huntington-esque civilizational struggle.[5] This rhetoric is nothing new. Shortly before Montenegro joined the alliance in 2017, the country's long-reigning premier, Milo Đukanović, said that the division was not "for NATO or against NATO," it was "civilizational and cultural."[6] Yet it is especially odd, and revealing, to encounter this same auto-orientalism in Scandinavia. One right-wing commentator recently wrote that by joining NATO, Sweden was at last becoming a "normal Western country." He then paused to consider whether the government would soon abolish the Systembolaget, or state liquor monopoly. Here we get a sense of what "joining the West" really means: binding oneself to a US-led power bloc and simultaneously doing away with any nominally socialist institutions —a process that has already been underway for decades.

The abandonment of principled neutrality as a moral option follows the changing meaning of internationalism, especially for the left in the Nordic

5　Linus Hagström, "Disciplinary Power: Text and Body in the Swedish NATO Debate," *Cooperation and Conflict* 56:2 (2021), pp. 141–62.

6　Filip Kovacevic, "NATO's Neocolonial Discourse and Its Resisters: The Case of Montenegro," *Socialism and Democracy* 31:1 (2017), pp. 43–59.

countries.[7] During the Cold War, the Swedish Social Democrats expressed the principle of international solidarity through their support for national liberation movements in the so-called Global South. No figure better embodied this spirit than Olof Palme, who posed for photos smoking cigars with Fidel Castro and famously excoriated the US aerial bombardment of Hanoi and Haiphong, comparing it to "Guernica, Oradour, Babi Yar, Katyn, Lidice, Sharpeville, [and] Treblinka." During the breakup of Yugoslavia in the 1990s, however, such "active internationalism" was reconceptualized as "responsibility to protect" certain non-Western victims of aggression. By the same logic, states are now expected to band together in an "alliance of democracies" to confront tyranny and terrorism—through regime change where necessary.

But the decision to join NATO does not just rely on a hollowed-out discourse of solidarity; it is also presented as a vital act of self-interest—a defensive response to the "Russian threat." In Sweden's case, we are asked to believe that the country is currently facing greater security risks than during both World Wars, and that the only way to address them is to enter a beefed-up military alliance. Although Russia is supposedly struggling to make headway against a much weaker opponent in Ukraine—unable to hold the capital, hemorrhaging troops and supplies—we are told that it poses an imminent threat to Stockholm and Helsinki. Amid such confected panic, genuine threats to the Nordic way of life have gone ignored: the withering away of the welfare state, the privatization and marketization of education, rising inequality and the weakening of the universal healthcare system. While rushing to align with "the West," the Swedish and Finnish governments have shown considerably less urgency in tackling these social crises.

2

In the EU-NATO protectorate of Kosovo, a small bureaucratic matter has provoked a spasm of violence. It was practically a routine occurrence, but trigger-happy Cold Warriors were quick to announce the beginning of a new Balkan war. The threat of a new conflict in the Balkans—to be instigated by Russia in concert with its Orthodox brothers in Serbia—has

---

7   Ann-Sofie Dahl, "Sweden: Once a Moral Superpower, Always a Moral Superpower?," *International Journal* 61:4 (2006), pp. 895–908.

proven to be a useful specter for the West, used to justify NATO expansion, distended budgets and the continued presence of the so-called international community. But it has also proven useful for Russia, allowing Moscow to claim that it still has a best friend in Europe, even as Belgrade moves quietly toward the West.

At issue this time were identification papers and license plates. At the end of June 2022, the government in Pristina announced plans to introduce new measures that would require the Serbian minority to obtain provisional, Kosovo-issued documents and plates for their vehicles. Kosovo today has a population of a little under 2 million, of which about 90 percent are Albanian; Serbs are the second biggest ethnic group, comprising between 4 and 7 percent. Pristina considers these reciprocal measures, as citizens of Kosovo need Serbian documents and plates in Serbia. The bureaucratic confusion is an outgrowth of Kosovo's contested status. Although Kosovo declared independence in 2008, Serbia still claims it as its southern province and holy Serbian land.

On July 31, in Serb-majority municipalities in Kosovo's north, locals expressed their discontent with the new rules by blocking roads near two border crossings with Serbia, now something of an annual ritual. Police were also reportedly shot at by unknown gunmen. Kosovo's imperial viceroy, the US ambassador Jeffrey Hovenier, brought the situation under control by directing Prime Minister Albin Kurti to delay implementation of the new measures by thirty days. The status quo—an uneasy but relatively durable peace—was restored. Observers in Kosovo remarked that the moment reflected Kurti's "political maturation." Tacit capitulation to the authority of the US embassy was an admission that all major government efforts require coordination with Kosovo's colonial administrators.

It has been a dramatic turn for "Kosovo's Che Guevara," who once led street protests against privatization and set off tear gas in parliament. Kurti's political philosophy was modeled on anticolonialist struggle in the so-called Global South; his party's name, *Lëvizja Vetëvendosje*, means "the movement for self-determination." A decade ago, the US ambassador accused the party of sending threats to former secretary of state Madeleine Albright, a champion of US intervention in Kosovo whose Albright Capital Management was controversially in the running to purchase the state telecommunications company. But those were different times. In July, Kurti was in Washington for the third time since April to sign the $202 million Kosovo Compact with the US government's Millennium

Challenge Corporation, represented by CEO Alice Albright, Madeleine's daughter.

The international community's decades-long tenure in Kosovo has long been the subject of considerable criticism, both from human rights organizations and within Kosovo. NATO's bombing of what remained of Yugoslavia in 1999 was purportedly to halt atrocities committed by Serbs, and initially met with much gratitude from the Albanian population. (Former Obama State Department official and current USAID head Samantha Power would later say that the bombing was also "partly about NATO credibility.") A number of international agencies, unaccountable to the population, were subsequently established to administer peace and democracy. The United Nations Interim Administration Mission in Kosovo (UNMIK) and NATO's Kosovo Force (KFOR) have been criticized for their failure to protect minorities from ethnic violence.[8] The Council of Europe would also accuse NATO of "obstructionism" in its investigation of alleged torture in KFOR detention camps, and its human rights envoy described Camp Bondsteel, the US military base in Kosovo, as a "smaller version of Guantanamo."[9] The European Union's Rule of Law Mission (EULEX), meanwhile, was dogged by serious accusations of corruption and bribery—exactly the kind of thing it was intended to combat. In 2020, the year its tenure was supposed to come to an end, Kosovo was ranked 104 out of 180 countries by Transparency International's Corruption Perceptions Index, a testament to EULEX's failures.

This recent controversy over papers and plates is compounded by wider tensions. Serbs in Kosovo say that the government in Pristina has not kept its promises, failing to implement a critical part of the 2013 Brussels Agreement with Belgrade: the creation of the Association of Serbian Municipalities, a political body that would govern the ten municipalities in Kosovo where Serbs comprise a majority. Much of the disagreement is rooted in the "constructive ambiguity" of the negotiations. For Serbia, the association is a third layer of government that should protect the rights of Serbs; for Kosovo, it is only a civic association, without any executive power. Kosovo's Albanians on the other hand feel they have waited far too long for full sovereignty. Although Kosovo declared independence fourteen years ago, it remains only partially recognized as a sovereign state.

---

8   "Failure to Protect: UNMIK and KFOR's Inability to Protect Serbs and Other Minorities," Human Rights Watch, July 2004; available at hrw.org.

9   "Questions Arise Over US Base in Kosovo," Deutsche Welle, December 10, 2005.

(Kosovo's Ministry of Foreign Affairs says that it is currently recognized by 117 countries; five of the EU's twenty-seven states do not recognize it.) Many also feel that the Serbs in the north have been treated well enough, pointing out that they have not paid for their own electricity in twenty-three years—in recent times it has been paid for by the government of Kosovo, at a cost of 40 million euros last year. Pristina is keen on resolving the issue, and local Serbs know that electricity bills are coming soon.

As the unrest in the north appeared to be stabilizing, a couple of well-known Cold War–mongers took to social media to report that Serbia, with backing from Russia, had just attacked Kosovo. A litany of unsubstantiated rumors spread: a new front in the confrontation between Russia and the West had opened; Serbia was invading; men wearing uniforms of the Russian paramilitary Wagner Group had been spotted. Francis Fukuyama joined the chorus, tweeting a recent photo of Kurti and himself with the comment that he "deserves our support in his present confrontation with Serbia." It was a fitting epitaph to the end of history, given the centrality of the Kosovo precedent in resurrecting it.[10]

It is important to pause here and say that in Kosovo, reckless rumor-mongering of this kind has gotten many people killed. In March of 2004, the drowning of three Albanian children—a day after a young Serbian man was shot—was erroneously blamed on local Serbs. Sensationalist media accounts followed. Over the next two days, Kosovo saw the worst ethnic violence since the war ended in 1999. When it was all over, nineteen people were dead and more than nine hundred injured. Some twenty-nine Serbian Orthodox churches and monasteries were severely damaged or destroyed. More than eight hundred homes belonging to Serbs, Roma, and Ashkali were attacked and destroyed. Over four thousand people were displaced. As an OSCE report detailing the media's role in fanning the flames of the violence states: "Without the reckless and sensationalist reporting on 16 and 17 March, events could have taken a different turn. They might not have reached the intensity and level of brutality that was witnessed or even might not have taken place at all."[11] Elsewhere the report issued a more general warning: "In a post-ethnic conflict society such as Kosovo, biased reporting alone can lead to

---

10   Masha Gessen, "How the Kosovo Air War Foreshadowed the Crisis in Ukraine," *New Yorker*, February 15, 2022.

11   "The Role of the Media in the March 2004 Events in Kosovo," OSCE, 2004; available at osce.org.

violence." Presumably, at least some keyboard Cold Warriors are aware of this, and yet they do it anyway.

Kurti has also been eager to invoke the specter of conflict. In recent months, he has realized that he can garner greater support in Western capitals by drawing parallels with Ukraine. He recently told Italian media that the risk of war was "very high" and emphasized that Kosovo, like Ukraine, was "a democracy bordering an autocracy." Critics of these ominous pronouncements argue that he is prioritizing pleasing the West and the diaspora over people living in Kosovo. Inflation is at 14.1 percent, while the unemployment rate is 25.9 percent (youth unemployment is particularly grim, at nearly 50 percent). Nemanja Starović, the state secretary of Serbia's Ministry of Foreign Affairs, argued last week that Pristina was trying to portray Serbian president Aleksandar Vučić as a "mini Putin" and Kurti as "petit Zelensky," in hopes that any escalation "would by default trigger US and NATO support for Kosovo" regardless of who started the violence.

Perhaps surprisingly, Ukraine is among the states that do not recognize Kosovo. But there have been new efforts to change that. Serbia has drawn Western criticism of late for its refusal to impose sanctions on Russia. There have been calls to revoke its EU candidate status. Images of football hooligans in Putin T-shirts marching in central Belgrade in support of Russia's "special military operation" have added to the outrage. Serbian public opinion is decidedly more sympathetic to Russia than that of any other country in Europe: according to recent polls, only 26 percent of Serbs view Russia as responsible for the invasion of Ukraine.[12] Serbian government media reproduces many Russian talking points about the war. Kurti has seized on these external markers of Russian-Serbian brotherhood to garner foreign support for his efforts to assert control over the north and advance Kosovo's independence. On August 6, 2022, an MP in the Ukrainian parliament registered a bill to recognize Kosovo as an independent country.

Upon closer inspection, however, the image of Serbia as a faithful servant of Moscow starts to fall apart. At the United Nations, Serbia has consistently voted to condemn Russia's invasion of Ukraine. Serbia has been a member of NATO's bilateral Partnership for Peace program since 2006. In recent years, Serbia has participated in more military exercises

12   Maxim Samorukov, "Last Friend in Europe: How Far Will Russia Go to Preserve Its Alliance with Serbia?," Carnegie Endowment for International Peace, October 6, 2022; available at carnegieendowment.org.

with NATO than it has with Russia. While Western media has fixated on the presence of Putin coffee mugs at tourist stands in Belgrade, Serbia has quietly held high-level meetings at NATO headquarters. Last year, NATO secretary general Jens Stoltenberg thanked President Vučić for his "personal commitment" to the partnership between Serbia and NATO. The Serbian armed forces have also worked closely with KFOR, the NATO security force in Kosovo, for many years. Serbia might be pro-Russia before the domestic public; but behind closed doors, it is closer to the West.

You wouldn't know any of this judging by media accounts from any side. The myth of eternal Serbian-Russian brotherhood is simply too useful to everyone: Russia, NATO, Kosovo and Serbia. But it is also possible that if Cold Warriors continue with the reckless dissemination of rumors of war, they will get the violence they want.

3

"The fantasy of an instinctively peaceful world may be comforting, but it is again coming to an end," Alex Karp, CEO of Peter Thiel's CIA-funded Palantir, wrote in an ominous open letter to European leaders a few weeks after the full-scale invasion of Ukraine. A co-founder of the company— and Thiel's Stanford roommate in the early nineties—Karp warned the continent of the high cost of complacency in the face of the "aspirations of autocratic rule," and reminded them that for the past two decades Europe "has stood on the sidelines of the digital revolution, whose principal participants are still essentially all based in the United States."

The message was straightforward: innovate or die. Adopt Palantir technologies as the US military has done, or risk domination. Elsewhere, Karp has been no less pointed. "Military AI will determine our lives, the lives of your kids," he said in an interview at Davos in 2020. "This is a zero-sum thing. The country with the most important AI, the most powerful AI, will determine the rules. That country should either be us or a Western country." At the beginning of June, Karp traveled to Ukraine to make a similar pitch about the role of technology in modern warfare to President Zelensky. The meeting marked the first visit of a CEO to Ukraine since the war began. (Karp would later gush that Zelensky was one of the very few heads of state he'd ever met whom he could imagine serving as a successful CEO.)

A few weeks later, a sprawling transatlantic "innovation" architecture was announced that will facilitate precisely what Karp and Palantir have been advocating. At NATO's summit in Madrid, the alliance declared the creation of "the world's first multi-sovereign venture capital fund" to invest in start-ups and other entities working on technologies "with great military potential"—including artificial intelligence, autonomy, big-data processing, biotechnology and human enhancement.[13] As Secretary General Jens Stoltenberg explained, "The NATO Innovation Fund will help bring to life those nascent technologies that have the power to transform our security in the decades to come, strengthening the alliance's innovation ecosystem and bolstering the security of our one billion citizens."

The fund is described as a complement to NATO's new Defense Innovation Accelerator of the North Atlantic, known by its unsettling anthropoid acronym, DIANA. Modeled on the US Defense Research Projects Agency, DARPA, whose best-known achievement is the creation of the internet, DIANA will encompass sixty innovation sites in twenty NATO member states. With its European headquarters at Imperial College London, the endeavor is said to be a "joint effort between private-sector entities, non-governmental entities, and academia" to ensure the alliance "can *harness the best of new technology for transatlantic security.*" A further ten accelerator sites will provide financing and mentorship to technology start-ups with potential application in warfare, and there will be more than fifty "dedicated test centres" spread across the alliance.

The news was met with enthusiasm by those in the habit of issuing grave pronouncements about the West "falling behind." A writer at the *National Interest* even declared that "innovation could save NATO."[14] These cyclical efforts to "save NATO" by finding a new raison d'être for it every decade or so brings to mind the quip about the alliance "attempting to justify its own existence in ever more imaginative ways."[15]

This push for "innovation" is the product of grander developments. Madrid saw the unveiling of NATO's new strategic concept, its first since 2010. The sixteen-page document describes a very different world than the last, one in which "the Euro-Atlantic area is not at peace," and—echoing

13   "NATO Launches Innovation Fund," NATO, June 30, 2022; available at the NATO website.

14   Zachary Kallenborn, "Can a Focus on Innovation Save NATO?," *National Interest*, June 23, 2022.

15   "Does NATO Have a Purpose Any Longer?," *Guardian*, June 12, 2011.

the Biden administration's rhetoric—"authoritarian" actors are threatening our democracies.[16] The Russian Federation represents "the most significant and direct threat to Allies' security and to peace and stability in the Euro-Atlantic area." But in a historic move, China is explicitly described as a "systemic challenge" for the first time. "The People's Republic of China's (PRC) stated ambitions and coercive policies challenge our interests, security and values," the concept states (relatedly, NATO invited the leaders of Japan, South Korea, Australia, and New Zealand to the summit—another historic first). While the document says that allies "remain open to constructive engagement with China," the intention is to reconfigure NATO as an anti-China military alliance, on belligerent US–UK lines.

That NATO identified China as a systemic challenge at the same time it announced a vast program to accelerate technological innovation is no coincidence. While NATO and companies like Palantir have seized on the invasion of Ukraine to push this agenda, Russia is not the West's main competitor in the field of new technology. "NATO is primarily concerned with Chinese (rather than Russian) innovation in the field of emerging and disruptive technologies," Simona Soares, a fellow of the International Institute for Strategic Studies wrote in a German Marshall Fund report last year. "China is the main geopolitical driver behind allied innovation plans."[17]

The reorientation is especially significant for the EU. "For the first time since the Mongol invasion of Europe in the 13th century, European powers now view an Asian power as a direct threat," Jo Inge Bekkevold, a former Norwegian intelligence official and fellow at its Institute for Defence Studies, proclaimed in a recent article for *Foreign Policy*. Bekkevold envisions an emerging division of labor for the alliance, with the US focused on China, the EU on Russia.[18]

Until recently, there had been optimism about the trajectory of EU–China relations. The draft of an ambitious comprehensive investment agreement was drawn up, after protracted negotiations. In 2018, EU military forces conducted a combined naval exercise with the People's Liberation Army at a Chinese military base in Djibouti. In 2020, China

---

16   "NATO 2022 Strategic Concept"; available on the NATO website.

17   Simona R. Soare, "Innovation as Adaptation: NATO and Emerging Technologies," German Marshall Fund of the United States, June 11, 2021.

18   Jo Inge Bekkevold, "NATO's New Division of Labor on Russia and China Won't Be Easy," *Foreign Policy*, July 11, 2022.

surpassed the United States to become the EU's largest trading partner. And while Beijing has repeatedly blamed "US-led NATO" for the war in Ukraine, it has largely refrained from directly criticizing the EU. Editorials in Chinese media assert that "a weaker Europe serves US interests" and describe the heavy price, in soaring food and energy prices, that Europeans are being made to pay for US imperial ambitions. "China and the EU should act as two major forces upholding world peace, and offset uncertainties in the international landscape," Xi Jinping told EU leaders at a summit in April, exhorting them to reject the "rival-bloc mentality" promoted by the US.

Relations, however, have been deteriorating in recent months, with many European countries abandoning their "tightrope diplomacy" with China and lining up decisively behind the United States and NATO.[19] The full-scale invasion of Ukraine, and Beijing's reticence to criticize Russia for it, has hastened this process. In April, EU chief diplomat Josep Borrell published a blog post titled "On China's Choices and Responsibilities" excoriating Beijing for its "pro-Russian neutrality."[20] All three Baltic states have pulled out of the 17+1 China-CEE initiative—established by Beijing a decade ago to strengthen relations with Central and Eastern Europe. The new German ambassador in Beijing used her first public speech in the country, in September 2022, to raise concerns about China's zero-Covid policy and tensions across the Taiwan Strait.

It is little wonder then that developments in Madrid have met with a frosty reception in Beijing. Chinese Foreign Ministry spokesperson Zhao Lijian condemned the new strategic concept, lambasting NATO for promoting conflict, confrontation and "a Cold War mentality." When Germany subsequently announced that it would send warplanes to take part in US-led exercises in the Indo-Pacific, the Chinese Foreign Ministry's response was mockery, saying that this "will probably lead to some bad memories and associations in many countries in the world."[21]

NATO member states may be more united behind the US than ever before, but there are likely to be disagreements over some of the

---

19   Philippe Le Corre, "Europe's Tightrope Diplomacy on China," Carnegie Endowment for International Peace, March 24, 2021.

20   Josep Borrell, "On China's Choices and Responsibilities," April 6, 2022; available at eeas.europa.eu.

21   Liu Zhen, "'Bad Memories': China Mocks Germany's Plans to Expand Military Presence in Asia," *South China Morning Post*, September 1, 2022.

technologies in development. Of greatest concern are lethal autonomous weapons systems (LAWS), or "slaughterbots," which can search for targets and kill entirely independently. Several NATO members, including Belgium and Germany, have been much more reticent about these than the US and UK. The rise of this kind of technology has conjured fears of a new arms race with China. Karp is unapologetic about this: he says that Palantir is working on "a new Manhattan Project." The company is certainly prepared to go further than most. In 2019, it took over the Pentagon's Project Maven after Google abandoned it over "ethical concerns." The controversial project, which prompted walkouts from Google employees, aims to construct AI-powered surveillance systems for unmanned aerial vehicles.

Dissenting voices have expressed serious concerns, though they have been given predictably little space in the media. "DIANA and the NATO innovation fund will divert researchers and research funding in key civilian areas—e.g., AI, big data—thus reducing the potential benefits for health and environment, at a time of increasing poverty, inequality, pandemics, and ecological disasters," Stuart Parkinson, director of Scientists for Global Responsibility, wrote in an email of September 2022. "Innovation programs like DIANA are most likely to increase and entrench militarism for decades to come, undermining security for all."

But all of this is welcome news for some. Europe is decisively lining up behind the United States and NATO; talk of "decoupling from China" abounds. There is little ambiguity about what is happening. With the vast majority of the Global South loath to impose sanctions on Russia, the current global competition is one of "the West" against the rest. This serves the interests of the US and Silicon Valley quite well. "The core mission of our company," Karp said at Davos in 2020, "always was to make the West, especially America, the strongest in the world, the strongest it's ever been."

21

Ottoman Revival?

Cihan Tuğal

In April 2022, as the world was occupied with Vladimir Putin's invasion of Ukraine, a NATO member launched an attack on two of its neighboring territories. In a bombing campaign, Turkey targeted the camps of Kurdish militants in Iraq and Syria, inflicting damage on shelters, ammunition depots, and bases.[1]

The irony went largely unnoticed. That's hardly a surprise: for a long time, the Western world has turned a blind eye to Turkey's heavy-handed treatment of the Kurds. Across decades, the Turkish state has persecuted the Kurdish minority—about 18 percent of the population—with devastating zeal. Thousands have perished and around a million have been displaced in a campaign of severe internal repression.[2] But Western nations, except for a brief spell when Kurdish resistance was holding back an ascendant Islamic State, have rarely seemed to care.

---

1 "Turkey Launches New Offensive against Kurdish Rebels in Iraq," Al Jazeera, April 18, 2022.
2 "Turkey," Internal Displacement Monitoring Center, October 26, 2009.

1

Turkey's treatment of the Kurds is now center stage—but not because allies have woken up to the injustice of Kurds' systematic oppression. Instead, it's because Turkey is effectively threatening to block the admittance of Finland and Sweden to NATO unless they agree to crack down on Kurdish militants. For President Recep Tayyip Erdoğan of Turkey, seeing an opportunity to further cement his nationalist agenda, it's a bold gambit. The tepid response from NATO allies so far suggests he might be successful.

However the situation shakes out, it's deeply revealing. For Turkey, it underlines once again the vigor with which Erdoğan is keen to stamp out the Kurds while asserting the country as a regional power. For the alliance itself, the impasse brings to light facts currently obscured by its makeover as a purely defensive organization. NATO, which has long acquiesced in the persecution of the Kurds, is far from a force for peace. And Turkey, a member since 1952, proves it.

Turkey's conflict with the Kurds goes back at least to the late nineteenth century, when Ottoman centralization led to tribal uprisings. The initial two decades of the Turkish Republic, founded in 1923, involved the denial of Kurdish identity, autonomy and language, all of which were mainstays of the Ottoman Empire. Rebellions ensued but were forcibly put down. After remaining largely dormant in the 1940s and 1950s, Kurdish militancy then experienced a revival, under revolutionary banners. The Kurdistan Workers' Party, or PKK, emerged in this atmosphere.

The organization is designated a terrorist group by Turkey, the United States, and the European Union—and its methods are indeed violent. Across four decades of conflict, the PKK has contributed to the bloodshed and is responsible for the deaths of civilians as well as security officials. Yet Turkey's militaristic approach to the Kurdish issue has left little room for other, more conciliatory Kurdish organizations.

The country experienced a spring of Kurdish activism in the late 1960s and 1970s, when many left-wing Turkish movements and organizations also expressed solidarity with the Kurds. But a coup d'état in 1980 heavily crushed these forces, with the exception of the PKK, most of whose camps were already outside Turkey. In the years after the coup, the heavy torture suffered by Kurdish activists of various organizations swelled the ranks of the PKK. More embittered against the Turkish state than ever, many activists saw no other effective home for their struggle.

Things today aren't much better: peaceful forms of Kurdish activism —such as those organized by the legal Peoples' Democratic Party, or HDP—are under constant attack, accused of affiliation with the PKK. The government also claims that the PKK is in cahoots with the Gulen movement, a former ally of the ruling party the government accuses of orchestrating a failed coup attempt in 2016. It is members of these two groups whom Erdoğan is demanding Sweden and Finland give up.[3]

Where was NATO in all of this? The 1980 military intervention, at least passively endorsed by the alliance, was led by Kenan Evren, a commander in NATO's counter-guerrilla forces.[4] Western countries kept on providing ample support for campaigns against the Kurds in the following years, even during the exceptionally violent clashes of 1993–95. As hostilities resumed in the 2010s, the West largely neglected internal waves of repression and Turkey's recurrent incursions into Syria and Iraq, where Kurds have long sought refuge.

If such enabling silence is so persistent, why did Erdoğan choose this particular time to ramp up military adventures? The answer is simple: elections are around the corner, and the government, overseeing the country's worst economic crisis in two decades, is counting on jingoism as a remedy for national ills. The ruling party has accordingly ratcheted up its moves against the Kurds, with imprisonment of politicians and journalists, military campaigns abroad and bans on concerts and plays at home.

Russia's invasion of Ukraine has apparently further emboldened Erdoğan. It has allowed Turkey to pose as a friend to the West, earning praise for its early blockade of the Black Sea while continuing to pursue its repressive agenda. What's more, by pushing Sweden and Finland— perceived to be longtime harborers of Kurdish militants—toward NATO, the war has handed Turkey a golden opportunity. If the United States were to pressure the two countries to accept Turkey's demands, as Secretary of State Antony Blinken has suggested might happen, it would be more than a policing victory.[5] It would be a rare symbolic triumph. Bombings and cultural bans would be nothing compared with an international admission, sealed by the world's most powerful country, that Kurdish rights can be waved aside.

----

3 "Turkey Sets Conditions for Nordic NATO Bid," *Deutsche Welle*, May 21, 2022.

4 John M. Goshko, "From the Allies: Patience," *New York Times*, September 13, 1980.

5 Olafimihan Oshin, "Blinken 'Confident' in NATO Consensus on Sweden, Finland Despite Turkey's Concerns," *The Hill*, May 14, 2022.

It's tempting to see Turkey as an exceptionally bellicose state. Labeled the "sick man of Europe" in the final days of the Ottoman Empire, the country now appears to be the continent's belligerent man. But it's wrong to look at the country in isolation. Erdoğan's aggression is not his alone. It is enabled, encouraged and buttressed by Western countries, as well as Russia. In Turkey, this is a provocative claim: the authorities want their citizens, and the world, to believe that "foreigners" and "outside powers" have always supported Kurdish separatism. This quite popular but highly twisted perception of reality says nothing about the weapons, logistical support and consent other countries have abundantly provided in the killing of Kurds.

The United States supplied weapons to Syrian Kurds during their fight against the Islamic State, it's true. But that's dwarfed by the sophistication and amount of military equipment that Turkey, home to NATO's second largest military, secures thanks to being part of the Western alliance. The truth is that Turkey's aggression has gone hand in hand with NATO acceptance, even complicity. It's no use for Western countries to be lecturing Turkey, or for Turkey to be complaining of Western hypocrisy: they are in it together. Whatever happens with the alliance's expansion—whether the Kurds are sacrificed on the altar of geopolitical expediency or not—this should be a moment of clarity. In a world of war, no country has a monopoly on violence.

2

During a war in which most countries have either taken sides or remained silent, Turkey has positioned itself as a mediator between Russia and Ukraine—seeking to negotiate with both Putin and Zelensky, and playing an important role in the semi-restitution of grain trade last summer. It has opposed Western sanctions on Russia, yet it has also limited Russian warships in the Black Sea. Such geopolitical maneuvering—treading a fine line between Great Powers—is not confined to the current crisis, nor to Turkey's bilateral relations with the two warring states. Rather, it is a reflection of Erdoğan's broader foreign policy direction.

Ever since the Arab Spring, Turkey's governing Justice and Development Party (AKP) has been reimagining the country as an independent actor: not simply a "bridge" between the West and the rest, but a force that both the declining American empire and its emergent competitors must reckon with. This, however, is more an expression of fantasy than fact. As we shall see, the material basis for an autonomous Turkish foreign policy is weak, and domestic class dynamics are unfavorable. No matter how much Islamist media outlets try to promote their thin and mostly antisemitic version of "anti-imperialism," it does not amount to a coherent overseas strategy. In the absence of such material and social anchors, the AKP's search for independence ultimately amounts to a haphazard series of short-termist adventures.

This is in marked contrast to the country's experience during the mid-to-late twentieth century. The Republic of Turkey's first two decades were an early harbinger of Third Worldism, with all its merits and demerits. The Republican People's Party (CHP, which ruled from 1923 to 1950) was dominated by Mustafa Kemal and his allies in the political center, but it also had a left wing that sympathized with the Soviet Union and a right wing that drew on the European traditions of corporatism and fascism. Kemal revered most aspects of Western civilization, but he believed that the best way to catch up with the developed world was for Turkey to retain its independence. He also viewed individualism and class struggle as undesirable aspects of Western capitalist culture, which he sought to banish from the Turkish body politic. This campaign for substantive autonomy largely succeeded, but at the cost of a stagnant illiberalism which left Turkey devoid of both entrepreneurialism and civic anticapitalism.

A principled alliance with the Soviet Union of the 1920s could have put Turkey on a steadier anti-imperialist path. Yet there was no proper class basis for such an alliance, since the breakup of the Ottoman Empire had decimated the bourgeoisie along with nascent labor movements, rendering the civic and military bureaucracy the most dynamic sector in this fledgling nation.[6] As such, the onset of the Cold War quickly marginalized Turkey's fragile anti-imperialist forces, while fear of Stalin drove the Kemalists into the arms of the West. This shift was not as abrupt as it appeared, though, since Kemal had himself always been hostile to Bolshevism—nipping left-wing organizing in the bud and restricting the space for trade union militancy.

The fruits of the CHP's alliance with the West were NATO membership

---

6   Fatma Muge Gocek, *Rise of the Bourgeoisie, Demise of Empire: Ottoman Westernization and Social Change* (Oxford: Oxford University Press, 1996).

in 1952 and a prolonged (and ultimately unrealized) process of European integration. But it had other manifestations as well, such as Turkey's vote against Algerian independence at the United Nations in 1955. With the rise of the Democrat Party—a liberal-conservative coalition opposed to the Kemalists' top-down modernization program, which governed between 1950 and 1960—a militant Atlanticism replaced the CHP's more cautious embrace of Western interests. Meanwhile, the 1940s and '50s witnessed the emergence of civic organizations of anticommunist militants, whose influence peaked over the following two decades. By then, Third Worldism had become an oppositional force, which the Turkish right lumped in with the "communist threat."

Long before their fateful splits, the Islamists and proto-fascist Grey Wolves banded together in violent anticommunist gangs, which fought with leftists and anti-imperialists on the streets of the major cities. In 1969, when thousands of students turned out to protest against the American navy's Sixth Fleet, these gangs assisted the police in suppressing the demonstration, killing two and injuring many more. Until the Turkish and Kurdish Islamists themselves took a quasi-Third Worldist turn toward the end of the 1970s, such armed groups served as the main "popular" bulwark against challenges to this alliance with the West.

Turkey's default center-right rulers of the last seventy-five years—the Democrat Party in the 1950s, Justice Party in the '60s and '70s, the Motherland Party in the '80s—mainstreamed this popular-reactionary anxiety concerning any kind of independence from the US empire. The most resonant political slogan of those decades, *Ortanın Sol'u, Moskova'nın Yolu* (which roughly translates as "Left of center, the path to Moscow"), captured the mood—implying that even a vote for the CHP would inevitably lead to Turkey's accession to the Eastern bloc. The political establishment thus gave a blank check to Grey Wolf militants in their campaign to violently eradicate the anti-imperialist left. They attacked coffee houses, bus stations, and homes, assassinating union leaders and socialist organizers throughout the 1970s. Toward the end of the decade, this terror campaign expanded to the provinces and countryside, culminating in ethnic and religious pogroms including the massacre of more than a hundred Alevis in two days in the provincial town of Maraş. Left-wing militants began to defend themselves, and their small armed units rapidly turned into undisciplined mass organizations.

The 1980 coup, led by Kenan Evren, the commander of a US-backed anticommunist guerrilla force, sealed Turkey's marriage to the West. Its explicit aim was to end "left–right clashes" (the official euphemism for the Grey Wolves' killing spree and the left's retaliation); but its real purpose was the implementation of a Chilean-style neoliberal policy package. To consolidate their power, the generals hanged and tortured several right-wing militants and leaders, but the left bore the brunt of their repression. Evren's coup was largely modeled on Pinochet's. Yet, thanks to the strong civic traditions of the Turkish right, the military ultimately agreed to govern alongside civilians from 1983, except in Turkish Kurdistan. At this point, military officers trained and funded by the US allied with burgeoning warlords and gained de facto control over the east and southeast of the country, deploying some of the most brutal counter-insurgency techniques of the Cold War against leftists and Kurdish insurgents. By the mid-1990s, this campaign had evolved into a full-scale civil war. The civilian government changed hands several times, but the elected administrations were either unable or unwilling to de-escalate the conflict.

After the fall of the Eastern bloc, the military's counterinsurgency campaign was rendered largely redundant in most of the country, as there was no longer an organized socialist movement to suppress. But the growing popularity of the Kurdish guerrilla forces extended its shelf life in the east. The Kurdistan Worker's Party (PKK) became the most powerful player in the Kurdish resistance, once all its competitors—armed or peaceful—were eradicated; and it remains locked in an ongoing conflict with the central government. All in all, the violence has left around forty thousand dead and created an ethnic rift between Turks and Kurds which remains unhealed today. It also served to marginalize the country's democratic forces. A brief upsurge of student, feminist, environmentalist, and labor movements, roughly spanning 1987–95, proved unable to sustain itself amid these harsh conditions, and failed to offer a unifying vision for the country.

The civil war thus unraveled any political bloc capable of questioning Turkey's submission to the West. Like black or Hispanic kids in white American schools, Turkey came to play the role of "token minority" in Fortress Europe and NATO. Its proximity to these institutions was held up as proof that liberal imperialism was more tolerant of religious, ethnic, and racial differences than it appeared. Turkey provided troops for the occupation of Afghanistan and played an auxiliary role in the conquest of Iraq—making it more difficult for critics to frame these wars as anti-Muslim crusades.

3

As the country's pro-Western consensus calcified in the new millennium, it became almost impossible to mount a progressive opposition to EU membership, viewed by both liberals and sections of the left as the most realistic hope for democratizing the Turkish political system. Criticism of the EU was mostly relegated to far-right nationalists and ultra-Kemalists, while NATO membership was considered non-negotiable. Thousands turned out to protest against the wars in Palestine, Iraq and Afghanistan, but most shied away from demanding Turkish withdrawal from Western-led military and security organizations.

At this juncture, Turkish Islamists began to outflank the pro-Westernism of the secular political class. From the seventies to the nineties, quasi–Third Worldist Islamists had organized under the banner of the National Salvation Party (MSP) and Welfare Party (RP), whereas pro-NATO Islamic communities had predominantly voted for the mainstream parties. Yet the integration of the small merchant base of the MSP-RP into world markets initiated a process of political and cultural liberalization, paving the way for the unabashedly pro-Western policies of the AKP.

Founded in 2001, the AKP managed to unite these two factions of the Muslim vote, bringing them together in a Western-oriented bloc. Whereas the previous Islamic establishment had given elaborate theological justifications for supporting NATO, the increasingly bourgeois AKP had less need for scriptural exegesis. Its ideology—more neo-Ottoman than Islamist—was a blend of pragmatic, conservative and imperial discourses. Ahmet Davutoğlu became the main ideologue of this new Islamism. A former professor of political science and international relations, he served as an adviser to Erdoğan in the 2000s, then as foreign minister between 2009 and 2014, and finally as prime minister until 2016.

However, two developments would alter the AKP's geopolitical calculus in the early 2010s. The first was the global financial crisis. After 2008, the government could no longer count on the flow of hot cash from abroad, and increasingly resorted to state-capitalist tools, which almost always went hand in hand with the expansion of the military apparatus.[7] This state-capitalist turn began to undermine Davutoğlu's liberal imperialism, if imperceptibly at first. Political-military control of industry eroded the formal independence of the pious bourgeoisie, on which Davutoğlu's pro-Western policy depended. Gradually, Turkey's overseas outlook began to shift with these domestic realignments.

The second decisive factor was the Arab Spring. In 2011, there initially appeared to be an opening for Davutoğlu's soft power approach, which aimed to peacefully export the Turkish model, first to Arab nations and then to the rest of the Muslim world. The AKP hoped that the uprisings would entrench its favorite binary opposition, between Islamic liberals and secular dictators. With this in mind, Erdoğan visited Egypt with an army of Turkish businessmen, hoping to gain greater access to Middle Eastern markets. Yet the sectarianization of the uprisings precluded this outcome. In Syria and Yemen, as elsewhere, civil unrest degenerated into wars between Sunni and Shia populations. This, in turn, prompted the AKP to abandon its dream of pan-Islamic influence and fall back on its default anti-Shiite position, arming murderous Sunni groups throughout the region. At the same time, the AKP responded to the growing movement for Kurdish regional autonomy by integrating the Grey Wolves—as well as some of the ultra-Kemalist soldiers it had purged in the late 2000s—into its governing coalition. These militarist forces proceeded to launch countless incursions into Iraqi and Syrian territory. In this new world, Davutoğlu's liberal-democratic project was rendered obsolete. His relations with Erdoğan deteriorated, and he was forced to resign in 2016.

In contrast to the Davutoğlu era, the latest iteration of the AKP lacks a sound ideological basis for its foreign policy. Erdoğanists have been forced to adopt the quasi–Third Worldist themes of yesteryear's Islamism, while attempting to reconcile them with the imperialist outlook of the Turkish right, which typically manifests in fantasies of reviving the Ottoman Empire, uniting Turkic nations of Asia with Turkey, or building pan-Islamist unity across the globe. In recent years, the AKP has drawn on these themes in an ad hoc and unsystematic manner. Turkey's Islamist newspapers are full of analyses of Chinese, Russian, Iranian, and Latin American alternatives to US hegemony, which haphazardly draw on World

---

7   Yahya M. Madra and Sedat Yılmaz, "Turkey's Decline into (Civil) War Economy: From Neoliberal Populism to Corporate Nationalism," *South Atlantic Quarterly* 118:1 (January 2019), pp. 41–59.

Systems Theory and other anti-imperialist schools of thought. None of these nations is glorified (indeed, Iran is viewed as Turkey's Shiite archenemy), but they are nevertheless seen as important experiments that Turkey could learn from and build on. One concrete policy that has emerged from this disjointed ideological landscape is the "Blue Homeland" project, which seeks to redefine the Eastern Mediterranean (including the Black Sea and Azov Sea, and stretching all the way to Tunisia) as a Sunni-Turkic possession.[8] The AKP's current ambition is to bring the natural resources and trade routes of this region under its control.

It is through this hodgepodge of references that Turkey can view Russia as a legitimate partner, yet retain a strong suspicion of its foreign policy decisions. The AKP claims that it does not have to choose between Russia and the US; it can strike deals with Putin while simultaneously presenting itself as Ukraine's savior. Yet such bombast flies in the face of Turkey's real geopolitical position. It remains militarily and economically dependent on the West—and, to a lesser extent, on the Russian energy sector and Arab oil wealth. The regime's state-capitalist turn may have freed up some resources for independent maneuvering; but the Turkish economy is still highly restricted by its existing trade routes and partnerships. It therefore lacks a reliable basis for imperial adventures. Without a sturdy state capitalism and a sound intellectual vision, the aspiring imperialists of the AKP cannot assert their control over the Eastern Mediterranean, nor over parts of the Middle East and Caucuses, into which they have made some brief and ineffective forays. When push comes to shove, Turkey's most consequential policies are decided elsewhere. For instance, in late September 2022, Erdoğan was forced to tow Washington's line and withdraw from a Russian-led payment system—despite the deleterious effects of this decision on the domestic economy.[9]

However, the AKP's disingenuous assertion of strategic independence still has obvious payoffs. Erdoğan's pledge that Turkey will become an imperial power—bolstered by its operations in Syria and Iraq—helps to galvanize his right-wing base and disarm the opposition. The Kemalists (still represented primarily by the CHP), the secular offshoots of the Grey Wolves (İyi Parti), and the liberal Islamists (Babacan's DEVA and Davutoğlu's Gelecek Partisi), all line up behind the AKP whenever

---

8   Süleyman Seyfi Öğün, "Yine ve yeniden Akdeniz," *Yeni Şafak*, October 6, 2022.

9   Firat Kozok, "Turkish State Banks Set to Exit Russia's Mir on US Warning," *Bloomberg*, September 27, 2022.

"national security" is at stake. By failing to articulate an alternative foreign policy, these doggedly pro-NATO forces offer little more than a revival of the AKP's early years, where liberal democracy, free markets and Atlanticism were articles of faith. Given how much the world has changed since 2002, it is doubtful whether this could constitute a governing vision fit for the 2020s.

Internationally, too, the major benefit of the AKP's foreign policy is buying time while the US empire declines and its rivals advance at an unpredictable pace. Erdoğanists hope that the Chinese Belt and Road Initiative will provide new resources for Turkey and more freedom from the West. Some in Erdoğan's coterie even think that Turkey could one day replicate the Chinese path to development. Yet the party has so far refrained from adopting any Chinese-style oversight of major industry. Here, too, postponing any reckoning with Turkey's place in the shifting sands of world capitalism is the greatest strength of the AKP's strategy. Where this will ultimately lead is still uncertain. But it's clear that neither a principled anti-imperialism, nor an ability to intervene in inter-imperialist rivalry, will flow from Erdoğan's confused worldview.

22

The EU after Ukraine

Wolfgang Streeck

War is father of all, and king of all.

—Heraclitus

Assuming that the history of the European Union begins with the European Economic Community (EEC), which was formed in 1958, it has now lasted almost two-thirds of a century. It started out as a six-country alliance jointly administering two key sectors of the postwar economy, coal and steel, making it unnecessary for France to repeat the occupation of the Ruhr Valley, which had contributed to the rise of German revanchism after the First World War. In the wake of the industrial strife of the late 1960s, and following the entry of three more countries, the United Kingdom, Ireland, and Denmark, the EEC turned into the European Community (EC). Dedicated to industrial policy and social democratic reform, the EC was to add a "social dimension" to what was on the way to becoming a common market. Later, after the neoliberal revolution and the collapse of Communism, what was now renamed the European Union (EU) became both a container for the newly independent nation-states in the east eager to join the capitalist world, and an engine of neoliberal reform, supply-side economics, and New Labourism in twenty-eight European countries. It also became firmly embedded in the American-dominated unipolar global order after the "end of history."

The European Union of the past three decades has served as a regional microcosm of what came to be called *hyperglobalization*.[1] Indeed, it was in a significant way a smaller-sized, continental model for the integrated global capitalism that was the ultimate objective of those subscribing at the time to the Washington Consensus. The EU offered a borderless internal market for goods, services, labor, and capital; rules-based economic governance was upheld by an almighty international court, the European Court of Justice (ECJ); and a common currency, the euro, was managed by an equally almighty central bank, the European Central Bank (ECB). The arrangement closely matched the Hayekian idea of an international federation designed to limit discretionary economic policy—an almost perfect approximation of what Hayek called *isonomy*: identical market-liberal laws in all states included in the system.[2] This no-more-political economy was ruled by a politically sterilized combination of technocracy—the ECB and the EU's pseudo-executive, the European Commission—and what might be called *nomocracy*—the ECJ—under an in-practice unchangeable de facto constitution. The latter consisted of two treaties,[3] unreadable for the normal citizen, among twenty-eight countries, each of them entitled to veto any change.[4] Anchoring the whole project within the global financial system dominated by the United States, the treaties provided for unlimited capital mobility, outlawing capital controls of any sort not just within the Union but also across its borders.[5]

---

1   This concept is from Dani Rodrik, *The Globalization Paradox* (New York: W. W. Norton, 2011).

2   F. A. Hayek, *The Constitution of Liberty* (Chicago: University of Chicago Press, 1960).

3   The two treaties are the Treaty on European Union (TEU) and the Treaty on the Functioning of the European Union (TFEU), the former also called the Maastricht Treaty, effective since 1993, the latter the Treaty of Rome, effective since 1958, both altered many times, for example by the Treaty of Lisbon of 2009. Moreover, according to Wikipedia, "there are 37 protocols, 2 annexes, and 65 declarations that are attached to the treaties to elaborate details, often in connection with a single country, without being in the full legal text."

4   In May 2005, a proposed "Constitution of the European Union" failed in a French referendum, after 55 percent of voters rejected it. The turnout was 69 percent. The rejection was attributed in part to the French government having made the mistake of distributing a copy of the draft constitution, hundreds of pages long and impossible to understand for nonspecialists, to every French household.

5   According to Article 63 of the Treaty on the Functioning of the European Union,

That this construction suffered from what came to be euphemistically called a "democratic deficit" did not go unnoticed. Indeed, among insiders in Brussels, the joke is often heard that, with its current constitution, the European Union would never be allowed to join itself. In recent years, efforts were made by the European Commission and, in particular, the so-called European Parliament to fill the democratic gap with a politics of "values" to be enforced by the EU upon its member states. Human rights, according to contemporary Western interpretations, would serve as a substitute for the debates over political economy that had become excluded from the Union's political system. Above all, this involved educational interventions in the countries of the former Soviet empire to convert governments, parties, and peoples to Western European liberalism, economic but also social, if need be by withholding part of the fiscal handouts that are intended to support these countries' transformation into bona fide market-economies-plus-capitalist-democracies. Increasingly top-down educational programs of this sort, the mandate for which was derived from ever more extensive and indeed intrusive interpretations of the declaratory sections of the EU treaties, culminated in a crusade against so-called anti-Europeans, identified by social scientists and political spin doctors as "populists."[6]

With time, the de facto centralization and depoliticization of the Union's political economy has inserted a hierarchical center–periphery dimension into the Union. The "rule of law" instituted as the rule of an all-powerful court; the formally rule-based but in practice increasingly discretionary economic policy of the politically independent European Central Bank;

"All restrictions on the movement of capital between Member States and between Member States and third countries shall be prohibited," the same applying to "all restrictions on payments," again both "between Member States and third countries."

6   Article 4, Section 1 of the TEU states, "In accordance with Article 5, competences not conferred upon the Union in the Treaties remain with the Member States." According to Article 5, Section 1, "The limits of Union competences are governed by the principle of conferral. The use of Union competences is governed by the principles of subsidiarity and proportionality." The European Commission and the ECJ have for some time been trying to get around Treaty restrictions of this kind by deriving specific powers for themselves from general clauses like, for example, Article 2 of the TEU: "The Union is founded on the values of respect for human dignity, freedom, democracy, equality, the rule of law and respect for human rights, including the rights of persons belonging to minorities. These values are common to the Member States in a society in which pluralism, non-discrimination, tolerance, justice, solidarity, and equality between women and men prevail."

and the sanction-supported reeducation in European "values" have led the EU increasingly to resemble a liberal empire, in both an economic and cultural sense, the latter as legitimation for the former.

Before Ukraine: Critical Fault Lines, Foreseeable Failure

Empires are at a congenital risk of overextension, in territorial, economic, political, cultural, and other respects. The larger they get, the more it costs to keep them together, as centrifugal forces grow and the center needs to mobilize ever more resources to contain them. After the global financial crisis of 2008 and its spread to Europe after 2009, the EU and the Economic Monetary Union (EMU) began to fracture along several dimensions, their economic, ideological, and coercive capacities for integration becoming increasingly overtaxed. On the EU's western flank, Brexit was the first case of a member state leaving a Union that ideologically considers itself permanent. There were many factors involved that contributed to the outcome of the Brexit referendum, which have been widely debated for almost a decade now. One major reason (less spectacular but certainly more fundamental than many others) why British membership proved unsustainable was a profound incompatibility of the British de facto constitution, and its parliamentary absolutism, with Brussels-style rule by judges and technocrats. Another reason, of course, was the inability and indeed unwillingness of Brussels to do something about the long-term neglect by British governments of the disintegration of the country's social fabric.

Turning to the south, entrenched national ways of doing capitalism proved incompatible with the prescriptions of the EMU and the internal market, leading Italy in particular down a path of prolonged and by all indications irreversible economic decline. Attempts at reversing the trend either through "structural reforms," according to neoliberal prescriptions, or via the ECB and the European Commission bending the anti-interventionist rules governing Monetary Union, silently tolerated by the French and German governments, failed dismally. By now it has become clear that even the European Union's Corona Recovery and Resilience Facility (RRF), and the subsidies it will provide to Italy, will not halt Italian decline either.[7] Among other things, the Italian case shows that

---

7   The RRF was set up in July 2020 to dispense €750 billion to member countries, proportionate to the losses they were found by the European Commission to have suffered

an effective regional policy aiming at economic convergence is even less feasible among, as compared to within, nation-states.

Furthermore, on the Union's eastern periphery, countries carry a historical legacy of cultural traditionalism, political authoritarianism, and nationalist resistance against international intervention in their internal life, the latter reinforced by their experience under the Soviet empire. Efforts to impose Western European mores and tastes on these societies, especially when accompanied by threats of economic sanctions (as in the case of the Union's so-called "rule of law" policies), caused "populist" opposition and resentment against what was perceived by many as an attempt to deprive them of their newly recovered national sovereignty.[8] Conflicts in the European Council over cultural issues went as far as western heads of governments more or less explicitly urging their eastern colleagues, in particular those from Hungary and Poland, to exit from the Union if they were unwilling to share its "values."[9] Combined with the threat of economic sanctions, this in effect amounted to nothing less than an attempt to bring about a regime change in fellow member states.

Finally, in the north, efforts of the European Union to preserve a memory of its older ambition to develop a "social dimension" are regularly

---

from the coronavirus pandemic. Italy is the leading beneficiary, with €192 billion (€69 billion in grants, the rest in loans). The RRF is the first time that the EU was allowed by its member states to take up debt; the fund is entirely debt financed. To get a sense of its effective magnitude, note that Germany, responding to American complaints over it not having spent enough on defense, set aside in early 2022, in a matter of a few days, a debt-financed fund of €100 billion for upgrading its military, to be spent immediately. This is more than half of what the entire country of Italy was allocated by the European Union, to be spent by 2023 (which turned out to be technically impossible).

8   On the politics of the "rule of law" controversy, see Wolfgang Streeck, "Ultra Vires," *Sidecar*, January 7, 2022; Wolfgang Streeck, "Rusty Charley," *Sidecar*, November 2, 2021.

9   At an EU summit meeting in June 2021, the Dutch prime minister, Mark Rutte, under pressure at home from a scandal over illegal punitive measures taken by his government against welfare recipients, told his Hungarian counterpart, Viktor Orbán, that Hungary had to leave the EU unless his government withdrew a law that bans schools from using materials seen as promoting homosexuality. From a Reuters report: "Several EU summit participants spoke of the most intense personal clash among the bloc's leaders in years ... 'It was really forceful, a deep feeling that this could not be. It was about our values; this is what we stand for,' Rutte told reporters on Friday. 'I said, "Stop this, you must withdraw the law and, if you don't like that and really say that the European values are not your values, then you must think about whether to remain in the European Union." '"

resisted by, of all countries, the Scandinavian member states, who insist upon their tradition of labor market regulation, including wage regulation, by collective bargaining rather than by state law. Recently, this resulted in some Scandinavian trade unions threatening to exit from the European trade union confederation, which they complained had not sufficiently respected their established national practice.

Further fault lines, both old and new, exist within the center of the liberal empire due to the fact that the European Union does not have a member state powerful enough to be its single hegemon. Instead, there are two leading countries, Germany and France, neither of which can alone dominate the Union. While each needs the other, they are unable to agree on central structures, interests, and policies of an integrated Europe. Traditionally, Franco-German differences are seen as deriving from differences between their national varieties of capitalism, with France cultivating a tradition of statist dirigisme and Germany insisting on its postwar invention of a "social market economy." As a result, France and Germany tend to be at odds in European Union and European Monetary Union policy, with France, among other things, favoring a more expansionary and politically discretionary fiscal and monetary policy.

More recently, especially after Brexit, differences in foreign and security policy have also come to the fore. While they already existed in the 1960s, they were thrown in sharper relief, first by the end of the bipolar world after 1989 and then by the fact that, since Brexit, France is the only European Union member state with nuclear arms and a permanent seat on the United Nations Security Council. Because France is unwilling to share either, Germany's nuclear dependence on the United States, which keeps roughly forty thousand troops on German soil, together with an uncounted number of nuclear warheads, effectively stands in the way of "European strategic sovereignty," as the French call it—a transfer of strategic sovereignty to "Europe" that is acceptable to French national security doctrine only under French leadership. Moreover, while France has strong interests in Africa and the Middle East, German national interests, as they relate to Europe, focus on Eastern Europe and the Balkans. As a result, disagreement, if carefully concealed, is endemic between the two would-be drivers of what is sometimes euphemistically called the French-German European tandem.

More Unity through Less Unity?

Before the war in Ukraine, there were two radically different projects in the air, or at least conceivable, for how to prevent the impending disintegration of the European Union due to overextension and overintegration. One may be summarized as a strategy of more unity through less unity, or of retrenchment—if not territorially, then functionally—by rolling back some major elements of the EU's "ever closer union of the peoples of Europe." Among others, it was the American sociologist Amitai Etzioni who had for some time advocated retrenchment as a way of deblocking European integration.[10] In many ways, his proposal was reminiscent of older concepts of an integrated West European state system as a Europe à la carte, or even as de Gaulle's "Europe of fatherlands."[11] What these notions had in common was a vision of a regional state system on the model of a cooperative rather than an empire, as recently outlined by Hans Joas in an important book on "Europe as a peace project."[12] In it, Joas refers to a debate on the possibilities of international peace between Carl Schmitt and the German historian Otto Hintze in the 1920s and 1930s. Schmitt believed that peace in a global region could be assured only by a central imperial power free to impose order on its periphery, its dependent states, essentially as it saw fit. His real-world model of a viable international order, incidentally, was the American hemisphere under the Monroe Doctrine. Arguing against him, Hintze, who had studied the German tradition of cooperative associations (*Genossenschaften*), insisted on the possibility of a social order based on voluntary cooperation within a framework that obliged participating countries to recognize each other's independence, or sovereignty. In various ways, this model came close to that of the Westphalian Peace of 1648, after the Thirty Years' War, with the creation of what later came to be named the "Westphalian state."

What would a European Union à la carte have looked like, if it had ever become a reality? It would, generally speaking, have provided for

---

10   See Amitai Etzioni, *Reclaiming Patriotism* (Charlottesville: University of Virginia Press, 2019), pp. 142ff.

11   Also in this category is the "Europe of different speeds" idea, which was intensely and successfully opposed by the EU's Eastern European countries.

12   Hans Joas, *Friedensprojekt Europa* (München: Kösel, 2020). I have greatly benefited from Joas; see Wolfgang Streeck, *Zwischen Globalismus und Demokratie: Politische Ökonomie im ausgehenden Neoliberalismus* (Berlin: Suhrkamp, 2020). An English translation is forthcoming from Verso.

more local, in the sense of national, autonomy, instead of insisting on political-economic uniformity among member states, with less centralized and hierarchical institutions and more space for national sovereignty.[13] The European Commission would have been turned into something like a platform for voluntary cooperation among member states, dropping its aspiration to grow into a pan-European executive; the same, mutatis mutandis, would have applied to the EU Parliament. The role of the European Court of Justice would also have had to be significantly reduced: it would no longer have been a constitutional legislator in disguise, in charge of everything it chose to be in charge of and intervening at its pleasure into national states, national law, and national politics. In some ways, a European Union of this sort would have looked like the Nordic Council formed by the Scandinavian states in the 1950s. Members are Denmark, Finland, Iceland, Norway, Sweden, the Faroe Islands, Greenland, and Åland. The bloc knows no equivalent to the European Court, the EU Parliament, or the European Commission. While member states keep borders open between them, they continue to have their own economic and social policies.[14]

In many ways, rolling back integration in order to preserve it was from the beginning an unrealistic project, if it could even be called a project at all. Most likely, to have any chance, it would have had to be preceded by a massive breakdown of the European Union, due to intensifying disruptions along its fault lines and, very likely, a state bankruptcy of Italy. None of this could have been ruled out, and more unity through less unity might have been realistic as a reconstruction project after an institutional collapse, rather than as a policy of reform to prevent such collapse. Under existing rules, it would have required an extensive treaty revision agreed to by all twenty-seven post-Brexit member states, some of them needing approval by popular vote. The practical impossibility of a meaningful revision of the governing treaties may be considered an essential feature of a European integration project intended to be irreversible (thereby unintentionally detracting from its democratic legitimacy).

---

13   See Streeck, *Zwischen Globalismus und Demokratie*.

14   According to its website, "The Nordic Council of Ministers is the official body for inter-governmental co-operation in the Nordic Region. It seeks Nordic solutions wherever and whenever the countries can achieve more together than by working on their own."

Integration by Militarization?

Another potential way out of the overextension malaise was suggested by a group of retired German politicians, from both major parties, led and inspired by the philosopher Jürgen Habermas. Among its members was Friedrich Merz, then chairman of the board of BlackRock Germany, a sidelined, longtime rival of Angela Merkel. (Surprisingly, Merz was recently resurrected to be Merkel's successor as leader of what is now Germany's main opposition party, CDU/CSU.) In October 2018, the group issued a public appeal titled, "For a Europe based on solidarity: Let's get serious about the will of our Constitution, now!"[15] Among other things, the group urged the creation of a European army ("We demand a European Army"), given that "Trump, Russia, and China" were "testing ever more severely ... Europe's unity, our willingness to stand up for our values together, to defend our way of life." To this there could be "only one answer: solidarity and the fight against nationalism and egoism internally, and unity and common sovereignty externally." Creating a European army was to be the first step toward a "deeper integration of foreign and security policy based on majority decisions" of the European Council. The group argued that a European army did not require "more money" as "the European NATO members together spend about three times as much on defense as Russia";[16] all that was needed was an end to national fragmentation, which would make for "much more defensive power without additional money." (No reason was given for why this was needed, given that the countries in question were already spending three times as much on their military as their designated enemy.) Moreover, "since Europe's defenses are not directed against anyone, the creation of a European army should be linked to arms control and disarmament initiatives," an effort in which Germany and France, "the founding states of Europe," should take the lead.

Like more unity through less unity, European state-building through militarization, somewhat reminiscent of the Prussian model, never had a

---

15   Hans Eichel et al., "Für ein solidarisches Europa—Machen wir Ernst mit dem Willen unseres Grundgesetzes, jetzt!," *Handelsblatt*, October 21, 2018.

16   SIPRI (Stockholm International Peace Research Institute) reports Russian military spending in 2018 of $62.4 billion. The UK, France, Germany, and Italy, the four largest European NATO members, were together spending $175.2 billion in 2018, 2.8 times as much as Russia.

chance.[17] This was in spite of the fact that on the surface, when its proponents pleaded for a "common sovereignty" for Europe, they were obviously catering to the French taste, as expressed in Macron's 2017 Sorbonne Speech, given a day after Angela Merkel's last reelection.[18] Also, by leaving open who the enemy was against which Europe needed to be defended, it did not preclude something like European equidistance to Russia and China, on the one hand, and "Trump" on the other, which would in principle be welcome in France. Moreover, NATO was never mentioned, and certainly not its revised doctrine, adopted in 1992, extending its mission worldwide to include "out of area" operations such as, presumably, humanitarian interventions in fulfillment of an alleged "duty to protect." In addition, by arguing that the new European army would not need higher defense spending, the appeal implicitly rejected the American demand that European NATO members, especially Germany, increase their military expenditures to 2 percent of GDP—which for Germany in 2018 would have meant an increase of no less than 50 percent.[19] Note that the first time that NATO had, following American pressure, discussed the 2 percent target was at a summit meeting in Prague in 2002. This was the same meeting at which the alliance opened accession talks with Bulgaria, Estonia, Latvia, Lithuania, Romania, Slovakia, and Slovenia, and confirmed an open-door policy for Eastern Europe, including Georgia and Ukraine, against strong public objections by the Russian government.

Even more importantly, the document failed to address the issue of nuclear arms—not least, one is led to believe, to make it possible for the German Greens to join the cause. Nevertheless, had the project ever become real, for Germany—committed to not having nuclear arms, and indeed forbidden to have them under the Nuclear Non-Proliferation Treaty of 1968—a European army entailed the risk of having to replace

17   As the French statesman Count Mirabeau allegedly put it in 1786, the year Frederick II of Prussia died: "Other states possess an army; Prussia is an army that possesses a state."

18   "In Europe, we are seeing a two-fold movement: gradual and inevitable disengagement by the United States, and a long-term terrorist threat with the stated goal of splitting our free societies ... In the area of defence, our aim needs to be ensuring Europe's autonomous operating capabilities, in complement to NATO." Emmanuel Macron, "Sorbonne Speech," September 26, 2017.

19   According to Statista, Germany in 2018 spent 1.2 percent of its GDP on its military, amounting to $44.7 billion. Targeting 2 percent, as asked by NATO, would have been equivalent to $74.5 billion, i.e., $12.1 billion more than Russia.

American with French nuclear protection. That risk would have seemed as unacceptable in Germany as was the idea in France of sharing its nuclear force with "Europe," meaning Germany sailing under a European flag. At bottom was the fundamental question of the extent to which a European army would be, or would have to be, integrated in the command structure of NATO—in effect, its "interoperability" with the military of the United States. Since Germany's rearmament in the 1950s, the Bundeswehr has been fully integrated in NATO, and the United States would likely have insisted that any European army, in particular its German contingent, would be integrated in NATO as well.

Had the Habermas appeal touched upon the nuclear question, it would have become obvious that, superficial similarities notwithstanding, it was incompatible with core elements of the French European security project. Like the United States, France wanted (and wants) Germany to spend more on defense. Rather than strengthening transatlantic American power, however, Germany's additional spending was to fill the conventional gap in the French military caused by the high costs of its nuclear force, so as to enable "Europe" to better serve French ambitions in Africa and the Middle East. For "European strategic sovereignty" of this kind, some form of détente with Russia would be helpful. A Eurasian settlement would, however, be at odds with American expansion through NATO on the Russian periphery. For the United States, the aim was to integrate the former Communist countries of Eastern Europe into an American-led "West." Making Europe through NATO take an adversarial position toward Russia would ensure European dependence on an alliance with the United States in the bipolar world growing out of George H. W. Bush's "New World Order." For France, to the contrary, a European army was of interest precisely to the extent that it would extract Europe from the close embrace in which the United States was holding it, among other things by keeping non-nuclear Germany dependent on American nuclear protection.

After Ukraine

War is the ultimate stochastic source of history, and once it is underway there is no limit to the surprises it may bring. Still, even though the war in Ukraine seems far from over at the time of writing, one may feel justified observing that it has put an end, at least for the foreseeable future, to any vision of an independent, non-imperial, cooperative state system in Europe. The war also seems to have dealt a death blow to the French dream of turning the liberal empire of the European Union into a strategically sovereign global force, credibly rivaling both a rising China and a declining United States. The Russian invasion of Ukraine seems to have answered the question of the European order by reinstating the model, long believed to be history, of the Cold War: a Europe united under American leadership as a transatlantic bridgehead for the United States in an alliance against a common enemy, then the Soviet Union and now Russia. Inclusion in and subordination to a resurrected, remilitarized "West," as a European subdepartment of NATO, seems to have saved, for the time being, the European Union from its destructive centrifugal forces, without however eliminating them. By restoring the West, the war neutralized the various fault lines where the EU was crumbling, some more and some less, while catapulting the United States into a position of renewed hegemony over Western Europe, including its regional organization, the European Union.

Above all, the reintegration of the West under American leadership settled the old issue of the relationship between NATO and the EU in favor of a division of labor that established the primacy of the former over the latter. In an interesting way, this seems to have healed the division between continental Europe and the United Kingdom that had opened in the course of Brexit. As NATO rose to supremacy, the fact that it includes the UK together with the leading member states of the EU restores a prominent European role for Britain through its special relationship with the United States. How this affects the international status of a country like France was recently illustrated by a strategic agreement—the so-called AUKUS pact—between the United States, Great Britain, and Australia. Under AUKUS, Australia canceled a 2016 deal with France on French diesel-powered submarines, instead committing itself to developing nuclear-powered submarines together with the United States and the United Kingdom—an event that showed France the limits of a French-led EU as a global power.

Regarding the EU, the rise of NATO implied its decline to the status of a NATO civil auxiliary, subservient to American strategic objectives, mostly but not exclusively in Europe. The United States had long thought about the EU as something like a waiting room or a prep school for future

NATO members, especially those neighboring Russia, like Georgia and Ukraine, but also the western Balkans.[20] The EU, for its part, had insisted on its own admissions procedures that included lengthy negotiations on national institutional and economic conditions that had to be met before formal accession. This was to reduce the burden that new countries would impose on the EU budget and to ensure that their political elites would be sufficiently "pro-European" so as not to rock the common boat. To the United States, with its geostrategic objectives, this typically appeared as overly pedantic if not obstructionist. Indeed, France in particular had resisted and still resists excessive "widening" of the Union, afraid that it might stand in the way of its "deepening." From an American perspective, burden-sharing with European countries meant that the latter were responsible for the provision of economic incentives for new states to join the West, and for helping them build the economic base of Westernization, for example through financial subsidies assisting aspiring member states in achieving social stability in a Western, liberal, democratic sense.

With the Ukrainian war, the American vision of the EU as a temporary home for future NATO members is rapidly becoming reality. Any negotiated settlement of the war will likely preclude Ukraine's accession to NATO in the near and not-so-near future. Fast-track admission to the European Union could be offered in compensation, not least because it would secure funds for repairing the damage caused by the war.[21] It also seems likely that France will no longer be allowed to block the accession of countries like Albania, Bosnia and Herzegovina (one country), North Macedonia, Montenegro, Kosovo, and Serbia (provided the European subsidies can make its political elite change its mind and turn "pro-European"). Depending on how the war develops, there may even be some sort of membership-like affiliation in store for Georgia and Armenia, all of which

---

20   After the accession of Croatia in 2013 and Montenegro in 2017, Serbia, North Macedonia, and Albania are currently official candidates for membership. Bosnia and Herzegovina and Kosovo are waiting in the wings.

21   In the past, Ukrainian requests for admission led to nothing as Brussels plainly felt the country to be unfit for membership. Strong doubts were expressed on the democratic nature of the Ukrainian state, the role of its oligarchs and their political power, and the treatment of minorities, including the Russian-speaking one in the eastern provinces; there was also a perception of rampant corruption. In part this may have been pretense, however, and the real reason for the rejection many have been the country's poverty, which would have imposed an enormous additional burden on the EU's internal finances, in particular its various assistance funds. The war may now override such concerns by making them less publicly presentable.

is likely to make significant demands on the EU's budget without making the EU any easier to govern.

In addition, during the war the European Commission was and continues to be in high demand as an agency for planning, coordinating, and monitoring European economic sanctions against Russia and, to be expected soon, China. Ultimately, sanctions imply a profound reorganization of the extended supply chains of the neoliberal age and the New World Order, in response to the multipolar world that is about to emerge, with its renewed emphasis on economic security and autonomy. What has for some time been an agency promoting globalization will then, in important respects, turn into one devoted to de-globalization—the latter up to a few weeks ago thought to be no more than a leftist (or maybe populist) absurdity. Shortening supply chains is a function less of government than of technocratic expertise, difficult enough given the high level of economic interdependence inherited from hyperglobalization. Politically, which sanctions are to be imposed, and which international supply chains are still to be considered safe, remains for national governments to determine; or more precisely, for their now principal organization, NATO, as controlled by its strongest nation-state, the United States, to determine. An example is the wrangling about German purchases of Russian natural gas and their replacement with American liquefied natural gas. Since NATO does not have the necessary expertise in economic matters to assess the effects of sanctions on Russia, on the one hand, and on Western Europe, on the other, the EU will continue to be needed as an administrative service provider in the management of a newly politicized European economy.

Finally, not to be underestimated, the EU is likely to play a major part in the generation of public money for rebuilding Ukraine once the war has ended. The same holds for the provision of financial support to other countries on the European periphery that will be candidates for European Union and, ultimately, NATO membership. The capacity of the EU to serve as a receptacle for public debt that is politically less noticeable—as in the case of the Corona Recovery and Resilience Facility, the first manifestation of the Commission's Next Generation EU (NGEU)—is likely to be permanently and extensively drawn upon for mobilizing European contributions to the long-term nonmilitary costs of the war, including for example the resettlement of Ukrainian refugees.[22] (Experience suggests

---

22   Projections by the Ukrainian government of the costs of repairing the damages caused by the war as of now are as high as $2 billion.

that the American contribution will be limited to and end with the military hostilities.)[23] For this, special services of the ECB will also be needed, as they were in the fight against "secular stagnation" and, later, the pandemic. NGEU debt does not appear in national budgets and is for this reason less politically controversial. This is similar to the ECB's purchases of government debt as a form of indirect state finance, in the context of quantitative easing, in circumvention of the European treaties.

Liabilities Old and New

The new functions that have accrued to the EU as a result of the Ukrainian war, and in particular in the course of its subordination to NATO, are far from resolving its old problems; in the longer run, in fact, they may add to and exacerbate them. On the EU's western flank, the United Kingdom has, via its close alliance with the United States under NATO, returned to the European flock with a vengeance, although more like a lieutenant than as one foot soldier among others. In the south, there is no reason to believe that NATO supremacy will help improve Italian economic performance; to the contrary, sanctions and shortened supply chains are likely to impose additional costs on the Mediterranean economies. These are certain to demand compensation—not from the United States but from the EU. Its rich member states, however, will be preoccupied with raising their defense spending to meet NATO demands, not to mention financing the accession of more EU member states on their way into NATO. Competition for EU subsidies, in particular for the EU's "Cohesion Fund,"[24] will further increase because of the new, war-related needs of eastern member states, for example the hosting of Ukrainian and, if

---

23   For example, in February 2022, the Biden administration confiscated one half of the frozen assets of the central bank of Afghanistan, deposited with the New York City branch of the Federal Reserve, to be set aside for the survivors of 9/11 and their lawyers. The impounded funds amounted to $3.5 billion. A few weeks later, an international donor conference organized by the United Nations, together with Germany, the UK, and Qatar, tried to raise $4.4 billion to help end mass starvation in Afghanistan, where the Taliban had returned to power after the American departure. Only $2.44 billion was contributed by the forty-one nations that were in (virtual) attendance.

24   The EU's "Cohesion Fund" supports member states with a GDP per capita below 90 percent of the EU average, "to strengthen the economic, social, and territorial cohesion of the EU."

the Western sanctions begin to bite, Russian refugees. Plans of the EU Parliament and the Commission to cut financial assistance to countries like Poland or Hungary for deficiencies in the "rule of law" will become increasingly obsolete as cultural conflicts between "liberal" and "illiberal" democracy will be eclipsed by the geostrategic objectives of NATO and the United States.[25]

As the costs of "cohesion" increase, a shift in political power inside the EU may be imminent in favor of the Union's eastern front states, resulting in higher financial obligations for the countries of the rich northwest. While Western European cultural education exercises have begun to appear petty in the face of millions of Ukrainian refugees arriving in a country like Poland, the United States has little reason to force its eastern allies to cater to German or Dutch liberal sensitivities. Efforts to make financial support for post-Communist countries conditional on their adherence to "democratic values" will come to naught as long as the United States is satisfied with their adherence to NATO and their willingness to fight the good pro-Western fight. As the United States, in its administration's own words at the time of writing, is preparing for a war lasting several years—which is only logical if the goal is regime change in Russia—a country's willingness to host American troops, planes, and missiles must take precedence over the EU treaties' (or the ECJ's) fine print of democratic conditionality. With the European Union facing a war lasting an uncertain number of years, its eastern front states are likely to dominate the common political agenda. In this they will be supported by

---

25 The politics of European "rule of law" are complicated. Since the beginning of the war the Commission seems to have postponed if not silently cancelled legal proceedings against Poland for its politicized judiciary and corrupt spending of EU money. This was different with Hungary, whose semi-dictatorial leader, Viktor Orbán, was reelected for the third time on April 3 this year, with a popular majority of 53 percent, bigger than in any of his previous elections. Unlike Poland, Hungary under Orbán has remained on a speaking relationship with the Russian president, Vladimir Putin, perhaps also because of discrimination in Ukraine against a sizable Hungarian-speaking, pro-Russian minority. Immediately after Orbán's election victory, the Commission started proceedings against Hungary, albeit only on the less severe of two alleged infringements, basically accusations of official corruption. The politicized nature of the matter is blatant as the EU Commission and Parliament are not particularly concerned about corruption in member states like Malta, Cyprus, Bulgaria, Romania, Slovenia, and Slovakia, which differ from Hungary and Poland not in their legal, or illegal, practices but in that their governments always vote "pro-European" in Brussels, as determined by the Commission. Incidentally, compared to the likely next member, Ukraine, a country like Hungary may be as clean as, say, Sweden or Denmark.

the United States, with its geostrategic interest in keeping Russia politically, economically, and militarily in check. Ultimately, this may result in the United States, acting through its Eastern European allies and NATO, growing into the place of the EU's all-too-often divided dual leadership, the French-German tandem.

American Dreams

One of the many remarkable developments around the Ukrainian war is how the dismal record of recent American military interventions has almost completely disappeared from European public memory. Until only a few months ago, the disastrous end of American nation-building in Afghanistan was a frequent theme for the European commentariat. Also present, if more in the background, were Syria, with Obama's "red lines" first drawn and then forgotten; Libya, which was abandoned after being turned into a living hell; and Iraq, with a conservatively estimated two hundred thousand civilian deaths since the American invasion. Nothing of this is mentioned these days in good European society, and if it is mentioned outside of it, it is immediately branded as an anti-American diversion from the evils committed by Putin and his army.

As the tensions increased around Ukraine, visible in the massing of Russian troops on the Ukrainian borders, Western European countries, apparently as a matter of course, handed the United States power of attorney, allowing it through NATO to act in their name and on their behalf. Now, with the war dragging on, Europe, organized in a European Union subordinate to NATO, will find itself dependent on the bizarreries of the domestic politics of the United States, a declining great power readying itself for global conflict with a rising great power, China. Iraq, Libya, Syria, and Afghanistan should have amply documented the American penchant to exit if their, always and by definition well-intentioned, efforts in other parts of the world fail for whatever reason, leaving behind a lethal mess that others must clean up if they require a minimum of international order at their doorsteps. Astonishingly, nowhere in Western Europe is the question asked what will happen if, in 2024, either Trump is reelected—which seems not at all impossible—or some ersatz Trump is elected in his place. But even with Biden or some moderate Republican, the notoriously short attention span of American imperial policy should, but does not, seem to enter into the strategic calculations, if there are any, of European governments.

One explanation that is too rarely invoked for the recklessness with which the United States all too often enters into and exits from far-flung military adventures is its location on a continent-sized island, away from those places where it might feel an urge to provide for what it considers political stability. Whatever the United States does or does not do abroad has few if any consequences for its citizens at home. (Iraqi troops will never march into Washington, DC, and arrest George W. Bush to deliver him to the International Criminal Court in The Hague.) When things go wrong, Americans can retreat to where they came from, where nobody can follow them. There is, if only for this reason, an enduring temptation in American foreign policy to be guided by wishful thinking, deficient intelligence, sloppy planning, and a fickle tailoring of international policies to domestic public sentiments. This makes it all the more amazing that European countries should, apparently without any debate, have so completely left the handling of Ukraine to the United States. In effect, this represents a principal turning the management of his vital interests over to an agent with a recent public record of incompetence and irresponsibility.

What will be the war aims of the United States, acting for and with Europe through NATO? Having left it to Biden to decide on its behalf, Europe's fate will depend on Biden's fate, that is, on the decisions, or non-decisions, of the US government. Short of what the Germans in the First World War called a *Siegfrieden*—a victorious peace imposed on a defeated enemy, as probably dreamed of in the United States by both neocons and the liberal imperialists of the Hillary Clinton school—Biden may go for, or even prefer, a drawn-out stalemate, a war of attrition keeping both Russia and Western Europe, in particular Germany, engaged with each other. A lasting confrontation between Russian and Ukrainian, or "Western," armies on Ukrainian soil would unite Europe under NATO and conveniently oblige European countries to maintain high levels of military spending. It would also force Europe to continue wide-ranging, indeed crippling, economic sanctions on Russia, as a side effect reinforcing the position of the United States as a supplier of energy and raw materials of various sorts to Europe. Moreover, an ongoing war, or almost-war, would stand in the way of Europe developing a Eurasian security architecture of its own, inclusive of Russia. It would cement American control over Western Europe and rule out French ideas of "European strategic sovereignty" as well as German hopes for détente, both presupposing some sort of Russian settlement. And not least, Russia would be occupied with preparations for Western military interventions, below the nuclear threshold, on its extended periphery.

Very likely, a protracted confrontation over Ukraine would force Russia into a close relationship of dependence on China, securing China a captive Eurasian ally and giving it assured access to Russian resources, at bargain prices as the West would no longer compete for them. Russia, in turn, could benefit from Chinese technology, to the extent that it would be made available. At first glance, an alliance like this might appear to be against the interests of the United States. It would, however, come with an equally close, and equally asymmetrical, American-dominated alliance between the United States and Western Europe, where what Europe can deliver to the United States would clearly exceed what Russia can deliver to China. Something like a stalemated phony war in Ukraine could be in the interest of a United States seeking to build global alliances for an imminent battle with China over the next New World Order, monopolar or bipolar in old or new ways, to be fought out in coming years, after the end of the end of history.

Conclusion

NATO and the Yeti

Thomas Meaney

NATO is back. With the invasion of Ukraine, Russian arms have revived the fortunes of the North Atlantic Treaty Organization. Nordic states that once prided themselves on independence from the alliance are eager to join. The German government has pledged an unprecedented increase in defense spending, which means increasing its contribution to NATO. US military strategists dream anew of opening a NATO franchise for the Pacific, while European boosters hail a NATO for the internet. Former liberal holdouts and skeptics of the alliance have learned to love NATO in much the same way they learned to love the CIA and the FBI during the Trump years. The old sheriff of the Cold War has regained its focus, and, to the surprise of many, has proved itself to be a remarkably spry and capable force in the fight against Russia.

NATO's return to the spotlight has been accompanied by a renewed debate about its history. But who can say exactly what NATO is? Crammed into a four-letter acronym is something more than a military alliance. NATO is no longer particularly "Northern," nor "Atlantic," nor bound to a "Treaty," while calling it an "Organization" makes it sound like a charitable enterprise. Part of the reason NATO's shape can be difficult to discern is that the alliance has, at least in the West, won a long war of public relations. In the 1950s, NATO sent traveling "caravans"—mass exhibitions and outdoor movie theaters—into the hinterlands of Europe to explain the benefits of the alliance to skeptical populations. Such a strenuous case for NATO no longer needs to be made, and opposition to it has vastly diminished since the 1980s. What was once presumed to be an artefact of the Cold War order sits so comfortably at the heart of the Western system that it is frequently mistaken for a natural feature in the geopolitical landscape.

1

On paper, NATO is an alliance of thirty nation-states committed to free institutions and bound together by Article 5 of its charter, which holds that—albeit conditionally—signatories will rally to defend any member that is attacked. Born in 1949, NATO sees itself as the younger sibling of other international institutions of midcentury vintage—the UN and the GATT, which became the World Trade Organization—and takes pride in having kept the European peace for more than half a century. Militarily, if not economically, NATO has largely fulfilled the mission its first secretary general, Hastings Ismay, is said to have set out for it: "To keep the Russians out, the Americans in, and the Germans down."

Though ostensibly a military alliance, NATO is also a culture, or as NATO's third Supreme Allied Commander, Alfred Gruenther, declared: "NATO is a state of mind." NATO company towns dot the continent (Brunssum, Ramstein, Geilenkirchen, Oberammergau, Uedem, Aviano, Świętoszów), there are NATO schools for NATO employees' children and NATO academies and centers where NATO military curriculums are taught ("smart training for smart defense"), the NATO Defense College in Rome, a NATO songbook, a NATO hymn, a Bing Crosby NATO ballad, a NATO phonetic alphabet ("Alpha, Bravo …"), NATO-funded grants and university chairs, an annual International Model NATO for university students, a NATO Hermès scarf, a NATO golf club in Belgium for handicap 36 and below, and a NATO headquarters in Brussels, which houses the British-funded "counter-propaganda" unit, as well as the NATO museum, or what is known in NATO-speak as an "arts heritage hub," which exhibits copies of Ancient Greek statuary and a large number of unremarkable wooden desks.

NATO's formal budget is a relatively modest €3.3 billion, with contributions from all member states, but the largesse of the Pentagon (allocated more than $800 billion for the 2023 fiscal year) guarantees that NATO can spend much of its own funds on bureaucratic upkeep. Despite some nods to how it produces all decisions by "consensus," NATO makes little attempt to hide the fact of American primacy in the alliance. In the official legal procedure for leaving NATO, the charter declares that a state must declare its intention not to NATO's secretary general, but to the president of the United States.

In practice, NATO is above all a political arrangement that guarantees US primacy in determining answers to European questions. The political headquarters of NATO are located in a modernist complex in Brussels, but its most significant military command center is in Norfolk, Virginia. Every SACEUR since 1949 has been an American military officer.[1] NATO itself has no forces of its own. It comprises about four thousand bureaucratic personnel who coordinate its activities around the world. NATO military forces at any given time are made up of contingents voluntarily seconded by member governments, with the US as the main contributor. NATO's wars and engagements—which have dragooned Luxembourgers and Turks into fighting in Korea, and Spaniards and Portuguese into fighting in Afghanistan—have typically been authored by Washington. Even wars primarily fought by Europeans—such as the NATO intervention in Libya—have relied overwhelmingly on American logistics, fueling stations, and hardware.

The crown jewels of NATO are its nuclear weapons. In theory, three NATO powers—Britain, France and the US—coordinate the nuclear defense for the rest of the alliance. NATO maintains nuclear forces on the continent, but they are largely ceremonial. If Moscow lobbed a warhead at Brussels, the initial response would come unilaterally from Washington since following actual NATO procedures involves laborious protocols. (The nuclear group in NATO would first have to confer and agree to respond, and then request Washington's portion of the relevant code in order to launch the missiles stationed on their territory.) Nuclear-capable aircraft in

---

1   Henry Kissinger, who has long worried that NATO is too bluntly synonymous with US power, once proposed a reversal of the traditional roles, mandating that NATO's military commander be a European and its secretary general an American. To date this radical proposal has been rebuffed. Kissinger, "A Plan to Reshape NATO," *Time*, March 5, 1984.

Belgium are flown and maintained by Belgians, as is the case in Germany, Italy, and the Netherlands. But none of these weapons systems are on the same high alert that the American president is capable of activating without any other NATO member's permission. France alone has a truly independent *force de frappe*.

2

"We've well overtaken the Athenian League against Sparta in the 4th century before Christ," Jamie Shea, NATO's longtime spokesman and in-house historian, declared in the lead-up to the alliance's diamond anniversary.[2] Ever since its birth in 1949, the funeral toll for NATO has been sounded many times, especially by those who forget that crises are its lifeblood. The alliance itself was very nearly stillborn. At the end of the Second World War, Franklin Roosevelt expected both American and Soviet troops to leave Central Europe within two years. But Western European statesmen wanted the US to provide a security guarantee while they rebuilt their economies.

There were many proposals for how this pact could be configured. The American strategist George Kennan proposed a "dumbbell" concept, in which Western Europe would have its own defense system, while Canada and the US had a separate one that could come to the Europeans' aid in the unlikely event of a Soviet invasion. The prominent liberal journalist Walter Lippmann argued that there was no point in the US stationing troops in Europe in a world in which nuclear weapons had rendered conventional forces redundant. But leading anti-communists such as Ernest Bevin and Dean Acheson rejected this vision. They knew that the Red Army, which had just vanquished the Nazis, was not only the strongest force on the continent, but also an alarmingly popular one in Western Europe.

Instead, Bevin and his European counterparts formed what they called the Western Union, which extended the postwar Dunkirk treaty between France and the United Kingdom to include Luxembourg, the Netherlands, and Belgium. When this organization asked Washington to provide a

---

2   One of Shea's many exaggerations. The Delian League led by Athens lasted seventy-four years, compared to NATO's sixty at the time of his encomium. Jamie Shea, "1949: NATO'S Anxious Birth," March 5, 2009; available on the NATO website.

binding security guarantee, American diplomats took control of the project and steered it into what would become NATO, a much more expansive security pact that included twelve member states, with the US in the lead. At the time, the debate about "enlargement" was about whether or not to include states like Italy in the alliance. Kennan believed NATO only made sense as a pact among what he saw as racially and culturally similar North Atlantic peoples, and bemoaned an alliance that would have the effect of freezing Cold War battle lines across the middle of Europe.[3] His State Department colleague Charles Bohlen thought the idea of NATO extension into southern Europe "weakly provocative" toward the Soviet Union, and that it set the stage for limitless expansion.[4]

From the start, NATO was unpopular with member publics. Harry Truman could not afford to risk mentioning his plans for the North Atlantic alliance to a war-weary America in his first campaign for the presidency. French Communists and nationalists—opposed on nearly every other issue—jointly protested France's entry into NATO in 1949. There were enormous anti-NATO insurrections across Italy. The largest uprising in Iceland's postwar history occurred when the island nation joined the alliance. An extensive repertory of Icelandic anti-NATO anthems and songs sprang up during the negotiations between Reykjavík and Washington. On the eve of Iceland's NATO membership, the great communist novelist Halldór Laxness published *The Atom Station*, an Icelandic *Remains of the Day*, in which a young serving woman from the north witnesses the Reykjavík elite sell out the country to NATO officials behind closed doors.[5]

The first postwar decade was tumultuous for NATO. With Europe's economic recovery in full swing, the conviction that the continent needed an American security guarantee was weakened. Truman's Korean war showed how easily the US could become overextended. In response, Western European leaders drew up plans for the European Defense Community, which would combine the fledgling armies of West Germany, France,

---

3 Anders Stephanson, *Kennan and the Art of Foreign Policy* (Cambridge, MA: Harvard University Press, 1989), pp. 143–4.

4 Cited in Lawrence S. Kaplan, *NATO 1948: The Birth of the Transatlantic Alliance* (Lanham, MD: Rowman & Littlefield, 2007), p. 118.

5 For an acute reading of this extraordinary novel in its Cold War context, see Giuliano D'Amico, "The Whole World Is One *Atom Station*: Laxness, the Cold War, Postcolonialism, and the Economic Crisis in Iceland," *Scandinavian Studies* 87:4 (Winter 2015), pp. 457–88.

Italy, and the Benelux countries. But this plan for a European army fell apart almost as soon as it was floated. Britain saw the combined force as a threat to national sovereignty. The French government, meanwhile, was more worried about a resurgent Germany than a Soviet invasion. Paradoxically, then, this early drive for autonomy from Washington on the part of Western European states ended up bringing them more tightly into the fold of NATO, which proved to be the only arrangement capable of plastering over their divisions.

NATO may have begun as a security stopgap, but it soon became a guarantor of Western stability in ways beyond the imagination of its architects. For the US, massive defense budgets became a way of life, and the least controversial way to facilitate public spending in a postwar economy that still aimed at full employment. That the country was never fully reconciled to this permanent war posture is neatly captured in the ritual of nearly every postwar American president promising, and failing, to reduce US troop levels in Europe.

The political stability that NATO achieved in the fifties was never free from ruptures. In 1955, Washington ushered West Germany into the alliance, to which the Soviets reacted with the creation of their own, anti-NATO security system, the Warsaw Pact.[6] A year later, NATO wobbled badly when the Suez Crisis exposed the divisions between members that wanted to cling to their colonial possessions and a Washington that was keen to win favor with Third World nationalists who might otherwise turn communist. (Belgium, France and the Netherlands initially hoped their colonies might be included in NATO, which was too much for Washington, although a concession had to be made for the French *départements* in North Africa.) NATO command had an ambivalent attitude toward the British Empire. On the one hand, NATO helped accelerate imperial decline

---

6   German Atlanticism has been a major preoccupation of postwar national culture, not least for the country's leading left-liberal intellectual, Jürgen Habermas, who has always detected in *Westbindung* both possibility and danger. "The unconditional opening of the Federal Republic to the political culture of the West is the greatest intellectual achievement of our postwar period," he wrote in 1986. "This event cannot and should not be stabilized by a kind of NATO philosophy colored with German nationalism." Jürgen Habermas, "Eine Art Schadensabwicklung: Die apologetischen Tendenzen in der deutschen Zeitgeschichtsschreibung," *Die Zeit*, July 11, 1986. After supporting NATO's campaigns in the Balkans the following decade, Habermas, in the face of calls for renewed German militarism in the wake of the war in Ukraine, has returned to form as a leading conscience of the nation. See in particular Habermas, "War and Indignation," *Süddeutsche Zeitung*, April 29, 2022.

by, for instance, demanding Britain fulfill its obligations to station thousands of British troops on the Rhine, at the cost of more critical colonial nodes such as Singapore. But American strategists were also worried that the British retreat from the resource-rich Middle East would leave behind a vacuum, which NATO tried to fill by spawning the Middle East Treaty Organization (METO), one of several failed attempts to replicate itself.

The sixties are remembered at NATO as a time of emergency. For years, Charles de Gaulle's patience with the alliance had been on a short fuse. "NATO is a subterfuge," he commented in 1963. "Thanks to NATO, Europe is placed under the dependence of the United States without appearing to be so."[7] Three years later de Gaulle withdrew France—and its nuclear weapons—from NATO's integrated command. (This withdrawal was more theatrical than actual: France remained a NATO member and continued to participate in NATO exercises and technology-sharing.)

De Gaulle's decision was partly the result of his delusion about the status of France as a great power. But he also—more imaginatively—viewed in Germany's inevitable resurrection as a power in Europe the possibility of forging a Franco-German alliance that might shake the yoke of US hegemony over the continent. He was prepared to view Russia as a natural part of Europe, one cordoned off by a Cold War that he believed would one day be over. In de Gaulle's assessment, American capitalism and Soviet communism were converging toward a remarkably similar technocratic society. NATO was a deliberate American attempt to slow down history, in order to prolong the moment when Washington was the leading world power.[8] But despite the uproar de Gaulle caused among Cold War stalwarts, and the bevy of NATO obituaries that followed, the alliance emerged intact, if not even strengthened, from France's semi-departure. This allowed NATO to integrate West Germany more fully into the alliance, and to sound the alarm for increased commitments from other member states.

In these decades, opposition to NATO was a rallying cry for the Western European left, which viewed it not only as an institutionalized form of nuclear brinkmanship, but as a class alliance between American and European establishments determined to shore up their rule against domestic

---

7   Quoted in Alain Peyrefitte, *C'était de Gaulle* (Paris: Gallimard, 2002), p. 385.

8   For the two classic overviews of de Gaulle's foreign policy, see Maurice Vaïsse, *La Grandeur: Politique étrangère du général de Gaulle* (Paris: CRNS Éditions, 2013), and Frédéric Bozo, *Two Strategies for Europe: De Gaulle, the United States, and the Atlantic Alliance*, trans. Susan Emanuel (Lanham, MD: Rowman & Littlefield, 2001).

opposition. The Communist parties of Western Europe were, in this sense, a more salient threat than the Red Army. Armed resistance to NATO was sporadic and paltry: in the late 1970s and early '80s, the Red Army Faction damaged a handful of installations and pipelines, and narrowly missed taking out Supreme Allied Commander Alexander Haig with a car bomb.

NATO was not particularly concerned about the domestic political arrangements of its member states, so long as they were implacably anti-communist. Portugal under Salazar's dictatorship was welcomed into NATO in 1949, and in 1967, when Greek colonels used NATO's own counter-insurgency blueprints to overthrow a democratically elected government, the legal claim, led by the Scandinavian members, that Athens should exit the alliance was never seriously entertained. In the following year, the Dutch government won a spat with West Germany when it successfully blocked Bonn's attempt to appoint Albert Schnez, the leader of a postwar, underground Waffen-SS and Wehrmacht-staffed anti-communist militia, to the post of NATO commander of Allied Land Forces Central Europe (LANDCENT).

There have been more serious threats to NATO unity, however. Greece and Turkey violently clashed over Cyprus in 1974. More recently, in the wake of NATO's 2011 intervention in Libya, militias backed by Turkey and Italy fought the French-backed Libyan army of General Haftar. NATO unity took another blow in 2019, when, after Turkey began besieging US and Western European Kurdish allies in Syria, Emmanuel Macron declared the alliance "brain-dead."[9] NATO also took a psychological hit during the presidency of Donald Trump, who publicly questioned the alliance's purpose and refused to mumble pieties about Article 5 during a visit to NATO headquarters, albeit all while *increasing* US expenditure and troop levels in Europe.

3

But NATO's most serious existential crisis came in the 1990s, when the raison d'être of the organization—the Soviet Union—collapsed. In this new environment, it was not clear even to NATO's own function-aries what its future would be. All that remained was the prospect of

---

9 "Emmanuel Macron Warns Europe: NATO Is Becoming Brain-Dead," *Economist*, November 7, 2019.

janitorial twilight, with NATO helping to mop up and dismantle the Soviet Union's nuclear arsenal. Not only had the organizing specter of the alliance vanished, but a series of new institutions in Europe—the European Union above all—seemed to proffer a European future of greater coherence and autonomy from the US. Even before the Soviet Union fell, there were proposals for new political arrangements, including François Mitterrand's short-lived idea of a European Confederation that would pointedly include the USSR and exclude the US. In 1989, Gorbachev appropriated de Gaulle's old dream of a Europe that stretched from the Atlantic to the Urals, which he called a "common European home," in which "a doctrine of restraint should take the place of the doctrine of deterrence."[10]

Several prominent participants and observers in the 1990s believed that NATO, its mission accomplished, would close shop. "Let's disband both NATO and the Warsaw Pact […] Let's release your allies and ours," Soviet foreign minister Eduard Shevardnadze gamely proposed to the US secretary of state in 1989. Later that same year, the Czech leader Václav Havel told George H. W. Bush that he expected American and Russian troops would soon be vacating Central Europe. Prominent American strategists agreed. With the collapse of the Soviet Union, it was time for Europeans to take their security back in their own hands, with the US withdrawing its troops from the continent. "The Soviet threat provides the glue that holds NATO together," John Mearsheimer, one of the US's leading international relations theorists, wrote in the *Atlantic Monthly* in 1990. "Take away that offensive threat and the United States is likely to abandon the continent."[11] To glance at the output of NATO bureaucracy from the 1990s is to witness a sea of panicked position papers outlining ways to prolong the life of an ailing patient.

But NATO's 1990s crisis turned out to be its greatest hour. Not only did it not shut down during the decade, it expanded. It did not fade into the background as a vestigial Cold War organ, but became more active. "NATO must go out of area or it will go out of business," became the mantra of NATO apparatchiks across the decade. In just a few short years, NATO mutated from a professedly defensive organization to an undeniably

---

10   Mikhail Gorbachev, Address to the Council of Europe in Strasbourg, July 6, 1989; available on the Council of Europe website.

11   John J. Mearsheimer, "Why We Will Soon Miss the Cold War," *Atlantic Monthly* (August 1990).

offensive one—from conservative custodian of the geopolitical status quo to agent of change in Eastern Europe. How did this happen?

As George H. W. Bush's advisers surveyed the ruins of the Soviet Union, they determined that the principal threat was not the nascent Russian Federation, but a unified Europe. "We must seek to prevent the emergence of European-only security arrangements which would undermine NATO," read the draft synopsis of Pentagon strategy that leaked to the press in 1992.[12] In public statements, the Bush administration was cautious about NATO expansion. But in practice, it was triumphalist: soon after NATO incorporated a newly unified Germany, the alliance began training Ukrainian troops. When Bill Clinton became president in 1992, the real difference was that the rhetoric of expansion matched the reality. Clinton oversaw the 1999 entry of Poland, Hungary, and the Czech Republic into NATO, and treated Russia as the wrecked state it was.

There was some irony in Clinton's doubling down on NATO. In many ways he had appeared to be the ideal figure to shutter the alliance. On the campaign trail in 1992, Clinton had made rumbles about downsizing NATO in favor of newer, sleeker "rapid-deployment" UN military units. Initially, Clinton was skeptical of NATO's extension eastward. "So let me get this straight," he reportedly said to his national security staff on being briefed of the expansion plan. All the Russians would get "out of this really great deal we're offering them" was an assurance "that we're not going to put our military stuff into their former military allies, who are now going to be our allies, unless we happen to wake up one morning and decide to change our minds?"[13]

But expansion recommended itself for a host of reasons. To begin with, governments in the former Warsaw Pact states were eager. For a country like Poland, NATO membership was the first step toward reorientation toward the wealthy West. "Let the Russian generals get upset," Polish president Lech Wałęsa chimed to his US counterpart in 1993. "They won't launch a nuclear war." There were also votes to be won among the large Eastern European émigré enclaves in the US rustbelt, not a minor consideration for a president primarily concentrated on domestic affairs.

---

12   See the excerpts of the FY 1994–1999 Defense Planning Guidance in Chapter 3 of this volume.

13   Mary E. Sarotte, *Not One Inch: America, Russia, and the Making of Post–Cold War Stalemate* (New Haven, CT: Yale University Press, 2021), p. 267.

More significant still was the crystallization of the ideology of human rights in the nineties, when the US exercised such a preponderance of power globally as to make concerns about impinging on a foreign nation's sovereignty beneath consideration. Many former NATO critics had come to embrace the organization by the end of the Cold War, seeing it as the only viable vehicle for their new program of humanitarian intervention. By the early 1990s, the most powerful factions of the German Greens were becoming NATO-holics, just in time to be party to bomb tests NATO was conducting in reindeer-calving reserves in Norway. By 1995, the office of secretary general was occupied by the Spanish Socialist Javier Solana, author of a 1982 tract titled "50 Reasons to Say No to NATO," who once himself figured on a US list of subversive agents.

The 1995 bombing of Bosnia and Herzegovina, and later Kosovo in 1999, were showcases of NATO's newfound place in the post–Cold War order. Not only did Clinton's decision to bomb the former Yugoslavia circumvent the UN Security Council, it demonstrated that the EU, and especially Germany, was incapable of solving security crises in its own neighborhood. But this was also a show of force that arguably shook the Kremlin more than NATO expansion itself. The war was a preview of coming attractions: the reliance on technological, "zero-casualty" (for allied forces) military operations that did not require US ground troops, and the expectation that NATO-led interventions could create instant American-aligned constituencies like the Kosovan Albanians, who continue to name their children after Clinton and Bush senior.

The Clinton administration's faith in NATO expansion and NATO warfare reflected its faith in capital and markets. NATO, in this view, came to act as something like a rating agency that would declare portions of Eastern Europe as safe zones for foreign investment and ultimately EU membership.[14] "We will seek to update NATO so that there continues behind the enlargement of market democracies an essential collective security," Clinton's national security adviser, Anthony Lake, declared in 1993. This cocktail of markets and democracy talk, along with geostrategic

---

14   Critics who point to the failure of Western European states to top off their military budgets at the NATO requirement of 2 percent of GDP may be misapprehending the wider symbiosis of NATO membership and European integration. For the US, NATO membership of Eastern European states presented no major increased financial burden, but their subsequent entry into the EU came at a high cost for Western European states, which footed the bill for the actual work of reconstructing societies that Washington had declared open for business. I owe this suggestion to Christopher Caldwell.

interests, proved very difficult for American politicians to resist: it appeared to be a perfect marriage of realism and idealism.

By the end of the decade, only an eccentric rump of "realists"—from the American statesman Paul Nitze to the conservative historian Richard Pipes—still held out against NATO expansion.[15] Early skeptics, such as Joe Biden, toured Eastern Europe and returned to Washington converts of the expansionist cause. Likewise, Republican opponents of Clinton's domestic policy, such as Newt Gingrich—who himself had once borrowed $13,000 from his friends to take a sabbatical in Europe to write a novel about NATO (still uncompleted)—were in full accord about expansion, which was duly enshrined in the Republican manifesto, the "Contract for America." Radicalizing Clinton's own position, they only wanted him to move faster.

Ukraine became a special point of interest during the Clinton years and was the third-largest recipient of US aid by the end of the 1990s, exceeded only by Egypt and Israel. Between the annexation of Crimea in 2014 and the Russian invasion six years later, Kiev received more than $3 billion in military assistance alone; since Russia went in, the figure has increased by orders of magnitude. NATO training of Ukrainian troops has also sharply increased over time.[16] Starting with Clinton's military intervention in Kosovo, Ukraine's troops could be counted in almost every US-led post–Cold War operation, including in Afghanistan and Iraq. The Ukrainian army's resistance to the Russian onslaught is perhaps less surprising than it appears: large segments of it are NATO-trained and capable of making effective use of NATO-grade weaponry.

By the time George W. Bush came to power in 2001, NATO was still basking in the glow of its war in the Balkans, where to this day it polices a statelet of its own making in Kosovo. In the wake of the attacks of 9/11, when the alliance invoked Article 5 for the first time, it added the coordination of counter-terrorism to its portfolio, a global struggle abetted by domestic crackdowns in Russia and China. By 2008, NATO had begun a decade-long series of anti-piracy missions—Operation Allied Provider,

---

15   See in particular the open letter to President Clinton from June 27, 1997, with its fifty signatories made up of former US senators, ambassadors, cabinet secretaries, and foreign policy specialists.

16   In the first weeks of the 2022 invasion, one of the first sites Russian forces targeted in western Ukraine was the Yavoriv army base near the Polish border west of Lviv, where NATO instructors began training Ukrainian soldiers in the early 1990s.

Operation Allied Protector, Operation Ocean Shield—off the coast of Somalia. But while Bush shared Clinton's faith in the inevitable triumph of the American way, he wanted to shed some of the multilateral pretense of the NATO alliance. If Washington was the only power in NATO that mattered, and humanity had already entered into a unipolar world order, what was the point of waiting for American desires to be seconded by Belgians?

Bush II's Iraq war was thus fought over the criticism of some NATO members, such as France and Germany, whose actual military forces the American president viewed as irrelevant. You were either with the US or against it, and quite evidently, the Eastern Europeans were with the US, and Bush wanted them amply rewarded. Despite German and French warnings, he thus saw no reason to heed Russian discontent over the prospect of NATO membership for Georgia and Ukraine, which he duly promised in 2008. In this period, as Eastern Europe and Washington grew closer, it was not lost on Warsaw, Budapest, and Prague—where there were nationalists who were much more comfortable with US-style nationalism than the post-nationalism vaunted by Brussels—that Washington could also be of aid in their own disputes within the European Union. Less remarked on, but no less central to the binding of US and Eastern European nations, is the fact the military leaders of these states have strong ties, via NATO, to both the US military and US defense industries. Were any political leadership in Poland, Romania, Hungary, or any other Eastern European state to become intolerable for Washington, it would have an open, exploitable channel to that country's military, greased by years of mutual exchanges, including stints at NATO headquarters, bevies of NATO conferences, retreats, and ceremonies, as well as wars fought together in the Middle East.[17]

4

America's most steadfast allies in NATO today are Poland and the Baltics. If forced to choose between the hegemony of Berlin (or Brussels) and that of Washington, Eastern European leaders will prefer Washington

---

17   General Daniel Petrescu, the current head of the Romanian military, was previously appointed to NATO headquarters and participated in the war in Afghanistan, as did his counterparts in Poland, General Rajmund Andrzejczak, and in Hungary, General Romulusz Ruszin-Szendi.

every time. Whereas Britain has specialized in hosting Russian capital, Germany in consuming Russian energy, and France has historically seen Russia as a potential strategic partner, Poland and the Baltics never cease to stress the threat to their hard-won sovereignty.[18] Washington has come to share their view of Russia: it is no longer worth "resetting" relations with a pariah. For many US hawks, Russia needs to stay irredeemable if NATO is to continue pointing to the vast gulf that separates states under its wing from the barbarians at the gate. From this perspective, a strong, liberal, democratic Russia would perhaps have posed an even greater challenge to American hegemony in Europe than an autocratic, revanchist, but ultimately weak Russia.

If Eastern European states are convinced that NATO safeguards their sovereignty, it would seem that the reverse applies to the continent more widely. Ever since the election of Donald Trump, when Angela Merkel announced that Europe may one day have to look after its own security, there has been renewed expectation that EU states might inch away from their US protectors, many of whom, at least in theory, would welcome the prospect of a stronger European partner. Hope springs eternal. But in practice NATO often tugs Europeans away from their own self-declared interests. In 2010, the government of the Netherlands fell when the public rejected its lock step obedience to NATO's Afghanistan mission. Under pressure from the US and Eastern European leaders—as well as from Greens in his own government—Chancellor Olaf Scholz has acquiesced in sending tanks and heavy weaponry to Ukraine and cutting Germany off from Russian energy altogether. This divergence of interests within the Atlantic Alliance continues to galvanize a handful of European thinkers. In 2018, Hans Magnus Enzensberger, grand old man of the German left, described NATO as a tributary system with member and associate states sending periodic offerings of soldiers for Washington's wars.[19] "NATO is harmful to any project of Europe as a power," echoes Enzensberger's French counterpart, Régis Debray. "If Europe wants a destiny, it will have

---

18   Polish fears of a Russian strike on, or invasion of, their territory reached a high point when, in the midst of a Russian missile onslaught in Ukraine, what was almost certainly a Ukrainian missile landed in the Polish village of Przewodów, killing two Polish citizens. Karolina Wigura and Jarosław Kuisz, "The Missile Strike Has Ignited Visceral Fear in Poland, and Poses Hard Questions for NATO," *Guardian*, November 22, 2022.

19   Hans Magnus Enzensberger, "Verdruss und Verdacht machen sich breit in Europa," *Neue Zürcher Zeitung*, September 9, 2018.

to take a different path from the NATO route that relegates it to the status of a dominion."[20]

For years in Europe there has been mesmerizingly vague talk of a new initiative called the European Security and Defense Identity, which is somehow meant to emerge, like Athena, from the head of NATO. But Russia's invasion of Ukraine has revealed how deceptive European steps toward autonomy are, and how deep-set the institutional lock of NATO is over the continent. "The 'defense identity of the EU' is like a yeti," the former foreign affairs minister of Poland declared in 2021. "Everyone is talking about it, but no one has seen it."[21] If anything, NATO's power and relevance is due to increase in the coming years, and the increase in European defense spending, which is still puny in comparison with Washington's, only means that there will be more materiel under NATO purview. Calls to adopt Kennan's old proposal of two separate defense systems, one North American, one European, with the EU further developing its own Rapid Reaction Force or its own armament union, appear destined to fall prey to the overriding command structure of NATO. From the expanses of the Sahel to the banks of the Dnieper, there is ever less wriggle room under Washington's supervision.

The trouble with the drive for European autonomy is not merely that—like the rollout of the European Defense Community in 1952—it could backfire. But rather that, considering what the European Union is today, if it ever did succeed in taking a more militarized form, this would hardly be a rosy prospect. A competent EU army patrolling the Mediterranean littoral for migrants, enforcing an elaborate repatriation system, and forcing regimes in Africa and Asia to serve in perpetuity as extraction points for its resources and receptacles of its trash would only clinch the status of "Fortress Europe" at the vanguard of xenophobic neoliberalism.

The English historian E. P. Thompson argued in 1978 that "Natopolitanism" was a form of extreme apathy, a pathology wrapped in an empty ideology that only knew what it was against. But Thompson was writing at a time when calls to abolish the alliance were not yet a weary incantation. In 1983, NATO's placement of cruise and Pershing missiles in Western Europe provoked the largest protests in postwar history. But if the institutionalization of nuclear brinksmanship was once considered

---

20   See Debray, Chapter 9, "Why France Should Leave NATO."
21   Kristina Zeleniuk, "Interview with Witold Waszczykowski," Friedrich Ebert Stiftung, *Blog i-E*, December 12, 2021.

a lethal gambit by many citizens of NATO states, recent wars in Libya and Afghanistan have proceeded without domestic hindrance, despite their abject failure. Russia's invasion of Ukraine has delivered NATO the grandest possible reprieve. Even so, some more belligerent US commentators see escalation in the European theater as yet another instance of Washington's inability to focus on the threat from Beijing. They need not worry. NATO's response and the West's state-of-the-art sanctions rollout have been a dress rehearsal for World NATO: an alliance with the ambition to encircle China. Nobody doubts the effectiveness of NATO support for Ukraine, though the war is not over. The lingering question is whether NATO is a Cold War corset that has constrained the freedom of the West—and imperiled populations around the world—more than it has secured either. At a time when there has never been more need for an alternative world order, NATO closes the door on that possibility. NATO may be back. But it is back only to hoist the old banner: "There is no alternative."

Acknowledgments

Tariq Ali's "Afghanistan: Mirage of the Good War," Peter Gowan's "The NATO Powers and the Balkan Tragedy," Susan Watkins's "Annexations" and "An Avoidable War?" and Tony Wood's "Matrix of War" were first published in *New Left Review* (II:50, Mar.–Apr. 2008; I:234 Mar.–Apr. 1999; II:86, Mar.–Apr. 2014; II:133–4, Jan.–Apr. 2022; II:133–4, Jan.–Apr. 2022). The essays by Richard Seymour, Alexander Zevin, and Lily Lynch originally ran on *Sidecar* (Ch. 18, Mar. 22, 2022; Ch. 19, Mar. 31, 2022; Ch. 20, May 20, Aug. 11, and Sept. 9, 2022). Parts of Cihan Tuğal's chapter first appeared on *Sidecar* and in the *New York Times* (May 26 and Oct. 14, 2022). Thomas Meaney's chapter is based on an article originally published by the *Guardian* (May 5, 2022). Benjamin C. Schwarz's essay was first published in the *Journal of Strategic Studies* (17:4, 1994). John Lewis Gaddis's "History, Grand Strategy, and NATO Enlargement" was first published in *Survival* (40:1, Spring 1998), and Alan J. Kuperman's chapter was published by *International Security* (38:1, Summer 2013). Michael T. Klare's contribution was first published in *Le Monde diplomatique* (September 2016), as was Régis Debray's (April 2013). Peter Gowan's "The Enlargement of NATO and the EU" appeared, in a different form, in *The Global Gamble: Washington's Faustian Bid for Global Dominance* (London: Verso, 1999). Wolfgang Streeck's essay was first published in *American Affairs* (VI:22, Summer 2022). An earlier version of Volodymyr Ishchenko's article appeared on *Truthout* (December 28, 2021). Both John J. Mearsheimer's and Mary E. Sarotte's essays were first published in *Foreign Affairs* (93:5, Sept.–Oct. 2014; 93:5, Sept.–Oct. 2014). For permission to publish the latter we would like to thank the author and the Wylie Agency. For the rest, we kindly thank the authors and original publishers for permission to republish.

The editor of this book would also like to thank Tariq Ali, Thomas Meaney, John Merrick, and Alexander Zevin for their suggestions and editorial help.